The History of Science in Western Civilization

Volume I
Antiquity and Middle Ages

L. Pearce Williams
Henry John Steffens

University Press of America™
division of
R.F. Publishing, Inc.
4710 Auth Place, S.E., Washington, D.C. 20023

Printed in the United States of America

0-8191-0191-5

THIS BOOK IS GRATEFULLY DEDICATED TO

HENRY GUERLAC

Preface

This work has originated from our participation, both as students and instructors, in the survey course at Cornell University in the history of science first offered by Professor Henry Guerlac in 1946. The problem that faces anyone rash enough to presume to offer an overview of the whole of Western science is how to fit the diversity and multiplicity of scientific endeavors, hypotheses, speculations and achievements into any kind of a coherent framework and within a reasonable scope. A narrative history of science must, necessarily, ignore dead ends and fruitless ideas if it is ever to achieve its goal of telling the story of the development of science. Monographs can and do focus upon the unique theory or discovery without bearing any responsibility for putting the single scientific event into a larger context. And, the original scientific works themselves lie scattered about like the bones of extinct dinosaurs. They are the mute testimony of generations of original thought, hard intellectual labor and, often, human drama. But, except for the specialist and the rare scientific antiquarian, they are ignored or piously misquoted in introductory chapters of science textbooks.

Each of these elements has an important place within the discipline of the history of science. There is a narrative history of science that does consist of more than "one damned thing after another." The adventure of ideas is exciting and ideas are linked to one another across both space and time. The story of these links and of the human beings caught up in the search for scientific truth is one well worth telling clearly and coherently. This we have tried to do in the narrative part of the text that follows. For those readers who wish a short but connected account of the development of Western science, this narrative, we trust, will serve their purpose.

The history of science is now a mature academic discipline. It calls upon the full panoply of the scholar's art and technique and its scholarly results are impressive. We have used the fruits of such mature scholarship to illuminate particular points that appeared to us worthy of more detailed treatment than could be offered in the narrative. We have sought different points of view and different approaches to the history of science in order to illustrate both the richness of this scholarly field and the complexities of the subject. It is our hope that these selections from scholars in the history of science may serve both to explain difficult points and to inspire some readers to participate actively in the uncovering of our scientific heritage.

Finally, we have drawn heavily from the mountain of original sources in the history of science. The history of science is particularly vulnerable to distortion through paraphrase. The modern scholar sees the world through modern spectacles and is always liable to read into an older author ideas that were not there. If one wants to know what Aristotle or Galileo or Einstein really meant, one had better read Aristotle or Galileo or Einstein and not rely upon second-hand reports. Yet, such sources are bare bones and require fleshing out by provision of a context and a description of the particular problem or problems with which each author was concerned. Thus, we have put the original sources into a matrix of narrative and monograph so that they may be read with a critical and an appreciative eye. By juxtaposing these three elements, we have hoped, as well, to lay bare some of the structure of the history of science as well as offer a panorama of the development of science itself.

Throughout the composition of this work, we have tried to keep two audiences in mind. Our primary concern has been with our students. We have long felt the need for a work of this kind that would bring students into intimate contact with science in Western Civilization. With C. P. Snow, we feel that some knowledge of our scientific heritage is as vital to the educated person as is an acquaintance with the humanities and the creative arts. Just because the history of science, in this sense, is not a narrow academic study but a vital tributary to our whole culture, we have also tried to serve the general reader as well. It has been our hope to produce a work that the intelligent and curious layman will read with both pleasure and profit. Perhaps we may even have conveyed our exuberance with the field, for after some 40 years collectively devoted to the study of the history of science, we each find the prospect of new researches as exciting as we did when first we heard of the subject.

Ithaca, New York
July 1977.

L. Pearce Williams
Henry John Steffens

TABLE OF CONTENTS

Chapter 1. Ancient Science. Narrative 1

Chapter 1. II. Readings in Ancient Science 34

A. Science in the Pre-Classical World 35

1. Medicine in Babylonia and Egypt 35

a. Babylonian Medical Texts 35

b. Egyptian Medicine 38

2. Babylonian Mathematics and Astronomy . . 41

a. Neugebauer on Mathematics in Mesopotamia 41

b. Neugebauer on Babylonian Astronomy . 50

B. The Philosophical Framework of Greek Science 55

1. Plato, *The Republic* 55

2. Aristotle, *Metaphysica* 61

3. Epicurus, *Letter to Herodotus* 75

C. The Apogee of Greek Science 85

1. Hippocratic Medicine 85

a. *On Ancient Medicine* 85

b. *Epidemics* 92

2. Astronomy and Cosmogony 96

a. Plato, *Timaeus* 96

b. Aristotle, *Metaphysica* 113

c. Ptolemy, *Almagest* 126

3. Physics 144

a. Archimedes, *On Floating Bodies* . . . 144

b. Hero, *Treatise on Pneumatics* 150

4. Galenic Medicine 156

a. *On Medical Experience* 156

b. *On the Natural Faculties* 167

Chapter 2. The Transmission of Ancient Science 170

Chapter 3. Medieval Science. Narrative 216

Chapter 3. II. Readings in Medieval Science 239

A. The Nature of Science in the Middle Ages 239

1. Charles Singer on the Dark Ages 239

2. Alistaire Crombie on the 12th Century Renaissance 251

3. Pope Gregory the Great on Secular Knowledge 263

4. Isidore of Seville, *Etymologia* 264

B. The Flowering of Medieval Science 275

1. Robert Grosseteste, *On Light* 275

2. Roger Bacon, *Opus Majus* 282

3. Adelard of Bath, *Quaestiones Naturales* . 293

4. St. Thomas Aquinas, *Commentary on Aristotle's Physics* 304

5. John Buridan, *Questions on the Eight Books of the Physics of Aristotle* . . . 316

6. John of St. Amand on Magnets 322

7. Peter of Limoges on the Comet of 1299 . 324

C. Marshall Clagett, Medieval Mechanics 326

CHAPTER ONE

ANCIENT SCIENCE

I. Narrative

Ever since man emerged as a separate species he has tried to make some sense of the world in which he lived. Primitive man built up an impressive intellectual treasure compounded of explanations of natural phenomena in the form of myths and detailed empirical knowledge of plants and the habits of animals upon which survival depended. This was undoubtedly the beginnings of science but it is its barest elements. The understanding of nature only gradually evolved from the level of myth to that of philosophy and physics. The control of nature by means of a truly scientific technology took even longer. The combination of the two, which is the hallmark of modern civilization, is of very recent origin, dating back no farther than a century or two.

As in most areas of development, the first steps are the crucial ones for the scientific quest, if not science itself, is one which is reinforced by tradition. It is of some importance to note that only Western Civilization developed this peculiar combination of intellectual and technological mastery of nature which we call science. Together with constitutional government, this is Western Civilization's major contribution to the modern world.

A. Science in Babylonia and Egypt.

The origins of science are to be found in the birthplace of Western Civilization itself. About 3500 B.C. a people of unknown origin settled in the lower reaches of the Tigris-Euphrates river system. The Sumerians, as they are known today, were faced with grim living conditions. Their cities were subject to flash floods, sudden, vicious storms, barbarian invasions from without and plague and famine from within. It was extraordinarily difficult to make any sense out of these sudden calamities without having recourse to the arbitrary will of supernatural beings. The gods, for the Sumerians and for their successors, the Babylonians, ran the world according to their whims. Man was but a puppet who could serve the gods and hope that this service might prevent catastrophe from striking. The Sumerian City was organized around this idea. In the center was the Temple and the City literally belonged to the patron god who, it was hoped, would extend his protection to his votaries on earth. All land belonged to the god and was administered for him by the priests of the Temple. It was the priests who allotted plots to the people to be tilled, figured the amount of seed corn necessary for the next year's planting, computed the amount of tillage of which every yoke of oxen was capable, calculated the manpower necessary to extend and repair the irrigation system upon which the agriculture of the City depended, and worked out a calendar by which the all-important time for sowing of seed could be determined. It was out of these activities that the first flourishing of mathematics occurred. Our source for knowledge of this mathematics is a rather large number of baked clay tablets about the size of one's hand inscribed with wedge-shaped marks made by a reed stylus. These cuneiform tablets date from around 1600 B.C., and represent the culmination of a mathematical tradition which must extend some way into the time before 1600 B.C. Babylonian mathematics was a highly sophisticated one. It was based on 60, rather than 10, and was extraordinarily supple. [Section II, A, 2a in Documents] Although its origins were undoubtedly practical, it soon transcended them and moved into the area of pure number theory. The Babylonians were the first people to become intoxicated with numbers and, motivated by the sheer joy of intellectual discovery, created an algebra that was not to be equalled for centuries.

In the other sciences there was not an equal advance in Old Babylonian times. Medicine, for example, was hopelessly demon-ridden. Illness was the result of sin or witchcraft and cures were to be sought in spells and incantations. There is an apparent exception in astronomy for Babylonian astronomy reached heights only equalled later in the Christian era. But chronology here is fundamental. Our astronomical texts date from ca. 300 B.C. to the beginning of the Christian era and cannot be considered as uniquely the products of Mesopotamian civilization. The conquests of Alexander the Great, who died in 323 B.C., brought Greek civilization into contact with Mesopotamian culture and the resultant stimulus probably accounts, in part, for the extraordinary achievements of the Mesopotamian mathematical astronomers. What was bequeathed to the Greeks was of fundamental importance for the further development of astronomy in the Hellenistic world.*

It was from Mesopotamia that the basic coordinates of Hellenistic astronomy were derived. The band of constellations through which the planets and particularly the sun appeared to move was divided into twelve zones called the Zodiac by the Greeks. The Zodiac centers about the ecliptic; the celestial equator, determined by the apparent rotation of the heavens about the pole star, is at an angle of 23½° to the ecliptic. Given these two great circles, the heavens could be mapped with confidence. Even more important was the mathematical heritage. When Babylonian mathematics was applied to observational astronomy, the result was a mathematical astronomy of considerable complexity. In the hands of Claudius Ptolemy in the second century of our era, Babylonian mathematics and Greek observations

---

* Classical scholars distinguish between the Hellenic and the Hellenistic periods. The Hellenic period extends from 1100 B.C. to the death of Alexander the Great; the Hellenistic period runs from 322 B.C. to the hegemony of Rome (ca. 146 B.C.) although, since the culture remained Hellenistic, it is sometimes extended into the period of the Roman Empire.

created an astronomical system which was only to be overthrown by Copernicus a millenium and a half later.

The other great pre-classical civilization of antiquity--Egypt--produced no such comparable scientific achievement. Egyptian mathematics remained primitive and its astronomy was rudimentary. Only the fact that the dog star, Sirius, rose just before the sun when the Nile flood began was noted by Egyptian astronomers as worthy of serious astronomical attention. Egyptian medicine, like its Babylonian counterpart, was filled with magic recipes, although the Edwin Smith Papyrus seems to be an exception. [Readings, p. 38] The considerable technical achievements of the Egyptians--the great pyramids and the numerous obelisks erected with apparent ease throughout Egypt--were accomplished with primitive tools and depended ultimately upon the availability of vast amounts of human labor.

It is difficult to call the achievements of the Babylonians and the Egyptians "science." Despite areas of striking clarity, in the last analysis natural events were controlled by supernatural powers whose wills could not be known. For "real science" to emerge, the gods had to be relegated to the background and an attempt made to explain the world in natural, rather than supernatural, terms. This was to be the great step taken by the Greeks. They invented philosophy and the task of philosophy was to lay bare the natural workings of the universe. The gods might still be present, as they were in Plato and, to a certain extent in Aristotle, but they differed in one fundamental respect from the gods of Mesopotamia. Their actions in the physical world were reasonable and capable of comprehension by man. But in the absence of their acts of intercession the universe continued to operate according to natural laws.

B. The Rise of Hellenic Science

The ancient Greeks were an amalgamation of a number of different but related Indo-European tribes that migrated from the Northeast into Greece over a long period of time. They make their first historical appearance in the records of the Kings of the Hittites who ruled over much of the Middle East during the years 1400-1200 B.C. There, reference is made to the Ahhiyawa who were probably Homer's Achaians, and to their ruler Atarshshiyash who has been tentatively identified as Atreus, the father of Agamemnon. The Achaians were followed by other Greek-speaking peoples, most important of which were those who spoke a dialect called Ionian and another, later, group which spoke the Dorian tongue. The Dorian Greeks were the last to arrive and moved into areas such as the Peloponnesus as conquerors.

Until the nineteenth century, the history of these early migrations was shrouded in myth. It was only the faith and monomaniacal efforts of a German businessman, Heinrich Schliemann, that brought these early years into the sphere of history. It was Schliemann, with Homer's *Iliad* clutched in one hand, who discovered and excavated the site of Troy and it was Schliemann also who discovered Mycenae, the hitherto legendary home of Agamemnon. We now know that Mycenaean civilization flourished from about 1600 to about 1200 B.C. when it was destroyed by the advance guard of the Dorians. Refugees fled to the Ionian stronghold of Athens in Attica where, perhaps because of its essential poverty and isolation, they were unmolested. From Attica, many of these people emigrated to the Eastern shore of the Aegean Sea (Ionia) where they founded cities. The Ionians kept alive the traditions of their past as best they could in the centuries that followed. But, for some three centuries after 1200 B.C. a Dark Age descended upon Greece and Ionia of such totality that these years still remain blank pages in history. Even the skill of writing disappeared so Ionian culture had to depend upon a purely oral tradition. It was from this tradition that the great poet, Homer, sprang and it was the Homeric epics--the *Iliad* and the *Odyssey*--which were to provide the basic framework for Hellenic civilization. We shall here have to ignore many aspects of the *Iliad* and the *Odyssey* in order to concentrate on those intellectual attributes which were later to characterize much of Greek science.

One of the most striking differences between the Homeric world and that of Mesopotamia or Egypt is the role the gods played in these societies. In Homer there is neither the terror felt by the Babylonian nor the almost smug confidence in divine beneficence experienced by the Egyptians. As Homer makes clear at the beginning of the *Iliad*, the gods could wreak havoc upon mortals as Apollo does by spreading a plague among the Achaians for having insulted one of his priests. But the gods were not so great that man could only implore their forgiveness and hope that catastrophe could be averted. The gods were very human and their intercourse, both social and sexual, with humanity was rather intense. Many of the Homeric heroes were confident of a divinity in their own ancestry. Achilles had a divine mother who intervened on Olympus for him. Odysseus is described as "Son of Laertes and seed of Zeus." Thus, the gods had supernatural powers but human attributes and were not above human defiance. Diomedes, Lord of Argos, did not shrink in terror from Apollo when the god tried to protect Aineias. Instead,

> Diomedes of the great war cry made for Aineias. Though he saw how Apollo himself held his hands over him he did not shrink even from the great god, but forever forward drove, to kill Aineias and strip his glorious armour. Three times, furious to cut him down, he drove forward, and three times Apollo battered aside the bright shield, but as a fourth time, like more than man, he charged, Apollo who strikes from afar cried out to him in the voice of terror: 'Take care, give back, son of Tydeus, and strive no longer to make yourself like the gods in mind, since never the same is the breed of gods, who are immortal, and men who walk groundling.'
>
> He spoke, and Tydeus' son gave backward, only a little, avoiding the anger of him who strikes from afar, Apollo. . . .*

---

* *The Iliad of Homer*, trans. by Richmond Lattimor, Phoenix Books, University of Chicago Press, Chicago & London, 1967. Lines 432-44.

The gulf which Apollo insisted upon between man and the Gods, however, was more apparent than real for as Greek mythology abundantly illustrated, the gods were all too human in their actions. They quarreled, committed adultery with one another and with humans, tricked one another, and generally gave the lie to Apollo's implication that to be "like the gods in mind" was a very lofty thing. Indeed, to be like the gods in mind might even be viewed as falling below the purely human standard. Xenophanes of Colophon (ca. 570-475 B.C.), one of the early pre-Socratic philosophers was persuaded that the gods were human inventions for whom little, if any respect, was due. "Homer and Hesiod," he wrote, "have attributed to the gods everything that is a shame and reproach among men, stealing and committing adultery and deceiving each other." And further, ". . . if cattle and horses or lions had hands, or were able to draw with their hands and do the works that men can do, horses would draw the forms of the gods like the horses, and cattle like cattle, and they would make their bodies such as they each had themselves."*

Such an attitude towards the gods left its impression on Hellenic culture. Man fell short of the gods but not by much. The result was the creation of two different ways of looking at man and the gods. On the one hand, man's divine ancestry and clear genetic relationship to the gods seemed to give him the necessary arrogance to inquire into divine things. There was, if you will, an intellectual as well as a social give and take between the human and the divine worlds. The actions and intentions of the gods were enshrined in myths but the myths could be questioned, their contradictions could be noted and the search for alternative explanations could be tolerated. What the Babylonian shrank from in fear of divine anger at human presumption, what the Egyptian avoided precisely because all the answers were available in theology, the Greek could and did attempt. Like so many other parts of Western Civilization, heresy was a Greek invention.

The other approach engendered by this critical appraisal of the gods was of more importance to the development of Greek Science. The Greeks, like almost all primitive peoples, attempted to account for their origins and the origins of the world. These attempts first took the form of myths in which the gods played primary roles. But could the gods of Homer and Hesiod *really* be the creators of the vast and orderly universe which even the most superficial study of natural phenomena revealed? It was the Greeks who first answered, No, to this question and sought to find the physical principle or principles which would explain the cosmos. The very word, cosmos, is Greek. Its original meaning was "order" and the first Greek contribution to the history of science was the recognition that there was an inherent order in the universe and that such order could be apprehended by the human mind.

Traditionally, the role of father of Greek philosophy is

---

* These citations are taken from G. S. Kirk and J. E. Raven, *The Pre-Socratic Philosophers*, Cambridge, 1957.

assigned to Thales of Miletus, about whom we know very little. We can date him by the solar eclipse of 584 B.C. which he is said to have predicted. He was a practical man, making a fortune in the Ionian city of Miletus by cornering all the olive presses in a bumper year. He was also reputed to be widely traveled, having visited Mesopotamia and Egypt. All these traditions have a certain air of plausibility about them. The prediction of the eclipse would only have been possible if Thales had access to the astronomical tables compiled by the Babylonians. From Egypt he is supposed to have brought back the knowledge of geometrical methods of measurement. There is a story that he was able to measure the height of the pyramids by comparing the length of their shadows and the length of the shadow of a stick (gnomon) stuck upright in the ground. The problem then reduced to one of similar triangles:

$$\frac{\text{Height of Pyramid}}{\text{Length of Pyramid Shadow}} = \frac{\text{Height of gnomon}}{\text{Length of gnomon shadow}}$$

Thales went beyond the purely metrical aspect of Egyptian geometry, however, by generalizing his results. The concept of geometrical proof is attributed to him. He is said to have proven a number of theorems: that a circle is bisected by its diameter, that the angles at the base of an isosceles triangle are equal, that the vertical angles of two intersecting lines are equal and that when two angles and a side of two triangles are equal, they are congruent. The science of geometry was born here.

Thales' most important contribution was his attempt to derive the multiplicity of phenomena from some underlying unity. What undoubtedly impressed him as he surveyed his surroundings was the ubiquity of water. The Aegean and Mediterranean Seas, together with the Homeric tradition of a great all-encircling Ocean were evidence that water was the preponderant element in purely quantitative terms. Perhaps Thales' visit to Egypt exposed him to the Egyptian view that the Nile was the source of all life, a view buttressed by the watery origins of man in the semen and the menstrual blood. Finally, water could take on various physical guises. It became vapor when heated and solid when frozen. Thus, Thales argued, water was the universal principle of all existing things. Everything that comes to be and passes away owes its existence ultimately to water. Precisely how different objects were, ultimately, water is a difficult question to answer. It is possible, for example, to say that something *comes from* water without meaning that it *is* water. This genealogical approach would be close to the older mythological accounts in which various parts of the world were engendered by the coupling of gods or emerged parthenogenetically from a single god. Athena "came from" Zeus' forehead but was not Zeus. Similarly, a worm or a frog could "come from" water yet not be water. For this to happen, however, water must contain some means for differentiation into different substances. If the primeval water were somehow alive, this difficulty could be removed. It is highly probably that Thales thought of his "water" as containing "soul," i.e., a material principle of motion and differentiation. The Greek metaphor for the universe tended to be an organic one, not the mechanical one that entered science during the Scientific Revolution of the Seventeenth Century.

Thales' attempts at cosmology and cosmogony were equally original and important. The world was a flat disc which floated upon the primeval waters "like a log." The "waters" simply extended downwards indefinitely, serving primarily to support the earth. It is, too, from the primeval water that the earth itself was formed. The Book of Genesis comes immediately to mind for there, too, there were waters which were divided to form the firmament above and the earth below (Genesis I, 6,7). But the difference is worth underlining. For Thales, the formation of the earth was a natural process following in some natural fashion from the nature of water itself. In Genesis, "God made the firmament and divided the waters." In the one account is the seed of philosophy, in the other, that of theology.

One further contribution by Thales should be noted. There is a modern school of the philosophy of science which insists that scientists deal less with the natural world per se than with the theories of nature proposed by their predecessors and colleagues. Science to these philosophers consists of the constant interplay between theory and criticism. Thales provided the first theory of the world which other philosophers could attack. There can be no doubt that Thales' achievement did stimulate thought and did provoke almost immediate attacks by his fellow Ionians and Milesians, Anaximander (ca. 600-545) and Anaximenes (ca. 585-525). Anaximander went beyond Thales both in the abstraction and the ambition of his philosophy. He diverged from his master on the fundamental question of the ultimate substance of nature. He doubted the ability of water to take up opposite qualities. How could water be the source, for example, of both wet and dry, since water was obviously and essentially wet. It plainly could not and Anaximander, therefore, assumed a new originative substance "the boundless" (*to apeiron*--the indefinite) which had no spatial limits and from which all the elements of the world were formed. The "boundless," it may be noted, was itself insensible but when endowed with qualities became the ordinary day to day objects of sense experience. The separation of qualities was an essential part of Anaximander's cosmogony. Part of the "boundless" was somehow put into vortex motion which produced the hot and the cold in the form of a ring in which the hot was on the outside and the cold was on the inside. Hot and cold could be identified with fire and air. Within the cold, the wet (or water) formed but under the influence of the hot condensed further into the dry (or earth). Further differentiation in the heavens led to the appearance of the celestial bodies. The original circle of fire broke into separate rings of the sun, the moon, and the stars. These rings were conceived by Anaximander as being tubes of fire veiled in mist so that the whole tube was never visible. There were, however, "breathing holes" by which the fire presumably kept burning and these holes were the heavenly bodies. Eclipses of the sun and the waxing and waning of the moon were explained by assuming that the breathing holes periodically become clogged with soot and are then reopened. Anaximander also estimated that the diameter of the sun's wheel was twenty-seven times the diameter of the earth, that of the moon was nineteen times the earth's diameter and the wheels of the stars were nine earth diameters across. The earth itself was a flat disc, three times as wide as it was deep and, since it was at the center of the fiery rings, in need of no support for it had no place to go. We have here materialism with a vengeance. There are no gods anywhere; everything comes to be and passes away through natural agencies.

There are, of course, many serious questions which may be addressed to Anaximander. Why, for example, does the original vortex motion begin? and how does it engender qualities? Why do the wheels of fire separate out from the "boundless" to form the sun, moon, and stars? It was to these questions that Anaximenes turned. It must have been with a triumphant note that he announced the solution to the problem of the origin of qualities. This origin should be sought in physical *process* not in physical *substance*. The same substance can, under different physical conditions, produce opposite qualities. If breath, for example, is expelled with the mouth wide open it is warm; if the lips are pursed, it is cold. Thus air could be both hot and cold depending on the physical circumstances. Air was also essential to life and Anaximenes made it the basic, universal substance. All things come from air by rarefaction and condensation and, since it is an observable fact that air is constantly in motion, rarefactions and condensations are always taking place. Thus Anaximenes had to call upon neither a watery "soul" nor arbitrary, unexplained movements of the "boundless" to explain his world. It all followed from the nature of air.

The earth, which had condensed from air, floated upon air like a leaf upon the wind. The heavenly bodies were discs (not spheres) of fire created by the rarefaction of vapors from the earth. They, too, like leaves were carried through the heavens but did not pass *under* the earth. Instead, upon "setting" they went around the earth's periphery, "just as if a felt cap turns round our head."

With Anaximenes, the Milesian school came to an end. Philosophical speculation became a more generally Hellenic pastime and the pace of intellectual development quickened. Two men, in particular, were to deepen the philosophical stream and raise questions of fundamental importance for the further development of philosophy and science.

Heraclitus of Ephesus (fl. 501 B.C.) took sharp issue with the Milesians, insisting that there was no underlying, unchanging substance from which all other things came. Instead, everything was constantly changing and the only unchanging principle was that the world was in constant flux. Heraclitus, therefore, raised the issue of how man could know anything about a world in which nothing remained constant. Heraclitus took fire as the fundamental element because fire was preeminently the symbol of change.

Exactly the opposite viewpoint was upheld by Parmenides of Elea in Southern Italy. Parmenides (fl. 475 B.C.) insisted that change is an illusion. In his argument, he presented the first conservation law in the history of science, the law of the Conservation of Being. Nothing, Parmenides insisted, can come into being from nothing, nor can anything pass away into nothing. Therefore, what is has always been and will always be. Hence change is impossible and reality must consist of an unchanging sphere. This is the real world. It is a world revealed by reason, not the senses. In fact, the senses are totally untrustworthy and never to be relied upon. Phenomena were not the proper object of science since they were merely fleeting images created by the senses. For Parmenides, only Being, not Becoming was real and once the essence of Being had been apprehended by the reason, that was the end of it. To a modern reader, this all seems rather fruitless. Parmenides, nevertheless, had a considerable impact in antiquity. He was the first philosopher to use reason systematically to prove a point and may be considered the father of formal logic. More importantly, he did raise a question that all other philosophers now had to attempt to answer. For those who rejected the idea that the sensible world was merely a mirage, the Parmenidean conservation of Being created an acute problem. How could Being be conserved and yet the world of change still be explained? There must be some unchanging entity out of which the world was constructed, not by transmutations as in Milesian philosophy, but by arrangements of some sort in which the elements of bodies remained unchanged.

Such a system had already been created before Parmenides. Pythagoras (fl. 530 B.C.) was the first to suggest that reality was the result of arrangements. For Pythagoras, the world consisted of number. He was led to this belief by a chance observation that, everything else being equal, the note produced by a lyre string was determined by its length. Moreover, the simple harmonies bore simple mathematical relations to one another. Thus the length of a string which produced a note an octave higher than another note was exactly half as long as the string for the lower note. This discovery is of basic importance in the history of science for it marks the first introduction of mathematics into physics. It is not self-evident that nature ought to contain mathematical relationships. Pythagoras' discovery created a whole new, and potentially extremely powerful, instrument for the analysis of the world. If a physical property could be expressed in mathematical terms, then it ought to be possible to operate upon this property with the full power of mathematical logic and mathematical relationships, in turn, could be correlated with physical phenomena. This was the method to be used by Archimedes in antiquity [see Readings, p. 144] and Galileo in the seventeenth century.

It was not difficult to construct the world of phenomena out of numbers. The number 1 could be represented by a dot and it is probable that the Pythagoreans considered this monad to have real physical existence. How the qualities of bodies could be derived from arrangements is seen at a glance in the following diagrams.

```
      .          . . . .
     . .         . . . .
    . . .        . . . .
   . . . .       . . . .
```

The qualitative differences between a square and a triangle are simply the results of the arrangement of the monads out of which they are constructed.

The Pythagorean intoxication with number had important cosmological consequences. The number 10 was of particular importance since it was the sum of the first four integers. It was argued that the universe (i.e., the solar system) must consist of ten bodies. Since there were only eight (Sun, moon, earth, Jupiter, Saturn, Mars, Mercury, and Venus) that could be observed, the Pythagoreans made up two--the central fire and a counter-earth. The central fire was, as the name implies, at the center of the universe and the earth went around it. It was not visible, however, because it was on the opposite side of the earth from the Mediterranean. The counter-earth was also invisible since it was always on the other side of the central fire from the earth. The idea that the center of the cosmos should be occupied by a pure body such as fire was to have a long history contributing to and culminating in the Copernican revolution of the sixteenth century. There were, however, few philosophers in antiquity outside the Pythagorean persuasion who took it seriously.

There were other philosophers who attempted to solve the Parmenidean problem. Empedocles (fl. ca. 450 B.C.) abandoned the monistic position of the Milesians and suggested that four elements were necessary. Given earth, air, fire, and water, the world of sense and change could be explained by various combinations, decompositions, and recombinations of these elements. The elements were brought together and separated by the forces of love and hate. Change, then, is simply rearrangement. Rearrangements take place by chance and Empedocles accounted for the order in the cosmos by means of a primitive doctrine of survival of the fittest. Thus in his discussion of the origin of organic beings, Empedocles states that the fortuitous combinations of the elements first produced separate organs--heads, arms, and legs which, unable to survive, soon perished. Some, however, joined together by chance and were viable. Thus were all living creatures first produced. What Empedocles' system could not explain was the stability of the world. Why, after all the limbs had either perished or been formed into complete organisms did order suddenly take over from the primeval chaos? Why did organisms reproduce their own kind and how did they transform food such as wheat or barley into *their* flesh and blood?

It was questions of this nature that led Anaxagoras of Clazomenae (ca. 500-428 B.C.) to insist that there must be more than four elements. Indeed, there must be as many elements as there were specific substances. For Anaxagoras, the creation of bone, say, from bread could only be explained by supposing that bread contained bone. Digestion separated out these bone "seeds" which then were incorporated into the bone structure of the organism. The order of the cosmos was not and could not be the result of chance. In an argument which was long to carry weight, Anaxagoras pointed out that the reasonableness of the universe implied a reason behind it. What kept everything orderly was a cosmic mind or *nous* which was all-pervading and which prevented the cosmos from collapsing into chaos.

Perhaps the most interesting doctrine devised to solve the Parmenidean problem was that of Leucippus (fl. ca. 440 B.C.) and Democritus of Abdera (fl. ca. 430 B.C.). It was they who created the atomic doctrine in which there are but two realities: atoms and the void. This was to grasp the Parmenidean nettle firmly for Parmenides had insisted that the void (non-Being) could not exist. By definition, non-Being could not logically Be. But, given the void and atoms, the world of change could be explained. Atoms came in all shapes and it was these shapes, as well as the shapes of clumps of atoms which accounted for the observed differences in bodies. All qualities can be explained by differences in shape, arrangement and position. Thus A differs from N in shape, AN from NA in arrangement and H from ⌶ in position. The atoms, themselves, were eternal and unchanging.

All these philosophical systems jostled one another in the marketplace of ideas. They represent the intellectual vigor of ancient Greece but they were, to be anachronistic, academic. Their concern was with the origin and composition of the universe, whereas it was the moral nature of man which increasingly preoccupied the average Greek. In the fifth century B.C., it was Socrates who pointed out that all the philosophical speculation in the world would not help to solve the urgent problems which pressed upon the citizens of the Polis, the Greek City-State. Philosophy, Socrates insisted, must be brought down from the heavens to the marketplace. This reorientation of philosophy is now known as the Socratic Revolt.

1. The Socratic Revolt and the Flowering of Greek Philosophy

Socrates (470-399 B.C.) was a stone-cutter in Athens during the most critical period of Athenian history. When he was born, Athens was just beginning her climb to greatness under the leadership of Pericles; when he was condemned to death by his fellow Athenians, Athens had just drained the cup of despair after total defeat by the Spartans in the Peloponnesian war. The successive crises which Athens underwent in these years provided the stimulus for the development of Socrates' thought. It should be noted that Socrates left no written remains. We know his ideas only through the writings of his diciples Plato and Xenophon.

The period of Socrates' life was one of intense political activity. Socrates' life was devoted to attempting to discover some intellectual guides to correct politics. Natural philosophy was irrelevant to such questions as "what is justice?" and "what is virtue?" and so Socrates abandoned it except insofar as he could use natural philosophy to illustrate man's rationality and the inherent order of the cosmos. His mortal enemies were the Sophists, a group of itinerant teachers who claimed the ability to be able to teach the art of political leadership. His method was to engage his opponent in debate and, through simple, but penetrating, questions, reduce him to a confession of ignorance. The recognition of ignorance is the first step in education and the Socratic method has been a favorite pedagogical device ever since Socrates invented it.

The discovery of the origin of knowledge was a more difficult task. Socrates appeared to believe (if we follow Plato) that the pursuit of Truth involved simply the process of recovering the memory of a previous state. Man's soul, before being united to the body, knew, in absolute terms, the True, the Good, and the Beautiful. Union with gross flesh, however, produced amnesia and the goal of education was to restore pre-natal memory. The first step was to clear the mind of illusions, of opinions, hence Socrates' relentless criticism of accepted notions. Only after this task was accomplished was the soul capable of contemplating the remembrance of things past. This was where the Socratic method created some problems which can best be illustrated by an example. In the *Meno*, a Platonic dialogue, Socrates, through clever questioning of a slave, leads him to the enunciation of the Pythagorean theorem. Socrates uses this example to prove his doctrine that knowledge is nothing but memory for it was certain that the slave had never received any instructions in geometry. But Socrates had, and without the proper questions which could be framed only through prior knowledge it is extremely doubtful that the slave would have "remembered" anything. The problem then shifts and we must ask *what* it was that Socrates had remembered that permitted him to lead the slave to truth? It was this question which Plato set out to answer in his doctrine of Ideas.

In a sense, Plato was faced with the old Parmenidean problem of finding an eternal, unchanging reality behind the daily flux of phenomena. But Plato had to account for eternal moral truths as well as physical ones so that the Parmenidean sphere was inapplicable. In its place Plato substituted eternal, unchanging Ideas. The phenomenal world was a flickering and corrupted version of this pure Ideal world. This is the message of the myth of the Cave [Readings, p 55 .]. The Ideas could be used to account for observable nature. Thus, for example, Plato could posit an Idea of a horse which was eternal and unchanging. Actual horses were horses because they participated in some mysterious fashion in the Idea. We recognize a horse as a horse because we dimly perceive the Idea. No two horses are exactly alike; some are large, some are small, some are white, others are chestnut, and so on. It is their common participation in the Idea of a horse which gives them their essential "horsiness." But this aspect of his theory was of relatively slight importance for Plato. The Ideas in which he was interested were moral ones: the Idea of Justice, Virtue, etc. To know these would be to be capable of setting absolute standards and, through them, creating the perfect Polis.

There were, however, two areas in which Plato's philosophy exerted great influence on the development of science. Plato was to set the fundamental problem in astronomy for the next 1800 years and he was also to stimulate the study of mathematics throughout antiquity and during the Platonic revival of the Renaissance.

In astronomy, Plato began with a fundamental postulate which he derived from his own political views. Plato was an aristocrat and a conservative in a period of demagoguery and corrupt democracy in Athens. In his view impiety led to anarchy and restoration of respect for the gods was the first step in the restoration of order. The old pantheon had lost its religious power so Plato attempted to create a new, astral religion. The heavens and the stars (including the planets) were divine. Being divine, they were perfect. They must, then, move in perfect motion. The only eternal, unchanging motion for Plato was circular motion. Hence, Plato insisted, all heavenly motion *must* be circular. But, very clearly, all heavenly motion was *not* circular, witness the planets. The planets do not simply circle the earth; they progress, slow down, retrogress and progress again. Plato set out to "save the phenomena," a wonderful phrase meaning that if observations do not fit a preconceived theory then the phenomena must be manipulated until they do. This, it might be added, is a common practice in science and is not unheard of even in the twentieth century. To "save the phenomena" it was necessary to devise some kind of mathematical model by which the apparently non-circular motion of the planets could be reduced to a more or less complex combination of circular motions. The problem intrigued Plato's contemporary, the mathematician Eudoxus (ca. 408-355 B.C.) whose doctrine of homocentric spheres was adopted by Aristotle [Readings, p. 113]. It continued to influence Ptolemy [Readings, p. 126], was basic to Copernicus in the sixteenth century A.D., and even blinded Galileo to the solution of the difficulty, finally offered by Johann Kepler in the early years of the seventeenth century. (See following illustrations.)

Plato's influence on mathematics was less specific but no less important. For Plato, mathematics dealt with eternal unchanging truths and was, therefore, the model of all sciences. The truths in themselves were unimportant but the habit of thought gained through the study of mathematics offered the student a guide to the road to truth. The apprehension of the Platonic Ideas could be achieved only when the soul was freed from its bondage to gross matter and the senses. Mathematics was the liberating agent. Thus those who would gaze upon naked Truth could do so only when prepared by a rigorous mathematical education. "Let no one enter here without geometry" was the motto of Plato's Academy. There were those who followed Plato who would take the argument even farther. They, like the Pythagoreans, would insist that the physical world was essentially mathematical. Mathematics, therefore, was not merely an intellectual purgative but *the* key to physical reality.

Plato's greatest pupil, Aristotle (384-322 B.C.), rejected both Plato's *via mathematica* and the doctrine of Ideas. Mathematics, for Aristotle, dealt and could deal only with quantity, thus neglecting the qualitative aspects of reality. The Ideas were too far removed from the world of the senses to satisfy Aristotle for Aristotle was a keen observer of living things and to him form was innate and in constant process of development,

ANCIENT SOLUTIONS TO THE PROBLEM OF HEAVENLY MOTION. Fig. 1 represents Eudoxus's solution of homocentric spheres. The planet is fixed to the innermost sphere whose axis connects with another sphere turning about its axis, and so on, until the resultant motion of the planet is that observed in the heavens. It was not a very good model. One of the things it could not explain was retrograde motion. Fig. 2 can. The large circle is called the deferent on which the smaller circle, or epicycle, revolves. If the angular velocities of the two circles are properly adjusted, then P will move backwards at various points in the epicycle's revolution around the deferent. Fig 3 is a geometrically equivalent model that uses another device, the eccentric. The Sun, in its annual path around the static earth, moves faster at some seasons than others. This can be represented by moving the position of the earth from the center, B, to A. Then, if P moves around B with constant angular velocity, it will move at varying velocities around A. Both epicycles and eccentrics were used by Ptolemy in his planetary theory, Fig. 4. The planet moves on an epicycle on a deferent with center at B', distant from the earth at A' by the eccentricity, e. The center of the epicycle, however, moves at equal angular velocity around C', opposite to A' and also distant e from B'. This point was later called the equant.

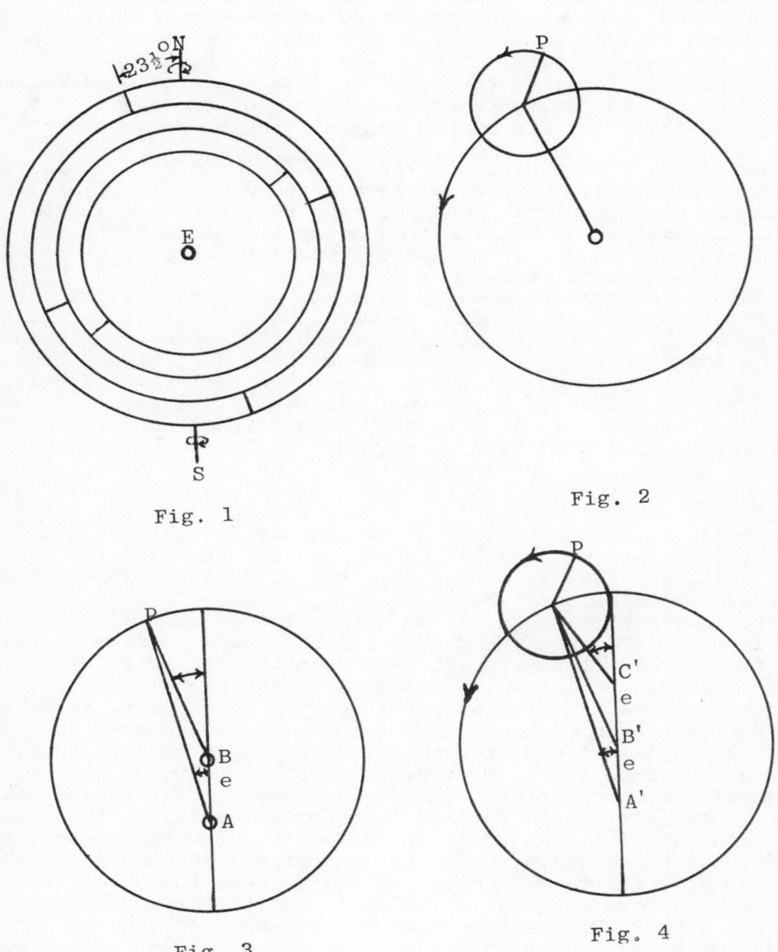

Fig. 1

Fig. 2

Fig. 3

Fig. 4

not a master blueprint imperfectly followed in matter.

Aristotle was born in Stagira in Macedonia, the son of the physician to Philip II, king of Macedonia. The earliest intellectual influence on him came from medicine with its emphasis upon close observation. He was keenly interested in living creatures and, unlike his master, Plato, felt it was in complete keeping with his intellectual dignity to spend his time observing them under natural conditions. His *History of Animals* is a classic in natural history and reveals his extraordinary ability as an observer. He knew and described the placental shark which brings forth its young alive and described a species of octopus in which the male inseminates the female by leaving the male organ within the female after coupling. This latter observation was derided by the "enlightened" scientists of the eighteenth century, until it was discovered that Aristotle was absolutely right.

Aristotle's thought was strongly influenced by his biological investigations. We have already alluded to the organic, as opposed to the mechanical, metaphor as a representation of the cosmos. Aristotle was to take this metaphor absolutely seriously. For him, the cosmos was alive and its elements were to be understood in biological terms.

Aristotle borrowed heavily from his predecessors for the parts of his system but he put them together in his own original way. He solved the Parmenidean problem by accepting the "boundless" of Anaximander as a sub-stratum without qualities. It was this sub-stratum, later named the *materia prima* (prime matter), which remained unchanged throughout all sensible change. It was Being. The *materia prima* could take on qualities and it was the *materia prima* plus qualities which made up the four elements. Thus fire was *materia prima* which had the qualities of hot and dry, water was wet and cold, air was wet and hot, and earth was cold and dry. The transmutation of one element into the other was a simple thing; one merely needed to substitute one quality for another. Thus water could be transmuted into air simply by substituting the quality of hot for that of cold, a process that occurred every time a pot began to boil.

Aristotle knew there was more to science than reducing objects to their elements. The real problem was to account for the different objects that were made from the elements. It is all well and good to say with Empedocles that a chair and a bed are both composed of varying proportions of earth, air, fire, and water but even a child knows that a chair is *not* a bed. Aristotle set out to explain the difference. To do so, he posited four causes which, when known, provided a *complete* solution to the problem of differentiation. These causes are: 1. the material cause; 2. the efficient cause; 3. the formal cause; 4. the final cause. These refer, in order, to the matter of which an object is made, the processes by which the matter has assumed the form of the object, the form itself, and the purpose the object serves. We can now answer the question, what is the difference between a chair and a bed? Both may be made of the same material and many of the processes--sawing, planing, joining--which went into their manufacture are the same. But they differ in form and their form is determined by their respective purposes. A bed is to sleep in and a chair is to sit in. Hence the final cause determines the formal and the formal determines both the material and the efficient for we would not make a bed out of a substance which would not bear our weight nor would we select a material which could not be worked into the form of a bed.

Aristotle's four causes also permitted him to discard Plato's Ideas. Plato would have argued that we recognize individual beds with vastly different shapes, as beds because we dimly apprehend the Idea of a bed and it is this Idea which is common to all the individual beds. Aristotle, on the other hand, would argue that we recognize that an object is a bed by recognizing its purpose. What is common to *all* beds is function and this is not a transcendant idea but a down-to-earth reality. Form and matter are united in Aristotelean science.

It should be noted that this approach is perfectly valid for those sciences in which a clear purpose can be discerned. The archaeologist, for example, upon uncovering an implement immediately seeks to determine its purpose for the rest of the causes will then follow logically. The anatomist, physiologist, and morphologist also still make excellent use of Aristotle's four causes to correlate form and function. When taken over into the realm of physics, however, the four causes are not so obviously applicable. If one asks why a stone falls to the earth, the answer may be difficult to find. Unless--unless one assumes that all Nature is purposive and this is precisely what Aristotle did assume. The cosmos *is* an organism in which order is maintained. God has so ordained it; without God and purpose the Aristotelean universe collapses.

Aristotle was perfectly aware of the difficulty and expended a good deal of effort to prove that there was a purposive, First Cause. If such a Cause be admitted, then it is possible to move into areas where purpose is not clearly evident. Such phenomena as that of motion, for example, can cause trouble.

For Aristotle, motion was synonymous with change of any kind. Motion from one place to another was locomotion; growth and decay were also motions which required explanation. Locomotion was of various kinds. The most obvious was the motion of one's own self from one place to another. This motion had a clear final cause. I go from my desk to the stove because I want to heat the coffee. My "soul" moves me and all voluntary motion is, by definition, purposive. It is somewhat more difficult to discern the purpose involved when a stone falls or fire flies upward. Aristotle provides one. The universe is so constructed that each element has its own place. Earth, being inert, is at the center; water lies on earth; air surrounds the water; and fire encompasses them all. When an element is displaced from its natural place, it strives to return to it. So, when released a stone falls to earth. Its purpose is to return to that space where it belongs. This motion Aristotle called natural motion. Aristotle's space is not the space of geometry where all places are equal. Aristotelean space has qualities; *here* is where earth belongs and *there* is where air belongs.

Another form of motion occurs when an object is displaced

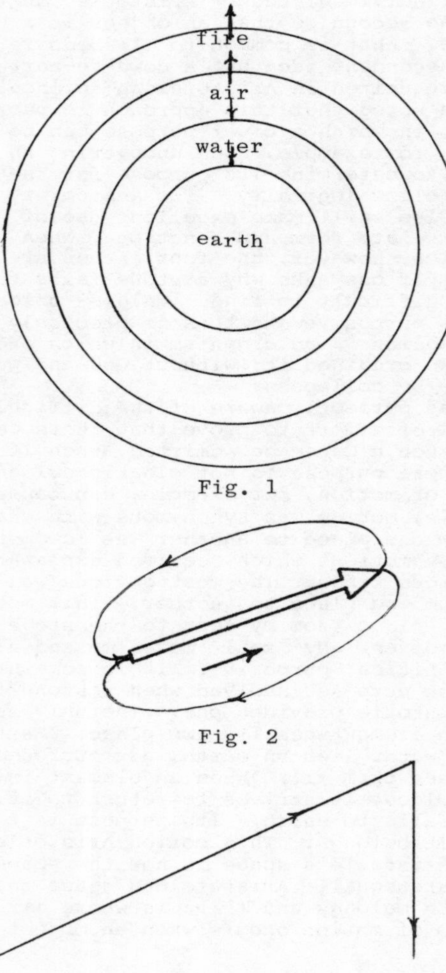

Fig. 1

Fig. 2

Fig. 3

NATURAL AND VIOLENT MOTION IN ARISTOTLE. Fig. 1 shows the sublunary world with the earth at the center. The elements have each their own sphere. Earth and water are heavy and move towards the center when displaced from their respective spheres. Air and fire move from the center when displaced. Fig. 2 represents Aristotle's theory of projectile motion. The spear forces air out from in front of it as it moves through the atmosphere and this air rushes behind the spear to prevent the formation of a vacuum, thus pushing the spear along. Fig. 3 shows the trajectory of a spear. It first suffers violent motion in a straight line; then it falls in natural motion to the earth. The two motions cannot mix.

from its natural place and forced to move contrary to its natural motion, as when a spear or ball is thrown upward or horizontally. Such motion is violent motion. It was not easy for Aristotle to explain it. Observation indicated that things move because they are pushed or pulled. Why should the object continue to move after the push or pull has ceased? Put in philosophical terms, this involves the question, "can the effect persist after the cause is removed?" If so, then cause and effect are not equal, a proposition which horrifies all philosophers. So Aristotle had to invent an explanation with which even he was not too happy. Nature, as we know from observing the rise of liquid in a straw when we suck on it, abhors a vacuum. When a projectile is hurled through the air, it creates a potential vacuum behind it. To prevent the vacuum, the air displaced from the front of the projectile rushes to the rear and thus pushes the projectile along. [See figure 2.]

There is a third kind of locomotion, namely that of the heavenly bodies. Here Aristotle accepted Plato's astral religion. The stars and planets move in circles because their souls direct them to move in circles in adoration of the Prime Mover, or God, who, unmoved, inspires this heavenly motion. That, at least, is Aristotle's belief in the *Metaphysics*. But in his *On the Heavens* he suggested that there might be a fifth element--a quintessence or aether--which was almost pure form and whose natural motion was circular.

Aristotle also agreed with Plato that the heavens were perfect and he was forced, accordingly, to divide the universe into two essentially distinct physical regions. Above the sphere of the moon, there was no generation or decay. All was perfect and unchanging. Below the moon, there was constant change. To account for this change, Aristotle introduced two new concepts: potentiality and actuality. These were of particular importance in explaining the development of organic forms (morphology). After all, an acorn does not resemble an oak tree in any way, but somehow it develops into an oak tree. How? Aristotle answered that the acorn was potentially an oak and that growth was the actualization of this potential. This is not a very satisfying explanation for the modern reader but it is worth noting that Aristotle here raised the fundamental question with which embryology had to deal from his own time to ours. Furthermore, Aristotle did more than raise the question. In his *History of Animals*, *On Generation*, and *The Parts of Animals* he recorded his own acute embryological and anatomical observations to document the actualization of morphological potential.

With Aristotle's death in 322 B.C., an era in Greek philosophy and science came to a close. The conquests of Alexander the Great, Aristotle's pupil who died in 323 B.C., opened the Greek world to a flood of knowledge and ideas from the conquered lands. And, Greek philosophy and science were among the most important exports to the Near East and Egypt. The Hellenistic world was a more cosmopolitan and infinitely more complex one than the Hellenic polis. Plato and Aristotle had drawn the large philosophical picture. Those who followed them felt their task to be the systematization of all the bits and pieces of science that had hitherto been produced and the intense investigation of smaller areas, rather than the production of rival philosophical systems. The intellectual center of gravity also shifted from Athens to the great Museum of Alexandria and, for a few decades, to the Syracuse of Archimedes.

C. Science in the Hellenistic Period

Within less than a decade after the death of Alexander his empire had split into three parts--Greece proper under the direct rule of Macedonia, Asia Minor and Egypt. Each fragment was ruled by one of Alexander's generals and each of these rulers quickly moved to make his rule permanent and hereditary.

In Greece, this meant repression of the City-state; the consequent intellectual atmosphere was not conducive to scientific thought. Philosophers turned, rather, to the problem of accommodating human life to the new conditions. New schools of philosophy sprang up almost overnight--Cynicism, Skepticism, Stoicism and Epicureanism were all devised to provide men with guides to conduct in the new world in which the polis was merely a component part of a larger and impersonal kingdom.

In Asia Minor, the successors of Seleucus, the general who seized power upon Alexander's death, were faced with extraordinary problems of government. The territory was vast, the population polyglot and the Greeks a small minority. Most energies had to be directed towards holding the Seleucid Empire together and little was left over for intellectual activity. The Greek conquest of Babylonia did have the effect of bringing Greeks into contact with the great mathematical and astronomical tradition of Mesopotamia. This knowledge was rapidly assimilated and was to influence Hellenistic developments in these fields. Otherwise, with but one exception, the Seleucid Empire was intellectually barren. The exception was the City of Pergamum, just inland of Ionia. There was a great library there (the word parchment comes from Pergamum) and it was a center of learning during the Hellenistic period. The great physician Galen [Readings, pp. 156, 157] was born there.

The third fragment of Alexander's Empire was seized by another of Alexander's generals, Ptolemy. He rapidly consolidated his power and Ptolemaic Egypt was the most unified and the most tranquil of all the Hellenistic states. Alexander himself had founded the city of Alexandria and Ptolemy and his successors set out to make it the most splendid city in the Middle East. Ptolemy II Philadelphus founded the Museum of Alexandria which contained the greatest library of antiquity. This was the center of scholarship in all fields and it was here that Hellenistic science flourished. With the exception of Archimedes, Galen and a few others, most of the scientific work of the Hellenistic period was accomplished by men who had some connection with the Museum of Alexandria.

The character of Hellenistic science differed markedly from that of the Hellenic period. The Hellenic philosophers of nature had attempted to encompass the whole of the physical world. Their goal was the explanation of the cosmos. The cosmos, like the polis, seemed to be a self-contained, internally regulated, ordered entity which could be understood in its entirety. The failure of the polis seems to have had the effect on philosophers of destroying their belief in the analogy, polis-cosmos. The Hellenistic world was politically infinitely larger and more complex than the Hellenic polis; so, too, was the Hellenistic universe larger and more complex than the Hellenic cosmos. There was, if you will, a certain failure of nerve. It seemed to most philosophers to be the better part of wisdom to leave aside the great cosmic questions that had inspired philosophers from Thales to Aristotle, and focus, instead, on smaller questions. One could either accept the grand philosophical synthesis of an Aristotle, and try to fill in the details, or one could consider philosophy irrelevant and attempt only to understand isolated aspects of reality, but understand these thoroughly and on the basis of the accurate determination of facts. Both approaches were to be followed. There was a third possibility. The sheer intellectual exuberance of the Hellenic period had brought forth a flood of works on all subjects from literature to mathematics. It would be a service to future generations to collect these works, subject them to critical analysis and bring the results together into some kind of synthetic whole. It was at the Museum of Alexandria, for example, that the variant texts of the Homeric epics were examined, critically assessed and synthesized into the version which has come down to us. Similarly, Euclid brought together the various theorems and proofs which had been formulated before him into a synthetic whole.

1. The Development of Mathematics and Astronomy

The great stimulus to the early development of Greek Mathematics was the Pythagorean discovery that musical intervals could be represented by numerical ratios and the discovery that the diagonal of a square could not be represented by the ratio of two integers. The first led to the theory of proportions which reached a high level of sophistication in the hands of Eudoxus, Plato's contemporary. What Eudoxus did, essentially, was to ring all the changes on the three basic Pythagorean ratios which he represented as follows (in modern notation):

The arithmetic: $a - b = b - c$

The geometric: $a/b = b/d$

The harmonic: $1/c - 1/b = 1/b - 1/a$

or $a/c = \frac{a-b}{b-c}$

From this latter, it was possible to develop an entire mathematical theory of music. If we take $a = 6$, $b = 8$, and $c = 12$ then the harmonic mean will be $1/12 - 1/8 = 1/8 - 1/6$ from which it is possible to deduce the principal musical intervals: a/c = the octave, c/b = the fifth, and b/a = the fourth. Music was the first mathematical science.

The discovery of irrational numbers led to the flourishing of geometry since the diagonal of a square can be simply represented geometrically, although it is impossible to represent it by number. The development of geometry, in turn, led to the recognition of certain geometrical problems of great difficulty. These were to serve as a challenge to geometers for centuries. The problems were:

1. The duplication of a cube.
2. Trisection of an angle using only compass and ruler.
3. The squaring of the circle.

The duplication of the cube involved finding the side of a cube whose volume would be double that of a given cube. In modern terms, this would be to find the solution to the equation $x^3 = 2a^3$. It can be attacked by finding two mean proportionals between x and a and this problem was solved by geometric means in antiquity.

The trisection of the angle led to very little original work and may be passed over here.

The squaring of the circle required the discovery of a method of reducing areas bounded by curves to rectilinear measure and was to stimulate the mathematical ingenuity of generations of mathematicians.

By the beginning of the Hellenistic period, then, there was a fairly high level of somewhat uncoordinated mathematical achievement. Isolated areas had been well investigated, problems had been set and the basic geometric method of deduction from axioms and theorems had been laid down. One of the fundamental conditions for further mathematical advance was the systematization of this knowledge so that the entire field of mathematics could be surveyed as a whole. This was the great achievement of Euclid (fl. ca. 300 B.C.).

Euclid's *Elements* in thirteen books, as every school boy used to know, begins with a statement of five axioms and five postulates which seem self-evident. From these, Euclid developed the whole of plane and solid geometry. In Book V, Euclid introduced Eudoxus' theory of proportions which served as the springboard for the study of number theory and proportion. Books XI-XIII dealt with solid geometry or constructions, Book XIII being particularly concerned with the inscription of the five regular solids (tetrahedron, cube, octahedron, dodecahedron, and icosahedron) in a sphere.

Euclid's *Elements* was the most popular textbook ever written. Generations of mathematicians and mathematical physicists were first awakened to the austere beauty and logic of mathematics by the *Elements*. Copernicus, Kepler, Galileo, Newton, and Einstein, to mention only a few, were brought up on Euclid. It took professional American educators of the twentieth century to discover that Euclid did not have a degree in education and that the *Elements* were pedagogically unsound.

One area that the *Elements* did not treat was the properties of curvilinear figures other than the circle. Solid geometry had led to the study of such solids as the cone and, in the Third century B.C., attention was focused on the curves produced when a right cone was cut by a plane at various angles to the bases.

These curves--the ellipse, parabola, and hyperbola--are known as conic sections and their properties were exhaustively analyzed by Apollonius of Perga (fl. 285 B.C.) using only geometric methods. It was Apollonius' treatise on conics which provided the basis of Kepler's work on the orbit of Mars in the early Seventeenth century. Apollonius' method was not displaced until the advent of the calculus at the end of the Seventeenth century.

Probably the greatest mathematician of antiquity was Archimedes (287-212 B.C.). In a treatise, *The Sand Reckoner*, Archimedes devised a numerical system for dealing with very large numbers, no mean feat when we reflect that the Greek number system was like the Roman. His most important contribution to mathematics was the development of the method of exhaustion for determining the area of a circle. This consisted of inscribing polygons of ever-increasing number of sides in a circle and circumscribing the circle with the same polygons. The areas of the inscribed and circumscribed polygons will approach the area of the circle as the number of sides increases. Since it is relatively easy to determine the area of any polygon, this provided a method of approximation to the problem of squaring the circle. More importantly, Archimedes introduced the embryo of the idea of the limit, the keystone of the calculus. With his method of exhaustion, Archimedes was able to find the volume of a cylinder inscribed in a sphere and the area of such curvilinear figures as the parabola.

Astronomy also flourished during the Hellenistic period. Contact with Babylonia made available the observations of Babylonian astronomers over the course of many years, and stimulated the compilation of observations by the Greeks. Hipparchus of Nicaea (ca. 190-120 B.C.) was the greatest astronomical observer of antiquity. He compiled the first stellar catalogue of some 850 stars, noting their positions with considerable accuracy and distinguishing them by assigning "magnitudes" of brightness to each. Using Babylonian star tables, Hipparchus also discovered the precession of the equinoxes, i.e., the fact that the equinoxes do not fall on the same days every year but vary slowly over the years. Hipparchus also applied the newly-discovered trigonometric methods of Babylonian mathematicians to astronomical problems. His is the first recorded table of chords without which it would be impossible to deal with planetary motion in mathematical detail.

Progress in observational astronomy created new problems for the philosophical astronomer who felt obliged to remain loyal to the Eudoxian-Aristotelean doctrine of homocentric spheres. As we have seen, this system could account for retrograde motion, but it could not easily deal with two other observations. Systematic observations revealed that the planets varied in brightness and that their motions were more complicated than the system of homocentric spheres could account for. A number of alternatives, then, were suggested. Heracleides of Pontus (ca. 388-310 B.C.) is credited with assuming that the "inferior" planets, Mercury and Venus, revolved around the sun while the sun revolved around the earth. The most conspicuous variation in planetary brightness is that of Venus and this system would account neatly for it. Heracleides also was the first astronomer to argue that it was fitter for the earth to turn on its axis than to require the immense vault of the heavens to revolve every 24 hours. A later astronomer, Aristarchus of Samos (fl. ca. 281 B.C.) took Heracleides' system to its logical conclusion. If the Sun were moved to the center of the cosmos and the earth and the other planets revolved around it, then most of the observational difficulties disappeared. The combination of the earth's annual revolution and diurnal rotation would make everything fit. This hypothesis was briefly summarized by Archimedes and may have been known to Copernicus. It was not accepted in antiquity for it not only violated all the then-known principles of philosophy (why should the earth revolve or rotate?) but it required a universe of such immense size that no one could take it seriously. If the earth revolved around the sun, there ought to be an observable stellar parallax Failure to detect this parallax either meant that the cosmos was almost infinitely large, or that the earth stood still, as Aristotle had said. Most philosophers opted for the latter explanation, as indeed they should have, for it was simpler and more in accord with common sense.

The failure of Heracleides and Aristarchus to be accepted still left the same problems outstanding. It was Hipparchus who first suggested a way out of the dilemma. Retrograde motion and difference in brightness could be accounted for mathematically by devising a system of circles upon one of which a point representing the planet moved. Later the difference in velocities of the planets and especially of the sun at different times of the year (the result of the fact that the earth, in its elliptical orbit moves more rapidly in the winter months when closer to the sun, than in the summer) could be accounted for by moving the center of the system of the circles from the earth to another point called the equant (see Fig. 4., p. 14).Hipparchus' suggestions were worked out in intricate mathematical detail by the last great astronomer of antiquity, Claudius Ptolemy (no relative of the rulers of Egypt). Ptolemy (fl. ca. 150 A.D.) did for astronomy what Euclid did for geometry. His work, *Mathematikei Syntaxis*, called by the Arabs al-Magesti (the greatest), put together the results of the mathematical and observational astronomers of antiquity [Readings, p. 126]. The *Almagest* preserved the philosophical requirement of circular motion at the same time that it offered a highly sophisticated mathematical treatment of planetary and heavenly motions. It was now possible to feel secure philosophically at the same time that one calculated planetary positions for astrological or calendrical purposes. It should, however, be noted what the *Almagest* did not do. It was a mathematical *representation* of heavenly motion not a physical theory of such motion. It dealt with points moving on circles, not planets moving in orbits and it made no attempt to answer the question of *why* the planets move as they do. This answer had been given by Aristotle and Ptolemy was content to leave the physics to Aristotle. The Middle Ages, then, inherited two cosmic schemes; the mathematical description by Ptolemy and the physical explanation by Aristotle. The two did not appear to conflict until quite late but when the conflict became evident, it created a considerable tension in astronomy. The tension was only to be relieved with the formulation and acceptance of the Copernican system.

2. The Development of Physics

The developments in physics during the Hellenistic period paralleled those in mathematics and astronomy. By and large the Hellenic philosophical framework of physics remained intact, although in specific and narrowly defined areas it was either ignored or challenged. By the end of the ancient world, the dominant philosophies of physics remained Hellenic--either Platonic or Aristotelian although the specific advances were later to offer alternatives to these philosophies.

Physics evolved along two rather distinct lines after the death of Aristotle. There was, on the one hand, the creation of a tradition of criticism of Aristotelian mechanics. This tradition was begun by the anonymous author of a treatise on the lever, the *Mechanica*, and continued by Strato of Lampsacus, and by the practical "mechanics" of the Hellenistic age such as Hero of Alexandria. The second path was that opened and explored by Archimedes.

The author of the *Mechanica* raises the question of why a weight on one end of a balance beam travels with greater velocity, the farther it is from the fulcrum. According to Aristotle, the velocity with which a body moves is determined solely by the force acting upon it and the resistance of the medium through which it travels. In the above case, this treatment leads to puzzlement for the force (weight) and the resistance of the air remain constant. All that changes is the length of the level arm. The fact that the author recognizes that there is a problem here casts doubt upon the Aristotelian doctrine.

This doubt was to be further amplified in the works of Strato of Lampsacus (fl. ca. 270 B.C.). Strato was a philosopher who became the head of the great school, the Lyceum, founded by Aristotle. It is possible that Strato was the author of the *Mechanica*; it is certain that he concerned himself with the question raised by that treatise. In a work, now lost, *On Motion*, Strato considered a more general case of the problem of the increase in velocity of bodies when acted upon by constant force. This was the question of uniformly accelerated motion in free fall. Again, by a strict application of Aristotelean mechanical principles, a body ought to fall at constant velocity since the cause of its motion--its weight--was constant. Strato could give no adequate explanation of uniform acceleration, but he did make the explanation of such motion of central concern to those interested in the laws of nature. Aristotelians in the Middle Ages were to wrestle long and hard with this problem and its resolution by Galileo and Newton was to be of central importance in the Scientific Revolution of the Seventeenth century.

Strato went beyond raising an important question; he also devised a general theory of physical reality which was directly opposed to Aristotle. He accepted the general tenets of

Democritus' atomic theory and, unlike Democritus, also suggested experiments by which this theory could be confirmed. The *Introduction* to Hero of Alexandria's *Pneumatica* [Readings, p. 150] is now generally believed to reflect accurately Strato's ideas on ultimate physical reality.

Hero of Alexandria represents an important part of the critical tradition in post-Aristotelean mechanics. Hero was not a philosopher but a practicing "mechanic." There had been such mechanics in the Hellenic period but their acquaintance with machinery had been slight, involving only such machines as the cranes with which actors were raised and lowered in the theaters. The *Deus ex machina* was a common character in Attic tragedy but the *machina* was fairly simple and little could be learned from it. This changed in the Hellenistic period. The conquests of Alexander the Great led to the rapid development of military engineering. Large and complicated siege engines were devised for such campaigns as the siege of Tyre and their construction and operation was in the hands of engineers of no mean ability. The consolidation of the Alexandrian conquests also required engineering ingenuity. One way to keep a conquered population under political control is by impressing upon them the fact that the gods are on the side of the ruler. Thus Ptolemy in Egypt devised the cult of Serapis and among the machines that Hero described are those which appeared to indicate the presence of the god. One such machine utilized the expansion of air from the heat of a burning sacrifice to work a series of pulleys which, in turn, caused the doors of the temple to open, seemingly without human agency. It was Hero's reflection on the causes of the action of such machines that led him to compose the *Pneumatica*. The treatise had little real impact in antiquity but its recovery and translation in the Renaissance was to have important consequences in the revolt against Aristotle.

With Archimedes, Mechanics reached its highest point in antiquity. The story of the machines that he devised for the defense of Syracuse against the Romans is widely known and illustrates the importance of military engineering in the development of ancient mechanics. Archimedes, however, had the advantage of being a mathematician as well as a mechanic and this union of talents was what permitted him to advance the science.

We know nothing of the chronology of Archimedes' work but the logic of its development may permit us to set an order. Archimedes was primarily a mathematician and one of the areas in which he was interested was the properties of conic sections. In particular, he set out to find the centers of gravity of such curves as the parabola and hyperbola. Thanks to a lucky discovery by J. L. Heiberg in 1896, we know how Archimedes proceeded. Heiberg discovered a parchment in a bazaar in Egypt which contained a letter by Archimedes in which he described his method. He first drew the curves on parchment and carefully cut them out. Using a pin, he found the center of gravity by trial and error (i.e., he found the point on which the curve balanced) and then, knowing where the point was, he "proved" it was the center of gravity by geometry. This was the application of mechanics to mathematics and it is not surprising to find Archimedes turning to the application of mathematics to mechanics. His method of discovering centers of gravity involved the law of the lever and so it was that Archimedes now turned to a mathematical investigation of that law. His work on conic sections had shown that mathematical properties (i.e., area) could be represented by a physical property (i.e., weight) and so Archimedes merely reversed the procedure. Weights could be represented by areas and the lever could be treated as a geometrical construction. The law of the lever could now be deduced geometrically. It was only a short step from this problem to Archimedes' greatest achievement in mechanics, his principles of floating bodies [Readings, pp. 144]. The procedure was the same; certain physical properties such as weight and specific gravity could be represented mathematically. Once so represented, they could be operated upon by mathematical principles and conclusions could be drawn which were mathematically correct. These conclusions, in turn, could be translated back into physics to establish a law of mechanics. The method was as important as the results. It was later to inspire Galileo. Archimedes, in a very real sense, may be regarded as one of the instigators of the Scientific Revolution.

Archimedes' results also provided an alternative to Aristotelean views. The discovery of specific gravity and the Archimedean principle potentially destroyed the Aristotelian distinction between heavy and light (i.e., earth and fire) and with it the doctrine of natural places. What if all bodies were heavy and the passage of air and fire upward was merely the result of difference in specific gravity? The whole qualitative structure of the Aristotelian sub-lunar world would be shaken if such were the case. Once again, Archimedes' ideas and the consequences that could be drawn from his results were relatively uninfluential in antiquity. It was not until the Renaissance that their full impact was to be felt.

3. Medicine and Biology in the Hellenistic Period

The origin of Greek medicine was traditionally assigned to Orpheus the son of Apollo. Orpheus dealt in drugs and pharmaceutical "simples" which produced hallucinogenic effects. The more practical side of mythological medicine was represented by Chiron the Centaur who specialized in military surgery. The synthesis of the two traditions was accomplished by the still mythological Aesculapius, a pupil of Chiron, who combined practical skill in leech-craft with a direct line to the gods who could be called in for consultations on difficult cases. The cult of Aesculapius became an important religious sect devoted to the art of healing. Aesculapian temples dotted the Aegean and the sick made pilgrimages to them in their search for health. The treatment combined some common sense with mystical mumbo jumbo. There was a preliminary examination which determined whether the patient should be admitted. It would be folly to admit someone who was obviously dying and the priests of Aesculapius became adept at recognizing morbid symptions. If admitted, the patient was placed on an ascetic diet and was cleansed externally, internally, and morally to prepare him for the visitation of the god. The patient was then drugged and passed into what was known as the incubation sleep during which the god visited him. Some form of hypnosis may have been used to suggest to the patient that he would recover and the priest would follow this up by interpreting the message of the god. Therapeutics was a combination of psychology and empirical treatment which did the patient no harm and might lead to the alleviation of his condition. The votive offerings at the Temples testified to the success of the Aesclepiads and they undoubtedly did develop a wide empirical knowledge of disease symptoms and clinical syndromes.

Medicine, like cosmology, could not but be affected by the rise of natural philosophy with the pre-Socratics. The basic question in medicine is what is disease and its converse what is health? The pre-Socratics were quick to answer these and their systems of medicine reflected their systems of the world. Nor was this unexpected, for man was felt to be a reflection of the cosmos in miniature. What obtained in the macrocosm of the universe should also be true in the microcosm of man. Thus, for example, we find the Empedoclean doctrine of the four elements reflected in the medical doctrine of the four humours. Blood, phlegm, black bile, and yellow bile were the elements of human physiology as fire, water, earth, and air were the elements of physics. We might note in passing that physiology and physics have the same etymological root. The Pythagorean doctrine of harmony and ratio also found a place in medicine with Alcmaeon of Croton who flourished at the beginning of the Fifth century B.C. Health, according to Alcmaeon, consisted of the proper balance or harmony among the humors. When this state of harmony, or isonomia, was disturbed, the patient fell ill. Humoral pathology was to enjoy a long vogue in the history of medicine.

The atomists were not to be out-done. To Democritus, health consisted of a state in which the atoms of the body could circulate freely. His clinical observations here seem to have focused on digestion. The healthy state was one in which the digestive process proceeded smoothly with regularity of elimination. The clogging of the bodily pores or constipation, led to illness.

Each of these systems implied a therapeutics. The imbalance of the humors which led to disease could, theoretically, be attacked by purging of the excess humor or restoration of those in deficit. It was simply not very clear how one went about this restoration of isonomia. Similarly, the opening of the pores might be accomplished by diet but not all diseases were characterized by constipation and what did one do then?

It was practical questions such as these that were attacked by the great physician Hippocrates of Cos (ca. 460-350 B.C.) and his school. In the treatise *On Ancient Medicine*, written by Hippocrates or one of his school, the philosophers are taken to task [Readings, p. 85]. Medicine is too complicated to be subsumed under any philosophical system. It may be intellectually satisfying to speak of humors and pores, but what do you do when faced with a sick patient? The Hippocratic physician treated people, he did not write speculative treatises. What was needed was some guide to medical practice. This came from close, clinical observation, hard-headed common sense and a recognition that the physician could do little except help his patients to get well, not cure them. The result was a sane approach to disease which was not bettered until the advent of modern medicine provided a scientific basis for the attack on disease.

The Hippocratic school took an immense step forward when it insisted that disease was a natural, not a super-natural, phenomenon. Epilepsy, for example, had been regarded as possession by a god and was, therefore, called the sacred disease. Not so, insisted the Hippocratics. Epilepsy was like any other disease; it had specific symptoms and ran its specific course. It could be described clinically, recognized as an entity by the physician, and the course of the seizure accurately predicted by a physician who had observed a sufficient number of cases. It was no more sacred than mumps. This example reveals one facet of Hippocratic medicine, namely its emphasis on clinical observation which permitted the physician to predict the future course of the disease. An important part of the Hippocratic corpus of writings is devoted to the careful description of specific cases [Readings, p. 92]. The Hippocratics also recognized that the best healing agent was nature herself. Purges and other strong medicaments often weakened the patient and hastened his demise. It was better to leave the patient alone, make him comfortable and feed him a simple but nutritious diet. His own restorative powers--what the Latin West later called the *vis medicatrix naturae* (the medical power of nature)--would bring him back to health.

Hippocratic medicine relied almost entirely upon clinical observations and implicit in it was the somewhat defeatist attitude that medicine could not be based upon an intimate knowledge of the workings of the body. Diseases were too varied ever to be understood; they could only be described. There were others who felt otherwise. Alcmaeon of Croton is reputed to be the first Greek to attempt to understand the body by taking it apart to see what makes it work. He is supposed to have dissected the eye and the brain in an attempt to understand how the senses worked. He had few followers in Hellenic Greece, however, since dissection involved desecration of the body. It was in Alexandria in Egypt, where the opening of the body for purposes of mummification was commonplace, that anatomy and physiology were advanced.

The two great pioneers were Herophilus (fl. 290 B.C.) and Erasistratus (fl. 260 B.C.), both of whom worked at the Museum of Alexandria. Herophilus systematically explored the various systems of the human body leaving descriptions (now lost) of the nerves, arteries and veins, the digestive tract and the skeleton. He paid particular attention to the brain, distinguishing the cerebrum from the cerebellum. He distinguished arteries from veins and named the duodenum, the first part of the small intestine. He was much like Hipparchus, content to describe accurately rather than erect a general system based upon his observations.

Herophilus' younger contemporary and rival Erasistratus was

not so restrained. He continued the work of Herophilus but also incorporated his observations into a general system of physiology based solely on mechanical principles. Thus Erasistratus attributed a mechanical grinding function to the stomach in digestion and also adopted a mechanical explanation for the mixture of blood and air (pneuma) in the arteries. His anatomical investigations led him to the understanding of the difference between the motor and sensory nerves, and to the mechanical function of the epiglottis in preventing the entrance of food and drink into the windpipe. He observed the heart in systole and diastole (contraction and relaxation) and distinguished the coronary valves. His work, together with that of Herophilus provided the basis for an Atlas of human anatomy and for a first step in the creation of a human physiology. The last step to be taken in antiquity in this task was that by Galen of Pergamum (130-200 A.D.).

Galen was a Greek, born and educated at Pergamum within the Greek tradition. Unlike Herophilus and Erasistratus, Galen did not have human cadavers at his disposal and was, therefore, forced to work on animals, particularly the pig and the Barbary ape. Some of his errors were due to this fact and his assumption that the anatomical features of his animals were duplicated in the human body. Galen was, nevertheless, one of the greatest anatomists of all time and his work remained basic to medicine until the Seventeenth century. He was also one of the first to devise a general physiology based on close observation of anatomical detail. Finally, he was an excellent experimenter and used experiment with great skill to prove his physiological points [Readings, p. 156].

Galen's work on anatomy led him to a fundamental point of central importance to physiology. Unlike Herophilus and Erasistratus who studied anatomical systems in isolation from one another, Galen recognized the importance of systemic interdependence. It was the organism as a whole which was alive and the individual systems were subordinate to the organism. Specific organs--the liver, kidney, stomach--were self-generating and drew their nutrition from the blood by attraction and coction. Each organ was the seat of a specific faculty which permitted it to perform its function. Thus the stomach was the seat of the digestive faculty, the brain contained the intellectual faculty, and so on. The whole organism was united by the various spirits which were central to Galenic physiology [see diagram]. Food from the intestine is carried via the portal vein to the liver. The liver manufactures blood and natural spirits which serve for growth and nutrition. The blood and natural spirits slosh back and forth in the veins and, in so doing enter the right ventricle of the heart where the blood is relieved of "soot" and impurities. Some of this blood seeps through minute pores in the septum of the heart to the left ventricle where it mixes with air carried from the lungs to the heart by the pulmonary vein. Here vital spirits are made which, passing through the arteries, endow the organs with their ability to function. Some blood also splashes into the brain where animal spirits are concocted and these spirits, passing through the nerves give rise to sensation and

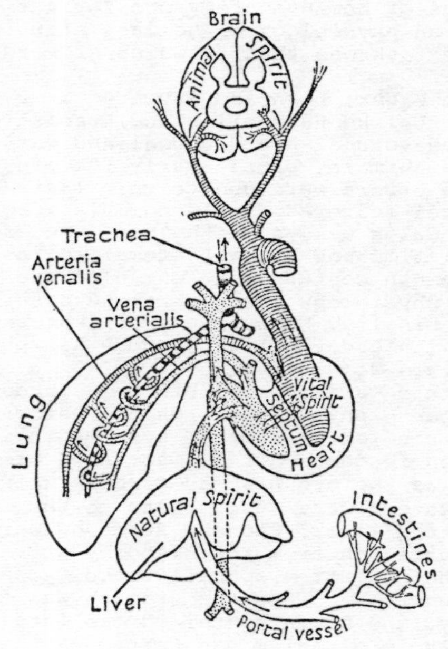
Brain
Animal Spirit
Trachea
Arteria venalis
Vena arterialis
Lung
Vital Spirit
Septum
Heart
Natural Spirit
Intestines
Liver
Portal vessel

motion. Galen was thus able to account for the action of the body on the basis of gross anatomy and the hypothetical spirits. Both his anatomy and physiology were to remain authoritative until successfully challenged in the seventeenth century. It might be noticed, however, that the flourishing of anatomy and physiology which culminated in Galen had little practical effect on the practice of medicine. In spite of the greatly expanded knowledge of anatomy and the sophisticated system of Galenic physiology, a sick person was well-advised to put himself in the hands of a Hippocratic physician who would regulate his diet and let Nature take its course.

There was not the same advance in biology as in anatomy and physiology for a number of reasons. The first was undoubtedly the fact that Aristotle had covered the field so thoroughly and so well. Descriptive zoology seemed covered once and for all by the *History of Animals*. Embryology had received authoritative treatment in the *On Generation* and animal anatomy and physiology were exhaustively considered in *The Parts of Animals*. The only thing left was botany. Aristotle's pupil and immediate successor at the Lyceum, Theophrastus (372-288 B.C.) did for botany what Aristotle had done for animals in his *Enquiry into Plants*. This was both a description and an analysis of plant life which also emphasized the practical side of plant culture. Theophrastus seems to have answered all the philosophical questions that anyone cared to ask in antiquity for after him the botanical tradition became completely practical. This involved treatises on agriculture which the Romans were particularly fond of, and works on the medical use of plants. Crateus (fl. 80 B.C.) was the founder of the "materia medica." His illustrated works described plants useful in medicine, as well as poisons and their antidotes. Dioscorides (fl. first century A.D.) wrote the first authoritative *materia medica* of antiquity which was basic to pharmacy for the next 1500 years.

A rapid survey of the names and dates of scientists of the Hellenistic period whom we have discussed reveals two interesting facts: the names are all Greek and the latest dates--Galen and Ptolemy--fall in the second century A.D. The rise of Rome was inimical to the advance of science. The Romans considered the Greeks to be ineffectual speculators whose great intellectual achievements had not prevented them from falling easy prey to the Legions of Rome. The Romans were, above all, practical men and they could see little of utility in Greek science. Some Greek philosophies, like Stoicism, might prepare a man to do his duty and could be naturalized in Rome. But, by and large, the Romans simply were not interested in the Greek scientific legacy. What little that was accepted was collected in the great encyclopedic works of Varro and Pliny and formed an important part of the scientific knowledge of the Middle Ages. But this heritage was pitiful. For science, the dark ages began some three centuries before the barbarian invasions brought the Roman Empire tumbling down.

CHAPTER ONE II.

READINGS ON ANCIENT SCIENCE

II. A. Science in the Pre-Classical World

1. Medicine in Babylonia and Egypt

a. Babylonian Medical Texts*

The personages of the myths were ever-present in Mesopotamian civilization. The Gods literally ruled the earth; they were to be flattered, appealed to, and prayed to if a man were to go through life with a minimum of catastrophe.

Document I provides some insight into Babylonian ideas on the origin of disease.

Document II illustrates the role of omens in medical lore.

Documents II and IV illustrate two approaches to healing.

I

Headache roameth over the desert, blowing like the wind,
Flashing like lightning, it is loosed above and below;
It cutteth off him who feareth not his god like a reed,
Like a stalk of henna it slitteth his thews.
It wasteth the flesh of him who hath no protecting goddess,
Flashing like a heavenly star, it cometh like the dew;
It standeth hostile against the wayfarer, scorching him like the day,
This man it hath struck and
Like one with heart disease he staggereth,
Like one bereft of reason he is broken,
Like that which has been cast into the fire he is shrivelled,
Like a wild ass . . . his eyes are full of cloud,
On himself he feedeth, bound in death;
Headache whose course like the dread windstorm none knoweth,
None knoweth its full time or its bond.

II

If a man go to the house of a sick man (and) a falcon goes along at his right, that sick man will get well.
If the falcon goes along on his left side, that sick man will die.
If in the morning in the rear of a sick man's house a falcon proceeds from an inclosure at the right to an inclosure at

---

* Henry E. Sigerist, *A History of Medicine*, Volume I: *Primitive and Archaic Medicine*, Oxford University Press, New York, 1951. Pp. 451; 456; 465; 470. Cited by permission of the Oxford University Press.

the left, that sick man will speedily recover.
If in the morning in the rear of a sick man's house a falcon proceeds from an inclosure at the left to an inclosure at the right, his sickness will be protracted.
If in the morning in the rear of a sick man's house a falcon flies away, that sick man will die.

* * * * *

If a scorpion falls upon a sick man, after the 10th day he will die.
If a scorpion drops itself on the sick man, his sickness will be long.
If a scorpion stands at the head of a sick man's bed, his sickness will quickly leave him.
If a scorpion stands on the wall before a sick man, his sickness will leave him.
If a scorpion enters a sick man's lap, that sick man will live.

III

Mighty Lord, thou exalted, first-born of Nunamnir,
First among the Anunnaki, Lord of the Battle,
Offspring of Kutushar, the great Queen,
Nergal, thou mightiest god, favorite of Ninmenna!
Thou art radiant in the bright Heavens, high is thy abode,
Great art thou in the Underworld, knowest no rival,
With Ea in the gods' assembly thy counsel is supreme,
With Sin in the Heavens thou seest all.
Thy father Enlil gave thee all, the black-headed ones, all that breatheth,
The cattle in the fields, he entrusted it all into thy hands.

* * * * *

Absolve my guilt, cancel my sin!
May the wrath of thy divine heart be appeased,
May the angered god and the angered goddess again be at peace with me!
Thy might I will proclaim and I will sing thy praise.

IV

Go, my son (Marduk),
Pull off a piece of clay from the deep,
Fashion a figure of his bodily form (therefrom) and
Place it on the loins of the sick man by night,
At dawn make the 'atonement' for his body,
Perform the Incantation of Eridu,
Turn his face to the west,
That the evil Plague-demon which hath seized upon him
May vanish away from him,

Fashion a figure of him in dough,
Put water upon the man and

Pour forth the water of the Incantation;
Bring forth a censer (and) a torch,
As the water trickleth away from his body
So may the pestilence in his body trickle away.
Return these waters into a cup and
Pour them forth in the broad places,
That the evil influence which hath brought low (his) strength
May be carried away into the broad places,
That the spittle which hath been spat
May be poured forth like the water,
That the magic which mingleth with the spat-forth spittle
May be turned back,
By the magic of the Word of Ea,
The chanting lips which have uttered the ban,--
May their bond be loosened!
That this man may be pure, be clean!
Into the kindly hands of his god may he be commended.

b. Egyptian Medicine*

CASE ONE

A Wound in the Head Penetrating to the Bone

Examination

[If thou examinest a man having a wound in his head, penetrating to the bone of his skull, (but) not having a gash, thou shouldst palpate his wound (or, thou shouldst lay thy hand upon it); shouldst thou find his skull uninjured, not having a perforation, a split, or a smash in it,] (conclusion in diagnosis).

Diagnosis

[Thou shouldst say regarding him: "One having a woun]d in his head, while his wound does [not] have two lips, . . . , nor a gash, although [it penetrates to the bone of] his head. An ailment which I will treat."

Treatment

Thou shouldst bind it with [fresh] meat [the first day] (and) treat afterward with grease, [honey] (and) lint every day until he recovers.

CASE THREE

A Gaping Wound in the Head Penetrating to the Bone and Perforating the Skull

Examination

[If thou examinest a man having a gaping wound] his [head], penetrating to the bone, (and) perforating his skull; thou shouldst palpate his wound; [shouldst thou find him unable to look at his two shoulders] and his [br]east, (and) suffering with stiffness in his neck, (conclusion in diagnosis).

Diagnosis

Thou shouldst say [regarding] him: "One having [a gaping wound in his head, penetrating to the bone, (and) per]forating his skull, while he suffers with stiffness in his neck. An ailment which I will treat."

---

* *The Edwin Smith Surgical Papyrus Published in Facsimile and Hieroglyphic Transliteration with Translation and Commentary in Two Volumes* by James Henry Breasted, published for the New York Historical Society by the University of Chicago Press, Chicago, Illinois, 1930. Pp. 429, 430, 431, 432, 435, 436, 439. Cited by permission of the University of Chicago Press.

Treatment

Now [after thou has stitched it, thou shouldst lay] fresh [meat] upon his wound the first day. Thou shouldst not bind it. Moor (him) [at his mooring stakes until the period of his injury passes by]. Thou shouldst [tre]at it afterward with grease, honey, and lint every day, until he recovers.

CASE SEVEN

A Gaping Wound in the Head Penetrating to the Bone and Perforating the Sutures

Examination

[If thou examinest a man having a gaping wound in his head, penetrating to the bone, (and) perforating the sutures of his skull], thou shouldst palpate his wound, (although) he shudders exceedingly. Thou shouldst cause him to lift his face; if it is painful for him to open his mouth, (and) his heart beats feebly; if thou observe his spittle hanging at his two lips and not falling off, while he discharges blood from both his nostrils (and) from both his ears; he suffers with stiffness in his neck, (and) is unable to look at his two shoulders and his breast, (conclusion in diagnosis).

First Diagnosis

Thou shouldst say regarding him: "One having a gaping wound in his head, penetrating to the bone, (and) perforating the sutures of his skull; the cord of his mandible is contracted; he discharges blood from both his nostrils (and) from both his ears, while he suffers with stiffness in his neck. An ailment with which I will contend."

First Treatment

Now as soon as thou findest that the cord of that man's mandible, his jaw, is contracted, thou shouldst have made for him something hot, until he is comfortable, so that his mouth opens. Thou shouldst bind it with grease, honey, (and) lint, until thou knowest that he has reached a decisive point.

Second Examination

If, then, thou findest that the flesh of that man has developed fever from that wound which is in the sutures of his skull, while that man has developed *ty'* from that wound, thou shouldst lay thy hand upon him. Shouldst thou find his countenance is clammy with sweat, the ligaments of his neck are tense, his face is ruddy, his teeth and his back [-], the odor of the chest of his head is like the *bkn* (urine) of sheep, his mouth is bound, (and) both his eyebrows are drawn, while his face is as if he wept, (conclusion in diagnosis).

Second Diagnosis

Thou shouldst say regarding him: "One having a gaping wound in his head, penetrating to the bone, perforating the sutures of his skull; he has developed *ty'*, his mouth is bound, (and) he suffers with stiffness in his neck. An ailment not to be treated."

Third Examination

If, however, thou findest that that man has become pale and has already [shown exhaustion].

Third Treatment

Thou shouldst have made for him a wooden brace padded with linen and put into his mouth. Thou shouldst have made for him a draught of *w ḥ*-fruit. His treatment is sitting, placed between two supports of brick, until thou knowest he has reached a decisive point.

CASE NINE

Wound in the Forehead Producing a Compound Comminuted Fracture of the Skull

Examination

If thou examinest a man having a wound in his forehead, smashing the shell of his head, (conclusion in treatment).

Treatment

Thou shouldst prepare for him the egg of an ostrich, triturated with grease (and) placed in the mouth of his wound. Now afterward thou shouldst prepare for him the egg of an ostrich, triturated and made into poultices for drying up that wound. Thou shouldst apply to it for him a covering for physician's use; thou shouldst uncover it the third day, (and) find it knitting together the shell, the color being like the egg of an ostrich.

That which is to be said as a charm over this recipe:

Repelled is the enemy that is in the wound!
Cast out is the evil that is in the blood,
The adversary of Horus, on every side of the mouth of Isis;
This temple does not fall down;
There is no enemy of the vessel therein.
I am under the protection of Isis;
My rescue is the son of Osiris.

Now afterward thou shouldst cool [it] for him [with] a compress of figs, grease, and honey, cooked, cooled, and applied to it.

2. Babylonian mathematics and astronomy

a. Mathematics in Mesopotamia

Otto Neugebauer of Brown University is one of the great pioneers in the study of ancient mathematics and astronomy. In 1949 he gave the Messenger Lectures at Cornell University on The Exact Sciences in Antiquity. *In these lectures Professor Neugebauer described the mathematical achievements of Mesopotamian civilization.**

The texts of which I speak are clay tablets, generally about the size of a hand, inscribed with signs which were pressed into the surface of the once soft clay by means of a sharpened stylus. This script is called "cuneiform," i.e. wedge-shaped, because the individual impressions have a deeper "head" and a finer line at the end, thus resembling a wedge. Cuneiform tablets with mathematical contents are known to us mostly from the so-called "Old-Babylonian" period, about 1600 B.C. No astronomical texts of any scientific significance exist from this period, while the mathematical texts already show the highest level ever attained in Babylonia.

The second period from which we have a larger number of texts is the latest period of Babylonian history, when Mesopotamia had become a part of the empire of Alexander's successors, the "Seleucids." This period, from about 300 B.C. to the beginning of our era, has furnished us with a great number of astronomical texts of a most remarkable mathematical character, fully comparable to the astronomy of the Almagest. Mathematical texts from this period are scarce, but they suffice nevertheless to demonstrate that the knowledge of Old-Babylonian mathematics had not been lost during the intervening 1300 years for which texts are lacking.

Thus it is essential to remember that we are dealing with mathematical texts from two periods, "Old-Babylonian" from about 1800 to 1600, and "Seleucid" from 300 to 0, whereas astronomical texts belong only to the second period.

The development of the numerical notations in Mesopotamia took as many centuries as the development of writing from a crude picture script to a well defined system of complicated signs. We shall for the moment deal only with the final product as it appears in the mathematical texts of the Old-Babylonian period. And we shall again use the most direct approach by deciphering an actual text.

Pl. 4,a shows a tablet whose size is about 3 1/8 by 2 inches (and about 3/4 of an inch thick). In the middle of the text is visible a column of signs which obviously represent

---

* Otto Neugebauer, *The Exact Sciences in Antiquity*, Ejnar Munksgaard, Copenhagen, 1951. Pp. 14-17; 20-22; 29-31; 33-35; 39-40; 43. Reprinted by permission of Munksgaard International Forlag and the author.

numbers in ascending order. The tablet is not quite cleaned from incrustation of salt or dirt but it is clear that the signs look about as follows:

Counting of the vertical wedges leads directly to the readings 1, 2, 3, etc. up to 9. Then follows which must be 10, and consequently we can also read the remaining signs as 11, 12, 13. Using this exceedingly plausible hypothesis, we should also be able to read the right-hand column of signs. The first five look as follows

Obviously we must read these signs as 10, 20, 30, 40, 50 if the first sign represents 10 as we have established in our first list. But what follows is

* * *

which we transcribe consistently as

1   1,10   1,20   *   *   *   2   2,10

each * indicating a broken line. These signs continue the previous ones if we interpret the first "1" as 60 and then read 1,10 as 60 + 10 = 70 and 1,20 as 60 + 20 = 80. The broken lines should contain 90, 100, and 110. The next sign "2" should be 120, in excellent agreement with our interpretation of "1" as 60, while the last sign 2,10 must be 120 + 10 = 130. Thus we have obtained all multiples of 10 from 10 to 130, line by line, corresponding to the numbers 1 to 13. In other words, our table is a multiplication table for 10, which we now can transcribe as follows:

1	10
2	20
3	30
4	40
5	50
6	1
7	1,10
8	1,20
9	1,30
10	1,40
11	1,50
12	2
13	2,10

The notation 1,10 = 70   1,20 = 80   2,10 = 130 etc. is "sexagesimal" in the sense that 60 units of one kind are written as 1 of the next higher order. This is exactly the same principle we found in Ptolemy's table of chords. The only difference consists in the fact that Old-Babylonian texts have not yet developed a special sign for "zero". This appears, however, in both mathematical and astronomical cuneiform texts of the Seleucid period, as we shall see in later examples. Thus we have reached complete identity of the principle of numerical notation for astronomical tables of the Hellenistic period, whether written in cuneiform or in Greek alphabetic numerals. Only in one point is the Greek notation less consistent than the Babylonian method. In the latter all numbers were written strictly sexagesimally, regardless of whether they were integers or fractions. In Greek astronomy, however, only the fractions were written sexagesimally, whereas for integer degrees or hours the ordinary alphabetic notation remained in use also for numbers from 60 onwards. Thus Ptolemy would write 130 17 20 where a cuneiform tablet would have 2 10 17 20. In other words, the Greeks already introduced the inconsistency which is still visible in modern astronomy, where one also would write 130°17'20". The other inconsistency of the modern astronomical notation, namely, to continue beyond the seconds with decimal fractions, is a recent invention. It is interesting to see that it took about 2000 years of migration of astronomical knowledge from Mesopotamia via Greeks, Hindus, and Arabs to arrive at a truly absurd numerical system.

* * * * *

The Babylonian place value notation shows in its earlier development two disadvantages which are due to the lack of a symbol for zero. The first difficulty consists in the possibility of misreading a number 1 20 as 1,20 = 80 when actually 1,0,20 = 3620 was meant. Occasionally this ambiguity is overcome by separating the two numbers very clearly if a whole sexagesimal place is missing. But this method is by no means strictly applied and we have many cases where numbers are spaced widely apart without any significance. In the latest period, however, when astronomical texts were computed, a special symbol for "zero" was used. This symbol also occurs earlier as a separation mark between sentences, and I therefore transcribe it by a "period." Thus we find in Seleucid astronomical texts many instances of numbers like 1,.,20 or even 1,.,.,20 which apply exactly the same principle as our 201 or 2001.

But even in the final phase of Babylonian writing we do not find any examples of zero signs at the end of numbers. Though there are many instances of cases like 1,20 there is no safe example of a writing like 20,. known to me. In other words, in all periods the context alone decides the absolute value of a sexagesimally written number. In Old-Babylonian mathematical texts we find several cases where a final result was written by means of individual symbols for the fractions, e.g., 1,30 might be called "1 and 1/2" which shows that we should transcribe 1;30 = 1 1/2 and not 1,30 = 90.

The ambiguity with respect to fractions and integers is of no importance for the practice of computation. Exactly as we multiply two numbers regardless of the position of the decimal point, one can also operate with the Babylonian numbers and determine the absolute value at the end if necessary. For the numerical process itself it is indeed a great advantage that one does not need to worry about special values for fractions and integers. It is precisely this feature which gave the Babylonian system its tremendous advantage over all other number systems in antiquity. Though this will become more obvious in the subsequent discussion of (and comparison between) Babylonian and Egyptian mathematics, one example may be given now to illustrate this point.

A multiplication by 12 would be performed by an Egyptian scribe in two steps. First he would multiply the other factor by 10 (simply by replacing each individual symbol by the next higher one) and then he would double the other factor. Finally he would add the two results. Thus for the multiplication of 12 by 12 he would arrange his figures as follows:

1	12
/ 10	120
/ 2	24
total	144

giving him 144 as the result of the addition of the two items marked by a stroke. Let us now assume that the other factor was a fraction, say the "unit fraction" 1/5, or, as we should write in imitation of the Egyptian notation, $\bar{5}$. The scribe would again proceed in two steps, namely, multiplication by 10 and by 2. The first gives the result 2. The second, however, would need a table of duplications of unit fractions where the double of $\bar{5}$ appears to be listed as $\bar{3}\ \overline{15}$ (indeed 2/5 = 1/3 + 1/15). Thus the computation would be

1	$\bar{5}$
/ 10	2
/ 2	$\bar{3}\ \overline{15}$
total	$2\ \bar{3}\ \overline{15}$

A contemporary Old-Babylonian scribe would solve the same problems by using a multiplication table for 12 exactly of the same type as we have described above for 10. In line 12 he would directly find the result 2,24. Of course, so far we have only established the fact of a better organized procedure in Mesopotamia but nothing intrinsically inherent in the Babylonian notation. This is different for the second problem, however. The Babylonian scribe would know (or take this information from a table of reciprocals) that 1/5 corresponds to "12" (0;12 = 12/60 in our notation when we use a zero symbol). Hence 12/5 leads again to finding the value of 12 times 12 or again to 2,24 (we would write 2;24). In other words the Babylonian process completely avoids special rules for computing with fractions, whether unit fractions or not, and requires only that one remember correctly the place value of each contributing number, exactly as we must do in placing the final decimal point. The historical consequences of this simplification can scarcely be overestimated.

* * * * *

The mathematical texts can be classified into two major groups: "table texts" and "problem texts". A typical representative of the first class is the multiplication table discussed above p. 42. The second class comprises a great variety of texts which are all more or less directly concerned with the formulation or solution of algebraic or geometrical problems. At present the number of problem texts known to us amounts to about one hundred tablets, as compared with more than twice as many table texts. The total amount of Babylonian tablets which have reached museums might be estimated to be at least 500,000 tablets and this is certainly only a small fraction of the texts which are still buried in the ruins of Mesopotamian cities. Our task can therefore properly be compared with restoring the history of mathematics from a few torn pages which have accidentally survived the destruction of a great library.

* * * * *

Though a single multiplication table is rather trivial in content, the study of a larger number of these texts soon revealed unexpected facts. Obviously a complete system of sexagesimal multiplication tables would consist of 58 tables, each containing all products from 1 to 59 with each of the numbers from 2 to 59. Thanks to the place value notation such a system of tables would suffice to carry out all possible multiplications exactly as it suffices to know our multiplication tables for all decimal products. At first this expectation seemed nicely confirmed except for the unimportant modification that each single tablet gave all products from 1 to 20 and then only the products for 30, 40, and 50. This is obviously nothing more than a space saving device because all 59 products can be obtained from such a tablet by at most one addition of two of its numbers. But a more disturbing fact soon became evident. On the one hand the list of preserved tables showed not only grave gaps but, more disconcertingly, there turned up tables which seemed to extend the expected scheme to an unreasonable size. Multiplication tables for 1,20 1,30 1,40 3,20 3,45 etc. seemed to compel us to assume the existence not of 59 single tables but of 3600 tables. The absurdity of this hypothesis became evident when tables for the multiples of 44,26,40 repeatedly appeared; obviously nobody would operate a library of $60^3 = 216,000$ tablets as an aid for multiplication. And it was against all laws of probability that we should have several copies of multiplication tables for 44,26,40 but none for 11, 13, 14, 17, 19 etc.

The solution of this puzzle came precisely from the number 44,26,40 which also appears in another type of tables, namely, tables of reciprocals. Ignoring variations in small details, these tables of reciprocals are lists of numbers as follows

2	30	16	3,45	45	1,20
3	20	18	3,20	48	1,15
4	15	20	3	50	1,12
5	12	24	2,30	54	1,6,40
6	10	25	2,24	1	1
8	7,30	27	2,13,20	1,4	56,15
9	6,40	30	2	1,12	50
10	6	32	1,52,30	1,15	48
12	5	36	1,40	1,20	45
15	4	40	1,30	1,21	44,26,40

The last pair contains the number 44,26,40 and also all the other two-place numbers mentioned above occur as numbers of the second column. On the other hand, with one single exception to be mentioned presently, the gaps in our expected list of multiplication tables correspond exactly to the missing numbers in our above table or reciprocals. Thus our stock of multiplication tables is not a collection of tables for all products $a \cdot b$, for a and b from 1 to 59, but tables for the products $a \cdot \overline{b}$ where $\overline{b}$ is a number from the right-hand side of our last list. The character of these numbers $\overline{b}$ is conspicuous enough; they are the reciprocals of the numbers b of the left column, written as sexagesimal fractions:

$$\frac{1}{2} = 0;30$$

$$\frac{1}{3} = 0;20$$

$$\frac{1}{4} = 0;15$$

etc.

$$\frac{1}{1,21} = 0;0,44,26,40.$$

We can express the same fact more simply and historically more correctly in the following form. The above "table of reciprocals" is a list of numbers, b and $\overline{b}$, such that the products $b \cdot \overline{b}$ are 1 or any other power of 60.

* * * * *

Very recently A. Sachs found a tablet which he recognized as having to do with the problem of evaluating the approximation of reciprocals of irregular numbers by a finite expression in sexagesimal fractions. The text deals with the reciprocals of 7, 11, 13, 14, and 17, in the last two cases in the form that $b \cdot \overline{b} = 10$ instead of $b \cdot \overline{b} = 1$ as usual. We here mention only the two first lines, which seem to state that

$$8,34,16,59 < \overline{7}$$

but

$$8,34,18 > \overline{7}.$$

Indeed, the correct expansion of $\overline{7}$ would be 8,34,17 periodically repeated. It is needless to underline the importance of a problem which is the first step toward a mathematical analysis of infinite arithmetical processes and of the concept of "number" in general. And it is equally needless to say that the new fragment raises many more questions than it solves. But it leaves no doubt that we must recognize an interest in problems of approximations for as early a period as Old-Babylonian times.

This is confirmed by a small tablet, now in the Yale Babylonian Collection. It shows a square with its two diagonals. The side shows the number 30, the diagonal the numbers 1,24,51,10 and 42,25,35. The meaning of these numbers becomes clear if we multiply 1,24,51,10 by 30, an operation which can be easily performed by dividing 1,24,51,10 by 2 because 2 and 30 are reciprocals of one another. The result is 42,25,35. Thus we have obtained from a = 30 the diagonal d = 42;25,35 by using

$$\sqrt{2} = 1;24,51,10.$$

The accuracy of this approximation can be checked by squaring 1;24,51,10. One finds

$$1;59,59,59,38,1,40$$

corresponding to an error of less than $22/60^4$. Expressed as a decimal fraction we have here the approximation 1.414213 . . instead of 1.414214 . . . This is indeed a remarkably good approximation. It was still used by Ptolemy in computing his table of chords almost two thousand years later.

* * * * *

The above example of the determination of the diagonal of the square from its side is sufficient proof that the "Pythagorean" theorem was known more than a thousand years before Pythagoras. This is confirmed by many other examples of the use of this theorem in problem texts of the same age, as well as from the Seleucid period. In other words it was known during the whole duration of Babylonian mathematics that the sum of the squares of the lengths of the sides of a right triangle equals the square of the length of the hypotenuse. This geometrical fact having once been discovered, it is quite natural to assume that all triples of numbers l, b, and d which satisfy the relation $l^2 + b^2 = d^2$ can be used as sides of a right triangle. It is furthermore a normal step to ask the question: When do numbers l, b, d satisfy the above relation? Consequently it is not too surprising that we find the Babylonian mathematicians investigating the number-theoretical problem of producing "Pythagorean numbers".

* * * * *

Pythagorean numbers were certainly not the only case of problems concerning relations between numbers. The tables for squares and cubes point clearly in the same direction. We also have examples which deal with the sum of consecutive squares or with arithmetic progressions. It would be rather surprising if the accidentally preserved texts should also show us the exact limits of knowledge which were reached in Babylonian mathematics. There is no indication, however, that the important concept of prime number was recognized.

All these problems were probably never sharply separated from methods which we today call "algebraic". In the center of this group lies the solution of quadratic equations for two unknowns. As a typical example might be quoted a problem from a Seleucid text. This problem requires the finding of a number such that a given number is obtained if its reciprocal is added to it.

Using modern notation we call the unknown number x, its reciprocal $\bar{x}$, and the given number b. Thus we have to determine x from

$$x\bar{x} = 1 \qquad x + \bar{x} = b.$$

In the text b has the value 2;0,0,33,20. The details of the solution are described step by step in the text as follows. Form

$$\left(\frac{b}{2}\right)^2 = 1;0,0,33,20,4,37,46,40.$$

Subtract 1 and find the square root

$$\sqrt{\left(\frac{b}{2}\right)^2 - 1} = \sqrt{0;0,0,33,20,4,37,46,40} = 0;0,44,43,20.$$

The correctness of this result is checked by squaring. Then add to and subtract from $b/2$ the result. This answers the problem:

$$x = \frac{b}{2} + \sqrt{} = 1;0,0,16,40 + 0;0,44,43,20 = 1;0,45$$

$$\bar{x} = \frac{b}{2} - \sqrt{} = 1;0,0,16,40 - 0;0,44,43,20 = 0;59,15,33,20.$$

Indeed, x and $\bar{x}$ are reciprocal numbers and their sum equals the given number b.

* * * * *

The extension of this "Babylonian algebra" is truly remarkable. Though the quadratic equations form obviously the most significant nucleus a great number of related problems were also considered. Linear problems for several unknowns are common in many forms, e.g., for "inheritance" problems where the shares of several sons should be determined from linear conditions which hold between these shares. Similar problems arise from divisions of fields or from general conditions in the framework of the above mentioned collections of algebraic examples.

On the other hand we know from these same collections series of examples which are equivalent to special types of equations of fourth and sixth order. Usually these problems are easily reducible to quadratic equations for x^2 or x^3 but we have also examples which lead to more general relations of 5th and 3rd order. In the latter case the tables for $n^2 + n^3$ seem to be useful for the actual numerical solution of such problems, but our source material is too fragmentary to give a consistent description of the procedure followed in cases which are no longer reducible to quadratic equations.

There is finally no doubt that problems were also investigated which transcend, in the modern sense, the algebraic character. This is not only clear from problems which have to do with compound interest but also from numerical tables for the consecutive powers of given numbers. On the other hand we have texts which concern the determination of the exponents of given numbers. In other words one had actually experimented with special cases of logarithms without, however, reaching any general use of this function. In the case of numerical tables the lack of a general notation appears to be much more detrimental than in the handling of purely algebraic problems.

* * * * *

However incomplete our present knowledge of Babylonian mathematics may be, so much is established beyond any doubt: we are dealing with a level of mathematical development which can in many aspects be compared with the mathematics, say, of the early Renaissance. Yet one must not overestimate these achievements. In spite of the numerical and algebraic skill and in spite of the abstract interest which is conspicuous in so many examples, the contents of Babylonian mathematics remained profoundly elementary. In the utterly primitive framework of Egyptian mathematics the discovery of the irrationality of $\sqrt{2}$ would be a strange miracle. But all the foundations were laid which could have given this result to a Babylonian mathematician, exactly in the same arithmetical form in which it was obviously discovered so much later by the Greeks. And even if it were only due to our incomplete knowledge of the sources that we assume that the Babylonians did not know that $p^2 = 2q^2$ had no solution in integer numbers p and q, even then the fact remains that the consequences of this result were not realized. In other words Babylonian mathematics never transgressed the threshold of pre-scientific thought. It is only in the last three centuries of Babylonian history and in the field of mathematical astronomy that the Babylonian mathematicians or astronomers reached parity with their Greek contemporaries.

b. Babylonian Astronomy*

Before describing the Babylonian planetary theory, we shall discuss the main features of the apparent movement of the planets from a modern point of view. We know that the planets move on ellipses around the sun, the earth being one of them. We shall derive from these facts the apparent motions as seen from the earth. In order to simplify our discussion, we shall replace all orbits by circles whose common center is the sun. The eccentricities of the elliptic orbits are so small that a scale drawing that would fit this page would not show the difference between the elliptic and the circular orbits.

We utilize furthermore the fact that the dimensions of our planetary system are so minute in comparison with the distances to the fixed stars which constitute the background of the celestial sphere that we commit no observable error at all if we keep either the sun or the earth in a fixed position with respect to the surrounding universe. Hence we will proceed in the following way. We shall start with the circular motion of the planets around the sun and then keep the earth fixed and ask for the resulting motion with respect to the earth. This will answer our question concerning the planetary phenomena.

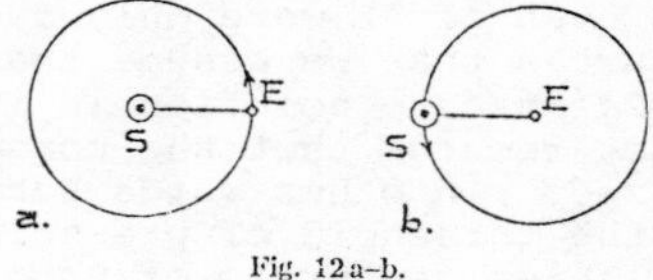

Fig. 12a–b.

The first step is absolutely trivial. We know that the earth is a satellite of the sun, moving around it once in a year. In order to obtain the appearances seen from the earth we subtract from all motions the motion of the earth. Thus we see that by arresting the motion of the earth we obtain the appearance that the sun moves around the earth once per year. Its apparent path is called the ecliptic (cf. Fig. 12a and b).

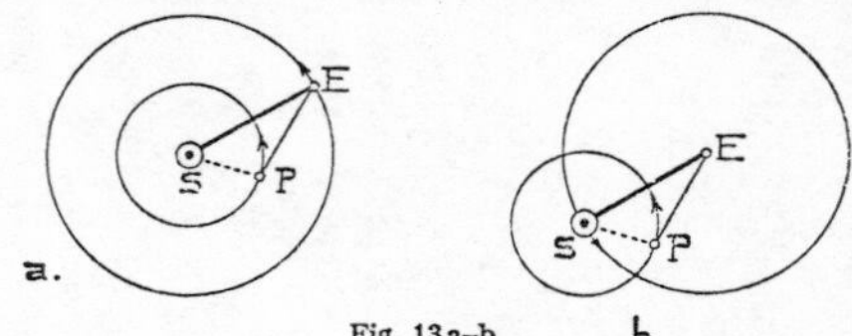

Fig. 13a–b

Secondly we consider an "inner" planet, Mercury or Venus, which moves closer to the sun than the earth (Fig. 13a). If we stop the earth we need only repeat Fig. 12 in order to obtain again the motion of the sun. The orbit of the planet remains a

---

* *Ibid.*, 117-123.

circle with the sun in its center. Hence the geocentric description of the motion of an inner planet is given by a planet which moves on a little circle whose center is carried on a larger circle whose center is the earth. The little circle is called an "epicycle", the large circle is the "deferent".

Finally we have an "outer" planet, Mars, Jupiter, or Saturn, whose orbit encloses the orbit of the earth (Fig. 14a). From the earth E the planet P appears to be moving on a circle whose center S moves around E. Thus we have again an epicyclic motion (Fig. 14b). In order to establish a closer similarity with the case of the inner planets we introduce a point C such that the four points S, E, P, and C always form a parellelogram.

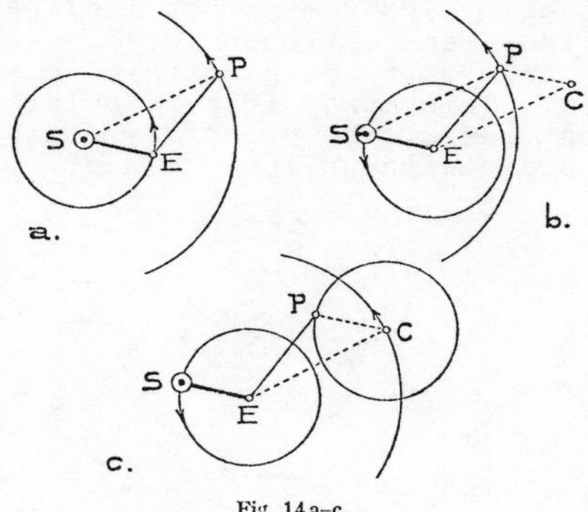

Fig. 14a–c.

SP is the radius of the planetary orbit; because EC = SP we see that C lies on a circle with center E. Similarly ES is the radius of the solar orbit, and, because ES = CP, we see that P lies on a circle around C. Thus the planet P moves on an epicycle whose center C travels on a deferent whose center is E (Fig. 14c). Thus we have established an exact analogue to the case of the inner planets. In both cases the planet has an epicyclic movement. In the case of the inner planets the center of the epicycle coincides with the sun. For the outer planets the center C of the epicycle moves around E with the same angular velocity as the planet moves around the sun, while the planet P moves on the epicycle around C with the same angular velocity as the sun moves around the earth.

In order to avoid misunderstandings, I shall repeat once more the assumptions upon which our above results rest. These assumptions were (a) that the planetary orbits are circles with the sun in their common center; (b) that all planetary orbits lie in the same plane. Accepting these two assumptions we have seen that the planetary orbits with respect to the earth consist of epicycles whose centers move with uniform velocity on deferents having the earth as center. In other words, if we disregard the small eccentricities of the planetary orbits, and if we also neglect the small inclinations of these orbits, then the epicylic motion gives a correct description of the planetary orbits with respect to the earth. Indeed it is only a matter of mathematical convenience whether one computes first the longitudes of the earth and the planets heliocentrically and then transforms to geocentric coordinates, or whether one carries out this transformation first and then operates with epicycles.

For a finer theory of the planetary plenomena the above assumptions are too crude. It is easy, however, to see in what directions one should move in order to reach higher accuracy. The eccentricity of the orbits can be taken into consideration by assuming slightly eccentric positions of the earth with respect to the centers of the deferents. The latitude can be accounted for by giving the epicycles the proper inclination. Both devices were followed by the Greek astronomers.

We have now seen that the planets move with respect to the earth on epicycles. This makes it particularly simple to understand the main features of the planetary motions as seen from the earth. We begin again with an inner planet. Its angular velo-

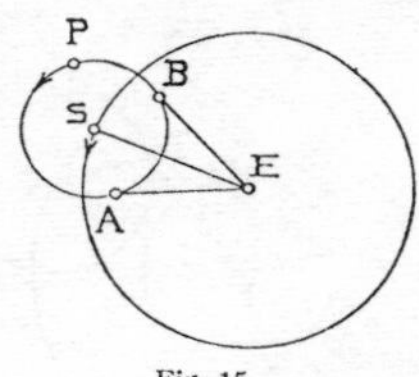

Fig. 15.

city about the center S of its epicycle (cf. Fig. 15) is greater than the angular velocity of S about the earth E. If the planet P is on the part of its epicycle which is removed from the earth, the motion of P is added to the motion of S and the planetary motion appears greater than the motion of S. We call this the "direct" motion. Between A and B, however, the planet moves backward faster than its epicycle is carried forward,* thus it appears to be "retrograde".

The same figure allows us also to describe the visibility conditions. If the planet P and the sun S are seen in the same, or in nearly the same, direction from E, the planet is invisible

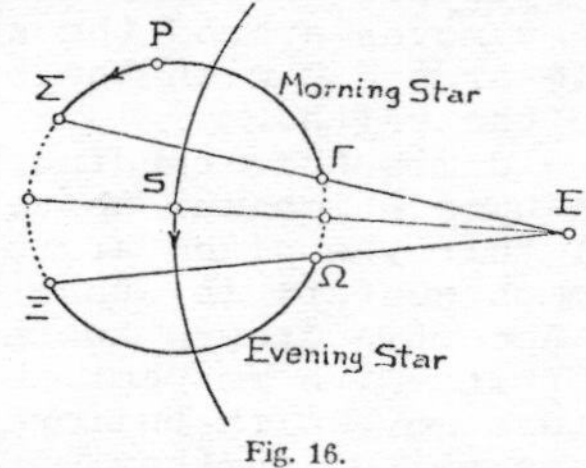

Fig. 16.

* It is easy to see that the points A and B lie somewhat inside the two points where the lines from E are tangential to the epicycle.

because of the brightness of the sun. Thus a certain "elongation" of the planet from the sun is required to make the planet visible. Fig. 16 shows that the arc of invisibility between Σ and Ξ near "superior conjunction" is much greater than between ω and Γ (near "inferior" conjunction). The visible arc from Γ to Σ rises before the sun; thus the planet is "morning star". Fig. 17 describes the same phenomena once more in a graph with the abscissa representing time whereas the ordinates represent geocentric longitudes. The straight line represents the motion of the sun.

In similar fashion one obtains for an outer planet a graph as given in Fig. 18. Now the motion of the planet is slower than the motion of the sun. Retrogradation occurs near opposition, Θ, when the sun and planet are seen in opposite directions from the earth. Consequently the retrogradation of an outer planet is fully visible in contrast to that of an inner planet, where a part of the retrograde motion becomes invisible near inferior conjunction. An outer planet becomes invisible only once: near conjunction, ω to Γ. The points Θ and Ψ, where direct motion changes to retrograde motion and vice versa, are called the "first" and "second" stationary points respectively.

It is in the theory of the planets that the contrast between the Babylonian approach and Ptolemy's theory as presented in the Almagest becomes most visible. In the Ptolemaic theory a

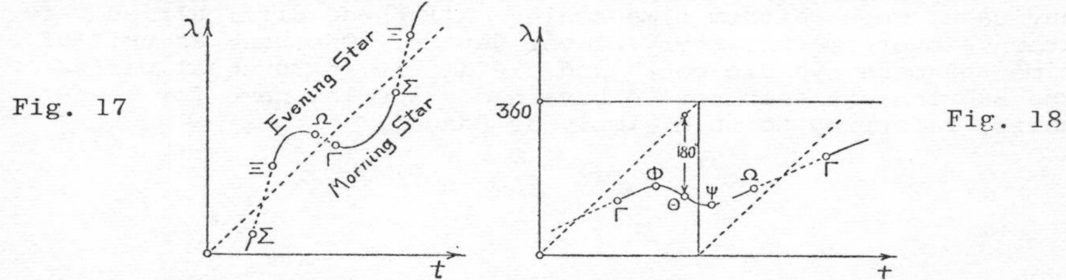

Fig. 17 Fig. 18

definite kinematic model is assumed, based on epicyclic motion, which closely corresponds to the description of the planetary motion given in the preceding sections. Thus the geocentric longitude of the planet can be computed for any given moment t. It is then a secondary problem to determine those values of t for which the planet is in one of the characteristic phenomena which we denoted by Greek letters.

The Babylonian method follows the exactly opposite arrangement. The first goal consists in determining the "Greek-letter phenomena", and thereafter the longitude of the planet for an arbitrary moment t is found by interpolation.

This difference in approach is, of course, the result of the historical development. The Babylonians were primarily interested in the appearance and disappearance of the planets in analogy to the first and last visibility of the moon. It was the periodic recurrence of these phenomena and their fluctuations which they primarily attempted to determine. When Ptolemy developed his planetary theory, he had already at his disposal the geometrical methods by means of which the solar and lunar anomalies were explained very satisfactorily, and similar models had been used also for an at least qualitative explanation of the apparent planetary orbits. Thus it had become an obvious goal of theoretical astronomy to offer a strictly geometrical theory of the planetary motions as a whole and the characteristic phenomena lost much of their specific interest, especially after the Greek astronomers had developed enough observational experience to realize that horizon phenomena were the worst possible choice to provide the necessary empirical data.

Whatever phenomenon the Babylonian astronomers wanted to predict, it had to be determined within the existing lunar calendar. Suppose one had found that a planet would reappear 100 days from a given date. What date should be assigned to this moment? Obviously one should know whether the three intermediate lunar months were, perhaps, all only 29 days long, or all three were 30 days long, etc. This question could be answered perfectly well by lunar ephemerides whose goal it was to determine whether a given month was 29 or 30 days long. But planetary phenomena proceed very slowly. One single table for Jupiter or Saturn could easily cover 60 years and more. To determine calendar dates so far in advance would have meant the computation of complete lunar ephemerides for several decades. Furthermore, the actual computation of the planetary motion had to be based, in any case, on a uniform time scale. All these difficulties were at once overcome by a very clever device. One used as unit of time the mean synodic month and divided it in 30 equal parts. The Babylonians seem not to have had a special name for these units, referring to them simply as "days".

B. The Philosophical Framework of Greek Science

Philosophy is a Greek invention. Whether or not it was beneficial to the growth of science is a question which has been debated now for generations. That it influenced the growth of science cannot be doubted. The three most important philosophers of antiquity, in terms of the development of scientific thought, were Plato, Aristotle and Epicurus. Each presented a metaphysics which each claimed was the only proper one to serve as a foundation of science. The selections that follow illustrate the Platonic, Aristotelian and Epicurean views of the nature of physical reality.

1. Plato*

Plato (429-347 B.C.) was primarily a political philosopher. But, in order to construct a political philosophy, he was forced to deal with such questions as the nature of reality and the means whereby men could gain knowledge of this reality. In the Republic *Plato spells out his ideas on the road to truth. The first speaker is Socrates.*

And now, I said, let me show in a figure how far our nature is enlightened or unenlightened:--Behold! human beings living in an underground den, which has a mouth open towards the light and reaching all along the den; here they have been from their childhood, and have their legs and necks chained so that they cannot move, and can only see before them, being prevented by the chains from turning round their heads. Above and behind them a fire is blazing at a distance, and between the fire and the prisoners there is a raised way; and you will see, if you look, a low wall built along the way, like the screen which marionette players have in front of them, over which they show the puppets.

I see.

And do you see, I said, men passing along the wall carrying all sorts of vessels, and statues and figures of animals made of wood and stone and various materials, which appear over the wall? Some of them are talking, others silent.

You have shown me a strange image, and they are strange prisoners.

Like ourselves, I replied; and they see only their own shadows, or the shadows of one another, which the fire throws on the opposite wall of the cave?

True, he said; how could they see anything but the shadows if they were never allowed to move their heads?

And of the objects which are being carried in like manner they would only see the shadows?

---

* *The Dialogues of Plato*, translated into English by B. Jowett, 4th ed., 1953, Vol. II, pp. 773-781. Reprinted by permission of the Clarendon Press, Oxford.

Yes, he said.

And if they were able to converse with one another, would they not suppose that they were naming what was actually before them?

Very true.

And suppose further that the prison had an echo which came from the other side, would they not be sure to fancy when one of the passers-by spoke that the voice which they heard came from the passing shadow?

No question, he replied.

To them, I said, the truth would be literally nothing but the shadows of the images.

That is certain.

And now look again, and see what will naturally follow if the prisoners are released and disabused of their error. At first, when any of them is liberated and compelled suddenly to stand up and turn his neck round and walk and look towards the light, he will suffer sharp pains; the glare will distress him, and he will be unable to see the realities of which in his former state he had seen the shadows; and then conceive some one saying to him, that what he saw before was an illusion, but that now, when he is approaching nearer to being and his eye is turned towards more real existence, he has a clearer vision,--what will be his reply? And you may further imagine that his instructor is pointing to the objects as they pass and requiring him to name them,--will he not be perplexed? Will he not fancy that the shadows which he formerly saw are truer than the objects which are now shown to him?

Far truer.

And if he is compelled to look straight at the light, will he not have a pain in his eyes which will make him turn away to take refuge in the objects of vision which he can see, and which he will conceive to be in reality clearer than the things which are now being shown to him?

True, he said.

And suppose once more, that he is reluctantly dragged up a steep and rugged ascent, and held fast until he is forced into the presence of the sun himself, is he not likely to be pained and irritated? When he approaches the light his eyes will be dazzled, and he will not be able to see anything at all of what are now called realities.

Not all in a moment, he said.

He will require to grow accustomed to the sight of the upper world. And first he will see the shadows best, next the reflections of men and other objects in the water, and then the objects themselves; then he will gaze upon the light of the moon and the stars and the spangled heaven; and he will see the sky and the stars by night better than the sun or the light of the sun by day?

Certainly.

Last of all he will be able to see the sun, and not mere reflections of him in the water, but he will see him in his own proper place, and not in another; and he will contemplate him as he is.

Certainly.

He will then proceed to argue that this is he who gives the season and the years, and is the guardian of all that is in the visible world, and in a certain way the cause of all things which he and his fellows have been accustomed to behold?

Clearly, he said, he would first see the sun and then reason about him.

And when he remembered his old habitation, and the wisdom of the den and his fellow-prisoners, do you not suppose that he would felicitate himself on the change, and pity them?

Certainly, he would.

And if they were in the habit of conferring honours among themselves on those who were quickest to observe the passing shadows and to remark which of them went before, and which followed after, and which were together; and who were therefore best able to draw conclusions as to the future, do you think that he would care for such honours and glories, or envy the possessors of them? Would he not say with Homer,

> 'Better to be the poor servant of a poor master,'

and to endure anything, rather than think as they do and live after their manner?

Yes, he said, I think that he would rather suffer anything than entertain these false notions and live in this miserable manner.

Imagine once more, I said, such an one coming suddenly out of the sun to be replaced in his old situation; would he not be certain to have his eyes full of darkness?

To be sure, he said.

And if there were a contest, and he had to compete in measuring the shadows with the prisoners who had never moved out of the den, while his sight was still weak, and before his eyes had become steady (and the time which would be needed to acquire this new habit of sight might be very considerable), would he not be ridiculous? Men would say of him that up he went and down he came without his eyes; and that it was better not even to think of ascending; and if any one tried to loose another and lead him up to the light, let them only catch the offender, and they would put him to death.

No question, he said.

This entire allegory, I said, you may now append, dear Glaucon, to the previous argument; the prison-house is the world of sight, the light of the fire is the sun, and you will not misapprehend me if you interpret the journey upwards to be the ascent of the soul into the intellectual world according to my poor belief, which, at your desire, I have expressed--whether rightly or wrongly God knows. But, whether true or false, my opinion is that in the world of knowledge the idea of good appears last of all, and is seen only with an effort; and, when seen, is also inferred to be the universal author of all things beautiful and right, parent of light and of the lord of light in this visible world, and the immediate source of reason and truth in the intellectual; and that this is the power upon which he who would act rationally either in public or private life must have his eye fixed.

I agree, he said, as far as I am able to understand you.

Moreover, I said, you must not wonder that those who attain to this beatific vision are unwilling to descend to human affairs; for their souls are ever hastening into the upper world where they desire to dwell; which desire of theirs is very natural, if our allegory may be trusted.

Yes, very natural.

And is there anything surprising in one who passes from divine contemplations to the evil state of man, misbehaving himself in a ridiculous manner; if, while his eyes are blinking and before he has become accustomed to the surrounding darkness, he is compelled to fight in courts of law, or in other places, about the images or the shadows of images of justice, and is endeavouring to meet the conceptions of those who have never yet seen absolute justice?

Anything but surprising, he replied.

Any one who has common sense will remember that the bewilderments of the eyes are of two kinds, and arise from two causes, either from coming out of the light or from going into the light, which is true of the mind's eye, quite as much as of the bodily eye; and he who remembers this when he sees any one whose vision is perplexed and weak, will not be too ready to laugh; he will first ask whether that soul of man has come out of the brighter life, and is unable to see because unaccustomed to the dark, or having turned from darkness to the day is dazzled by excess of light. And he will count the one happy in his condition and state of being, and he will pity the other; or, if he have a mind to laugh at the soul which comes from below into the light, there will be more reason in this than in the laugh which greets him who returns from above out of the light into the den.

That, he said, is a very just distinction.

But then, if I am right, certain professors of education must be wrong when they say that they can put a knowledge into the soul which was not there before, like sight into blind eyes.

They undoubtedly say this, he replied.

Whereas, our argument shows that the power and capacity of learning exists in the soul already; and that just as the eye was unable to turn from darkness to light without the whole body, so too the instrument of knowledge can only by the movement of the whole soul be turned from the world of becoming into that of being, and learn by degrees to endure the sight of being, and of the brightest and best of being, or in other words, of the good.

Very true.

And must there not be some art which will effect conversion in the easiest and quickest manner; not implanting the faculty of sight, for that exists already, but has been turned in the wrong direction, and is looking away from the truth?

Yes, he said, such an art may be presumed.

* * * * *

And now shall we consider in what way such guardians will be produced, and how they are to be brought from darkness to light,--as some are said to have ascended from the world below to the gods?

By all means, he replied.

The process, I said, is not the turning over of an oyster-shell, but the turning round of a soul passing from a day which is little better than night to the true of being, that is, the ascent from below, which we affirm to be true philosophy?

Quite so.

And should we not enquire what sort of knowledge has the power of effecting such a change?

Certainly.

What sort of knowledge is there which would draw the soul from becoming to being? And another consideration has just occurred to me: You will remember that our young men are to be warrior athletes?

Yes, that was said.

Then this new kind of knowledge must have an additional quality?

What quality?

Usefulness in war.

Yes, if possible.

There were two parts in our former scheme of education, were there not?

Just so.

There was gymnastic which presided over the growth and decay of the body, and may therefore be regarded as having to do with generation and corruption?

True.

Then that is not the knowledge which we are seeking to discover?

No.

But what do you say of music, what also entered to a certain extent into our former scheme?

Music, he said, as you will remember, was the counterpart of gymnastic, and trained the guardians by the influences of habit, by harmony making them harmonious, by rhythm rhythmical, but not giving them science; and the words, whether fabulous or possibly true, had kindred elements of rhythm and harmony in them. But in music there was nothing which tended to that good which you are now seeking.

You are most accurate, I said, in your recollection; in music there certainly was nothing of the kind. But what branch of knowledge is there, my dear Glaucon, which is of the desired nature; since all the useful arts were reckoned mean by us?

Undoubtedly; and yet if music and gymnastic are excluded, and the arts are also excluded, what remains?

Well, I said, there may be nothing left of our special subjects; and then we shall have to take something which is not special, but of universal application.

What may that be?

A something which all arts and sciences and intelligences use in common, and which every one first has to learn among the elements of education.

What is that?

The little matter of distinguishing one, two, and three--in a word, number and calculation:--do not all arts and sciences necessarily partake of them?

Yes.

2. Aristotle*

Aristotle (384-322 B.C.) was Plato's pupil. He took all knowledge for his province, writing on physics, biology, ethics, aesthetics and political theory. In his Metaphysics *Aristotle laid out the definitions necessary for the creation of the science of physics.*

We are seeking the principles and the causes of the things that are, and obviously of them *qua* being. For, while there is a cause of health and of good condition, and the objects of mathematics have first principles and elements and causes, and in general every science which is ratiocinative or at all involves reasoning deals with causes and principles, more or less precise, all these sciences mark off some particular being--some genus, and inquire into this, but not into being simply nor *qua* being, nor do they offer any discussion of the essence of the things of which they treat; but starting from the essence--some making it plain to the senses, others assuming it as a hypothesis--they then demonstrate, more or less cogently, the essential attributes of the genus with which they deal. It is obvious, therefore, that such an induction yields no demonstration of substance or of the essence, but some other way of exhibiting it. And similarly the sciences omit the question whether the genus with which they deal exists or does not exist, because it belongs to the same kind of thinking to show what it is and that it is.

And since natural science, like other sciences, is in fact about one class of being, i.e. to that sort of substance which has the principle of its movement and rest present in itself, evidently it is neither practical nor productive. For in the case of things made the principle is in the maker--it is either reason or art or some faculty, while in the case of things done it is in the doer--viz. will, for that which is done and that which is willed are the same. Therefore, if all thought is either practical or productive or theoretical, physics must be a theoretical science, but it will theorize about such being as admits of being moved, and about substance-as-defined for the most part only as not separable from matter. Now, we must not fail to notice the mode of being of the essence and of its definition, for, without this, inquiry is but idle. Of things defined, i.e. of 'whats', some are like 'snub', and some like 'concave'. And these differ because 'snub' is bound up with matter (for what is snub is a concave *nose*), while concavity is independent of perceptible matter. If then all natural things are analogous to the snub in their nature--e.g. nose, eye, face, flesh, bone, and, in general, animal; leaf, root, bark, and, in

---

* *The Works of Aristotle*, translated into English under the editorship of W. D. Ross, Volume VIII, *Metaphysica* (Oxford, Clarendon Press, 1928), pp. 1025b-1026b; 1064a-1065b; 1069a-1070a; 1032a-1032b; 999a-999b; 1013a; 1014a-1015a; 1017b; 1019a-1019b; 1020a-1020b; 1025a. Reprinted by permission of the Clarendon Press, Oxford.

general, plant (for none of these can be defined without reference to movement--they always have matter), it is clear how we must seek and define the 'what' in the case of natural objects, and also that it belongs to the student of nature to study even soul in a certain sense, i.e. so much of it as is not independent of matter.

That physics, then, is a theoretical science, is plain from these considerations. Mathematics also, however, is theoretical; but whether its objects are immovable and separable from matter, is not at present clear; still, it is clear that *some* mathematical theorems *consider* them *qua* immovable and *qua* separable from matter. But if there is something which is eternal and immovable and separable, clearly the knowledge of it belongs to a theoretical science,--not, however, to physics (for physics deals with certain movable things) nor to mathematics, but to a science prior to both. For physics deals with things which exist separately but are not immovable, and some parts of mathematics deal with things which are immovable but presumably do not exist separately, but as embodied in matter; while the first science deals with things which both exist separately and are immovable. Now all causes must be eternal, but especially these; for they are the causes that operate on so much of the divine as appears to us. There must, then, be three theoretical philosophies, mathematics, physics, and what we may call theology, since it is obvious that if the divine is present anywhere, it is present in things of this sort. And the highest science must deal with the highest genus. Thus, while the theoretical sciences are more to be desired than the other sciences, this is more to be desired than the other theoretical sciences. For one might raise the question whether first philosophy is universal, or deals with one genus, i.e. some one kind of being; for not even the mathematical sciences are all alike in this respect,--geometry and astronomy deal with a certain particular kind of thing, while universal mathematics applies alike to all. We answer that if there is no substance other than those which are formed by nature, natural science will be the first science; but if there is an immovable substance, the science of this must be prior and must be first philosophy, and universal in this way, because it is first. And it will belong to this to consider being *qua* being--both what it is and the attributes which belong to it *qua* being.

* * * * *

Every science seeks certain principles and causes for each of its objects--e.g. medicine and gymnastics and each of the other sciences, whether productive or mathematical. For each of these marks off a certain class of things for itself and busies itself about this as about something existing and real,--not however *qua* real; the science that does *this* is another distinct from these. Of the sciences mentioned each gets somehow the 'what' in some class of things and tries to prove the other truths, with more or less precision. Some get the 'what' through perception, others by hypothesis; so that it is clear from an induction of this sort that there is no *demonstration* of the substance or 'what'.

There is a science of nature, and evidently it must be different both from practical and from productive science. For in the case of productive science the principle of movement is in the producer and not in the product, and is either an art or some other faculty. And similarly in practical science the movement is not in the thing done, but rather in the doers. But the science of the natural philosopher deals with the things that have *in themselves* a principle of movement. It is clear from these facts, then, that natural science must be neither practical nor productive, but theoretical (for it must fall into some one of these classes). And since each of the sciences must somehow know the 'what' and use this as a principle, we must not fail to observe how the natural philosopher should define things and how he should state the definition of the essence--whether as akin to 'snub' or rather to 'concave'. For of these the definition of 'snub' includes the matter of the thing, but that of 'concave' is independent of the matter; for snubness is found in a nose, so that we look for its definition without eliminating the nose, for what is snub is a concave nose. Evidently then the definition of flesh also and of the eye and of the other parts must always be stated without eliminating the matter.

Since there is a science of being *qua* being and capable of existing apart, we must consider whether this is to be regarded as the same as physics or rather as different. Physics deals with the things that have a principle of movement in themselves; mathematics is theoretical, and *is* a science that deals with things that are at rest, but its subjects cannot exist apart. Therefore about that which can exist apart and is unmovable there is a science different from both of these, if there *is* a substance of this nature (I mean separable and unmovable), as we shall try to prove there is. And if there is such a kind of thing in the world, here must surely be the divine, and this must be the first and most dominant principle. Evidently, then, there are three kinds of theoretical sciences--physics, mathematics, theology. The class of theoretical sciences is the best, and of these themselves the last named is best; for it deals with the highest of existing things, and each science is called better or worse in virtue of its proper object.

One might raise the question whether the science of being *qua* being is to be regarded as universal or not. Each of the mathematical sciences deals with some one determinate class of things, but universal mathematics applies alike to all. Now if natural substances are the first of existing things, physics must be the first of sciences; but if there is another entity and substance, separable and unmovable, the knowledge of it must be different and prior to physics and universal because it is prior.

Since 'being' in general has several senses, of which one is 'being by accident', we must consider first that which 'is' in this sense. Evidently none of the traditional sciences busies itself about the accidental. For neither does architecture consider what will happen to those who are to use the house (e.g. whether they will have a painful life in it or not), nor does weaving, or shoemaking, or the confectioner's art, do the like; but each of these sciences considers only what is peculiar to it, i.e. its proper end. And as for the argument that 'when he who is musical becomes lettered he will be both at once, not having been, must have come to be; therefore he must have at once become musical and lettered',--this none of the recognized sciences considers, but only sophistic; for this alone busies itself about the accidental, so that Plato is not far wrong when he says that the sophist spends his time on non-being.

That a science of the accidental is not even possible will be evident if we try to see what the accidental really is. We say that everything either is always and of necessity (necessity not in the sense of violence, but that which we appeal to in demonstrations), or is for the most part, or is neither for the most part, nor always and of necessity, but merely as it chances; e.g. there might be cold in the dog-days, but this occurs neither always and of necessity, nor for the most part, though it might happen sometimes. The accidental, then, is what occurs, but not always nor of necessity, nor for the most part. Now we have said what the accidental is, and it is obvious why there is no science of such a thing; for all science is of that which is always or for the most part, but the accidental is in neither of these classes.

Evidently there are not causes and principles of the accidental, of the same kind as there are of the essential; for if there were, everything would be of necessity. If *A* is when *B* is, and *B* is when *C* is, and if *C* exists not by chance but of necessity, that also of which *C* was cause will exist of necessity, down to the last *causatum* as it is called (but this was supposed to be accidental). Therefore all things will be of necessity, and chance and the possibility of a thing's either occurring or not occurring are removed entirely from the range of events. And if the cause be supposed not to exist but to be coming to be, the same results will follow; everything will occur of necessity. For to-morrow's eclipse will occur if *A* occurs, and *A* if *B* occurs, and *B* if *C* occurs; and in this way if we subtract time from the limited time between now and to-morrow we shall come sometime to the already existing condition. Therefore since this exists, everything after this will occur of necessity, so that all things occur of necessity.

As to that which 'is' in the sense of being true or of being by accident, the *former* depends on a combination in thought and is an affection of thought (which is the reason why it is the principles, not of that which 'is' in this sense, but of that which is outside and can exist apart, that are sought); and the *latter* is not necessary but indeterminate (I mean the accidental); and of such a thing the causes are unordered and indefinite.

Adaptation to an end is found in events that happen by nature or as the result of thought. It is 'luck' when one of these events happens by accident. For as a thing may exist, so it may be a cause, either by its own nature or by accident. Luck is an accidental cause at work in such events adapted to an end as are usually effected in accordance with purpose. And so luck and thought are concerned with the same sphere; for purpose cannot exist without thought. The causes from which lucky results might happen are indeterminate: and so luck is obscure to human calculation and is a cause by accident, but in the unqualified sense a cause of nothing. It is good or bad luck when the result is good or evil; and prosperity or misfortune when the scale of the results is large.

Since nothing accidental is prior to the essential, neither are accidental causes prior. If, then, luck or spontaneity is a cause of the material universe, reason and nature are causes before it.

* * * * *

The subject of our inquiry is substance; for the principles and the causes we are seeking are those of substances. For if the universe is of the nature of a whole, substance is its first part; and if it coheres merely by virtue of serial succession, on this view also substance is first, and is succeeded by quality, and then by quantity. At the same time these latter are not even being in the full sense, but are qualities and movements of it,--or else even the not-white and the not-straight would be being; at least we say even these *are*, e.g. 'there is a not-white'. Further, none of the categories other than substance can exist apart. And the early philosophers also in practice testify to the primacy of substance; for it was of substance that they sought the principles and elements and causes. The thinkers of the present day tend to rank universals as substances (for genera are universals, and these they tend to describe as principles and substances, owing to the abstract nature of their inquiry); but the thinkers of old ranked particular things as substances, e.g. fire and earth, not what is common to both, body.

There are three kinds of substance--one that is sensible (of which one subdivision is eternal and another is perishable; the latter is recognized by all men, and includes e.g. plants and animals), of which we must grasp the elements, whether one or many; and another that is immovable, and this certain thinkers assert to be capable of existing apart, some dividing it into two, others identifying the Forms and the objects of mathematics, and others positing, of these two, only the objects of mathematics. The former two kinds of substance are the subject of physics (for they imply movement); but the third kind belongs to another science, if there is no principle common it it and to the other kinds.

Sensible substance is changeable. Now if change proceeds from opposites or from intermediates, and not from all opposites (for the voice is not-white[,but it does not therefore change to white]), but from the contrary, there must be something underlying which changes into the contrary state; for the *contraries* do not change. Further, something persists, but the contrary does not persist; there is, then, some third thing besides the contraries, viz. the matter. Now since changes are of four kinds--either in respect of the 'what' or of the quality or of the quantity or of the place, and change in respect of 'thisness' is simple generation and destruction, and change in quantity is increase and diminution, and change in respect of an affection is alteration, and change of place is motion, changes will be from given states into those contrary to them in these several respects. The matter, then, which changes must be capable of both states. And since that which 'is' has two senses, we must say that everything changes from that which is potentially to that which is actually, e.g. from potentially white to actually white, and similarly in the case of increase and diminution. Therefore not only can a thing come to be, incidentally, out of that which is not, but also all things come to be out of that which is, but is potentially, and is not actually. And this is the 'One' of Anaxagoras; for instead of 'all things were together'--and the 'Mixture' of Empedocles and Anaximander and the account given by Democritus--it is better to say 'all things were together potentially but not actually'. Therefore these thinkers seem to have had some notion of matter. Now all things that change have matter, but different matter; and of eternal things those which are not generable but are movable in space have matter--not matter for generation, however, but for motion from one place to another.

One might raise the question from what sort of non-being generation proceeds; for 'non-being' has three senses. If, then, one form of non-being exists potentially, still it is not by virtue of a potentiality for any and every thing, but different things come from different things; nor is it satisfactory to say that 'all things were together'; for they differ in their matter, since otherwise why did an infinity of things come to be, and not one thing? For 'reason' is one, so that if matter also were one, that must have come to be in actuality which the matter was in potency. The causes and the principles, then, are three, two being the pair of contraries of which one is definition and form and the other is privation, and the third being the matter.

Note, next, that neither the matter nor the form comes to be--and I mean the last matter and form. For everything that changes is something and is changed by something and into something. That by which it is changed is the immediate mover; that which is changed, the matter; that into which it is changed, the form. The process, then, will go on to infinity, if not only the bronze comes to be round but also the round or the bronze comes to be; therefore there must be a stop.

Note, next, that each substance comes into being out of something that shares its name. (Natural objects and other things both rank as substances.) For things come into being either by art or by nature or by luck or by spontaneity. Now art is a principle of movement in something other than the thing moved, nature is a principle in the thing itself (for man begets man), and the other causes are privations of these two.

There are three kinds of substance--the matter, which is a 'this' in appearance (for all things that are characterized by contact and not by organic unity are matter and substratum, e.g. fire, flesh, head; for these are all matter, and the last matter is the matter of that which is in the full sense substance); the nature, which is a 'this' or positive state towards which movement takes place; and again, thirdly, the particular substance which is composed of these two, e.g. Socrates or Callias. Now in some cases the 'this' does not exist apart from the composite substance, e.g. the form of house does not so exist, unless the art of building exists apart (nor is there generation and destruction of these forms, but it is in another way that the house apart from its matter, and health, and all ideals of art, exist and do not exist); but if the 'this' exists apart from the concrete thing, it is only in the case of natural objects. And so Plato was not far wrong when he said that there are as many Forms as there are kinds of natural object (if there *are* Forms distinct from the things of this earth). The moving causes exist as things preceding the effects, but causes in the sense of definitions are simultaneous with their effects. For when a man is healthy, then health also exists; and the shape of a bronze sphere exists at the same as the bronze sphere. (But we must examine whether any form also survives afterwards. For in some cases there is nothing to prevent this; e.g. the soul may be of this sort--not all soul but the reason; for presumably it is impossible that *all* soul should survive.) Evidently then there is no necessity, on this ground at least, for the existence of the Ideas. For man is begotten by man, a given man by an individual father; and similarly in the arts; for the medical art is the formal cause of health.

* * * * *

Of things that come to be, some come to be by nature, some by art, some spontaneously. Now everything that comes to be comes to be by the agency of something and from something and comes to be something. And the something which I say it comes to be may be found in any category; it may come to be either a 'this' or of some size or of some quality or somewhere.

Now natural comings to be are the comings to be of those things which come to be by nature; and that out of which they come to be is what we call matter; and that by which they come to be is something which exists naturally; and the something which they come to be is a man or a plant or one of the things of this kind, which we say are substances if anything is--all things produced either by nature or by art have matter; for each of them is capable both of being and of not being, and this capacity is the matter in each--and, in general, both that from which they are produced is nature, and the type according to which they are produced is nature (for that which is produced, e.g. a plant or an animal, has a nature), and so is that by which they are produced--the so-called 'formal' nature, which is specifically the same (though this is in another individual); for man begets man.

Thus, then, are natural products produced; all other productions are called 'makings'. And all makings proceed either from art or from a faculty or from thought. Some of them happen also spontaneously or by luck just as natural products sometimes do; for there also the same things sometimes are produced without seed as well as from seed. Concerning these cases, then, we must inquire later, but from art proceed the things of which the form is in the soul of the artist. (By form I mean the essence of each thing and its primary substance.) For even contraries have in a sense the same form; for the substance of a privation is the the opposite substance, e.g. health is the substance of disease (for disease is the absence of health); and health is the formula in the soul or the knowledge of it. The healthy subject is produced as the result of the following train of thought:--since *this* is health, if the subject is to be healthy *this* must first be present, e.g. a uniform state of body, and if this is to be present, there must be heat; and the physician goes on thinking thus until he reduces the matter to a final something which he himself can produce. Then the process from this point onward, i.e. the process towards health, is called a 'making'. Therefore it follows that in a sense health comes from health and house from house, that with matter from that without matter; for the medical art and the building art are the form of health and of the house, and when I speak of substance without matter I mean the essence.

* * * * *

There is a difficulty . . . the hardest of all and the most necessary to examine, and of this the discussion now awaits us. If, on the one hand, there is nothing apart from individual things, and the individuals are infinite in number, how then is it possible to get knowledge of the infinite individuals? For all things that we come to know, we come to know in so far as they have some unity and identity, and in so far as some attribute belongs to them universally.

But if this is necessary, and there must be something apart from the individuals, it will be necessary that the genera exist apart from the individuals,--either the lowest or the highest genera; but we found by discussion just now that this is impossible.

Further, if we admit in the fullest sense that something exists apart from the concrete thing, whenever something is predicated of the matter, must there, if there is something apart, be something apart from each set of individuals, or from some and not from others, or from none? (A) If there is nothing apart from individuals, there will be no object of thought, but all things will be objects of sense, and there will not be knowledge of anything, unless we say that sensation is knowledge. Further, nothing will be eternal or unmovable; for all perceptible things perish and are in movement. But if there is nothing eternal, neither can there be a process of coming to be; for there must be something that comes to be, i.e. from which something comes to be, and the ultimate term in this series cannot have come to be, since the series has a limit and since nothing can come to be out of that which is not. Further, if generation and movement exist there must also be a limit; for no movement is infinite, but every movement has an end, and that which is incapable of complating its coming to be cannot be in process of coming to be; and that which has completed its coming to be must *be* as soon as it has come to be. Further, since the matter exists, because it is ungenerated, it is *a fortiori* reasonable that the substance or essence, that which the matter is at any time coming to be, should exist; for if neither essence nor matter is to be, nothing will be at all, and since this is impossible there must be something besides the concrete thing, viz. the shape or form.

But again (B) if we are to suppose this, it is hard to say in which cases we are to suppose it and in which not. For evidently it is not possible to suppose it in all cases; we could not suppose that there is a house besides the particular houses.--Besides this, will the substance of all the individuals, e.g. of all men, be one? This is paradoxical, for all the things whose substance is one are one. But are the substances many and different? This also is unreasonable.--At the same time, how does the matter become each of the individuals, and how *is* the concrete thing these two elements?

* * * * *

'BEGINNING' means (1) that part of a thing from which one would start first, e.g. a line or a road has a beginning in either of the contrary directions. (2) That from which each thing would best be originated, e.g. even in learning we must sometimes begin not from the first point and the beginning of the subject, but from the point from which we should learn most easily. (3) That from which, as an immanent part, a thing first comes to be, e.g. as the keel of a ship and the foundation of a house, while in animals some suppose the heart, others the brain, others some other part, to be of this nature. (4) That from which, *not* as an immanent part, a thing first comes to be, and from which the movement or the change naturally first begins, as a child comes from its father and its mother, and a fight from abusive language. (5) That at whose will that which is moved is moved and that which changes changes, e.g. the magistracies in cities, and oligarchies and monarchies and tyrannies, are called ἀρχαί, and so are the arts, and of these especially the architectonic arts. (6) That from which a thing can first be known,--this also is called the beginning of the thing, e.g. the hypotheses are the beginnings of demonstrations. (Causes are spoken of in an equal number of senses; for all causes are beginnings.) It is common, then, to all beginnings to be the first point from which a thing either is or comes to be or is known; but of these some are immanent in the thing and others are outside. Hence the nature of a thing is a beginning, and so is the element of a thing, and thought and will, and essence, and the final cause--for the good and the beautiful are the beginnings both of the knowledge and of the movement of many things.

'Cause' means (1) that from which, as immanent material, a thing comes into being, e.g. the bronze is the cause of the statue and the silver of the saucer, and so are the classes which include these. (2) The form or pattern, i.e. the definition of the essence, and the classes which include this (e.g. the ratio 2 : 1 and number in general are causes of the octave), and the parts included in the definition. (3) That from which the change or the resting from change first begins; e.g. the adviser is a cause of the action, and the father a cause of the child, and in general the maker a cause of the thing made and the change-producing of the changing. (4) The end, i.e. that for the sake of which a thing is; e.g. health is the cause of walking. For 'Why does one walk?' we say; 'that one may be healthy'; and in speaking thus we think we have given the cause. The same is true of all the means that intervene before the end, when something else has put the process in motion, as e.g. thinning or purging or drugs or instruments intervene before health is reached; for all these are for the sake of the end, though they differ from one another in that some are instruments and others are actions.

*   *   *   *   *

'Element' means (1) the primary component immanent in a thing, and indivisible in kind into other kinds; e.g. the elements of speech are the parts of which speech consists and into which it is ultimately divided, while *they* are no longer divided into other forms of speech different in kind from them. If they *are* divided, their parts are of the same kind, as a part of water is water (while a part of the syllable is not a syllable). Similarly those who speak of the elements of bodies mean the things into which bodies are ultimately divided, while *they* are no longer divided into other things differing in kind; and whether the things of this sort are one or more, they call these elements. The so-called elements of geometrical proofs, and in general the elements of demonstrations, have a similar character; for the primary demonstrations, each of which is implied in many demonstrations, are called elements of demonstrations; and the primary syllogisms, which have three terms and proceed by means of one middle, are of this nature.

(2) People also transfer the word 'element' from this meaning and apply it to that which, being one and small, is useful for many purposes; for which reason what is small and simple and indivisible is called an element. Hence come the facts that the most universal things are elements (because each of them being one and simple is present in a plurality of things, either in all or in as many as possible), and that unity and the point are thought by some to be first principles. Now, since the so-called genera are universal and indivisible (for there is no definition of them), some say the genera are elements, and more so than the differentia, because the genus is more universal; for where the differentia is present the genus accompanies it, but where the genus is present the differentia is not always so. It is common to all the meanings that the element of each thing is the first component immanent in each.

'Nature' means (1) the genesis of growing things--the meaning which would be suggested if one were to pronounce the υ in φύσιζ long. (2) That immanent part of a growing thing from which its growth first proceeds. (3) The source from which the primary movement in each natural object is present in it in virtue of its own essence. Those things are said to grow which derive increase from something else by contact and either by organic unity, or by organic adhesion as in the case of embryos. Organic unity differs from contact; for in the latter case there need not be anything besides the contact, but in organic unities there is something identical in both parts, which makes them grow together instead of merely touching, and be one in respect of continuity and quantity, though not of quality.--(4) 'Nature' means the primary material of which any natural object consists or out of which it is made, which is relatively unshaped and cannot be changed from its own potency, as e.g. bronze is said to be the nature of a statue and of bronze utensils, and wood the nature of wooden things; and so in all other cases; for when a product is made out of these materials, the first matter is preserved throughout. For it is in this way that people call the elements of natural objects also their nature, some naming fire, others earth, others air, others water, others something else of the sort, and some naming more than one of these, and others all of them.--(5) 'Nature' means the *essence* of natural objects, as with those who say the nature is the primary mode of composition, or as Empedocles says:--

Nothing that is has a nature,
But only mixing and parting of the mixed,
And nature is but a name given them by men.

Hence as regards the things that are or come to be by nature, though that *from which* they naturally come to be or are is already present, we say they have not their nature yet, unless they have their form or shape. That which comprises both of these exists *by* nature, e.g. the animals and their parts; and not only is the first matter nature (and this in two senses, either the first, counting from the thing, or the first in general; e.g. in the case of works in bronze, bronze is first with reference to them, but in general perhaps water is first, if all things that can be melted are water), but also the form or essence, which is the end of the process of becoming.--(6) By an extension of meaning from this sense of 'nature' every essence in general has come to be called a 'nature', because the nature of a thing is one kind of essence.

From what has been said, then, it is plain that nature in the primary and strict sense is the essence of things which have in themselves, as such, a source of movement; for the matter is called the nature because it is qualified to receive this, and processes of becoming and growing are called nature because they are movements proceeding from this. And nature in this sense is the source of the movement of natural objects, being present in them somehow, either potentially or in complete reality.

* * * * *

We call 'substance' (1) the simple bodies, i.e. earth and fire and water and everything of the sort, and in general bodies and the things composed of them, both animals and divine beings, and the parts of these. All these are called substance because they are not predicated of a subject but everything else is predicated of them.--(2) That which, being present in such things as are not predicated of a subject, is the cause of their being, as the soul is of the being of an animal.--(3) The parts which are present in such things, limiting them and marking them as individuals, and by whose destruction the whole is destroyed, as the body is by the destruction of the plane, as some say, and the plane by the destruction of the line; and in general number is thought by some to be of this nature; and in general number is thought by some to be of this nature; for if it is destroyed, they say, nothing exists, and it limits all things.--(4) The essence, the formula of which is a definition, is also called the substance of each thing.

It follows, then, that 'substance' has two senses, (A) the ultimate substratum, which is no longer predicated of anything else, and (B) that which, being a 'this', is also separable--and of this nature is the shape or form of each thing.

* * * * *

'Potency' means (1) a source of movement or change, which is in another thing than the thing moved or in the same thing *qua* other; e.g. the art of building is a potency which is not in the thing built, while the art of healing, which is a potency, may be in the man healed, but not in him *qua* healed. 'Potency' then means the source, in general of change or movement in another thing or in the same thing *qua* other, and also (2) the source of a thing's being moved by another thing or by itself *qua* other. For in virtue of that principle, in virtue of which a patient suffers anything, we call it 'capable' of suffering; and this we do sometimes if it suffers anything at all, sometimes not in respect of everything it suffers, but only if it suffers a change for the better.--(3) The capacity of performing this well or according to intention; for sometimes we say of those who merely can walk or speak but not well or not as they intend, that they cannot speak or walk. So too (4) in the case of passivity.--(5) The states in virtue of which things are absolutely impassive or unchangeable, or not easily changed for the worse, are called potencies; for things are broken and crushed and bent and in general destroyed not by having a potency but by not having one and by lacking something, and things are impassive with respect to such processes if they are scarcely and slightly affected by them, because of a 'potency' and because they 'can' do something and are in some positive state.

'Potency' having this variety of meanings, so too the 'potent' or 'capable' in one sense will mean that which can begin a movement (or a change in general, for even that which can bring things to rest is a 'potent' thing) in another thing or in itself *qua* other; and in one sense that over which something else has such a potency; and in one sense that which has a potency of changing into something, whether for the worse or for the better (for even that which perishes is thought to be 'capable' of perishing, for it would not have perished if it had not been capable of it' but, as a matter of fact, it has a certain disposition and cause and principle which fits it to suffer this; sometimes it is thought to be of this sort because it has something, sometimes because it is deprived of something; but if privation is in a sense 'having' or 'habit', everything will be capable by having something, so that things are capable both by having a positive habit and principle, and by having the privation of this, if it is possible to *have* a privation; and if privation is *not* in a sense 'habit', 'capable' is used in two distinct senses); and a thing is capable in another sense because neither any other thing, nor itself *qua* other, has a potency or principle which can destroy it. Again, all of these are capable either merely because the thing might chance to happen or not to happen, or because it might do so *well*. This sort of potency is found even in lifeless things, e.g. in instruments; for we say one lyre can speak, and another cannot speak at all, if it has not a good tone.

'Quality' means (1) the differentia of the essence, e.g. man is an animal of a certain quality because he is two-footed, and the horse is so because it is four-footed; and a circle is a figure of particular quality because it is without angles,--which shows that the essential differentia is a quality.--This, then, is one meaning of quality--the differentia of the essence, but (2) there is another sense in which it applies to the unmovable objects of mathematics, the sense in which the numbers have a certain quality, e.g. the composite numbers which are not in one dimension only, but of which the plane and the solid are copies (these are those which have two or three factors); and in general that which exists in the essence of numbers besides quantity is quality; for the essence of each is what it is once, e.g. that of 6 is not what it is twice or thrice, but what it is once; for 6 is once 6.

(3) All the modifications of substances that move (e.g. heat and cold, whiteness and blackness, heaviness and lightness, and the others of the sort) in virtue of which, when they change, bodies are said to alter. (4) Quality in respect of virtue and vice and, in general, of evil and good.

Quality, then, seems to have practically two meanings, and one of these is the more proper. The primary quality is the differentia of the essence, and of this the quality in numbers is a part; for it is a differentia of essences, but either not of things that move or not of them *qua* moving. Secondly, there are the modifications of things that move, *qua* moving, and the differentiae of movements. Virtue and vice fall among these modifications; for they indicate differentiae of the movement or activity, according to which the things in motion act or are acted on well or badly; for that which can be moved or act in one way is good, and that which can do so in another--the contrary--way is vicious. Good and evil indicate quality especially in living things, and among these especially in those which have purpose.

* * * * *

'Accident' means (1) that which attaches to something and can be truly asserted, but neither of necessity nor usually, e.g. if some one in digging a hole for a plant has found treasure. This--the finding of treasure--is for the man who dug the hole an accident; for neither does the one come of necessity from the other or after the other, nor, if a man plants, does he usually find treasure. And a musical man *might* be pale; but since this does not happen of necessity nor usually, we call it an accident. Therefore since there are attributes and they attach to subjects, and some of them attach to these only in a particular place and at a particular time, whatever attaches to a subject, but not because it was this subject, or the time this time, or the place this place, will be an accident. Therefore, too, there is no definite cause for an accident, but a chance cause, i.e. an indefinite one. Going to Aegina was an accident for a man, if he went not in order to get there, but because he was carried out of his way by a storm or captured by pirates. The accident has happened or exists,--not in virtue of the subject's nature, however, but of something else; for the *storm* was the cause of his coming to a place for which he was not sailing, and this was Aegina.

'Accident' has also (2) another meaning, i.e. all that attaches to each thing in virtue of itself but is not in its essence, as having its angles equal to two right angles attaches to the triangle. And accidents of this sort may be eternal, but no accident of the other sort is. This is explained elsewhere.

3. Epicurus*

Epicurus (341-270 B.C.) based his philosophy on the atomic doctrine first proposed by Leucippus and Democritus in the preceding century. The atomic theory was to have a long history but it smacked of atheism and was, therefore, suspect. In his letter to Herodotus, Epicurus explains the atomic theory and its place in the Epicurean philosophy.

Epicurus to Herodotus

For those who are unable, Herodotus, to work in detail through all that I have written about nature, or to peruse the larger books which I have composed, I have already prepared at sufficient length an epitome of the whole system, that they may keep adequately in mind at least the most general principles in each department, in order that as occasion arises they may be able to assist themselves on the most important points, in so far as they undertake the study of nature. But those also who have made considerable progress in the survey of the main principles ought to bear in mind the scheme of the whole system set forth in its essentials. For we have frequent need of the general view, but not so often of the detailed exposition. Indeed it is necessary to go back on the main principles, and constantly to fix in one's memory enough to give one the most essential comprehension of the truth. And in fact the accurate knowledge of details will be fully discovered, if the general principles in the various departments are thoroughly grasped and borne in mind; for even in the case of one fully initiated the most essential feature in all accurate knowledge is the capacity to make a rapid use of observation and mental apprehension, and (this can be done if everything) is summed up in elementary principles and formulae. For it is not possible for any one to abbreviate the complete course through the whole system, if he cannot embrace in his own mind by means of short formulae all that might be set out with accuracy in detail. Wherefore since the method I have described is valuable to all those who are accustomed to the investigation of nature, I who urge upon others the constant occupation in the investigation of nature, and find my own peace chiefly in a life so occupied, have composed for you another epitome on these lines, summing up the first principles of the whole doctrine.

First of all, Herodotus, we must grasp the ideas attached to words, in order that we may be able to refer to them and so to judge the inferences of opinion or problems of investigation or reflection, so that we may not either leave everything uncertain and go on explaining to infinity or use words devoid of meaning. For this purpose it is essential that the first mental image associated with each word should be regarded, and that there

---

* *Epicurus, The Extant Remains*, with Short Critical Apparatus. Translation and Notes by Cyril Bailey, Oxford at the Clarendon Press, 1926. Pp. 19; 21; 23; 25; 31; 33; 35; 37; 39; 41; 43; 45; 47; 49; 51; 53. Reprinted by permission of the Clarendon Press, Oxford.

should be no need of explanation, if we are really to have a standard to which to refer a problem of investigation or reflection or a mental inference. And besides we must keep all our investigations in accord with our sensations, and in particular with the immediate apprehensions whether of the mind or of any one of the instruments of judgement, and likewise in accord with the feelings existing in us, in order that we may have indications whereby we may judge both the problem of sense-perception and the unseen.

Having made these points clear, we must now consider things imperceptible to the senses. First of all, that nothing is created out of that which does not exist: for if it were, everything would be created out of everything with no need of seeds. And again, if that which disappears were destroyed into that which did not exist, all things would have perished, since that into which they were dissolved would not exist. Furthermore, the universe always was such as it is now, and always will be the same. For there is nothing into which it changes: for outside the universe there is nothing which could come into it and bring about the change.

Moreover, the universe is (bodies and space): for that bodies exist, sense itself witnesses in the experience of all men, and in accordance with the evidence of sense we must of necessity judge of the imperceptible by reasoning, as I have already said. And if there were not that which we term void and place and intangible existence, bodies would have nowhere to exist and nothing through which to move, as they are seen to move. And besides these two nothing can even be thought of either by conception or on the analogy of things conceivable such as could be grasped as whole existences and not spoken of as the accidents or properties of such existences. Furthermore, among bodies some are compounds, and others those of which compounds are formed. And these latter are indivisible and unalterable (if, that is, all things are not to be destroyed into the non-existent, but something permanent is to remain behind at the dissolution of compounds): they are completely solid in nature, and can by no means be dissolved in any part. So it must needs be that the first-beginnings are indivisible corporeal existences.

Moreover, the universe is boundless. For that which is bounded has an extreme point: and the extreme point is seen against something else. So that as it has no extreme point, it has no limit; and as it has no limit, it must be boundless and not bounded. Furthermore, the infinite is boundless both in the number of the bodies and in the extent of the void. For if on the one hand the void were boundless, and the bodies limited in number, the bodies could not stay anywhere, but would be carried about and scattered through the infinite void, not having other bodies to support them and keep them in place by means of collisions. But if, on the other hand, the void were limited, the infinite bodies would not have room wherein to take their place.

Besides this the indivisible and solid bodies, out of which too the compounds are created and into which they are dissolved, have an incomprehensible number of varieties in shape: for it is not possible that such great varieties of things should arise from the same (atomic) shapes, if they are limited in number. And so in each shape the atoms are quite infinite in number, but their differences of shape are not quite infinite, but only incomprehensible in number.

And the atoms move continuously for all time, some of them (falling straight down, others swerving, and others recoiling from their collisions. And of the latter, some are borne on) separating to a long distance from one another, while others again recoil and recoil, whenever they chance to be checked by the interlacing with others, or else shut in by atoms interlaced around them. For on the one hand the nature of the void which separates each atom by itself brings this about, as it is not able to afford resistance, and on the other hand the hardness which belongs to the atoms makes them recoil after collision to as great a distance as the interlacing permits separation after the collision. And these motions have no beginning, since the atoms and the void are the cause.

These brief sayings, if all these points are borne in mind, afford a sufficient outline for our understanding of the nature of existing things.

Furthermore, there are infinite worlds both like and unlike this world of ours. For the atoms being infinite in number, as was proved already, are borne on far out into space. For those atoms, which are of such nature that a world could be created out of them or made by them, have not been used up either on one world or on a limited number of worlds, nor again on all the worlds which are alike, or on those which are different from these. So that there nowhere exists an obstacle to the infinite number of the worlds.

* * * * *

Moreover, we must suppose that the atoms do not possess any of the qualities belonging to perceptible things, except shape, weight, and size, and all that necessarily goes with shape. For every quality changes; but the atoms do not change at all, since there must needs be something which remains solid and indissoluble at the dissolution of compounds, which can cause changes; not changes into the non-existent or from the non-existent, but changes effected by the shifting of position of some particles, and by the addition or departure of others. For this reason it is essential that the bodies which shift their position should be imperishable and should not possess the nature of what changes, but parts and configuration of their own. For thus much must needs remain constant. For even in things perceptible to us which change their shape by the withdrawal of matter it is seen that shape remains to them, whereas the qualities do not remain in the changing object in the way in which shape is left behind, but are lost from the entire body. Now these particles which are left behind are sufficient to cause the differences in compound bodies, since it is essential that some things should be left behind and not be destroyed into the non-existent.

Moreover, we must not either suppose that every size exists among the atoms, in order that the evidence of phenomena may not contradict us, but we must suppose that there are some variations of size. For if this be the case, we can give a better account of what occurs in our feelings and sensations. But the existence of atoms of every size is not required to explain the differences of qualities in things, and at the same time some atoms would be bound to come within our ken and be visible; but this is never seen to be the case, nor is it possible to imagine how an atom could become visible.

Besides this we must not suppose that in a limited body there can be infinite parts or parts of every degree of smallness. Therefore, we must not only do away with division into smaller and smaller parts to infinite, in order that we may not make all things weak, and so in the composition of aggregate bodies be compelled to crush and squander the things that exist into non-existent, but we must not either suppose that in limited bodies there is a possibility of continuing to infinity in passing even to smaller and smaller parts. For if once one says that there are infinite parts in a body or parts of any degree of smallness, it is not possible to conceive how this should be, and indeed how could the body any longer be limited in size? (For it is obvious that these infinite particles must be of some size or other; and however small they may be, the size of the body too would be infinite.) And again, since the limited body has an extreme point, which is distinguishable, even though not perceptible by itself, you cannot conceive that the succeeding point to it is not similar in character, or that if you go on in this way from one point to another, it should be possible for you to proceed to infinity marking such points in your mind. We must notice also that the least thing in sensation is neither exactly like that which admits of progression from one part to another, nor again is it in every respect wholly unlike it, but it has a certain affinity with such bodies, yet cannot be divided into parts. But when on the analogy of this resemblance we think to divide off parts of it, one on the one side and another on the other, it must needs be that another point like the first meets our view. And we look at these points in succession starting from the first, not within the limits of the same point nor in contact part with part, but yet by means of their own proper characteristics measuring the size of bodies, more in a greater body and fewer in a smaller. Now we must suppose that the least part in the atom too bears the same relation to the whole; for though in smallness it is obvious that it exceeds that which is seen by sensation, yet it has the same relations. For indeed we have already declared on the ground of its relation to sensible bodies that the atom has size, only we placed it far below them in smallness. Further, we must consider these least indivisible points as boundary-marks, providing in themselves as primary units the measure of size for the atoms, both for the smaller and the greater, in our contemplation of these unseen bodies by means of thought. For the affinity which the least parts of the atom have to the homogeneous parts (of sensible things) is sufficient to justify our conclusion to this extent: but that they should ever come together as bodies with motion is quite impossible.

[Furthermore, in the infinite we must not speak of 'up' or

'down', as though with reference to an absolute highest or lowest--and indeed we must say that though it is possible to proceed to infinity in the direction above our heads from wherever we take our stand, the absolute highest point will never appear to us--nor yet can that which passes beneath the point thought of to infinity be at the same time both up and down in reference to the same thing: for it is impossible to think this. So that it is possible to consider as one single motion that which is thought of as the upwards motion to infinity and as another the downward motion, even though that which passes from us into the regions above our heads arrives countless times at the feet of beings above and that which passes downwards from us at the head of beings below; for none the less the whole motions are thought of as opposed, the one to the other, to infinity.]

Moreover, the atoms must move with equal speed, when they are borne onwards through the void, nothing colliding with them. For neither will the heavy move more quickly than the small and light, when, that is, nothing meets them: nor again the small more quickly than the great, having their whole course uniform, when nothing collides with them either: nor is the motion upwards or sideways owing to blows (quicker), nor again that downwards owing to their own weight. For as long as either of the two motions prevails, so long will it have a course as quick as thought, until something checks it either from outside or from its own weight counteracting the force of that which dealt the blow. Moreover, their passage through the void, when it takes place without meeting any bodies which might collide, accomplishes every comprehensible distance in an inconceivably short time. For it is collision and its absence which take the outward appearance of slowness and quickness. Moreover, it will be said that in compound bodies too one atom is faster than another, though as a matter of fact all are equal in speed: this will be said because even in the least period of continuous time all the atoms in aggregate bodies move towards one place, even though in moments of time perceptible only by thought they do not move towards one place but are constantly jostling one against another, until the continuity of their movement comes under the ken of sensation. For the addition of opinion with regard to the unseen, that the moments perceptible only by thought will also contain continuity of motion, is not true in such cases; for we must remember that it is what we observe with the senses or grasp with the mind by an apprehension that is true. Nor must it either be supposed that in moments perceptible only by thought the moving body too passes to the several places to which its component atoms move (for this too is unthinkable, and in that case, when it arrives all together in a sensible period of time from any point that may be in the infinite void, it would not be taking its departure from the place from which we apprehend its motion); for the motion of the whole body will be the outward expression of its internal collisions, even though up to the limits of perception we suppose the speed of its motion not to be retarded by collision. It is of advantage to grasp this first principle as well.

Next, referring always to the sensations and the feelings

(for in this way you will obtain the most trustworthy ground of belief), you must consider that the soul is a body of fine particles distributed throughout the whole structure, and most resembling wind with a certain admixture of heat, and in some respects like to one of these and in some to the other. There is also the part which is many degrees more advanced even than these in fineness of composition, and for this reason is more capable of feeling in harmony with the rest of the structure as well. Now all this is made manifest by the activities of the soul and the feelings and the readiness of its movements and its processes of thought and by what we lose at the moment of death. Further, you must grasp that the soul possesses the chief cause of sensation: yet it could not have acquired sensation, unless it were in some way enclosed by the rest of the structure. And this in its turn having afforded the soul this cause of sensation acquires itself too a share in this contingent capacity from the soul. Yet it does not acquire all the capacities which the soul possesses: and therefore when the soul is released from the body, the body no longer has sensation. For it never possessed this power in itself, but used to afford opportunity for it to another existence, brought into being at the same time with itself: and this existence, owing to the power now consummated within itself as a result of motion, used spontaneously to produce for itself the capacity of sensation and then to communicate it to the body as well, in virtue of its contact and correspondence of movement, as I have already said. Therefore, so long as the soul remains in the body, even though some other part of the body be lost, it will never lose sensation; nay more, whatever portions of the soul may perish too, when that which enclosed it is removed either in whole or in part, if the soul continues to exist at all, it will retain sensation. On the other hand the rest of the structure, though it continues to exist either as a whole or in part, does not retain sensation, if it has once lost that sum of atoms, however small it be, which together goes to produce the nature of the soul. Moreover, if the whole structure is dissolved, the soul is dispersed and no longer has the same powers nor performs its movements, so that it does not possess sensation either. For it is impossible to imagine it with sensation, if it is not in this organism and cannot effect these movements, when what encloses and surrounds it is no longer the same as the surroundings in which it now exists and performs these movements. Furthermore, we must clearly comprehend as well, that the incorporeal in the general acceptation of the term is applied to that which could be thought of as such as an independent existence. Now it is impossible to conceive the incorporeal as a separate existence, except the void: and the void can neither act nor be acted upon, but only provides opportunity of motion through itself to bodies. So that those who say that the soul is incorporeal are talking idly. For it would not be able to act or be acted on in any respect, if it were of this nature. But as it is, both these occurrences are clearly distinguished in respect of the soul. Now if one refers all these reasonings about the soul to standards of feeling and sensation and remembers what was said at the outset, he will see that they are sufficiently embraced in these general formulae to enable him to work out with certainty on this basis the details of the system as well.

Moreover, as regards shape and colour and size and weight and all other things that are predicated of body, as though they were concomitant properties either of all things or of things visible or recognizable through the sensation of these qualities, we must not suppose that they are either independent existences (for it is impossible to imagine that), nor that they absolutely do not exist, nor that they are some other kind of incorporeal existence accompanying body, nor that they are material parts of body: rather we should suppose that the whole body in its totality owes its own permanent existence to all these, yet not in the sense that it is composed of properties brought together to form it (as when, for instance, a larger structure is put together out of the parts which compose it, whether the first units of size or other parts smaller than itself, whatever it is), but only, as I say, that it owes its own permanent existence to all of them. All these properties have their own peculiar means of being perceived and distinguished, provided always that the aggregate body goes along with them and is never wrested from them, but in virtue of its comprehension as an aggregate of qualities acquires the predicate of body.

Furthermore, there often happen to bodies and yet do not permanently accompany them (accidents, of which we must suppose neither that they do not exist at all nor that they have the nature of a whole body), nor that they can be classed among unseen things nor as incorporeal. So that when according to the most general usage we employ this name, we make it clear that accidents have neither the nature of the whole, which we comprehend in its aggregate and call body, nor that of the qualities which permanently accompany it, without which a given body cannot be conceived. But as the result of certain acts of apprehension, provided the aggregate body goes along with them, they might each be given this name, but only on occasions when each one of them is seen to occur, since accidents are not permanent accompaniments. And we must not banish this clear vision from the realm of existence, because it does not possess the nature of the whole to which it is joined nor that of the permanent accompaniments, nor must we suppose that such contingencies exist independently (for this is inconceivable both with regard to them and to the permanent properties), but, just as it appears in sensation, we must think of them all as accidnets occurring to bodies, and that not as permanent accompaniments, or again as having in themselves a place in the ranks of material existence; rather they are seen to be just what our actual sensation shows their proper character to be.

Moreover, you must firmly grasp this point as well; we must not look for time, as we do for all other things which we look for in an object, by referring them to the general conceptions which we perceive in our own minds, but we must take the direct intuition, in accordance with which we speak of 'a long time' or 'a short time', and examine it, applying our intuition to time as we do to other things. Neither must we search for expressions as likely to be better, but employ just those which are in common use about it. Nor again must we predicate of time anything else as having the same essential nature as this special perception, as some people do, but we must turn our thoughts particularly to that only with which we associate this peculiar perception and by which we measure it. For indeed this requires no demonstration, but only reflection, to show that it is with days and nights and their divisions that we associate it, and likewise also with internal feelings or absence of feeling, and with movements and states of rest; in connexion with these last again we think of this very perception as a peculiar kind of accident, and in virtue of this we call it time.

And in addition to what we have already said we must believe that worlds, and indeed every limited compound body which continuously exhibits a similar appearance to the things we see, were created from the infinite, and that all such things, greater and less alike, were separated off from individual agglomerations of matter; and that all are again dissolved, some more quickly, some more slowly, some suffering from one set of causes, others from another. And further we must believe that these worlds were neither (created) all of necessity with one configuration (nor yet with every kind of shape. Furthermore, we must believe that in all worlds there are living creatures and plants and other things we see in this world;_ for indeed no one could prove that in a world of one kind there might or might not have been included the kinds of seeds from which living things and plants and all the rest of the things we see are composed, and that in a world of another kind they could not have been.

*　　*　　*　　*　　*

Furthermore, the motions of the heavenly bodies and their turnings and eclipses and risings and settings, and kindred phenomena to these, must not be thought to be due to any being who controls and ordains or has ordained them and at the same time enjoys perfect bliss together with immortality (for trouble and care and anger and kindness are not consistent with a life of blessedness, but these things come to pass where there is weakness and fear and dependence on neighbours). Nor again must we believe that they, which are but fire agglomerated in a mass, possess blessedness, and voluntarily take upon themselves these movements. But we must preserve their full majestic significance in all expressions which we apply to such conceptions, in order that there may not arise out of them opinions contrary to this notion of majesty. Otherwise this very contradiction will cause the greatest disturbance in men's souls. Therefore we must believe that it is due to the original inclusion of matter in such agglomerations during the birth-process of the world that this law of regular succession is also brought about.

Furthermore, we must believe that to discover accurately the cause of the most essential facts is the function of the science of nature, and that blessedness for us in the knowledge of celestial phenomena lies in this and in the understanding of the nature of the existences seen in these celestial phenomena, and of all else that is akin to the exact knowledge requisite for our happiness: in knowing too that what occurs in several ways or is capable of being otherwise has no place here, but that nothing which suggests doubt or alarm can be included at all in that which is naturally immortal and blessed. Now this we can ascertain by our mind is absolutely the case. But what falls within the investigation of risings and settings and turnings and eclipses, and all that is akin to this, is no longer of any value for the happiness which knowledge brings, but persons who have perceived all this, but yet do not know what are the natures of these things and what are the essential causes, are still in fear, just as if they did not know these things at all: indeed, their fear may be even greater, since the wonder which arises out of the observation of these things cannot discover any solution or realize the regulation of the essentials. And for this very reason, even if we discover several causes for turnings and settings and risings and eclipses and the like, as has been the case already in our investigation of detail, we must not suppose that our inquiry into these things has not reached sufficient accuracy to contribute to our peace of mind and happiness. So we must carefully consider in how many ways a similar phenomenon is produced on earth, when we reason about the causes of celestial phenomena and all that is imperceptible to the senses; and we must despise those persons who do not recognize either what exists or comes into being in one way only, or that which may occur in several ways in the case of things which can only be seen by us from a distance, and further are not aware under what conditions it is impossible to have peace of mind. If, therefore, we think that a phenomenon probably occurs in some such particular way, and that in circumstances under which it is equally possible for us to be at peace, when we realize that it may occur in several ways, we shall be just as little disturbed as if we know that it occurs in some such particular way.

And besides all these matters in general we must grasp this point, that the principal disturbance in the minds of men arises because they think that these celestial bodies are blessed and immortal, and yet have wills and actions and motives inconsistent with these attributes; and because they are always expecting or imagining some everlasting misery, such as is depicted in legends, or even fear the loss of feeling in death as though it would concern them themselves; and, again, because they are brought to this pass not by reasoned opinion, but rather by some irrational presentiment, and therefore, as they do not know the limits of pain, they suffer a disturbance equally great or even more extensive than if they had reached this belief by opinion. But peace of mind is being delivered from all this, and having a constant memory of the general and most essential principles.

Wherefore we must pay attention to internal feelings and to external sensations in general and in particular, according as the subject is general or particular, and to every immediate intuition in accordance with each of the standards of judgement. For if we pay attention to these, we shall rightly trace the causes whence arose our mental disturbance and fear, and, by learning the true causes of celestial phenomena and all other occurrences that come to pass from time to time, we shall free ourselves from all which produces the utmost fear in other men.

C. The Apogee of Greek Science

Greek philosophy was always closely related to Greek science. In some cases, the science remained within the bounds of philosophy, as was the case in the astronomy of Plato and Aristotle. In other cases, philosophy seemed of lesser importance to the questions at hand, and science developed without its aid or hindrance. Hippocratic medicine and Hellenistic mathematical physics are but two instances of science developing with a diminishing reliance upon philosophy. The sections that follow illustrate the achievements of Greek science at its apogee.

1. Hippocratic medicine

1.a)

The greatest physician of antiquity was Hippocrates of Cos (460-375 B.C.). The school he founded produced some of the greatest medical treatises in the history of medicine. On Ancient Medicine* *is one such treatise in which the author (perhaps Hippocrates himself) comes to grips with the problem of the relation between philosophy and experience in the practice of medicine.*

Whoever having undertaken to speak or write on Medicine, have first laid down for themselves some hypothesis to their argument, such as hot, or cold, or moist, or dry, or whatever else they choose, (Thus reducing their subject within a narrow compass, and supposing only one or two original causes of diseases or of death among mankind,) are all clearly mistaken in much that they say; and this is the more reprehensible as relating to an art which all men avail themselves of on the most important occasions, and the good operators and practitioners, some bad and some far otherwise, which, if there had been no such thing as Medicine, and if nothing had been investigated or found out in it, would not have been the case, but all would have been equally unskilled and ignorant of it, and everything concerning the sick would have been directed by chance. But now it is not so; for, as in all the other arts, those who practise them differ much from one another in dexterity and knowledge, so is it in like manner with Medicine. Wherefore I have not thought that it stood in need of an empty hypothesis, like those subjects which are occult and dubious, in attempting to handle which it is necessary to use some hypothesis; as, for example, with regard to things above us and things below the earth; if any one should treat of these and undertake to declare how they are constituted, the reader or hearer could not find out, whether

---

* *The Genuine Works of Hippocrates*, translated from the Greek with a preliminary discourse and annotations by Francis Adams, Vol. I. (London: Printed for the Sydenham Society, 1849). Pp. 161-162; 169-172; 175-178.

what is delivered be true or false; for there is nothing which can be referred to in order to discover the truth.

But all these requisites belong of old to Medicine, and an origin and way have been found out, by which many and elegant discoveries have been made, during a length of time, and others will yet be found out, if a person possessed of the proper ability, and knowing those discoveries which have been made, should proceed from them to prosecute his investigations. But whoever, rejecting and despising all these, attempts to pursue another course and form of inquiry, and says he has discovered anything, is deceived himself and deceives others, for the thing is impossible. And for what reasons it is impossible, I will now endeavour to explain, by stating and showing what the art really is. From this it will be manifest that discoveries cannot possibly be made in any other way. And most especially, it appears to me, that whoever treats of this art should treat of things which are familiar to the common people. For of nothing else will such a one have to inquire or treat, but of the diseases under which the common people have laboured, which diseases and the causes of their origin and departure, their increase and decline, illiterate persons cannot easily find out themselves, but still it is easy for them to understand these things when discovered and expounded by others. For it is nothing more than that every one is put in mind of what had occurred to himself. But whoever does not reach the capacity of the illiterate vulgar, and fails to make them listen to him, misses his mark. Wherefore, then, there is no necessity for any hypothesis.

*   *   *   *   *

But I wish the discourse to revert to the new method of those who prosecute their inquiries in the Art by hypothesis. For if hot, or cold, or moist, or dry, be that which proves injurious to man, and if the person who would treat him properly just apply cold to the hot, hot to the cold, moist to the dry, and dry to the moist--let me be presented with a man, not indeed one of a strong constitution, but one of the weaker, and let him eat wheat, such as it is supplied from the thrashing-floor, raw and unprepared, with raw meat, and let him drink water. By using such a diet I know that he will suffer much and severely, for he will experience pains, his body will become weak, and his bowels deranged, and he will not subsist long. What remedy, then, is to be provided for one so situated? Hot? or cold? or moist? or dry? For it is clear that it must be one or other of these. For, according to this principle, if it is one of these which is injuring the patient, it is to be removed by its contrary. But the surest and most obvious remedy is to change the diet which the person used, and instead of wheat to give bread, and instead of raw flesh, boiled, and to drink wine in addition to these: for by making these changes it is impossible but that he must get better, unless completely disorganised by time and diet. What, then, shall we say? whether that, as he suffered from cold, these hot things being applied were of use to him, or the contrary? I should think this question must prove a puzzler to whomsoever it is put. For whether did he who prepared bread out of wheat remove the hot, the cold, the moist, or the dry principle in it?--for the bread is consigned both to fire and to water, and is wrought with many things, each of which has its peculiar property and nature, some of which it loses, and with others it is diluted and mixed.

And this I know, moreover, that to the human body it makes a great difference whether the bread be fine or coarse; of wheat with or without the hull, whether mixed with much or little water, strongly wrought or scarcely at all, baked or raw--and a multitude of similar differences; and so, in like manner, with the cake (maza); the powers of each, too, are great, and the one nowise like the other. Whoever pays no attention to these things, or, paying attention, does not comprehend them, how can he understand the diseases which befall a man? For, by every one of these things, a man is affected and changed this way or that, and the whole of his life is subjected to them, whether in health, convalescence, or disease. Nothing else, then, can be more important or more necessary to know than these things. So that the first inventors, pursuing their investigations properly, and by a suitable train of reasoning, according to the nature of man, made their discoveries, and thought the Art worthy of being ascribed to a god, as is the established belief. For they did not suppose that the dry or the moist, the hot or the cold, or any of these, are either injurious to man, or that man stands in need of them; but whatever in each was strong, and more than a match for a man's constitution, whatever he could not manage, that they held to be hurtful, and sought to remove. Now, of the sweet, the strongest is that which is intensely sweet; of the bitter, that which is intensely bitter; of the acid, that which is intensely acid; and of all things that which is extreme, for these things they saw both existing in man, and proving injurious to him. For there is in man the bitter and the salt, the sweet and the acid, the sour and the insipid, and a multitude of other things having all sorts of powers, both as regards quantity and strength. These, when all mixed and mingled up with one another, are not apparent, neither do they hurt a man; but when any of them is separate, and stands by itself, then it becomes perceptible, and hurts a man. And thus, of articles of food, those which are unsuitable and hurtful to man when administered, every one is either bitter, or intensely so, or saltish or acid, or something else intense and strong, and therefore we are disordered by them in like manner as we are by the secretions in the body. But all those things of which a man eats and drinks are devoid of any such intense and well-marked quality, such as bread, cake, and many other things of a similar nature which man is accustomed to use for food, with the exception of condiments and confectionaries, which are made to gratify the palate and for luxury. And from those things, when received into the body abundantly, there is no disorder nor dissolution of the powers belonging to the body; but strength, growth, and nourishment result from them, and this for no other reason than because they are well mixed, have nothing in them of an immoderate character, nor anything strong, but the whole forms one simple and not strong substance.

I cannot think in what manner they who advance this doctrine, and transfer the Art from the cause I have described to hypothesis, will cure men according to the principle which they have laid down. For, as far as I know, neither the hot nor the cold, nor the dry, nor the moist, has ever been found unmixed with any other quality; but I suppose they use the same articles of meat and drink as all we other men do. But to this substance they give the attribute of being hot, to that cold, to that dry, and to that moist. Since it would be absurd to advise the patient to take something hot, for he would straightway ask what it is? so that he must either play the fool, or have recourse to some one of the well-known substances: and if this hot thing happen to be sour, and that hot thing insipid, and this hot thing has the power of raising a disturbance in the body (and there are many other kinds of heat, possessing many opposite powers), he will be obliged to administer some one of them, either the hot and the sour, or the hot and the insipid, or that which, at the same time, is cold and sour (for there is such a substance), or the cold and the insipid. For, as I think, the very opposite effects will result from either of these, not only in man, but also in a bladder, a vessel of wood, and in many other things possessed of far less sensibility than man; for it is not the heat which is possessed of great efficacy, but the sour and the insipid, and other qualities as described by me, both in man and out of man, and that whether eaten or drunk, rubbed in externally, and otherwise applied.

But I think that of all the qualities heat and cold exercise the least operation in the body, for these reasons: as long time as hot and cold are mixed up with one another they do not give trouble, for the cold is attempered and rendered more moderate by the hot, and the hot by the cold; but when the one is wholly separate from the other, then it gives pain; and at that season when cold is applied it creates some pain to a man, but quickly, for that very reason, heat spontaneously arises in him without requiring any aid or preparation. And these things operate thus both upon men in health and in disease. For example, if a person in health wishes to cool his body during winter, and bathes either in cold water or in any other way, the more he does this, unless his body be fairly congealed, when he resumes his clothes and comes into a place of shelter, his body becomes more heated than before. And thus, too, if a person wish to be warmer thoroughly either by means of a hot bath or strong fire, and straightway having the same clothing on, takes up his abode again in the place he was in when he became congealed, he will appear much colder, and more disposed to chills than before. And if a person fan himself on account of a suffocating heat, and having procured refrigeration for himself in this manner, cease doing so, the heat and suffocation will be ten times greater in his case than in that of a person who does nothing of the kind. And, to give a more striking example, persons travelling in the snow, or otherwise in rigorous weather, and contracting great cold in their feet, their hands, or their head, what do they not suffer from inflammation and tingling when they put on warm clothing and get into a hot place? In some instances, blisters arise as if from burning with fire, and they do not suffer from any of those unpleasant symptoms until they become heated. So readily does either of these pass into the other; and I could mention many other examples. And with regard to the sick, is it not in those who experience a rigor that the most acute fever is apt to break out? And yet not so strongly neither, but that it ceases in a short time, and, for the most part, without having occasioned much mischief; and while it remains, it is hot, and passing over the whole body, ends for the most part in the feet, where the chills and cold were most intense and lasted longest; and, when sweat supervenes, and the fever passes off, the patient is much colder than if he had not taken the fever at all. Why then should that which so quickly passes into the opposite extreme, and loses its own powers spontaneously, be reckoned a mighty and serious affair? And what necessity is there for any great remedy for it?

* * * * *

Certain sophists and physicians say that it is not possible for any one to know medicine who does not know what man is [and how he was made and how constructed], and that whoever would cure men properly, must learn this in the first place. But this saying rather appertains to philosophy, as Empedocles and certain others have described what man in his origin is, and how he first was made and constructed. But I think whatever such has been said or written by sophist or physician concerning nature has less connexion with the art of medicine than with the art of painting. And I think that one cannot know anything certain respecting nature from any other quarter than from medicine; and that this knowledge is to be attained when one comprehends the whole subject of medicine properly, but not until then; and I say that this history shows what man is, by what causes he was made, and other things accurately. Wherefore it appears to me necessary to every physician to be skilled in nature, and strive to know, if he would wish to perform his duties, what man is in relation to the articles of food and drink, and to his other occupations, and what are the effects of each of them to every one. And it is not enough to know simply that cheese is a bad article of food, as disagreeing with whoever eats of it to satiety, but what sort of disturbance it creates, and wherefore, and with what principle in man it disagrees; for there are many other articles of food and drink naturally bad which affect man in a different manner. Thus, to illustrate my meaning by an example, undiluted wine drunk in large quantity renders a man feeble; and everybody seeing this knows that such is the power of wine, and the cause thereof; and we know, moreover, on what parts of a man's body it principally exerts its action; and I wish the same certainty to appear in other cases. For cheese (since we used it as an example) does not prove equally injurious to all men, for there are some who can take it to satiety without being hurt by it in the least, but, on the contrary, it is wonderful what strength it imparts to those it agrees with; but there are some who do not bear it well, their constitutions are different, and they differ in this respect, that what in their body is incompatible with cheese, is roused and put in commotion by such a thing; and those in whose bodies such a humour happens to prevail in greater quantity and intensity, are likely to suffer the more from it. But if the thing had been pernicious to the whole nature of man, it would have hurt all. Whoever knows these things will not suffer from it.

* * * * *

And it appears to me that one ought also to know what diseases arise in man from the powers, and what from the structures. What do I mean by this? By powers, I mean intense and strong juices; and by structures, whatever conformations there are in man. For some are hollow, and from broad contracted into narrow; some expanded, some hard and round, some broad and suspended, some stretched, some long, some dense, some rare and succulent, some spongy and of loose texture. Now, then, which of these figures is the best calculated to suck to itself and attract humidity from another body? Whether what is hollow and expanded, or what is solid and round, or what is hollow, and from broad, gradually turning narrow? I think such as from hollow and broad are contracted into narrow: this may be ascertained otherwise from obvious facts: thus, if you gape wide with the mouth you cannot draw in any liquid; but by protruding, contracting, and compressing the lips, and still more by using a tube, you can readily draw in whatever you wish. And thus, too, the instruments which are used for cupping are broad below and gradually become narrow, and are so constructed in order to suck and draw in from the fleshy parts. The nature and construction of the parts within a man are of a like nature; the bladder, the head, the uterus in women; these parts clearly attract, and are always filled with a juice which is foreign to them. Those parts which are hollow and expanded are most likely to receive any humidity flowing into them, but cannot attract it in like manner. Those parts which are solid and round could not attract a humidity, nor receive it when it flows to them, for it would glide past, and find no place of rest on them. But spongy and rare parts, such as the spleen, the lungs, and the breasts, drink up especially the juices around them, and become hardened and enlarged by the accession of juices. Such things happen to these organs especially. For it is not with the spleen as with the stomach, in which there is a liquid, which it contains and evacuates every day; but when it (the spleen) drinks up and receives a fluid into itself, the hollow and lax parts of it are filled, even the small interstices; and, instead of being rare and soft, it becomes hard and dense, and it can neither digest nor discharge its contents: these things it suffers, owing to the nature of its structure. Those things which engender flatulence or tormina in the body, naturally do so in the hollow and broad parts of the body, such as the stomach and chest, where they produce rumbling noises; for when they do not fill the parts so as to be stationary, but have changes of place and movements, there must necessarily be noise and apparent movements from them.

But such parts as are fleshy and soft, in these there occur torpor and obstructions, such as happen in apoplexy. But when it (the flatus?) encounters a broad and resisting structure, and rushes against such a part, and this happens when it is by nature not strong so as to be able to withstand it without suffering injury; nor soft and rare, so as to receive or yield to it, but tender, juicy, full of blood, and dense, like the liver, owing to its density and broadness, it resists and does not yield. But flatus, when it obtains admission, increases and becomes stronger, and rushes towards any resisting object; but owing to its tenderness, and the quantity of blood which it (the liver) contains, it cannot be without uneasiness; and for these reasons the most acute and frequent pains occur in the region of it, along with suppurations and chronic tumours (phymata). These symptoms also occur in the site of the diaphragm, but much less frequently; for the diaphragm is a broad, expanded, and resisting substance, of a nervous (tendinous?) and strong nature, and therefore less susceptible of pain; and yet pains and chronic abscesses do occur about it.

There are both within and without the body many other kinds of structure, which differ much from one another as to sufferings both in health and disease; such as whether the head be small or large; the neck slender or thick, long or short; the belly long or round; the chest and ribs broad or narrow; and many others besides, all which you ought to be acquainted with, and their differences; so that knowing the causes of each, you may make the more accurate observations.

1.b) Hippocratic Medicine, From *Epidemics**

After theories of disease had been examined and criticized, there always remained the patient suffering from some malady. In most cases, neither diet nor a consideration of the humors permitted the physician to do much. The best he could expect was to predict the outcome of the disease. Prediction, or prognosis, was the result of experience of a large number of cases. The case history became a standard part of the physician's practice.

Case IV

Philistes in Thasos had for a long time pain in the head, and at last fell into a state of stupor and took to his bed. Heavy drinking having caused continuous fevers the pain grew worse. At night he grew hot at the first.

First day. Vomited bilious matters, scanty, at first yellow, afterwards increasing and of the colour of verdigris; solid motions from the bowels; an uncomfortable night.

Second day. Deafness; acute fever; tension of the right hypochondrium, which fell inwards. Urine thin, transparent, with a small quantity of substance, like semen, floating in it. About mid-day became raving.

Third day. Uncomfortable.

Fourth day. Convulsions; exacerbation.

Fifth day. Died early in the morning.

Case V

Chaerion, who lay sick in the house of Demaenetus, was seized with fever after drinking. At once there was painful heaviness of the head; no sleep; bowels disturbed with thin, rather bilious stools.

Third day. Acute fever, trembling of the head, particularly of the lower lip; after a while rigor, convulsions, complete delirium; an uncomfortable night.

Fourth day. Quiet; snatches of sleep; wandering.

Fifth day. Pain; general exacerbation; irrational talk; uncomfortable night; no sleep.

Sixth day. The same symptoms.

Seventh day. Rigor; acute fever; sweating all over; crisis.

This patient's stools were throughout bilious, scanty and uncompounded. Urine thin, not of a good colour, with a cloudy substance floating in it. About the eighth day the urine had a better colour, with a slight, white sediment; quite rational and no fever; an intermission.

Ninth day. Relapse.

About the fourteenth day acute fever.

Sixteenth day. Vomited bilious, yellow matters rather

---

* *Hippocrates*, with an English translation by W. H. S. Jones (London: William Heinemann, 1923; New York, G. P. Putnam's Sons, 1923). Pp. 227, 229, 231, 233, 275, 277.

frequently.

Seventeenth day. Rigor; acute fever; sweating; crisis ended the fever.

Urine after relapse and crisis of a good colour, with a sediment; no delirium during the relapse.

Eighteenth day. Slight heat; rather thirsty; urine thin, with cloudy substance floating in it; slight delirium.

Nineteenth day. No fever; pain in the neck; sediment in urine.

Twentieth day. Complete crisis.

Case VI

The maiden daughter of Euryanax was seized with fever. Throughout the illness she suffered no thirst and had no inclination for food. Slight alvine discharges; urine thin, scanty, and not of a good colour. At the beginning of the fever suffered pain in the seat. On the sixth day did not sweat, being without fever; a crisis. The sore near the seat suppurated slightly, and burst at the crisis. After the crisis, on the seventh day, she had a rigor; grew slightly hot; sweated. Afterwards the extremities always cold. About the tenth day, after the sweating that occurred, she grew delirious, but was soon rational again. They said that the trouble was due to eating grapes. After an intermission, on the twelfth day she again wandered a great deal; the bowels were disturbed, with bilious, uncompounded, scanty, thin, irritating stools, which frequently made her get up. She died the seventh day from the second attack of delirium. This patient at the beginning of the illness had pain in the throat, which was red throughout. The uvula was drawn back. Many fluxes, scanty and acrid. She had a cough with signs of coction, but brought up nothing. No appetite for any food the whole time, nor did she desire anything. No thirst, and she drank nothing worth mentioning. She was silent, and did not converse at all. Depression, the patient despairing of herself. There was also some inherited tendency to consumption.

Case VII

The woman suffering from angina who lay sick in the house of Aristion began her complaint with indistinctness of speech. Tongue red, and grew parched.

First day. Shivered, and grew hot.

Third day. Rigor; acute fever; a reddish, hard swelling in the neck, extending to the breast on either side; extremities cold and livid, breathing elevated; drink returned through the nostrils--she could not swallow--stools and urine ceased.

Fourth day. General exacerbation.

Fifth day. Death.

Case VIII

The youth who lay sick by the Liars' Market was seized with fever after unaccustomed fatigue, toil and running.

First day. Bowels disturbed with bilious, thin, copious stools; urine thin and blackish; no sleep; thirst.

Second day. General exacerbation; stools more copious and more unfavourable. No sleep; mind disordered; slight sweating.

Third day. Uncomfortable; thirst; nausea; much tossing; distress; delirium; extremities livid and cold; tension, soft underneath, of the hypochondrium on both sides.

Fourth day. No sleep; grew worse.

Seventh day. Died, being about twenty years old.

Case IX

The woman who lodged with Tisamenus was in bed with a troublesome attack of inflammation of the upper bowel. Copious vomits; could not retain her drink. Pains in the region of the hypochondria. The pains were also lower, in the region of the bowels. Constant tormina. No thirst. She grew hot, though the extremities were cold all the time.

Case X

In Abdera Nicodemus after venery and drunkenness was seized with fever. At the beginning he had nausea and cardialgia; thirst; tongue parched; urine thin and black.

Second day. The fever increased; shivering; nausea; no sleep; bilious, yellow vomits; urine the same; a quiet night; sleep.

Third day. All symptoms less severe; relief. But about sunset he was again somewhat uncomfortable; painful night.

Fourth day. Rigor; much fever; pains everywhere; urine thin, with floating substance in it; the night, on the other hand, was quiet.

Fifth day. All symptoms present, but relieved.

Sixth day. Same pains everywhere; substance floating in urine; much delirium.

Seventh day. Relief.

Eighth day. All the other symptoms less severe.

Tenth day and following days. The pains were present, but all less severe. The exacerbations and the pains in the case of this patient tended throughout to occur on the even days.

Twentieth day. Urine white, having consistency; no sediment on standing. Copious sweating; seemed to lose his fever, but towards evening grew hot again, with pains in the same parts; shivering; thirst; slight delirium.

Twenty-fourth day. Much white urine, with much sediment. Hot sweating all over; the fever passed away in a crisis.

Case XI

In Thasos a woman of gloomy temperament, after a grief with a reason for it, without taking to bed lost sleep and appetite, and suffered thirst and nausea. She lived near the place of Pylades on the plain.

First day. As night began there were fears, much rambling, depression and slight feverishness. Early in the morning frequent convulsions; whenever these frequent convulsions intermitted, she wandered and uttered obscenities; many pains, severe and continuous.

Second day. Same symptoms; no sleep; fever more acute.

Third day. The convulsions ceased, but were succeeded by coma and oppression, followed in turn by wakefulness. She would jump up; could not restrain herself; wandered a great deal; fever acute; on this night a copious, hot sweating all over; no fever; slept, was perfectly rational, and had a crisis. About the third day urine black and thin, with particles mostly round floating in it, which did not settle. Near the crisis copious menstruation.

2. Astronomy and Cosmogony

2.a) From Plato's *Timaeus**

The two giants of Greek philosophy, Plato and Aristotle, did not confine their attention to the purely philosophical aspects of science. They also attempted to describe and explain the natural world. Plato's dialogue, the Timaeus, *was an attempt at cosmogony. The dialogue form is not the best suited for such a subject, the language is metaphorical and often obscure, yet the dialogue was one which was of considerable influence in antiquity and was known to the Middle Ages.*

Crit. Let me proceed to explain to you, Socrates, the order in which we have arranged our entertainment. Our intention is, that Timaeus, who is the most of an astronomer amongst us, and has made the nature of the universe his special study, should speak first, beginning with the generation of the world and going down to the creation of man; next, I am to receive the men whom he has created of whom some will have profited by the excellent education which you have given them; and then, in accordance with the tale which you have given them; and then, in accordance with the tale of Solon, and equally with his law, we will bring them into court and make them citizens, as if they were those very Athenians whom the sacred Egyptian record has recovered from oblivion, and thenceforward we will speak of them as Athenians and fellow-citizens.

Soc. I see that I shall receive in my turn a perfect and splendid feast of reason. And now, Timaeus, you, I suppose, should speak next, after duly calling upon the Gods.

Tim. All men, Socrates, who have any degree of right feeling, at the beginning of every enterprise, whether small or great, always call upon God. And we, too, who are going to discourse of the nature of the universe, how created or how existing without creation, if we be not altogether out of our wits, must invoke the aid of Gods and Goddesses and pray that our words may be acceptable to them and consistent with themselves. Let this, then, be our invocation of the Gods, to which I add an exhortation of myself to speak in such manner as will be most intelligible to you, and will most accord with my own intent.

First then, in my judgment, we must make a distinction and ask, What is that which always is and has no becoming; and what is that which is always becoming and never is? That which is apprehended by intelligence and reason is always in the same state; but that which is conceived by opinion with the help of sensation and without reason, is always in a process of becoming and perishing and never really is. Now everything that becomes of is created must of necessity be created by some cause, for without a cause nothing can be created. The work of the creator,

---

* *The Dialogues of Plato*, translated into English by Benjamin Jowett, 4th edition, 1953, Vol. II, pp. 12-25; 28-37. Reprinted by permission of the Clarendon Press, Oxford.

whenever he looks to the unchangeable and fashions the form and nature of his work after an unchangeable pattern, must necessarily be made fair and perfect; but when he looks to the created only, and uses a created pattern, it is not fair or perfect. Was the heaven then or the world, whether called by this or by any other more appropriate name--assuming the name, I am asking a question which has to be asked at the beginning of an enquiry about anything--was the world, I say, always in existence and without beginning? or created, and had it a beginning? Created, I reply, being visible and tangible and having a body, and therefore sensible; and all sensible things are apprehended by opinion and sense and are in a process of creation and created. Now that which is created must, as we affirm, of necessity be created by a cause. But the father and maker of all this universe is past finding out; and even if we found him, to tell of him to all men would be impossible. And there is still a question to be asked about him: Which of the patterns had the artificer in view when he made the world,--the pattern of the unchangeable, or of that which is created? If the world be indeed fair and the artificer good, it is manifest that he must have looked to that which is eternal; but if what cannot be said without blasphemy is true, then to the created pattern. Every one will see that he must have looked to the eternal; for the world is the fairest of creations and he is the best of causes. And having been created in this way, the world has been framed in the likeness of that which is apprehended by reason and mind and is unchangeable, and must therefore of necessity, if this is admitted, be a copy of something. Now it is all-important that the beginning of everything should be according to nature. And in speaking of the copy and the original we may assume that words are akin to the matter which they describe; when they relate to the lasting and permanent and intelligible, they ought to be lasting and unalterable, and, as far as their nature allows, irrefutable and immovable--nothing less. But when they express only the copy or likeness and not the eternal things themselves, they need only be likely and analogous to the real words. As being is to becoming, so is truth to belief. If then, Socrates, amid the many opinions about the gods and the generation of the universe, we are not able to give notions which are altogether and in every respect exact and consistent with one another, do not be surprised. Enough, if we adduce probabilities as likely as any others; for we must remember that I who am the speaker, and you who are the judges, are only mortal men, and we ought to accept the tale which is probable and enquire no further.

Soc. Excellent, Timaeus; and we will do precisely as you bid us. The prelude is charming, and is already accepted by us--may we beg of you to proceed to the strain?

Tim. Let me tell you then why the creator made this world of generation. He was good, and the good can never have any jealousy of anything. And being free from jealousy, he desired that all things should be as like himself as they could be. This is in the truest sense the origin of creation and of the world, as we shall do well in believing on the testimony of wise men: God desired that all things should be good and nothing bad, so far as this was attainable. Wherefore also finding the whole visible sphere not at rest, but moving in an irregular and disorderly fashion, out of disorder he brought order, considering that this was in every way better than the other. Now the deeds of the best could never be or have been other than the fairest; and the creator, reflecting on the things which are by nature visible, found that no unintelligent creature taken as a whole was fairer than the intelligent taken as a whole; and that intelligence could not be present in anything which was devoid of soul. For which reason, when he was framing the universe, he put intelligence in soul, and soul in body, that he might be the creator of a work which was by nature fairest and best. Wherefore, using the language of probability, we may say that the world became a living creature truly endowed with soul and intelligence by the providence of God.

This being supposed, let us proceed to the next stage: In the likeness of what animal did the Creator make the world? It would be an unworthy thing to liken it to any nature which exists as a part only; for nothing can be beautiful which is like any imperfect thing; but let us suppose the world to be the very image of that whole of which all other animals both individually and in their tribes are portions. For the original of the universe contains in itself all intelligible beings, just as this world comprehends us and all other visible creatures. For the Deity, intending to make this world like the fairest and most perfect of intelligible beings, framed one visible animal comprehending within itself all other animals of a kindred nature. Are we right in saying that there is one world, or that they are many and infinite? There must be one only, if the created copy is to accord with the original. For that which includes all other intelligible creatures cannot have a second or companion; in that case there would be need of another living being which would include both, and of which they would be parts, and the likeness would be more truly said to resemble not them, but that other which included them. In order then that the world might be solitary, like the perfect animal, the creator made not two worlds or an infinite number of them; but there is and ever will be one only-begotten and created heaven.

Now that which is created is of necessity corporeal, and also visible and tangible. And nothing is visible where there is no fire, or tangible which has no solidity, and nothing is solid without earth. Wherefore also God in the beginning of creation made the body of the universe to consist of fire and earth. But two things cannot be rightly put together without a third; there must be some bond of union between them. And the fairest bond is that which makes the most complete fusion of itself and the things which it combines; and proportion is best adapted to effect such a union. For whenever in any three numbers, whether cube or square, there is a mean, which is to the last term what the first term is to it; and again, when the mean is to the first term as the last term is to the mean,--then the mean becoming first and last, and the first and last both becoming means, they will all of them of necessity come to be the same, and having become the same with one another will be all one. If the universal frame had been created a surface only and having no depth, a single mean would have sufficed to bind together itself and the terms; but now, as the world must be solid, and solid bodies are always compacted not by one mean but by two, God placed water and air in the mean between fire and earth, and made them to have the same proportion so far as was possible (as fire is to air so is air to water, and as air is to water so is water to earth); and thus he bound and put together a visible and tangible heaven. And for these reasons, and out of such elements which are in number four, the body of the world was created, and it was harmonized by proportion, and therefore has the spirit of friendship; and having been reconciled to itself, it was indissoluble by the hand of any other than the framer.

* * * * *

. . . And he gave to the world the figure which was suitable and also natural. Now to the animal which was to comprehend all animals, that figure was suitable which comprehends within itself all other figures. Wherefore he made the world in the form of a globe, round as from a lathe, having its extremes in every direction equidistant from the centre, the most perfect and the most like itself of all figures; for he considered that the like is infinitely fairer than the unlike. This he finished off, making the surface smooth all around for many reasons; in the first place, because the living being had no need of eyes when there was nothing remaining outside him to be seen; nor of ears when there was nothing to be heard; and there was no surrounding atmosphere to be breathed; nor would there have been any use of organs by the help of which he might receive his food or get rid of what he had already digested, since there was nothing which went from him or came into him: for there was nothing beside him. Of design he was created thus, his own waste providing his own food, and all that he did or suffered taking place in and by himself. For the Creator conceived that a being which was self-sufficient would be far more excellent than one which lacked anything; and, as he had no need to take anything or defend himself against any one, the Creator did not think it necessary to bestow upon him hands: nor had he any need of feet, nor of the whole apparatus of walking; but the movement suited to his spherical form was assigned to him, being of all the seven that which is most appropriate to mind and intelligence; and he was made to move in the same manner and on the same spot, within his own limits revolving in a circle. All the other six motions were taken away from him, and he was made not to partake of their deviations. And as this circular movement required no feet, the universe was created without legs and without feet.

Such was the whole plan of the eternal God about the god that was to be, to whom for this reason he gave a body, smooth and even, having a surface in every direction equidistant from the centre, a body entire and perfect, and formed out of perfect bodies. And in the centre he put the soul, which he diffused throughout the body, making it also to be the exterior environment of it; and he made the universe a circle moving in a circle, one and solitary, yet by reason of its excellence able to converse with itself, and needing no other friendship or acquaintance. Having these purposes in view he created the world a blessed god.

Now God did not make the soul after the body, although we are speaking of them in this order; for having brought them together he would never have allowed that the elder should be ruled by the younger; but this is a random manner of speaking which we have, because somehow we ourselves too are very much under the domination of chance. Whereas he made the soul in origin and excellence prior to and older than the body, to be the ruler and mistress, of whom the body was to be the subject. And he made her out of the following elements and on this wise: Out of the indivisible and unchangeable, and also out of that which is divisible and has to do with material bodies, he compounded a third and intermediate kind of essence, partaking of the nature of the same and of the other, and this compound he placed accordingly in a mean between the indivisible, and the divisible and material. He took the three elements of the same, the other, and the essence, and mingled them into one form, compressing by force the reluctant and unsociable nature of the other into the same. When he had mingled them with the essence and out of three made one, he again divided this whole into as many portions as was fitting, each portion being a compound of the same, the other, and the essence. And he proceeded to divide after this manner:--First of all, he took away one part of the whole [1], and then he separated a second part which was double the first [2], and then he took away a third part which was half as much again as the second and three times as much as the first [3], and then he took a fourth part which was twice as much as the second [4], and a fifth part which was three times the third [9], and a sixth part which was eight times the first [8], and a seventh part which was twenty-seven times the first [27]. After this he filled up the double intervals [i.e. between 1, 2, 4, 8] and the triple [i.e. between 1, 3, 9, 27], cutting off yet other portions from the mixture and placing them in the intervals, so that in each interval there were two kinds of means, the one exceeding and exceeded by equal parts of its extremes [as for example 1, $\frac{4}{3}$, 2, in which the mean $\frac{4}{3}$ is one-third of 2 less than 2], the other being that kind of mean which exceeds and is exceeded by an equal number.* Where there were intervals of $\frac{3}{2}$ and of $\frac{4}{3}$ and of $\frac{9}{8}$, made by the connecting terms in the former intervals, he filled up all the intervals of $\frac{4}{3}$ with the interval of $\frac{9}{8}$, leaving a fraction over; and the interval which this fraction expressed was in the ratio of 256 to

---

* E.g. $\overline{1}, \frac{4}{3}, \frac{3}{2}, \overline{2}, \frac{8}{3}, 3, \overline{4}\ \frac{16}{3}, 6, \overline{8}$; and

$\overline{1}, \frac{3}{2}, 2, \overline{3}, \frac{9}{2}, 6, \overline{9}, \frac{27}{2}, 18, \overline{27}$.

243.* And thus the whole mixture out of which he cut these portions was all exhausted by him. This entire compound he divided lengthways into two parts, which he joined to one another at the centre like the letter X, and bent them into a circular form, connecting them with themselves and each other at the point opposite to their original meeting-point; and, comprehending them in a uniform revolution upon the same axis, he made the one the outer circle he called the motion of the same, and the motion of the inner circle the motion of the other or diverse. The motion of the same he carried round by the side to the right, and the motion of the diverse diagonally to the left. And he gave dominion to the motion of the same and like, for that he left single and undivided; but the inner motion he divided in six places and made seven unequal circles having their intervals in ratios of two and three, three of each, and bade the orbits proceed in a direction opposite to one another; and three [Sun, Mercury, Venus] he made to move with equal swiftness, and the remaining four [Moon, Saturn, Mars, Jupiter] to move with unequal swiftness to the three and to one another, but in due proportion.

* * * * *

When the father and creator saw the creature which he had made moving and living, the created image of the eternal gods, he rejoiced, and in his joy determined to make the copy still more like the original; and as this was eternal, he sought to make the universe eternal, so far as might be. Now the nature of the ideal being was everlasting, but to bestow this attribute in its fulness upon a creature was impossible. Wherefore he resolved to have a moving image of eternity, and when he set in order the heaven, he made this image eternal but moving according to number, while eternity itself rests in unity; and this image we call time. For there were no days and nights and months and years before the heaven was created, but when he constructed the heaven he created them also. They are all parts of time, and the past and future are created species of time, which we unconsciously but wrongly transfer to the eternal essence; for we say that he 'was,' he 'is,' he 'will be,' but the truth is that 'is' alone is properly attributed to him, and that 'was' and 'will be' are only to be spoken of becoming in time, for they are motions, but that which is immovably the same cannot become older or younger by time, nor ever did or has become, or hereafter will be, older or younger, nor is subject at all to any of those states which affect moving and sensible things and of which generation is the cause. These are the forms of time, which imitates eternity and revolves according to a law of number. Moreover, when we say that what has become *is* become and what becomes *is* becoming, and that what will become *is* about to become and that the non-existent *is* non-existent,--all these are inaccurate modes of expression. But perhaps this whole subject will be more suitably discussed on

---

* E.g. $243:256::\frac{81}{64}:\frac{4}{3}::\frac{243}{128}:2::\frac{81}{32}:\frac{8}{3}::\frac{243}{64}:4::\frac{81}{16}:\frac{16}{3}::\frac{242}{32}:8.$

some other occasion.

Time, then, and the heaven came into being at the same instant in order that, having been created together, if ever there was to be a dissolution of them, they might be dissolved together. It was framed after the pattern of the eternal nature, that it might resemble this as far as was possible; for the pattern exists from eternity, and the created heaven has been, and is, and will be, in all time. Such was the mind and thought of God in the creation of time. The sun and moon and five other stars, which are called the planets, were created by him in order to distinguish and preserve the numbers of time; and when he had made their several bodies, he placed them in the orbits in which the circle of the other was revolving,--in seven orbits seven stars. First, there was the moon in the orbit nearest the earth, and next the sun, in the second orbit above the earth; then came the morning star and the star sacred to Hermes, moving in orbits which have an equal swiftness with the sun, but in an opposite direction; and this is the reason why the sun and Hermes and Lucifer overtake and are overtaken by each other. To enumerate the places which he assigned to the other stars, and to give all the reasons why he assigned them, although a secondary matter, would give more trouble than the primary. These things at some future time, when we are at leisure, may have the consideration which they deserve, but not at present.

Now, when all the stars which were necessary to the creation of time had attained a motion suitable to them, and had become living creatures having bodies fastened by vital chains, and learnt their appointed task, moving in the motion of the diverse, which is diagonal, and passes through and is governed by the motion of the same, they revolved, some in a larger and some in a lesser orbit,--those which had the lesser orbit revolving faster, and those which had the larger more slowly. Now by reason of the motion of the same, those which revolved fastest appeared to be overtaken by those which moved slower although they really overtook them; for the motion of the same made them all turn in a spiral, and, because some went one way and some another, that which receded most slowly from the sphere of the same, which was the swiftest, appeared to follow it most nearly. That there might be some visible measure of their relative swiftness and slowness as they proceeded in their eight courses, God lighted a fire, which we now call the sun, in the second from the earth of these orbits, that it might give light to the whole of heaven, and that the animals, as many as nature intended, might participate in number, learning arithmetic from the revolution of the same and the like. Thus, then, and for this reason the night and the day were created, being the period of the one most intelligent revolution. And the month is accomplished when the moon has completed her orbit and overtaken the sun, and the year when the sun has completed his own orbit. Mankind, with hardly an exception, have not remarked the periods of the other stars, and they have no name for them, and do not measure them against one another by the help of number, and hence they can scarcely be said to know that their wanderings, being infinite in number and admirable for their variety, make up time.

And yet there is no difficulty in seeing that the perfect number of time fulfils the perfect year when all the eight revolutions, having their relative degrees of swiftness, are accomplished together and attain their completion at the same time, measured by the rotation of the same and equally moving. After this manner, and for these reasons, came into being such of the stars as in their heavenly progress received reversals of motion, to the end that the created heaven might imitate the eternal nature, and be as like as possible to the perfect and intelligible animal.

Thus far and until the birth of time the created universe was made in the likeness of the original, but inasmuch as all animals were not yet comprehended therein, it was still unlike. What remained, the creator then proceeded to fashion after the nature of the pattern. Now as in the ideal animal the mind perceives ideas or species of a certain nature and number, he thought that this created animal ought to have species of a like nature and number. There are four such; one of them is the heavenly race of the gods; another, the race of birds whose way is in the air; the third, the watery species; and the fourth, the pedestrian and land creatures. Of the heavenly and divine, he created the greater part out of fire, that they might be the brightest of all things and fairest to behold, and he fashioned them after the likeness of the universe in the figure of a circle, and made them follow the intelligent motion of the supreme, distributing them over the whole circumference of heaven, which was to be a true cosmos or glorious world spangled with them all over. And he gave to each of them two movements: the first, a movement on the same spot after the same manner, whereby they ever continue to think consistently the same thoughts about the same things; the second, a forward movement, in which they are controlled by the revolution of the same and the like; but by the other five motions they were unaffected, in order that each of them might attain the highest perfection. And for this reason the fixed stars were created, to be divine and eternal animals, ever-abiding and revolving after the same manner and on the same spot; and the other stars which reverse their motion and are subject to deviations of this kind, were created in the manner already described. The earth, which is our nurse, clinging around the pole which is extended through the universe, he framed to be the guardian and artificer of night and day, first and eldest of gods that are in the interior of heaven. Vain would be the attempt to tell all the figures of them circling as in dance, and their juxtapositions, and the return of them in their revolutions upon themselves, and their approximations, and to say which of these deities in their conjunctions meet, and which of them are in opposition, and in what order they get behind and before one another, and when they are severally eclipsed to our sight and again reappear, sending terrors and intimations of the future to those who cannot calculate their movements--to attempt to tell of all this without a visible representation of the heavenly system would be labour in vain. Enough on this head; and now let what we have said about the nature of the created and visible gods have an end.

To know or tell the origin of the other divinities is beyond us, and we must accept the traditions of the men of old time who affirm themselves to be the offspring of the gods--that is what they say--and they must surely have known their own ancestors. How can we doubt the word of the children of the gods? Although they give no probably or certain proofs, still, as they declare that they are speaking of what took place in their own family, we must conform to custom and believe them. In this manner, then, according to them, the genealogy of these gods is to be received and set forth.

Oceanus and Tethys were the children of Earth and Heaven, and from these sprang Phorcys and Cronos and Rhea, and all that generation; and from Cronos and Rhea sprang Zeus and Here, and all those who are said to be their brethren, and others who were the children of these.

Now, when all of them, both those who visibly appear in their revolutions as well as those other gods who are of a more retiring nature, had come into being, the creator of the universe addressed them in these words: 'Gods, children of gods, who are my works, and of whom I am the artificer and father, my creations are indissoluble, if so I will. All that is bound may be undone, but only an evil being would wish to undo that which is harmonious and happy. Wherefore, since ye are but creatures, ye are not altogether immortal and indissoluble, but ye shall certainly not be dissolved, nor be liable to the fate of death, having in my will a greater and mightier bond than those with which ye were bound at the time of your birth. And now listen to my instructions:--Three tribes of mortal beings remain to be created--without them the universe will be incomplete, for it will not contain every kind of animal which it ought to contain, if it is to be perfect. On the other hand, if they were created by me and received life at my hands, they would be on an equality with the gods. In order then that they may be mortal, and that this universe may be truly universal, do ye, according to your natures, betake yourselves to the formation of animals, imitating the power which was shown by me in creating you. The part of them worthy of the name immortal, which is called divine and is the guiding principle of those who are willing to follow justice and you--of that divine part I will myself sow the seed, and having made a beginning, I will hand the work over to you. And do ye then interweave the mortal with the immortal, and make and beget living creatures, and give them food, and make them to grow, and receive them again in death.

Thus he spake, and once more into the cup in which he had previously mingled the soul of the universe he poured the remains of the elements, and mingled them in much the same manner; they were not, however, pure as before, but diluted to the second and third degree. And having made it he divided the whole mixture into souls equal in number to the stars, and assigned each soul to a star; and having there placed them as in a chariot, he showed them the nature of the universe, and declared to them the laws of destiny, according to which their first birth would be one and the same for all,--no one should suffer a disadvantage at his hands; they were to be sown in the instruments of time severally adapted to them, and to come forth the most religious of animals;

and as human nature was of two kinds, the superior race would hereafter be called man. Now, when they should be implanted in bodies by necessity, and be always gaining or losing some part of their bodily substance, then in the first place it would be necessary that they should all have in them one and the same faculty of sensation, arising out of irresistible impressions; in the second place, they must have love, in which pleasure and pain mingle; also fear and anger, and the feelings which are akin or opposite to them; if they conquered these they would live righteously, and if they were conquered by them, unrighteously. He who lived well during his appointed time was to return and dwell in his native star, and there he would have a blessed and congenial existence. But if he failed in attaining this, at the second birth he would pass into a woman, and if, when in that state of being, he did not desist from evil, he would continually be changed into some brute who resembled him in the evil nature which he had acquired, and would not cease from his toils and transformations until he followed the revolution of the same and the like within him, and overcame by the help of reason the turbulent and irrational mob of later accretions, made up of fire and air and water and earth, and returned to the form of his first and better state. Having given all these laws to his creatures, that he might be guiltless of future evil in any of them, the creator sowed some of them in the earth, and some in the moon, and some in the other instruments of time; and when he had sown them he committed to the younger gods the fashioning of their mortal bodies, and desired them to furnish what was still lacking to the human soul, and having made all the suitable additions, to rule over them, and to pilot the mortal animal in the best and wisest manner which they could, and avert from him all but self-inflicted evils.

When the creator had made all these ordinances he remained in his own accustomed nature, and his children heard and were obedient to their father's word, and receiving from him the immortal principle of a mortal creature, in imitation of their own creator they borrowed portions of fire, and earth, and water, and air from the world, which were hereafter to be restored--these they took and welded them together, not with the indissoluble chains by which they were themselves bound, but with little pegs too small to be visible, making up out of all the four elements each separate body, and fastening the courses of the immortal soul in a body which was in a state of perpetual influx and efflux. Now these courses, detained as in a vast river, neither overcame nor were overcome; but were hurrying and hurried to and fro, so that the whole animal was moved and progressed, irregularly however and irrationally and anyhow, in all the six directions of motion, wandering backwards and forwards, and right and left, and up and down, and in all the six directions. For great as was the advancing and retiring flood which provided nourishment, the affections produced by external contact caused still greater tumult--when the body of any one met and came into collision with some external fire, or with the solid earth or the gliding waters, or was caught in the tempest borne on the air, and the motions produced by any of these impulses were carried through the body to the soul. All such motions have consequently received the general name of 'sensations,' which they still retain. And they did in fact at that time create a very great and mighty movement; uniting with the everflowing stream in stirring up and violently shaking the courses of the soul, they completely stopped the revolution of the same by their opposing current, and hindered it from predominating and advancing; and they so disturbed the nature of the other or diverse, that the three double intervals [i.e. between 1, 2, 4, 8], and the three triple intervals [i.e. between 1, 3, 9, 27], together with the mean terms and connecting links which are expressed by the ratios of 3 : 2, and 4 : 3, and of 9 : 8,--these, although they cannot be wholly undone except by him who united them, were twisted by them in all sorts of ways, and the circles were broken and disordered in every possible manner, so that when they moved they were tumbling to pieces, and moved irrationally, at one time in a reverse direction, and then again obliquely, and then upside down, as you might imagine a person who is upside down and has his head leaning upon the ground and his feet up against something in the air; and when he is in such a position, both he and the spectator fancy that the right of either is his left, and left right. If, when powerfully experiencing these and similar effects, the revolutions of the soul come in contact with some external thing, either of the class of the same or of the other, they speak of the same or of the other in a manner the very opposite of the truth; and they become false and foolish, and there is no course or revolution in them which has a guiding or directing power; and if again any sensations enter in violently from without and drag after them the whole vessel of the soul, then the courses of the soul, though they seem to conquer, are really conquered.

And by reason of all these affections, the soul, when encased in a mortal body, now, as in the beginning, is at first without intelligence; but when the flood of growth and nutriment abates, and the courses of the soul, calming down, go their own way and become steadier as time goes on, then the several circles return to their natural form, and their revolutions are corrected, and they call the same and the other by their right names, and make the possessor of them to become a rational being. And if these combine in him with any true nurture or education, he attains the fulness and health of the perfect man, and escapes the worst disease of all; but if he neglects education he walks lame to the end of his life, and returns imperfect and good for nothing to the world below.

* * * * *

Thus far in what we have been saying, with small exception, the works of intelligence have been set forth; and now we must place by the side of them in our discourse the things which come into being through necessity--for the creation is mixed, being made up of necessity and mind.

* * * * *

This new beginning of our discussion of the universe requires a fuller division than the former; for then we made two classes, now a third must be revealed. The two sufficed for the former discussion: one, which we assumed, was a pattern intelligible and always the same; and the second was only the imitation of the pattern, generated and visible. There is also a third kind which we did not distinguish at the time, conceiving that the two would be enough. But now the argument seems to require that we should set forth in words another kind, which is difficult of explanation and dimly seen. What nature are we to attribute to this new kind of being? We reply, that it is the receptacle, and in a manner the nurse, of all generation. I have spoken the truth; but I must express myself in clearer language, and this will be an arduous task for many reasons, and in particular because I must first raise questions concerning fire and the other elements, and determine what each of them is; for to say, with any probability or certitude, which of them should be called water rather than fire, and which should be called any of them rather than all or some one of them, is a difficult matter. How, then, shall we settle this point, and what questions about the elements may be fairly raised?

In the first place, we see that what we just now called water, by condensation, I suppose, becomes stone and earth; and this same element, when melted and dispersed, passes into vapour and air. Air, again, when inflamed, becomes fire; and again fire, when condensed and extinguished, passes once more into the form of air; and once more, air, when collected and condensed, produces cloud and mist; and from these, when still more compressed, comes flowing water, and from water comes earth and stones once more; and thus generation appears to be transmitted from one to the other in a circle. Thus, then, as the several elements never present themselves in the same form, how can any one have the assurance to assert positively that any of them, whatever it may be, is one thing rather than another? No one can.

* * * * *

Let us consider this question more precisely. Is there any self-existent fire? and do all those things which we call self-existent exist? or are only those things which we see, or in some way perceive through the bodily organs, truly existent, and nothing whatever besides them? And is all that which we call an intelligible essence nothing at all, and only a name? Here is a question which we must not leave unexamined or undetermined, nor must we affirm too confidently that there can be no decision; neither must we interpolate in our present long discourse a digression equally long, but if it is possible to set forth a great principle in a few words, that is just what we want.

Thus I state my view:--If mind and true opinion are two distinct classes, then I say that there certainly are these self-existent ideas unperceived by sense, and apprehended only by the mind; if however, as some say, true opinion differs in no respect from mind, then everything that we perceive through the body is to be regarded as most real and certain. But we must affirm them to be distinct, for they have a distinct origin and are of a different nature; the one is implanted in us by instruction, the other by persuasion; the one is always accompanied by true reason, the other is without reason; the one cannot be overcome by persuasion, but the other can: and lastly, every man may be said to share in true opinion, but mind is the attribute of the gods and of very few men. Wherefore also we must acknowledge that there is one kind of being which is always the same, uncreated and indestructible, never receiving anything into itself from without, nor itself going out to any other, but invisible and imperceptible by any sense, and of which the contemplation is granted to intelligence only. And there is another nature of the same name with it, and like to it, perceived by sense, created, always in motion, becoming in place and again vanishing out of place, which is apprehended by opinion and sense. And there is a third nature, which is space, and is eternal, and admits not of destruction and provides a home for all created things, and is apprehended without the help of sense, by a kind of spurious reason, and is hardly real; which we beholding as in a dream, say of all existence that it must of necessity be in some place and occupy a space, but that what is neither in heaven nor in earth has no existence. . . .

* * * * *

Thus have I concisely given the result of my thoughts; and my verdict is that being and space and generation, these three, existed in their three ways before the heaven; and that the nurse of generation, moistened by water and inflamed by fire, and receiving the forms of earth and air, and experiencing all the affections which accompany these, presented a strange variety of appearances; and being full of powers which were neither similar nor equally balanced, was never in any part in a state of equipoise, but swaying unevenly hither and thither, was shaken by them, and by its motion again shook them; and the elements when moved were separated and carried continually, some one way, some another; as, when grain is shaken and winnowed by fans and other instruments used in the threshing of corn, the close and heavy particles are borne away and settle in one direction, and the loose and light particles in another. In this manner, the four kinds or elements were then shaken by the receiving vessel, which, moving like a winnowing machine, scattered far away from one another the elements most unlike, and forced the most similar elements into close contact. Wherefore also the various elements had different places before they were arranged so as to form the universe. At first, they were all without reason and measure. But when the world began to get into order, fire and water and earth and air had only certain faint traces of themselves, and were altogether such as everything might be expected to be in the absence of God; this, I say, was their nature at that time, and God fashioned them by form and number. Let it be consistently maintained by us in all that we say that God made them as far as possible the fairest and best, out of things which were not fair and good. And now I will endeavour to show you the disposition and generation of them by an unaccustomed argument, which I am compelled to use; but I believe that you will be able to follow me, for your education has made you familiar with the methods of science.

In the first place, then, as is evident to all, fire and earth and water and air are bodies. And every sort of body possesses solidity, and every solid must necessarily be contained in planes; and every plane rectilinear figure is composed of triangles; and all triangles are originally of two kinds, both of which are made up of one right and two acute angles; one of them has at either end of the base the half of a divided right angle, having equal sides, while in the other the right angle is divided into unequal parts, having unequal sides. These, then, proceeding by a combination of probability with demonstration, we assume to be the original elements of fire and the other bodies; but the principles which are prior to these God only knows, and he of men who is the friend of God. And next we have to determine what are the four most beautiful bodies which are unlike one another, and of which some are capable of resolution into one another; for having discovered thus much, we shall know the true origin of earth and fire and of the proportionate and intermediate elements. And then we shall not be willing to allow that there are any distinct kinds of visible bodies fairer than these. Wherefore we must endeavour to construct the four forms of bodies which excel in beauty, and then we shall be able to say that we have sufficiently apprehended their nature. Now of the two triangles, the isosceles has one form only; the scalene or unequal-sided has an infinite number. Of the infinite forms we must select the most beautiful, if we are to proceed in due order, and any one who can point out a more beautiful form than ours for the construction of these bodies, shall carry off the palm, not as an enemy, but as a friend. Now, the one which we maintain to be the most beautiful of all the many triangles (and we need not speak of the others) is that of which the double forms a third triangle which is equilateral; the reason of this would be long to tell; he who disproves what we are saying, and shows that we are mistaken, may claim a friendly victory. Then let us choose two triangles, out of which fire and the other elements have been constructed, one isosceles, the other having the square of the longer side equal to three times the square of the lesser side.

Now is the time to explain what was before obscurely said: there was an error in imagining that all the four elements might be generated by and into one another; this, I say, was an erroneous supposition, for there are generated from the triangles which we have selected four kinds--three from the one which has the sides unequal; the fourth alone is framed out of the isosceles triangle. Hence they cannot all be resolved into one another, a great number of small bodies being combined into a few large ones, or the converse. But three of them can be thus resolved and compounded, for they all spring from one, and when the greater bodies are broken up, many small bodies will spring up out of them and take their own proper figures; or, again, when many small bodies are dissolved into their triangles, if they become one, they will form one large mass of another kind. So much for their passage into one another. I have now to speak of their several kinds, and show out of what combinations of numbers each of them was formed. The first will be the simplest and smallest construction, and its element is that triangle which has its hypotenuse twice the lesser side. When two such triangles are joined at the diagonal, and this is repeated three times, and the triangles rest their diagonals and shorter sides on the same point as a centre, a single equilateral triangle is formed out of six triangles; and four equilateral triangles, if put together, make out of every three plane angles one solid angle, being that which is nearest to the most obtuse of plane angles; and out of the combination of these four angles arises the first solid form which distributes into equal and similar parts the whole circle in which it is inscribed. The second species of solid is formed out of the same triangles, which unite as eight equilateral triangles and form one solid angle out of four plane angles, and out of six such angles the second body is completed. And the third body is made up of 120 triangular elements, forming twelve solid angles, each of them included in five plane equilateral triangles, having altogether twenty bases, each of which is an equilateral triangle. The one element [that is, the triangle which has its hypotenuse twice the lesser side] having generated these figures, generated no more; but the isosceles triangle produced the fourth elementary figures, which is compounded of four such triangles, joining their right angles in a centre, and forming one equilateral quadrangle. Six of these united form eight solid angles, each of which is made by the combination of three plane right angles; the figure of the body thus composed is a cube, having six plane quadrangular equilateral bases. There was yet a fifth combination which God used in the delineation of the universe.

* * * * *

To earth, then, let us assign the cubical form; for earth is the most immoveable of the four and the most plastic of all bodies, and that which has the most stable bases must of necessity be of such a nature. Now, of the triangles which we assumed at first, that which has two equal sides is by nature more firmly based than that which has unequal sides; and of the compound figures which are formed out of either, the plane equilateral quadrangle has necessarily a more stable basis than the equilateral triangle, both in the whole and in the parts. Wherefore, in assigning this figure to earth, we adhere to probability; and to water we assign that one of the remaining forms which is the least moveable; and the most moveable of them to fire; and to air that which is intermediate. Also we assign the smallest body to fire, and the greatest to water, and the intermediate in size to air, and the third to water. Of all these elements, that which has the fewest bases must necessarily be the most moveable, for it must be the acutest and most penetrating in every way, and also the lightest as being composed of the smallest number of similar particles: and the second body has similar properties in a second degree, and the third body in the third degree. Let it be agreed, then, both according to strict reason and according to probability, that the pyramid is the solid which is the original element and seed of fire; and let us assign the element which was next in the order of generation to air, and the third to water. We must imagine all these to be so small that no single particle of any of the four kinds is seen by us on account of their smallnexx: but when many of them are collected together their aggregates are seen. And the ratios of their numbers, motions, and other properties, everywhere God, as far as necessity allowed or gave consent, has exactly perfected, and harmonized in due proportion.

From all that we have just been saying about the elements or kinds, the most probable conclusion is as follows:--earth, when meeting with fire and dissolved by its sharpness, whether the dissolution take place in the fire itself or perhaps in some mass of air or water, is borne hither and thither, until its parts, meeting together and mutually harmonizing, again become earth; for they can never take any other form. But water, when divided by fire or by air, on re-forming, may become one part fire and two parts air; and a single volume of air divided becomes two of fire. Again, when a small body of fire is contained in a larger body of air or water or earth, and both are moving, and the fire struggling is overcome and broken up, then two volumes of fire form one volume of air; and when air is overcome and cut up into small pieces, two and a half parts of air are condensed into one part of water. Let us consider the matter in another way. When one of the other elements is fastened upon by fire, and is cut by the sharpness of its angles and sides, it coalesces with the fire, and is cut by the sharpness of its angles and sides, it coalesces with the fire, and then ceases to be cut by them any longer. For no element which is one and the same with itself can be changed by or change another of the same kind and in the same state. But so long as in the process of transition the weaker is fighting against the stronger, the dissolution continues. Again, when a few small particles, enclosed in many larger ones, are in process of decomposition and extinction, they only cease from their tendency to extinction when they consent to pass into the conquering nature, and fire becomes air and air water. But if bodies of another kind go and attack them [i.e. the small particles], the latter continue to be dissolved until, being completely forced back and dispersed, they make their escape to their own kindred, or else, being overcome and assimilated to the conquering power, they remain where they are and dwell with their victors, and from being many become one. And owing to these affections, all things are changing their place, for by the motion of the receiving vessel the bulk of each class is distributed into its proper place; but those things which become unlike themselves and like other things, are hurried by the shaking into the place of the things to which they grow like.

Now all unmixed and primary bodies are produced by such causes as these. As to the subordinate species which are included in the greater kinds, they are to be attributed to the varieties in the structure of the two original triangles. For either structure did not originally produce the triangle of one size only, but some larger and some smaller, and there are as many sizes as there are species of the four elements. Hence when they are mingled with themselves and with one another there is an endless variety of them, which those who would arrive at the probably truth of nature ought duly to consider.

2.b.) From Aristotle's *De Caelo* and *Metaphysica**

In the De Caelo *(On the Heavens) and the* Metaphysica *Aristotle tried to make sense out of the Platonic (and poetic) account of creation. In the* De Caelo *Aristotle came to grips with the physics of the problem, namely why things move as they do in the universe, with particular attention given to the cause of the motion of the heavenly spheres. This problem was to continue to be a crucial one in Astronomy until Isaac Newton dealt with it in the 17th century. It should be noted here that it was to be central to the acceptance of the Copernican theory. In the* Metaphysica, *Aristotle showed how his physics of celestial motion could be treated mathematically so as to give results which were in accordance with observations.*

We will now speak of those parts of the whole which are specifically distinct. Let us take this as our starting-point. All natural bodies and magnitudes we hold to be, as such, capable of locomotion; for nature, we say, is their principle of movement. But all movement that is in place, all locomotion, as we term it, is either straight or circular or a combination of these two, which are the only simple movements. And the reason of this is that these two, the straight and the circular line, are the only simple magnitudes. Now revolution about the centre is circular motion, while the upward and downward movements are in a straight line, 'upward' meaning motion away from the centre, and 'downward' motion towards it. All simple motion, then, must be motion either away from or towards or about the centre. This seems to be in exact accord with what we said above: as body found its completion in three dimensions, so its movement completes itself in three forms.

Bodies are either simple or compounded of such; and by simple bodies I mean those which possess a principle of movement in their own nature, such as fire and earth with their kinds, and whatever is akin to them. Necessarily, then, movements also will be either simple or in some sort compound--simple in the case of the simple bodies, compound in that of the composite--and in the latter case the motion will be that of the simple body which prevails in the composition. Supposing, then, that there is such a thing as simple movement, and that circular movement is an instance of it, and that both movement of a simple body is simple and simple movement is of a simple body (for if it is movement of a compound it will be in virtue of a prevailing simple element), then there must necessarily be some simple body which revolves naturally and in virute of its own nature with a circular movement. By constraint, of course, it may be brought

---

* *The Works of Aristotle*, translated into English under the editorship of W. D. Ross. Volume II, *De Caelo* (Oxford: Clarendon Press, 1930). Pp. 268b; 269a-270b; 283b-284a; 287b-290a; 291a. Reprinted by permission of the Clarendon Press, Oxford.

to move with the motion of something else different from itself, but it cannot so move naturally, since there is one sort of movement natural to each of the simple bodies. Again, if the unnatural movement is the contrary of the natural and a thing can have no more than one contrary, it will follow that circular movement, being a simple motion, must be unnatural, if it is not natural, to the body moved. If then (1) the body, whose movement is circular, is fire or some other element, its natural motion must be the contrary of the circular motion. But a single thing has a single contrary; and upward and downward motion are the contraries of one another. If, on the other hand, (2) the body moving with this circular motion which is unnautral to it is something different from the elements, there will be some other motion which is natural to it. But this cannot be. For if the natural motion is upward, it will be fire or air, and if downward, water or earth. Further, this circular motion is necessarily primary. For the perfect is naturally prior to the imperfect, and the circle is a perfect thing. This cannot be said of any straight line:--not of an infinite line; for, if it were perfect, it would have a limit and an end: nor of any finite line; for in every case there is something beyond it, since any finite line can be extended. And so, since the prior movement belongs to the body which is naturally prior, and circular movement is prior to straight, and movement in a straight line belongs to simple bodies--fire moving straight upward and earthy bodies straight downward towards the centre--since this is so, it follows that circular movement also must be the movement of some simple body. For the movement of composite bodies is, as we said, determined by that simple body which preponderates in the composition. These premises clearly give the conclusion that there is in nature some bodily substance other than the formations we know, prior to them all and more divine than they.

* * * * *

In consequence of what has been said, in part by way of assumption and in part by way of proof, it is clear that not every body either possesses lightness or heaviness. As a preliminary we must explain in what sense we are using the words 'heavy' and 'light', sufficiently, at least, for our present purpose: we can examine the terms more closely later, when we come to consider their essential nature. Let us then apply the term 'heavy' to that which naturally moves towards the centre, and 'light' to that which moves naturally away from the centre. The heaviest thing will be that which sinks to the bottom of all things that move downward, and the lightest that which rises to the surface of everything that moves upward. Now, necessarily, everything which moves either up or down possesses lightness or heaviness of both--but not both relatively to the same thing: for things are heavy and light relatively to one another; air, for instance, is light relatively to water, and water light relatively to earth. The body, then, which moves in a circle cannot possibly possess either heaviness or lightness. For neither naturally nor unnaturally can it move either towards or away from the centre. Movement in a straight line certainly does not belong to it *naturally*, since one sort of movement is, as we saw, appropriate to each simple body, and so we should be compelled to identify it with one of the bodies which move in this way. Suppose, then, that the movement is *unnatural*. In that case, if it is the downward movement which is unnatural, the upward movement will be natural; and if it is the upward which is unnatural, the downward will be natural. For we decided that of contrary movements, if the one is unnatural to anything, the other will be natural to it. But since the natural movement of the whole and of its part--of earth, for instance, as a whole and of a small clod--have one and the same direction, it results, in the first place, that this body can possess no lightness or heaviness at all (for that would mean that it could move by its own nature either from or towards the centre, which, as we know, is impossible); and, secondly, that it cannot possibly move in the way of locomotion by being forced violently aside in an upward or downward direction. For neither naturally nor unnaturally can it move with any other motion but its own, either itself or any part of it, since the reasoning which applies to the whole applies also to the part.

It is equally reasonable to assume that this body will be ungenerated and indestructible and exempt from increase and alteration, since everything that comes to be comes into being from its contrary and in some substrate, and passes away likewise in a substrate by the action of the contrary into the contrary, as we explained in our opening discussions. Now the motions of contraries are contrary. If then this body can have no contrary, because there can be no contrary motion to the circular, nature seems justly to have exempted from contraries the body which was to be ungenerated and indestructible. For it is in contraries that generation and decay subsist. Again, that which is subject to increase increases upon contact with a kindred body, which is resolved into its matter. But there is nothing out of which this body can have been generated. And if it is exempt from increase and diminution, the same reasoning leads us to suppose that it is also unalterable. For alteration is movement in respect of quality; and qualitative states and dispositions, such as health and disease, do not come into being without changes of properties. But all natural bodies which change their properties we see to be subject without exception to increase and diminution. This is the case, for instance, with the bodies of animals and their parts and with vegetable bodies, and similarly also with those of the elements. And so, if the body which moves with a circular motion cannot admit of increase or diminution, it is reasonable to suppose that it is also unalterable.

The reasons why the primary body is eternal and not subject to increase or diminution, but unaging and unalterable and unmodified, will be clear from what has been said to any one who believes in our assumptions. Our theory seems to confirm experience and to be confirmed by it. For all men have some conception of the nature of the gods, and all who believe in the existence of gods at all, whether barbarian or Greek, agree in allotting the highest place to the deity, surely because they suppose that immortal is linked with immortal and regard any other supposition as inconceivable. If then there is, as there certainly is, anything divine, what we have just said about the primary bodily substance was well said. The mere evidence of the senses is enough to convince us of this, at least with human certainty. For in the whole range of time past, so far as our inherited records reach, no change appears to have taken place either in the whole scheme of the outermost heaven or in any of its proper parts. The common name, too, which has been handed down from our distant ancestors even to our own day, seems to show that they conceived of it in the fashion which we have been expressing. The same ideas, one must believe, recur in men's minds not once or twice but again and again. And so, implying that the primary body is something else beyond earth, fire, air, and water, they gave the highest place a name of its own, *aither*, derived from the fact that it 'runs always' for an eternity of time. Anaxagoras, however, scandalously misuses this name, taking *aither* as equivalent to fire.

It is also clear from what has been said why the number of what we call simple bodies cannot be greater than it is. The motion of a simple body must itself be simple, and we assert that there are only these two simple motions, the circular and the straight, the latter being subdivided into motion away from and motion towards the centre.

* * * * *

That the heaven as a whole neither came into being nor admits of destruction, as some assert, but is one and eternal, with no end or beginning of its total duration, containing and embracing in itself the infinite of time, we may convince ourselves not only by the arguments already set forth but also by a consideration of the views of those who differ from us in providing for its generation. If our view is a possible one, and the manner of generation which they assert is impossible, this fact will have great weight in convincing us of the immortality and eternity of the world. Hence it is well to persuade oneself of the truth of the ancient and truly traditional theories, that there is some immortal and divine thing which possesses movement, but movement such as has no limit and is rather itself the limit of all other movement. A limit is a thing which contains; and this motion, being perfect, contains those imperfect motions which have a limit and a goal, having itself no beginning or end, but unceasing through the infinity of time, and of other movements, to some the cause of their beginning, to others offering the goal. The ancients gave to the Gods the heaven or upper place, as being alone immortal; and our present argument testifies that it is indestructible and ungenerated. Further, it is unaffected by any mortal discomfort, and, in addition, effortless; for it needs no constraining necessity to keep it to its path, and prevent it from moving with some other movement more natural to itself. Such a constrained movement would necessarily involve effort--the more so, the more eternal it were--and would be inconsistent with perfection. Hence we must not believe the old tale which says that the world needs some Atlas to keep it safe--a tale composed, it would seem, by men who, like later thinkers, conceived of all the upper bodies as earthy and endowed with weight, and therefore supported it in their fabulous way upon animate necessity. We must no more believe that than follow Empedocles when he says that the world, by being whirled round, received a movement quick enough to overpower its own downward tendency, and thus has been kept from destruction all this time. Nor, again, is it conceivable that it should persist eternally by the necessitation of a soul. For a soul could not live in such conditions painlessly or happily, since the movement involves constraint, being imposed on the first body, whose natural motion is different, and imposed continuously. It must therefore be uneasy and devoid of all rational satisfaction; for it could not even, like the soul of mortal animals, take recreation in the bodily relaxation of sleep. An Ixion's lot must needs possess it, without end or respite. If then, as we said, the view already stated of the first motion is a possible one, it is not only more appropriate so to conceive of its eternity, but also on this hypothesis alone are we able to advance a theory consistent with popular divinations of the divine nature. But of this enough for the present.

* * * * *

The shape of the heaven is of necessity spherical; for that is the shape most appropriate to its substance and also by nature primary. . . .

Corroborative evidence may be drawn from the bodies whose position is about the centre. If earth is enclosed by water, water by air, air by fire, and these similarly by the upper bodies--which while not continuous are yet contiguous with them--and if the surface of water is spherical, and that which is continuous with or embraces the spherical must itself be spherical, then on these grounds also it is clear that the heavens are spherical. But the surface of water is seen to be spherical if we take as our starting-point the fact that water naturally tends to collect in a hollow place--'hollow' meaning 'nearer the centre'. Draw from the centre the lines *AB*, *AC*, and let their extremities be joined by the straight line *BC*. The line *AD*, drawn to the base of the triangle, will be shorter than either of the radii. Therefore the place in which it terminates will be a hollow place. The water then will collect there until equality is established, that is until the line *AE* is equal to the two radii. Thus water forces its way to the ends of the radii, and there only will it rest: but the line which connects the extremities of the radii is circular: therefore the surface of the water *BEC* is spherical.

It is plain from the foregoing that the universe is spherical. It is plain, further, that it is turned (so to speak) with a finish which no manufactured thing nor anything else within the range of our observation can even approach. For the matter of which these are composed does not admit of anything like the same regularity and finish as the substance of the enveloping body; since with each step away from earth the matter manifestly becomes finer in the same proportion as water is finer than earth.

We have next to show that the movement of the heaven is regular and not irregular. This applies only to the first heaven and the first movement; for the lower spheres exhibit a composition of several movements into one. If the movement is uneven, clearly there will be acceleration, maximum speed, and retardation, since these appear in all irregular motions. The maximum may occur either at the starting-point or at the goal or between the two; and we expect natural motion to reach its maximum at the goal, unnatural motion at the starting-point, and missiles midway between the two. But circular movement, having no beginning or limit or middle in the direct sense of the words, has neither whence nor whither nor middle: for in time it is eternal, and in length it returns upon itself without a break. If then its movement has no maximum,it can have no irregularity, since irregularity is produced by retardation and acceleration. Further, since everything that is moved is moved by something, the cause of the irregularity of movement must lie either in the mover or in the moved or in both. For if the mover moved not always with the same force, or if the moved were altered and did not remain the same, or if both were to change, the result might well be an irregular movement in the moved. But none of these possibilities can be conceived as actual in the case of the heavens. As to that which is moved, we have shown that it is primary and simple and ungenerated and indestructible and generally unchanging; and the mover has an even better right to these attributes. It is the primary that moves the primary, the simple the simple, the indestructible and ungenerated that which is indestructible and ungenerated. Since then that which is moved, being a body, is nevertheless unchanging, how should the mover, which is incorporeal, be changed?

It follows, then, further, that the motion cannot be irregular. For if irregularity occurs, there must be change either in the movement as a whole, from fast to slow and slow to fast, or in its parts. That there is no irregularity in the parts is obvious, since, if there were, some divergence of the stars would have taken place before now in the infinity of time, as one moved slower and another faster: but no alteration of their intervals is ever observed. Nor again is a change in the movement as a whole admissible. Retardation is always due to incapacity, and incapacity is unnatural. The incapacities of animals, age, decay, and the like, are all unnatural, due, it seems, to the fact that the whole animal complex is made up of materials which differ in respect of their proper places, and no single part occupies its own place. If therefore that which is primary contains nothing unnatural, being simple and unmixed and in its proper place and having no contrary, then it has no place for incapacity, nor, consequently, for retardation or (since acceleration involves retardation) for acceleration. Again, it is inconceivable that the mover should first show incapacity for an infinite time, and capacity afterwards for another infinity.

For clearly nothing which, like incapacity, is unnatural ever continues for an infinity of time; nor does the unnatural endure as long as the natural, or any form of incapacity as long as the capacity. But if the movement is retarded it must necessarily be retarded for an infinite time. Equally impossible is perpetual acceleration or perpetual retardation. For such movement would be infinite and indefinite, but every movement, in our view, proceeds from one point to another and is definite in character. Again, suppose one assumes a minimum time in less than which the heaven could not complete its movement. For, as a given walk or a given exercise on the harp cannot take any and every time, but every performance has its definite minimum time which is unsurpassable, so, one might suppose, the movement of the heaven could not be completed in any and every time. But in that case perpetual acceleration is impossible (and, equally, perpetual retardation: for the argument holds of both and each), if we may take acceleration to proceed by identical or increasing additions of speed and for an infinite time. The remaining alternative of slower and faster: but this is a mere fiction and quite inconceivable. Further, irregularity of this kind would be particularly unlikely to pass unobserved, since contrast makes observation easy.

That there is one heaven, then, only, and that it is ungenerated and eternal, and further that its movement is regular, has now been sufficiently explained.

We have next to speak of the stars, as they are called, of their composition, shape, and movements. It would be most natural and consequent upon what has been said that each of the stars should be composed of that substance in which their path lies, since, as we said, there is an element whose natural movement is circular. In so saying we are only following the same line of thought as those who say that the stars are fiery because they believe the upper body to be fire, the presumption being that a thing is composed of the same stuff as that in which it is situated. The warmth and light which proceed from them are caused by the friction set up in the air by their motion. Movement tends to create fire in wood, stone, and iron; and with even more reason should it have that effect on air, a substance which is closer to fire than these. An example is that of missiles, which as they move are themselves fired so strongly that leaden balls are melted; and if they are fired the surrounding air must be similarly affected. Now while the missiles are heated by reason of their motion in air, which is turned into fire by the agitation produced by their movement, the upper bodies are carried on a moving sphere, so that, though they are not themselves fired, yet the air underneath the sphere of the revolving body is necessarily heated by its motion, and particularly in that part where the sun is attached to it. Hence warmth increases as the sun gets nearer or higher or overhead. Of the fact, then, that the stars are neither fiery nor move in fire, enough has been said.

Since changes evidently occur not only in the position of the stars but also in that of the whole heaven, there are three possibilities. Either (1) both are at rest, or (2) both are in motion, or (3) the one is at rest and the other in motion.

(1) That both should be at rest is impossible; for, if the earth is at rest, the hypothesis does not account for the observations; and we take it as granted that the earth is at rest. It remains either that both are moved, or that the one is moved and the other at rest.

(2) On the view, first, that both are in motion, we have the absurdity that the stars and the circles move with the same speed, i.e. that the pace of every star is that of the circle in which it moves. For star and circle are seen to come back to the same place at the same moment; from which it follows that the star has traversed the circle and the circle has completed its own movement, i.e. traversed its own circumference, at one and the same moment. But it is difficult to conceive that the pace of each star should be exactly proportioned to the size of its circle. That the pace of each circle should be proportionate to its size is not absurd but inevitable: but that the same should be true of the movement of the stars contained in the circles is quite incredible. For if, on the one hand, we suppose that the star which moves on the greater circle is necessarily swifter, clearly we also admit that if stars shifted their position so as to exchange circles, the slower would become swifter and the swifter slower. But this would show that their movement was not their own, but due to the circles. If, on the other hand, the arrangement was a chance combination, the coincidence in every case of a greater circle with a swifter movement of the star contained in it is too much to believe. In one or two cases it might not inconceivably fall out so, but to imagine it in every case alike is a mere fiction. Besides, chance has no place in that which is natural, and what happens everywhere and in every case is no matter of chance.

(3) The same absurdity is equally plain if it is supposed that the circles stand still and that it is the stars themselves which move. For it will follow that the outer stars are the swifter, and that the pace of the stars corresponds to the size of their circles.

Since, then, we cannot reasonably suppose either that both are in motion or that the star alone moves, the remaining alternative is that the circles should move, while the stars are at rest and move with the circles to which they are attached. Only on this supposition are we involved in no absurd consequence. For, in the first place, the quicker movement of the larger circle is natural when all the circles are attached to the same centre. Whenever bodies are moving with their proper motion, the larger moves quicker. It is the same here with the revolving bodies: for the arc intercepted by two radii will be larger in the larger circle, and hence it is not surprising that the revolution of the larger circle should take the same time as that of the smaller. And secondly, the fact that the heavens do not break in pieces follows not only from this but also from the proof already given of the continuity of the whole.

Again, since the stars are spherical, as our opponents assert and we may consistently admit, inasmuch as we construct them out of the spherical body, and since the spherical body has two movements proper to itself, namely rolling and spinning, it follows that if the stars have a movement of their own, it will be one of these. But neither is observed. (1) Suppose them to *spin*. They would then stay where they were, and not change their place, as, by observation and general consent, they do. Further, one would expect them all to exhibit the same movement: but the only star which appears to possess this movement is the sun, at sunrise or sunset, and this appearance is due not to the sun itself but to the distance from which we observe it. The visual ray being excessively prolonged becomes weak and wavering. The same reason probably accounts for the apparent twinkling of the fixed stars and the absence of twinkling in the planets. The planets are near, so that the visual ray reaches them in its full vigour, but when it comes to the fixed stars it is quivering because of the distance and its excessive extension; and its tremor produces an appearance of movement in the star: for it makes no difference whether movement is set up in the ray or in the object of vision.

(2) On the other hand, it is also clear that the stars do not *roll*. For rolling involves rotation: but the 'face', as it is called, of the moon is always seen. Therefore, since any movement of their own which the stars possessed would presumably be one proper to themselves, and no such movement is observed in them, clearly they have no movement of their own.

There is, further, the absurdity that nature has bestowed upon them no organ appropriate to such movement. For nature leaves nothing to chance, and would not, while caring for animals, overlook things so precious. Indeed, nature seems deliberately to have stripped them of everything which makes self-originated progression possible, and to have removed them as far as possible from things which have organs of movement. This is just why it seems proper that the whole heaven and every star should be spherical. For while of all shapes the sphere is the most convenient for movement in one place, making possible, as it does, the swiftest and most self-contained motion, for forward movement it is the most unsuitable, least of all resembling shapes which are self-moved, in that it has no dependent or projecting part, as a rectilinear figure has, and is in fact as far as possible removed in shape from ambulatory bodies. Since, therefore, the heavens have to move in one place, and the stars are not required to move themselves forward, it is natural that both should be spherical--a shape which best suits the movement of the one and the immobility of the other.

* * * * *

With their order--I mean the position of each, as involving the priority of some and the posteriority of others, and their respective distances from the extremity--with this astronomy may be left to deal, since the astronomical discussion is adequate. This discussion shows that the movements of the several stars depend, as regards the varieties of speed which they exhibit, on the distance of each from the extremity. It is established that the outermost revolution of the heavens is a simple movement and swiftest of all, and that the movement of all other bodies is composite and relatively slow, for the reason that each is moving on its own circle with the reverse motion to that of the heavens. This at once leads us to expect that the body which is nearest to that first simple revolution should take the longest time to complete its circle, and that which is farthest from it the shortest, the others taking a longer time the nearer they are and a shorter time the farther away they are. For it is the nearest body which is most strongly influenced, and the most remote, by reason of its distance, which is least affected, the influence on the intermediate bodies varying, as the mathematicians show, with their distance.

From Aristotle's *Metaphysica**

It is clear then from what has been said that there is a substance which is eternal and unmovable and separate from sensible things. It has been shown also that this substance cannot have any magnitude, but is without parts and indivisible (for it produces movement through infinite time, but nothing finite has infinite power; and, while every magnitude is either infinite or finite, it cannot, for the above reason, have finite magnitude, and it cannot have infinite magnitude because there is no infinite magnitude at all). But it has also been shown that it is impassive and unalterable; for all the other changes are posterior to change of place.

It is clear, then, why these things are as they are. But we must not ignore the question whether we have to suppose one such substance or more than one, and if the latter, how many; we must also mention, regarding the opinions expressed by others, that they have said nothing about the number of the substances that can even be clearly stated. For the theory of Ideas has no special discussion of the subject; for those who speak of Ideas say the Ideas are numbers, and they speak of numbers now as unlimited, now as limited by the number 10: but as for the reason why there should be just so many numbers, nothing is said with any demonstrative exactness. We however must discuss the subject, starting from the presuppositions and distinctions we have mentioned. The first principle or primary being is not movable either in itself or accidentally, but produces the primary eternal and single movement. But since that which is moved must be moved by something, and the first mover must be in itself unmovable, and eternal movement must be produced by something eternal and a single movement by a single thing, and since we see that besides the simple spatial movement of the universe, which we say the first and unmovable substance produces, there are other spatial movements--those of the planets--which are eternal (for a body which moves in a circle is eternal and unresting; we have proved these points in the physical treatises), each of *these* movements also must be caused by a substance both unmovable in itself and eternal. For the nature of the stars is eternal just because it is a certain kind of substance, and the mover is eternal and prior to the moved, and that which is prior to a substance must be a substance. Evidently, then, there must be substances which are of the same number as the movements of the stars, and in their nature eternal, and in themselves unmovable, and without magnitude, for the reason before mentioned.

That the movers are substances, then, and that one of these is first and another second according to the same order as the movements of the stars, is evident. But in the number of the movements we reach a problem which must be treated from the standpoint of that one of the mathematical sciences which is most

---

* *The Works of Aristotle*, translated into English under the editorship of W. D. Ross. Volume VIII, *Metaphysica* (Oxford: Clarendon Press, 1908). Pp. 1073a-1073b. Reprinted by permission of the Clarendon Press, Oxford.

akin to philosophy--viz. of astronomy; for this science speculates about substance which is perceptible but eternal, but the other mathematical sciences, i.e. arithmetic and geometry, treat of no substance. That the movements are more numerous than the bodies that are moved is evident to those who have given even moderate attention to the matter; for each of the planets has more than one movement. But as to the actual number of these movements, we now--to give some notion of the subject--quote what some of the mathematicians say, that our thought may have some definite number to grasp; but, for the rest, we must partly investigate for ourselves, partly learn from other investigators, and if those who study this subject form an opinion contrary to what we have now stated, we must esteem both parties indeed, but follow the more accurate.

Eudoxus supposed that the motion of the sun or of the moon involves, in either case, three spheres, of which the first is the sphere of the fixed stars, and the second moves in the circle which runs along the middle of the zodiac, and the third in the circle which is inclined across the breadth of the zodiac; but the circle in which the moon moves is inclined at a greater angle than that in which the sun moves. And the motion of the planets involves, in each case, four spheres, and of these also the first and second are the same as the first two mentioned above (for the sphere of the fixed stars is that which moves all the other spheres, and that which is placed beneath this and has its movement in the circle which bisects the zodiac is common to all), but the *poles* of the third sphere of each planet are in the circle which bisects the zodiac, and the motion of the fourth sphere is in the circle which is inclined at an angle to the equator of the third sphere; and the poles of the third sphere are different for each of the other planets, but those of Venus and Mercury are the same.

Callippus made the position of the spheres the same as Eudoxus did, but while he assigned the same number as Eudoxus did to Jupiter and to Saturn, he thought two more spheres should be added to the sun and two to the moon, if one is to explain the observed facts; and one more to each of the other planets.

But it is necessary, if all the spheres combined are to explain the observed facts, that for each of the planets there should be other spheres (one fewer than those hitherto assigned) which counteract those already mentioned and bring back to the same position the outermost sphere of the star which in each case is situated below the star in question; for only thus can all the forces at work produce the observed motion of the planets. Since, then, the spheres involved in the movement of the planets themselves are--eight for Saturn and Jupiter and twenty-five for the others, and of these only those involved in the movement of the lowest-situated planet need not be counteracted, the spheres which counteract those of the outermost two planets will be six in number, and the spheres which counteract those of the next four planets will be sixteen; therefore the number of all the spheres--both those which move the planets and those which counteract these--will be fifty-five. And if one were not to add to the moon and to the sun the movements we mentioned, the whole set of spheres will be forty-seven in number.

C. From Ptolemy's *Almagest**

The astronomical tradition of antiquity culminated in the work of Ptolemy of Alexandria (fl. A.D. 140). His Mathematikei syntaxis *was an eclectic summary of centuries of observational and mathematical astronomy and cosmogony. When it was discovered by Islam and translated into Arabic, it was given the name of "The Greatest" by prefixing the Arabic* al *to the Greek* megiste *to form the title which it has borne ever since, the* Almagest. *In the Almagest, Ptolemy confronted the separate demands of Greek philosophy, observational astronomy and Babylonian mathematics to produce a synthesis which was to influence the development of astronomy down to the time of Johann Kepler (1571-1630).*

1. Preface

Those who have been true philosophers, Syrus, seem to me to have very wisely separated the theoretical part of philosophy from the practical. For even if it happens the practical turns out to be theoretical prior to its being practical, nevertheless a great difference would be found in them; not only because some of the moral virtues can belong to the everyday ignorant man and it is impossible to come by the theory of whole sciences without learning, but also because in practical matters the greatest advantage is to be had from a continued and repeated operation upon the things themselves, while in theoretical knowledge it is to be had by a progress onward. We accordingly thought it up to us so to train our actions even in the application of the imagination as not to forget in whatever things we happen upon the consideration of their beautiful and well-ordered disposition, and to indulge in meditation mostly for the exposition of many beautiful theorems and especially of those specifically called mathematical.

For indeed Aristotle quite properly divides also the theoretical into three immediate genera: the physical, the mathematical, and the theological. For given that all beings have their existence from matter and form and motion, and that none of these can be seen, but only thought, in its subject separately from the others, if one should seek out in its simplicity the first cause of the first movement of the universe, he would find God invisible and unchanging. And the kind of science which seeks after Him is the theological; for such an act [ενεργεια] can only be thought as high above somewhere near the loftiest things of the universe and is absolutely apart from sensible things. But the kind of science which traces through the material and ever moving quality, and has to do with the white, the hot, the sweet, the soft, and such things, would be called physical; and such an

---

* Ptolemy, *The Almagest*, trans. by R. C. Taliaferro, in *Great Books of the Western World*, editor R. M. Hutchins (Chicago: Encyclopedia Britannica, Inc., 1939, 1952), Volume 16. Pp. 5-8; 12-14; 270-273; 291-296. Reprinted by permission of Encyclopedia Britannica, Inc.

essence [ουσια], since it is only generally what it is, is to be found in corruptible things and below the lunar sphere. And the kind of science which shows up quality with respect to forms and local motions, seeking figure, number, and magnitude, and also place, time, and similar things, would be defined as mathematical. For such an essence falls, as it were, between the other two, not only because it can be conceived both through the senses and without the senses, but also because it is an accident in absolutely all beings both mortal and immortal, changing with those things that ever change, according to their inseparable form, and preserving unchangeable the changelessness of form in things eternal and of an ethereal nature.

And therefore meditating that the other two genera of the theoretical would be expounded in terms of conjecture rather than in terms of scientific understanding: the theological because it is in no way phenomenal and attainable, but the physical because its matter is unstable and obscure, so that for this reason philosophers could never hope to agree on them; and meditating that only the mathematical, if approached enquiringly, would give its practitioners certain and trustworthy knowledge with demonstration both arithmetic and geometric resulting from indisputable procedures, we were led to cultivate most particularly as far as lay in our power this theoretical discipline [θεωρια]. And especially were we led to cultivate that discipline developed in respect to divine and heavenly things as being the only one concerned with the study of things which are always what they are, and therefore able itself to be always what it is--which is indeed the proper mark of a science--because of its own clear and ordered understanding, and yet to cooperate with the other disciplines no less than they themselves. For that special mathematical theory would most readily prepare the way to the theological, since it alone could take good aim at that unchangeable and separate act, so close to that act are the properties having to do with translations and arrangements of movements, belonging to those heavenly beings which are sensible and both moving and moved, but eternal and impassible. Again as concerns the physical there would not be just chance correspondances. For the general property of the material essence is pretty well evident from the peculiar fashion of its local motion--for example, the corruptible and incorruptible from straight and circular movements, and the heavy and light or passive and active from movement to the center and movement from center. And indeed this same discipline would more than any other prepare understanding persons with respect to nobleness of actions and character by means of the sameness, good order, due proportion, and simple directness contemplated in divine things, making its followers lovers of that divine beauty, and making habitual in them, and as it were natural, a like condition of the soul.

And so we ourselves try to increase continuously our love of the discipline of things which are always what they are, by learning what has already been discovered in such sciences by those really applying themselves to them, and also by making a small original contribution such as the period of time from them to us could well make possible. And therefore we shall try and set forth as briefly as possible as many theorems as we recognize to have come to light up to the present, and in such a way that those who have already been initiated somewhat may follow, arranging in proper order for the completeness of the treatise all matters useful to the theory of heavenly things. And in order not to make the treatise too long we shall only report what was rigorously proved by the ancients, perfecting as far as we can what was not fully proved or not proved as well as possible.

2. On the Order of the Theorems

A view, therefore, of the general relation of the whole earth to the whole of the heavens will begin this composition of ours. And next, of things in particular, there will first be an account of the ecliptic's position and of the places of that part of the earth inhabited by us, and again of the difference, in order, between each of them according to the inclinations of their horizons. For the theory of these, once understood, facilitates the examination of the rest. And, secondly, there will be an account of the solar and lunar movements and of their incidents. For without a prior understanding of these one could not profitably consider what concerns the stars. The last part, in view of this plan, will be an account of the stars. Those things having to do with the sphere of what are called the fixed stars would reasonably come first, and then those having to do with what are called the five planets. And we shall try and show each of these things using as beginnings and foundations for what we wish to find, the evident and certain appearances from the observations of the ancients and our own, and applying the consequences of these conceptions by means of geometrical demonstrations.

And so, in general, we have to state that the heavens are spherical and move spherically; that the earth, in figure, is sensibly spherical also when taken as a whole; in position, lies right in the middle of the heavens, like a geometrical centre; in magnitude and distance, has the ratio of a point with respect to the sphere of the fixed stars, having itself no local motion at all. And we shall go through each of these points briefly to bring them to mind.

3. That the Heavens Move Spherically

It is probable the first notions of these things came to the ancients from some such observation as this. For they kept seeing the sun and moon and other stars always moving from rising to setting in parallel circles, beginning to move upward from below as if out of the earth itself, rising little by little to the top, and then coming around again and going down in the same way until at last they would disappear as if falling into the earth. And then again they would see them, after remaining some time invisible, rising and setting as if from another beginning; and they saw that the times and also the places of rising and setting generally corresponded in an ordered and regular way.

But most of all the observed circular orbit of those stars, which are always visible, and their revolution about one and the same centre, led them to this spherical notion. For necessarily this point became the pole of the heavenly sphere; and the stars nearer to it were those that spun around in smaller circles, and those farther away made greater circles in their revolutions in proportion to the distance, until a sufficient distance brought one to the disappearing stars. And then they saw that those near the always-visible stars disappeared for a short time, and those farther away for a longer time proportionately. And for these reasons alone it was sufficient for them to assume this notion as a principle, and forthwith to think through also the other things consequent upon these same appearances, in accordance with the development of the science. For absolutely all the appearances contradict the other opinions.

If, for example, one should assume the movement of the stars to be in a straight line to infinity, as some have opined, how could it be explained that each star will be observed daily moving from the same starting point? For how could the stars turn back while rushing on to infinity? Or how could they turn back without appearing to do so? Or how is it they do not disappear with their size gradually diminishing, but on the contrary seem larger when they are about to disappear, being covered little by little as if cut off by the earth's surface? But certainly to suppose that they light up from the earth and then again go out in it would appear most absurd. For if anyone should agree that such an order in their magnitudes and number, and again in the distances, places, and times is accomplished in this way at random and by chance, and that one whole part of the earth has an incandescent nature and another a nature capable of extinguishing, or rather that the same part lights the stars up for some people and puts them out for others, and that the same stars happen to appear to some people either lit up or put out and to others not yet so--even if anyone, I say, should accept all such absurdities, what could we say about the always-visible stars which neither rise nor set? Or why don't the stars which light up and go out rise and set for every part of the earth, and why aren't those which are not affected in this way always above the earth for every part of the earth? For in this hypothesis the same stars will not always light up and go out for some people, and never for others. But it is evident to everyone that the same stars rise and set for some parts, and do neither of these things for others.

In a word, whatever figure other than the spherical be assumed for the movement of the heavens, there must be unequal linear distances from the earth to parts of the heavens, wherever or however the earth be situated, so that the magnitudes and angular distances of the stars with respect to each other would appear unequal to the same people within each revolution, now larger now smaller. But this is not observed to happen. For it is not a shorter linear distance which makes them appear larger at the horizon, but the steaming up of the moisture surrounding the earth between them and our eyes, just as things put under water appear larger the farther down they are placed.

The following considerations also lead to the spherical notion: the fact that instruments for measuring time cannot agree with any hypothesis save the spherical one; that, since the movement of the heavenly bodies ought to be the least impeded and most facile, the circle among plane figures offers the easiest path of motion, and the sphere among solids; likewise that, since of different figures having equal perimeters those having the more angles are the greater, the circle is the greatest of plane figures and the sphere of solid figures, and the heavens are greater than any other body.

Moreover, certain physical considerations lead to such a conjecture. For example, the fact that of all bodies the ether has the finest and most homogeneous parts; but the surfaces of homogeneous parts must have homogeneous parts, and only the circle is such among plane figures and the sphere among solids. And since the ether is not plane but solid, it can only be spherical. Likewise the fact that nature has built all earthly and corruptible bodies wholly out of rounded figures but with heterogeneous parts, and all divine bodies in the ether out of spherical figures with homogeneous parts, since if they were plane or disclike they would not appear circular to all those who see them from different parts of the earth at the same time. Therefore it would seem reasonable that the ether surrounding them and of a like nature be also spherical, and that because of the homogeneity of its parts it moves circularly and regularly.

4. That also the Earth, Taken as a Whole, Is Sensibly Spherical

Now, that also the earth taken as a whole is sensibly spherical, we could most likely think out in this way. For again it is possible to see that the sun and moon and the other stars do not rise and set at the same time for every observer on the earth, but always earlier for those living towards the orient and later for those living towards the occident. For we find that the phenomena of eclipses taking place at the same time, especially those of the moon, are not recorded at the same hours for everyone--that is, relatively to equal intervals of time from noon; but we always find later hours recorded for observers towards the orient than for those towards the occident. And since the differences in the hours is found to be proportional to the distances between the places, one would reasonably suppose the surface of the earth spherical, with the result that the general uniformity of curvature would assure every part's covering those following it proportionally. . . .

* * * * *

5. That There Are Two Different Prime Movements in the Heavens

It will be sufficient for these hypotheses, which have to be assumed for the detailed expositions following them, to have been outlined here in such a summary way since they will finally be established and confirmed by the agreement of the consequent proofs with the appearances. In addition to those already mentioned, this general assumption would also be rightly made that there are two different prime movements in the heavens. One is that by which everything moves from east to west, always in the same way and at the same speed with revolutions in circles parallel to each other and clearly described about the poles of the regularly revolving sphere. Of these circles the greatest is called the equator, because it alone is always cut exactly in half by the horizon which is a great circle of the sphere, and because everywhere the sun's revolution about it is sensibly equinoctial. The other movement is that according to which the spheres of the stars make certain local motions in the direction opposite to that of the movement just described and around other poles than those of that first revolution. And we assume that it is so because, while, from each day's observation, all the heavenly bodies are seen to move generally in paths sensibly similar and parallel to the equator and to rise, culminate, and set (for such is the property of the first movement), yet from subsequent and more continuous observation, even if all the other stars appear to preserve their angular distances with respect to each other and their properties as regards their places within the first movement, still the sun and moon and planets make certain complex movements unequal to each other, but all contrary to the general movement, towards the east opposite to the movement of the fixed stars which preserve their respective angular distances and are moved as if by one sphere.

If, then, this movement of the planets also took place in circles parallel to the equator--that is, around the same poles as those of the first revolution--it would be sufficient to assume for them all one and the same revolving movement in conformity with the first. For it would then be plausible to suppose that their movement was the result of a lag and not of a contrary movement. But they always seem, at the same time they move towards the east, to deviate towards the north and south poles without any uniform magnitude's being observed in this deviation, so that this seems to befall them through impulsions. But although this deviation is irregular on the hypothesis of one prime movement, it is regular when effected by a circle oblique to the equator. And so such a circle is conceived one and the same for, and proper to, the planets, quite exactly expressed and as it were described by the motion of the sun, but traveled also by the moon and planets which ever turn about it with every deviation from it on the part of any planet either way, a deviation within a prescribed distance and governed by rule. And since this is seen to be a great circle also because of the sun's equal oscillation to the north and south of the equator, and since the eastward movements of all the planets (as we said) take place on one and the same circle, it was necessary to suppose a second movement different from the general one, a movement about the poles of this oblique circle or ecliptic in the direction opposite to that of the first movement.

Then if we think of a great circle described through the poles of both the circles just mentioned, which necessarily cuts each of them--that is, the equator and the circle inclined to it--exactly in half and at right angles, there will be four points on the oblique circle or ecliptic: the two made by the equator diametrically opposite each other and called the equinoxes of which the one guarding the northern approach is called spring, and the opposite one autumn. And the two made by the circle drawn through both sets of poles, also clearly diametrically opposite each other, are called the tropics, of which the one to the south of the equator is called winter, and the one to the north summer.

The one first movement which contains all the others will be thought of then as described and as if defined by the great circle, through both sets of poles, which is carried around and carries with it all the rest from east to west about the poles of the equator. And these poles are as if they were on what is called the meridian, which differs from the circle through both sets of poles in this alone: that it is not always drawn through the poles of the ecliptic, but is conceived as continuously at right angles to the horizon and therefore called the meridian, since such a position cutting in half as it does each of the two hemispheres, that below the earth and that above, provides midday and midnight. But the second movement, consisting of many parts and contained by the first, and embracing itself all the planetary spheres, is carried by the first as we said, and revolves about the poles of the ecliptic in the opposite direction. And these poles of the ecliptic being on the circle effecting the first revolution--that is, on the circle drawn through all four poles together--are carried around with it as one would expect; and, moving therefore with a motion opposite to the second prime movement, in this way keep the position of the great circle which is the ecliptic ever the same with respect to the equator.

9. On the Particular Notions

A summary and general preliminary explanation would contain some such exposition as the foregoing of the things to be presupposed. But now we are going to begin the detailed proofs. And we think the first of these is that by means of which is calculated the length of the arc between the poles of the equator and the ecliptic, lying on the great circle drawn through these poles. To this end we must first see expounded the method of computing the size of chords inscribed in a circle, and we are now going to demonstrate this geometrically for each case, once for all.

10. On the Size of Chords in a Circle

With an eye to immediate use, we shall now make a tabular exposition of the size of these chords by dividing the circumference into 360 parts and setting side by side the chords as the arcs subtended by them increase by a half part. That is, the diameter of the circle will be cut into 120 parts for ease in calculation; [and we shall take the arcs, considering them with respect to the number they contain of the circumference's 360 parts, and compare them with the subtending chords by finding out the number the chords contain of the diameter's 120 parts.] But first we shall show how, with as few theorems as possible and the same ones, we make a methodical and rapid calculation of their sizes so that we may not only have the magnitudes of the chords set out without knowing the why and wherefore but so that we may also easily manage a proof by means of a systematic geometrical construction. In general we shall use the sexagesimal system because of the difficulty of fractions, and we shall follow out the multiplications and divisions, aiming always at such an approximation as will leave no error worth considering as far as the accuracy of the senses is concerned.

* * * * *

1. Concerning the Order of the Spheres of the Sun and Moon and Five Planets

Now, certainly whatever one could say in general about the fixed stars, to the extent that the appearances up until now fall under our apprehension, would be pretty much like this. But since this Composition still lacks a treatment of the five planets, we shall give an exposition of them, going as far as possible with what they have in common to avoid repetition, and then adding on the plan of each one in particular.

First, then, concerning the order of their spheres, all of which have their positions about the poles of the ecliptic, we see the foremost mathematicians agree that all these spheres are nearer the earth than the sphere of the fixed stars, and farther from the earth than that of the moon; that the three--of which Saturn's is the largest, Jupiter's next earthward, and Mars' below that--are all farther from the earth than the others and that of the sun. On the other hand, the spheres of Venus and Mercury are placed by the earlier mathematicians below the sun's, but by some of the later ones above the sun's because of their never having seen the sun eclipsed by them. But this judgment seems to us unsure since these planets could be below the sun and never yet have have been in any of the planes through the sun and our eye but in another, and therefore not have appeared in a line with it; just as in the case of the moon's conjunctive passages there are for the most part no eclipses.

Since there is no other way of getting at this because of the absence of any sensible parallax in these stars, from which appearance alone linear distances are gotten, the order of the earlier mathematicians seems the more trustworthy, using the sun as a natural dividing line between those planets which can be any angular distance from the sun and those which cannot but which always move near it. Besides, it does not place them far enough at their perigees to produce a sensible parallax.

2. On the Aim of the Planetary Hypotheses

So much, then, for the orders of the spheres. Now, since our problem is to demonstrate, in the case of the five planets as in the case of the sun and moon, all their apparent irregularities as produced by means of regular and circular motions (for these are proper to the nature of divine things which are strangers to disparities and disorders) the successful accomplishment of this aim as truly belonging to mathematical theory in philosophy is to be considered a great thing, very difficult and as yet unattained in a reasonable way by anyone. For, since, in the case of the researches about the periodic movements of each planet, whatever slight error the eye makes in systematic observations produces a sensible difference more quickly when the examination has been over a shorter interval than when over a greater one, the time for which we have observations of. . . . In the case of research about the anomalies, the fact that there are two anomalies appearing for each of the planets, and that they are unequal in magnitude and in the times of their returns, works a good deal of confusion. For one of the anomalies is seen to have relation to the sun, and the other to the parts of the zodiac, but both are mixed together so it is very hard to determind what belongs to each*; and most of the old observations were

---

* It is important to notice that all the five planets, just like the moon, have an anomaly with respect to the sun as well as an anomaly with respect to the zodiac. Since Ptolemy merely expounds the theory as a deduction, it might be well to explain the appearances from which these things could be gotten. It must be remembered that Ptolemy had long astronomical tables of data which had been kept for nearly a thousand years, and which served as appearances over a long period of time.

The appearances of Venus and Mercury are fairly simple. These two stars move on the ecliptic, more of less, and swing back and forth from one side of the sun to the other, Mercury never getting more than some 25° from the sun, and Venus never more than some 45°. This makes them alternately morning and evening stars. This swinging is the heliacal anomaly and, from a greatest elongation from the mean sun (say eastern) back to the next greatest eastern elongation, is called one cycle of heliacal anomaly. Furthermore the time from a western elongation to an eastern is longer than from the eastern to the next western. It is also observed that, for different positions of the mean sun on the ecliptic, the greatest elongations are smaller or larger, but always the same for the same position.

It is further observed that, if one considers the sum of the greatest eastern and greatest western elongation for each position of the mean sun, this sum is greatest at one position, and on either side gets smaller and smaller until it is least at the position exactly opposite on the ecliptic. This variation of the apparent heliacal anomaly is called the zodiacal anomaly.

The appearances of Mars, Jupiter, and Saturn are more complicated. These planets move generally from west to east along the ecliptic more or less at different speeds, Mars making a complete circuit through the fixed stars in about 2 years, Jupiter in about 11, and Saturn in about 30. They can be at any angular distance from the sun, unlike Venus and Mercury which are constrained to remain within certain bounds. But they are tied to

thrown together carelessly and grossly. The more continuous of them contain stations and apparitions, and the apprehension of these properties is not certain. The stations cannot indicate the exact time, since the planet's local motion remains imperceptible for many days before and after its station; and the apparitions not only make the places immediately disappear along with the stars as they are seen for the first or last time, but also can be utterly misleading as to the times because of the differences in the atmosphere and in the eye of the observer. In general, the observations made with reference to some fixed star at a rather great angular distance, unless because of these things one attends to them wisely and clear-sightedly, furnish a magnitude from their measurements hard to calculate and subject to guesswork. And this is so, not only because the lines between the observed stars make different angles with the ecliptic and by no means right angles--whence in the variety of the zodiac's inclinations a great uncertainty is apt to follow in the determination of the longitudinal and latitudinal positions--but also because the same angular distances appear to the eye greater near the horizon and smaller near the culminations, and so they can be measured as sometimes greater and sometimes smaller than the real angular distance.

And so I consider Hipparchus to have been most zealous after the truth, both because of all these things and especially because of his having left us more examples of accurate observations than he ever got from his predecessors. He sought out the hypotheses of the sun and moon, and demonstrated as far as possible and by every available means that they were accomplished through uniform circular movements, but he did not attempt to give the principle of the hypotheses of the five planets, as far as we can tell from those memoirs of his which have come down to us, but only arranged the observations in a more useful way and showed the appearances to be inconsistent with the hypotheses of the mathematicians of that time. For not only did he think it

---

the sun in a different way. Whenever the mean sun is nearly opposite any one of these three planets, the planet stops its eastward motion, and this is called a station. And then, as the mean sun gets more directly opposite, the planet moves westward, and this is called a regression or retrogradation. As the mean sun moves on, the planet appears to stop again, and then move eastward again. As the mean sun moves toward the planet, the planet moves faster and faster eastward until the mean sun has overtaken it; then it moves more and more slowly eastward until it again appears to stop. The time from a station to a corresponding station is one cycle of heliacal anomaly. Furthermore, the time from a station through the eastward motion of the planet to the next station is much longer than that from a station through the westward or regressive motion of the planet to the next station.

Again these speeds vary for different positions of the mean sun on the ecliptic. And this variation is called the zodiacal anomaly.

All the planets wander slightly from one side of the ecliptic to the other. The theory of this latitudinal anomaly is explained in Book XIII.

necessary as it seemed to declare that, because of the double anomaly of each planet, the regressions of each are unequal and of such and such a magnitude, while the other mathematicians gave their geometrical demonstrations on one and the same anomaly and regression, but he also thought that these movements could not be effected either by eccentric circles, or by circles concentric with the ecliptic but bearing epicycles, or even by both together, although the zodiacal anomaly was of one magnitude and the anomaly with respect to the sun of another. For these are the means used by nearly all those who have wished to demonstrate uniform circular movement by the so-called perpetual table, but in a false and inconsequential way, some getting nowhere at all, some following the problem to a limited extent. But Hipparchus reasoned that no one who has progressed through the whole of mathematics to such a point of accuracy and zeal for truth would be content to stop at this like the rest; but that anyone who was to persuade himself and those in touch with him would have to demonstrate the magnitude and periods of each of the anomalies by clear and consistent appearances; and, putting both together, he would have to find out the position and order of the circles by which these anomalies are produced and the mode of their movement and finally show about all the appearances to be consistent with the peculiar property of this hypothesis of the circles. I think this is difficult, and it seemed so to him. We have said all this not through ostentation, but in order that, if we are forced by the problem itself either (1) to use something contrary to the general argument, as when, for example, for ease we make our demonstrations of the circles described by the movement in the planetary spheres as if they were simple and in the same plane with the ecliptic; or if we are forced (2) to presuppose something without immediate foundation in the appearances, an apprehension gotten from continuous trial and adjustment; or (3) to suppose not everywhere the same mode of movement or inclination of the circles--in order that, I say, we may then reasonably agree that (1) using something of the sort that no appreciable difference is to result from it will not falsify the subject in hand; (2) that things supposed without proof, once they are conceived in such a way as to be consistent with appearances, cannot be found without some plan and knowledge even if the way of getting hold of them is hard to explain (after all, generally speaking, the cause of first principles is either nothing or hard to interpret in its nature); and (3) that, since the appearances relative to the stars are also found to be dissimilar, one should not reasonably think it strange or absurd to vary the mode of the hypotheses of the circles, especially when, along with saving the regular circular movement absolutely everywhere, each of the appearances is demonstrated in its more lawful and general character.

And so we have used for the demonstrations of each planet only those observations which cannot be disputed, that is those taken at contact or great proximity with the stars or even with the moon, above all those taken with the astrolabe where the eye is lined up with the diametrically opposite sights in the circles, sees on every side equal angular distances by means of similar arcs, and can accurately apprehend the passages relative to the middle of each star in longitude and latitude by moving to and fro to the observed stars the astrolabe's ecliptic circle and the diametrically opposite sights in the circles through its poles.

* * * * *

5. Preliminaries of the Hypotheses of the Five Planets

Now, the relation of the anomalies to the longitudinal passage of the five planets follows the exposition of these mean movements, and we have attempted a general outline of it in the vollowing way.

For, as we said, the very simple movements together sufficient for the problem in hand are two: one effected by circles eccentric to the ecliptic, and the other by circles concentric with the ecliptic but bearing epicycles. And likewise also the apparent anomalies for each star considered singly are two: one observed with respect to the parts of the zodiac and the other with respect to the configurations observed in contiguity and in the same parts of the zodiac, that, for the five planets, the time from the greatest movement to the mean movement is always longer than from the mean to the least. And such a property cannot follow from the hypothesis of eccentricity, but its contrary follows, because the greatest passage is always effected at the perigee, and in both hypotheses the arc from the perigee to the point of mean passage is less than that from this point to the apogee. But it can occur in the hypothesis of epicycles when the greatest passage is not effected at the perigee as in the case of the moon, but at the apogee--that is, when the star, starting from the apogee, moves not westward as the moon, but eastward in the opposite direction. And so we suppose this anomaly to be produced by epicycles.

But in the case of the anomaly observed with respect to the parts of the zodiac, we find, by means of the arcs of the zodiac taken at the same phases or configurations, that, on the contrary, the time from the least movement to the greatest. But this property can follow from either hypothesis, and at the beginning of the composition of the sun we showed how they were alike in this. But since it is more proper to the eccentric hypothesis, we suppose this anomaly is effected according to it, and also because the other anomaly is peculiar to the epicyclic hypothesis.

But immediately on applying the particular positions observed to the courses constructed from the combination of both hypotheses and continually examining these together, we find things cannot proceed so simply: (1) The planes in which we describe the eccentric circles are not immobile, so that the straight line through both their centres and the ecliptic's centre, along which the apogees and perigees are sighted, always remains at the same angular distances from the tropic and equinoctial points. (2) The epicycles do not have their centres borne on the eccentric circles whose centres are those with respect to which the epicycles' centres revolve in a regular eastward motion and cut off equal angles in equal times. But (1) the eccentrics' apogees make a slight regular shift eastward from the tropic points around the ecliptic's centre and nearly as much for each planet as the sphere of the fixed stars is found to make--that is, one degree in a hundred years, as far as one can detect from present data. And (2) the epicycles' centres are borne on circles equal to the eccentrics effecting the anomaly, but described about other centres. And these other centres, in the case of all except Mercury, bisect the straight lines between the centres of the eccentrics effecting the anomaly and the centre of the ecliptic. But in the case of Mercury alone, this other centre is the same distance from the centre revolving it [centre of equant] as this centre revolving it is in turn from the centre effecting the anomaly on the side of the apogee, and as this last centre effecting the anomaly is in turn from the centre placed at the eye. For, in the case of that star alone as also with the moon, we find the eccentric circle revolved by the aforesaid centre, contrariwise to the epicycle, back westward one revolution in a year's time, since it appears to be twice perigee in one revolution, just as the moon is also twice so in one month's time.

6. On the Mode and Difference of these Hypotheses

The mode of the hypotheses just derived would be more easy to understand in this way:

In the case of the hypothesis of all planets except Mercury, first let there be conceived the eccentric circle *ABC* about the centre *D*, and the diameter *ADC* through *D* and the centre of the ecliptic. And on this diameter let *E* be made the centre of the ecliptic, the point *A* the apogee, and *C* the perigee. And let *DE* be bisected at *F*; and with *F* as centre and *DA* as radius, let circle *GHK* be drawn, equal of course to circle *ABC*. And with *H* as centre let the epicycle *LM* be drawn, and let the straight line *LHMD* be joined.

Then first we suppose the plane of the eccentric circles to be inclined to that of the ecliptic, and again the plane of the epicycle to that of the eccentric, because of the latitudinal passage of the stars to be demonstrated by us hereafter. But to make things easy as far as the longitudinal passages are concerned, we suppose that they are all conceived in the one plane of the ecliptic, since there will be no appreciable difference in longitude resulting from such inclinations as will be found for each of the stars.

Then we say that the whole plane revolves eastward in the direction of the signs about centre *E*, moving the apogees and perigees one degree in a hundred years; that the epicycle's diameter *LHM* in turn is revolved regularly by centre *D* eastward in the direction of the signs at the rate of the star's longitudinal return; and that at the same time it revolves the points of the epicycle *L* and *M*, its centre *H* always borne on the eccentric *GHK*, and the star itself. And the star in turn moves on the epicycle *LM*, regularly with respect to the diameter always pointing to centre *D*, and makes its returns at the rate of the mean

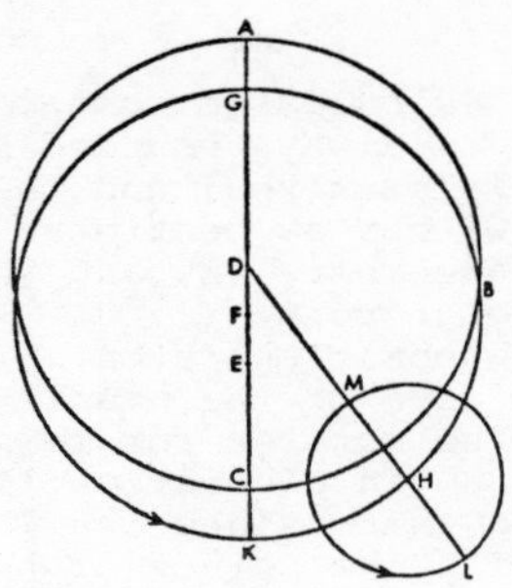

cycle of the anomaly with respect to the sun, moving eastward in the order of the signs at the apogee *L*.

And we could visualize the characteristic property of the hypothesis of Mercury in this way.

For let there be the eccentric circle of anomaly *ABC* about centre *D*, and the diameter *ADEC* through *D*, the ecliptic's centre *E*, and the apogee *A*. And let *DF* be taken on *AC* in the direction of the apogee *A* and equal to *DE*.

Then, other things remaining the same (that is, the whole plane shifting the apogee eastward about *E* and a centre the same amount as for the other stars, and the epicycle being revolved regularly eastward about *D* as centre by the straight line *DB*, and again the star moving on the epicycle in the same way as the others), here the centre of the other eccentric, equal to the first and on which the epicycle's centre will always lie, will be revolved by the straight line *FGH* about point *F* contrariwise to the epicycle--that is, westward in the direction opposite to the signs--regularly and at the same speed as the epicycle, so that each of the straight lines *DB* and *FGH*, in one year's time, is restored once with respect to the points of the ecliptic, and twice with respect to each other. And this centre of the other eccentric will always be a distance from the point *F* equal to either of the straight lines *DB* or *FGH*(for instance, *FG*) so that

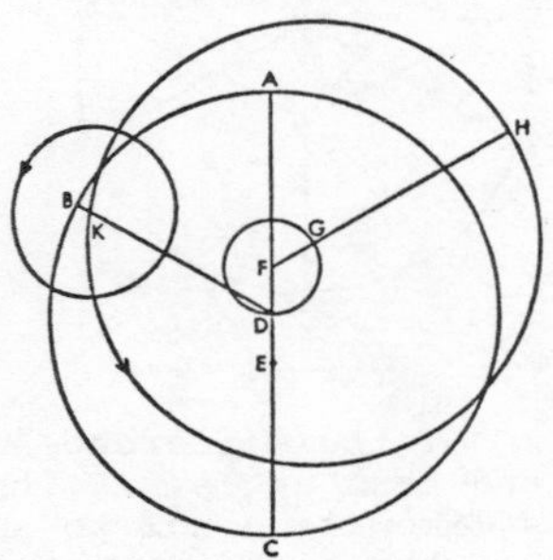

the little circle described by its movement westward, with *F* as centre and *FG* as radius, is always bounded by the centre of the first eccentric which remains fixed; and the moving eccentric is described in every case with *G* as centre and with radius *GH*, equal to *DA*, as for instance here *HK*, and the epicycle always has its centre on it, as here at point *K*.

We can follow the suppositions even more precisely from the demonstrations we are to give of the magnitudes for each planet. In these demonstrations the motives for formulating the hypotheses will somehow show up in clearer outline.

Yet one must premise that, since the longitudinal cycles do not make their returns with the points of the zodiac and with the apogees or perigees of the eccentric circles, because of their shift, therefore the longitudinal movements set out by us in the foregoing manner do not contain returns considered with respect to the apogees of the eccentrics but returns that are relative to the tropic and equinoctial points in accordance with our year.

Then it must be shown first that, also according to these hypotheses, whenever the mean longitudinal position of the star is equidistant from the apogees and perigees in either direction, the difference of zodiacal anomaly is equal for either distance, and also the greatest elongation on the epicycle on the corresponding side of the mean position.

For about centre *E* and diameter *AEC*, let there be the eccentric circle *ABC* on which the epicycle's centre is borne. On this diameter let *F* be taken as the ecliptic's centre, and *G* as the centre of the eccentric making the anomaly--that is, the centre around which we say the epicycle's mean passage is regularly effected. And let the straight lines *BGH* and *DGK* be drawn through, both the same angular distance from the apogee *A*, so *A* that angles *AGB* and *AGD* are equal. And let epicycles be described about points *B* and *D*, and let straight lines *BF* and *BD* be joined, and from *F* the eye-point let the straight lines *FL* and *FM* be drawn tangent to the epicycles on the corresponding sides.

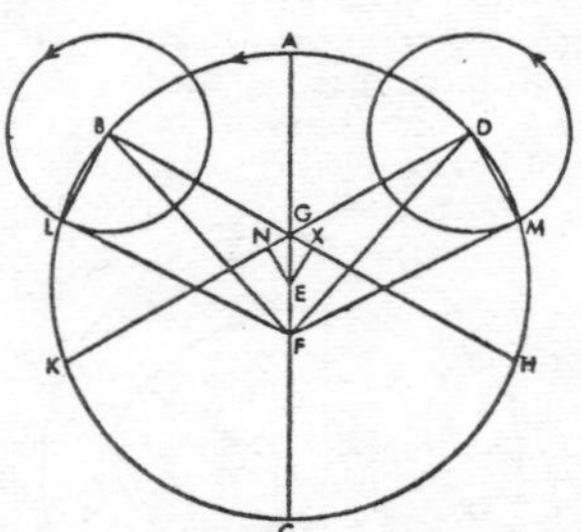

I say that angle *FBG* of the difference of zodiacal anomaly is equal to angle *GDF*; and that angle *BFL*, the greatest elongation on the epicycle, is likewise equal to angle *DFM*. For in this way the magnitudes of the elongations resulting from the combination of the eccentric and of the greatest elongations from the mean position will also be equal.

Then let the straight lines *BL* and *DM* be drawn from *B* and *D* perpendicular to *FL* and *FM*, and straight lines *EN* and *EX* from *E* perpendicular to *BH* and *DK*. Since

angle *XGE*=angle *NGE*,

and the angles at *N* and *X* are right, and *EG* is common to the equiangular triangles, therefore

NG=*XG*,

EN=*EX*.

Therefore *BH* and *DK* are chords equidistant from the centre *E*; therefore they are equal and their halves also. And so, by subtraction,

BG=*DG*.

But *GF* is common, and

angle *BGF*=angle *DGF*,

and are within equal sides; therefore also

base *BF*=base *DF*,

and

angle *GBF*=angle *DGF*.

And also, as radii of the epicycles,

BL=*DM*,

and the angles at *L* and *M* are right; therefore also

angle *BFL*=angle *DFM*.

Which things it was required to prove.

Then again, for the hypothesis of Mercury, let there be the diameter *ABC* through the circles' centres and apogee; and let *A* be supposed the centre of the ecliptic; *B* the centre of the eccentric effecting the anomaly, and *C* the point about which moves the centre of the eccentric bearing the epicycle. And again let the straight lines *BD* and *BE* of the epicycle's regular eastward motion be drawn through on either side, and the straight lines *CF* and *CG* of the eccentric's westward revolution at the same rate, so that of course the angles at *C* and *B* are equal, and *BD* parallel to *CF*, and *BE* to *CG*. And let the centres of the eccentrics be taken on *CF* and *CG*, and let them be *H* and *K*. And let the eccentrics described about these centres, eccentrics bearing the

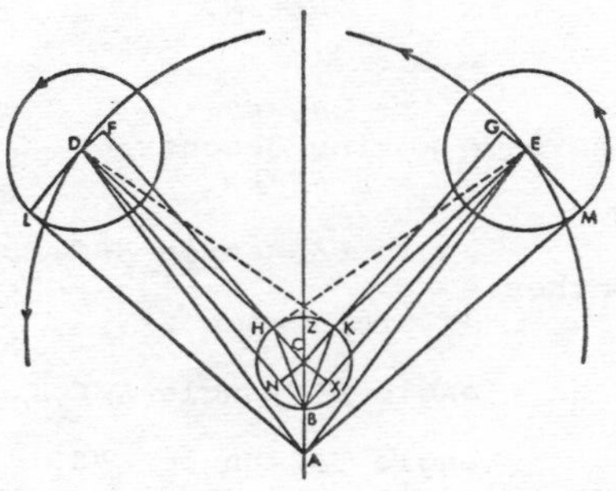

epicycles, pass through the points D and E. Again, with equal epicycles described about points D and E, let the straight lines AD and AE be joined, and let the straight lines AL and AM be drawn tangent to the corresponding sides of the epicycles.

Then it must be proved that the angle of zodiacal anomaly ADB is equal to angle AEB; and that the angle of greatest elongation for the epicycle DAL is equal to angle EAM.

For let the straight lines BH, BK, HD, and KE be joined; and let CN and CX be drawn from C perpendicular to BD and BE; and DF and EG from D and E perpendicular to CF and CG; and DL and EM perpendicular to AL and AM. Since then

angle CBN=angle CBX,

and the angles at N and X are right, and the straight line CB is common, therefore

$CN=CX$,

that is

$DF=EG$.

But also

$HD=KE$,*

and the angles at F and G are right. And so

angle DHF=angle EKG;

and

angle CHB=angle CKB,

because it is supposed

$HC=CK$,

CB is common, and

angle HCB=angle KCB.

And so also, by subtraction,

angle BHD=angle BKE,

and

base BD=base BE.

But again BA is also common, and

angle DBA=angle EBA.

And so

base AD=base AE,

and

angle ADB=angle AEB

And is the same way, since

$DL=EM$,

---

* For, as below,

$HB=KB$,

and as radii of the same moving eccentric

$HE=KD$.

And by hypothesis

angle DBC=angle EBC;

and, since by hypothesis

arc HZ=arc ZK,

therefore

angle HBC=angle KBC,

and by addition

angle DBZ=angle EBZ.

Hence, by congruent triangles and ,

$HD=KE$.

and the angles at L and M are right, therefore also

$$\text{angle } DAL = \text{angle } EAM.$$

Which things it was required to prove.

3. Physics

3.a. From Archimedes' *On Floating Bodies**

Archimedes (287-212 B.C.) was one of the greatest mathematical physicists of all time. Gottfried Wilhelm Leibnitz wrote of Archimedes in the early eighteenth century: "Whoever gets to the bottom of the works of Archimedes will admire the discoveries of the moderns less." Archimedes attempted to separate mathematical problems from metaphysical concerns. His treatise, On Floating Bodies, *illustrates the power of such an approach.*

On Floating Bodies.

Book I.

Postulate 1.

"Let it be supposed that a fluid of such a character that, its parts lying evenly and being continuous, that part which is thrust the less is driven along by that which is thrust the more; and that each of its parts is thrust by the fluid which is above it in a perpendicular direction if the fluid be sunk in anything and compressed by anything else."

Proposition 1.

If a surface be cut by a plane always passing through a certain point, and if the section be always a circumference [of a circle] whose centre is the aforesaid point, the surface is that of a sphere.

For, if not, there will be some two lines drawn from the point to the surface which are not equal.

Suppose O to be the fixed point, and A,B to be two points on the surface such that OA, OB are unequal. Let the surface be cut by a plane passing through OA, OB. Then the section is, by hypothesis, a circle whose centre is O.

Thus $OA=OB$; which is contrary to the assumption. Therefore the surface cannot but be a sphere.

Proposition 2.

The surface of any fluid at rest is the surface of a sphere whose centre is the same as that of the earth.

Suppose the surface of the fluid cut by a plane through O, the centre of the earth, in the curve $ABCD$.

$ABCD$ shall be the circumference of a circle.

For, if not, some lines drawn from O to the curve will be unequal. Take one of them, OB, such that OB is greater than some of the lines from O to the curve and less than others. Draw a circle with OB as radius. Let it be EBF, which will therefore

---

* *The Works of Archimedes*, by T. L. Heath, Pp. 253-259; 261-262. *On Floating Bodies*. Dover Publications, Inc., New York. Reprinted through permission of the publisher.

fall partly within and partly without the surface of the fluid.

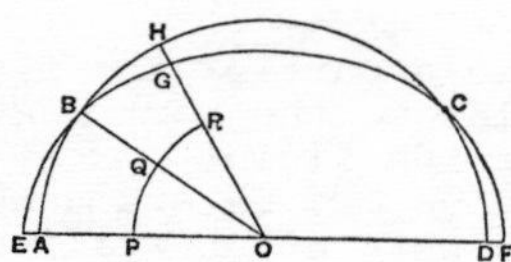

Draw *OGH* making with *OB* an angle equal to the angle *EOB*, and meeting the surface in *H* and the circle in *G*. Draw also in the plane an arc of a circle *PQR* with centre *O* and within the fluid.

Then the parts of the fluid along *PQR* are uniform and continuous, and the part *PQ* is compressed by the part between it and *AB*, while the part *QR* is compressed by the part between *QR* and *BH*. Therefore the parts along *PQ*, *QR* will be unequally compressed, and the part which is compressed the less will be set in motion by that which is compressed the more.

Therefore there will not be rest; which is contrary to the hypothesis.

Hence the section of the surface will be the circumference of a circle whose centre is *O*; and so will all other sections by planes through *O*.

Therefore the surface is that of a sphere with centre *O*.

Proposition 3.

Of solids those which, size for size, are of equal weight with a fluid will, if let down into the fluid, be immersed so that they do not project above the surface but do not sink lower.

If possible, let a certain solid *EFHG* of equal weight, volume for volume, with the fluid remain immersed in it so that part of it, *EFHG*, projects above the surface.

Draw through *O*, the centre of the earth, and through the solid a plane cutting the surface of the fluid in the circle *ABCD*.

Conceive a pyramid with vertex *O* and base a parallelogram at the surface of the fluid, such that it includes the immersed portion of the solid. Let this pyramid be cut by the plane of *ABCD* in *OL*, *OM*. Also let a sphere within the fluid and below *GH* be described with centre *O*, and let the plane of *ABCD* cut this sphere in *PQR*.

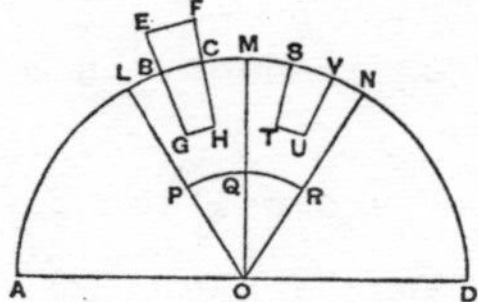

Conceive also another pyramid in the fluid with vertex *O*, continuous with the former pyramid and equal and similar to it. Let the pyramid so described be cut in *OM*, *ON* by the plane of *ABCE*.

Lastly, let *STUV* be a part of the fluid within the second pyramid equal and similar to the part *BGHC* of the solid, and let *SV* be at the surface of the fluid.

Then the pressures on *PQ*, *QR* are unequal, that on *PQ* being the greater. Hence the part at *QR* will be set in motion by that at *PQ*, and the fluid will not be at rest; which is contrary to the hypothesis.

Therefore the solid will not stand out above the surface.

Nor will it sink further, because all the parts of the fluid will be under the same pressure.

Proposition 4.

A solid lighter than a fluid will, if immersed in it, not be completely submerged, but part of it will project above the surface.

In this case, after the manner of the previous proposition, we assume the solid, if possible to be completely submerged and the fluid to be at rest in that position, and we conceive (1) a pyramid with its vertex at *O*, the centre of the earth, including the solid, (2) another pyramid continuous with the former and equal and similar to it, with the same vertex *O*, (3) a portion of the fluid within this latter pyramid equal to the immersed solid in the other pyramid, (4) a sphere with centre *O* whose surface is below the immersed solid and the part of the fluid in the second pyramid corresponding thereto. We suppose a plane to be drawn through the centre *O* cutting the surface of the fluid in the circle *ABC*, the solid in *S*, the first pyramid in *OA*, *OB*, the second pyramid in *OB*, *OC*, the portion of the fluid in the second pyramid in *K*, and the inner sphere in *PQR*.

Then the pressures on the parts of the fluid at *PQ*, *QR* are unequal, since *S* is lighter than *K*. Hence there will not be rest; which is contrary to the hypothesis.

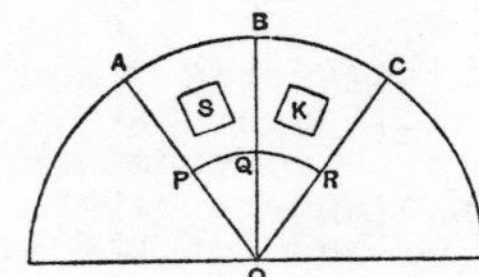

Therefore the solid *S* cannot, in a condition of rest, be completely submerged.

Proposition 5.

Any solid lighter than a fluid will, if placed in the fluid be so far immersed that the weight of the solid will be equal to the weight of the fluid displaced.

For let the solid be *EGHF*, and let *BGHC* be the portion of it immersed when the fluid is at rest. As in Prop. 3 conceive a pyramid with vertex *O* including the solid, and another pyramid with the same vertex continuous with the former and equal and similar to it. Suppose a portion of the fluid *STUV* at the base of the second pyramid to be equal and similar to the immersed portion of the solid; and let the construction be the same as in Prop. 3.

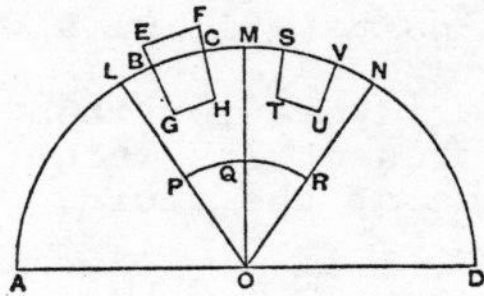

Then, since the pressure on the parts of the fluid at *PQ*,*QR* must be equal in order that the fluid may be at rest, it follows that the weight of the portion *STUV* of the fluid must be equal to the weight of the solid *EGHF*. And the former is equal to the weight of the fluid displaced by the immersed portion of the solid *BGHC*.

Proposition 6.

If a solid lighter than a fluid be forcibly immersed in it, the solid will be driven upwards by a force equal to the difference between its weight and the weight of the fluid displaced.

For let *A* be completely immersed in the fluid, and let *G* represent the weight of *A*, and (*G*+*H*) the weight of an equal volume of the fluid. Take a solid *D*, whose weight is *H* and add it to *A*. Then the weight of (*A*+*D*) is less than that of an equal volume of the fluid; and, if (*A*+*D*) is immersed in the fluid, it will project so that its weight will be equal to the weight of the fluid displaced. But its weight is (*G*+*H*).

Therefore the weight of the fluid displaced is (*G*+*H*), and hence the volume of the fluid displaced is the volume of the solid *A*. There will accordingly be rest with *A* immersed and *D* projecting.

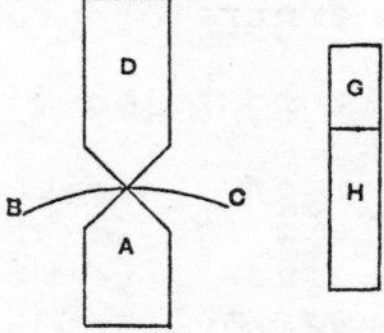

Thus the weight of *D* balances the upward force exerted by the fluid on *A*, and therefore the latter force is equal to *H*, which is the difference between the weight of *A* and the weight of the fluid which *A* displaces.

Proposition 7.

A solid heavier than a fluid will, if placed in it, descend to the bottom of the fluid, and the solid will, when weighed in the fluid, be lighter than its true weight by the weight of the fluid displaced.

(1) The first part of the proposition is obvious, since the part of the fluid under the solid will be under greater pressure, and therefore the other parts will give way until the solid reaches the bottom.

(2) Let A be a solid heavier than the same volume of the fluid, and let $(G+H)$ represent its weight, while G represents the weight of the same volume of the fluid.

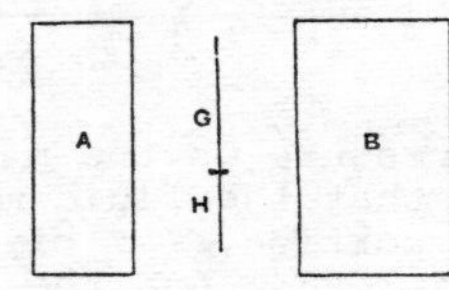

Take a solid B lighter than the same volume of the fluid, and such that the weight of B is G, while the weight of the same volume of the fluid is $(G+H)$.

Let A and B be now combined into one solid and immersed. Then, since $(A+B)$ will be of the same weight as the same volume of fluid, both weights being equal to $(G+H)+G$, it follows that $(A+B)$ will remain stationary in the fluid.

Therefore the force which causes A by itself to sink must be equal to the upward force exerted by the fluid on B by itself. This latter is equal to the difference between $(G+H)$ and G [Prop. 6]. Hence A is depressed by a force equal to H, i.e. its weight in the fluid is H, or the difference between $(G+H)$ and G.

* * * * *

Postulate 2.

"Let it be granted that bodies which are forced upwards in a fluid are forced upwards along the perpendicular [to the surface] which passes through their centre of gravity."

Proposition 8.

If a solid in the form of a segment of a sphere, and of a substance lighter than a fluid, be immersed in it so that its base does not touch the surface, the solid will rest in such a position that its axis is perpendicular to the surface; and, if the solid be forced into such a position that its base touches the fluid on one side and be then set free, it will not remain in that position but will return to the symmetrical position.

[The proof of this proposition is wanting in the Latin version of Tartaglia. Commandinus supplied a proof of his own in his edition.]

Proposition 9.

If a solid in the form of a segment of a sphere, and of a substance lighter than a fluid, be immersed in it so that its base is completely below the surface, the solid will rest in such a position that its axis is perpendicular to the surface.

[The proof of this proposition has only survived in a mutilated form. It deals moreover with only one case out of three which are distinguished at the beginning, viz. that in which the segment is greater than a hemisphere, while figures only are given for the cases where the segment is equal to, or less than, a hemisphere.]

Suppose, first, that the segment is greater than a hemisphere. Let it be cut by a plane through its axis and the centre of the earth; and, if possible, let it be at rest in the position shown in the figure, where *AB* is the intersection of the plane with the base of the segment, *DE* its axis, *C* the centre of the sphere of which the segment is a part, *O* the centre of the earth.

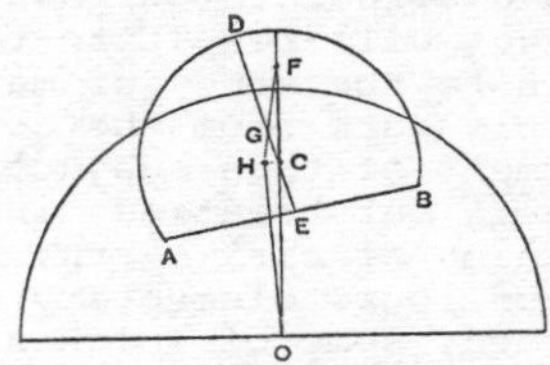

The centre of gravity of the portion of the segment outside the fluid, as *F*, lies on *OC* produced, its axis passing through *C*.

Let *G* be the centre of gravity of the segment. Join *FG*, and produce it to *H* so that

FG:*GH*=(volume of immersed portion):(rest of solid). Join *OH*.

Then the weight of the portion of the solid outside the fluid acts along *FO*, and the pressure of the fluid on the immersed portion along *OH*, while the weight of the immersed portion acts along *HO* and is by hypothesis less than the pressure of the fluid acting along *OH*.

Hence there will not be equilibrium, but the part of the segment towards *A* will ascend and the part towards *B* descend, until *DE* assumes a position perpendicular to the surface of the fluid.

3.b. From Hero's *Treatise on Pneumatics**

Hero of Alexandria (ca. 62 A.D.) produced important treatises on mechanics and optics, but had a special interest in inventing unusual and entertaining mechanical contrivances. His Pneumatica *was a treatise on gadgets run by the condensation and rarefaction of air. But, more than this, it was the most famous and influential attempt to apply the atomic hypothesis to physics. It begins with a consideration of the physics of air which was to influence scientific thought as late as the Scientific Revolution of the seventeenth century.*

The investigation of the properties of Atmospheric Air having been deemed worthy of close attention by the ancient philosophers and mechanists, the former deducing them theoretically, the latter from the action of sensible bodies, we also have thought proper to arrange in order what has been handed down by former writers, and to add thereto our own discoveries: a task from which much advantage will result to those who shall hereafter devote themselves to the study of mathematics. We are further led to write this work from the consideration that it is fitting that the treatment of this subject should correspond with the method given by us in our treatise, in four books, on water-clocks. For, by the union of air, earth, fire and water, and the concurrence of three, or four, elementary principles, various combinations are effected, some of which supply the most pressing wants of human life, while others produce amazement and alarm.

But, before proceeding to our proper subject, we must treat of the vacuum. Some assert that there is absolutely no vacuum; others that, while no continuous vacuum is exhibited in nature, it is to be found distributed in minute portions through air, water, fire and all other substances: and this latter opinion, which we will presently demonstrate to be true from sensible phenomena, we adopt. Vessels which seem to most men empty are not empty, as they suppose, but full of air. Now the air, as those who have treated of physics are agreed, is composed of particles minute and light, and for the most part invisible. If, then, we pour water into an apparently empty vessel, air will leave the vessel proportioned in quantity to the water which enters it. This may be seen from the following experiment. Let the vessel which seems to be empty be inverted, and, being carefully kept upright, pressed down into water; the water will not enter it even though it be entirely immersed: so that it is manifest that the air, being matter, and having itself filled all the space in the vessel, does not allow the water to enter. Now, if we bore the bottom of the vessel, the water will enter through the mouth, but the air will escape through the hole. Again, if, before perforating the bottom, we raise the vessel vertically, and turn it up,

---

* Hero of Alexandria, *The Pneumatics*, from the Original Greek, translated for and edited by Bennet Woodcroft (London, Taylor, Walton & Maberly, 1851), pp. 1-10.

we shall find the inner surface of the vessel entirely free from moisture, exactly as it was before immersion. Hence it must be assumed that the air is matter. The air when set in motion becomes wind, (for wind is nothing else but air in motion), and if, when the bottom of the vessel has been pierced and the water is entering, we place the hand over the hole, we shall feel the wind escaping from the vessel; and this is nothing else but the air which is being driven out by the water. It is not then to be supposed that there exists in nature a distinct and continuous vacuum, but that it is distributed in small measures through air and liquid and all other bodies. Adamant alone might be thought not to partake of this quality, as it does not admit of fusion or fracture, and, when beaten against anvils or hammers, buries itself in them entire. This peculiarity however is due to its excessive density: for the particles of fire, being coarser than the void spaces in the stone, do not pass through them, but only touch the outer surface; consequently, as they do not penetrate into this, as into other substances, no heat results. The particles of the air are in contact with each other, yet they do not fit closely in every part, but void spaces are left between them, as in the sand on the sea shore: the grains of sand must be imagined to correspond to the particles of air, and the air between the grains of sand to the void spaces between the particles of air. Hence, when any force is applied to it, the air is compressed, and, contrary to its nature, falls into the vacant spaces from the pressure exerted on its particles: but when the force is withdrawn, the air returns again to its former position from the elasticity of its particles, as is the case with horn shavings and sponge, which, when compressed and set free again, return to the same position and exhibit the same bulk. Similarly, if from the application of force the particles of air be divided and a vacuum be produced larger than is natural, the particles unite again afterwards; for bodies will have a rapid motion through a vacuum, where there is nothing to obstruct or repel them, until they are in contact. Thus, if a light vessel with a narrow mouth be taken and applied to the lips, and the air be sucked out and discharged, the vessel will be suspended from the lips, the vacuum drawing the flesh towards it that the exhausted space may be filled. It is manifest from this that there was a continuous vacuum in the vessel. The same may be shown by means of the egg-shaped cups used by physicians, which are of glass, and have narrow mouths. When they wish to fill these with liquid, after sucking out the contained air, they place the finger on the vessel's mouth and invert them into the liquid; then, the finger being withdrawn, the water is drawn up into the exhausted space, though the upward motion is against its nature. Very similar is the operation of cupping-glasses, which, when applied to the body, not only do not fall though of considerable weight, but even draw the contiguous matter toward them through the apertures of the body. The explanation is that the fire placed in them consumes and rarefies the air they contain, just as other substances, water, air or earth are consumed and pass over into more subtle substances.

That something is consumed by the action of fire is manifest from coal-cinders, which, preserving the same bulk as they had before combustion, or nearly so, differ very much in weight. The consumed parts pass away with the smoke into a substance of fire or air or earth: the subtlest parts pass into the highest region where fire is; the parts somewhat coarser than these into air, and those coarser still, having been borne with the others a certain space by the current, descend again into the lower regions and mingle with earthy substances. Water also, when consumed by the action of fire, is transformed into air; for the vapour arising from cauldrons placed upon flames is nothing but the evaporation from the liquid passing into air. That fire, then, dissolves and transforms all bodies grosser than itself is evident from the above facts. Again, in the exhalations that rise from the earth the grosser kinds of matter are changed into subtler substances; for dew is sent up from the evaporation of the water contained in the earth by exhalation; and this exhalation is produced by some igneous substance, when the sun is under the earth and warms the ground below, especially if the soil be sulphureous or bituminous, and the ground thus warmed increases the exhalation. The warm springs found in the earth are due to the same cause. The lighter portions of the dew, then, pass into air; the grosser, after being borne upwards for a certain space from the force of the exhalation, when this has cooled at the return of the sun, descend again to the surface.

Winds are produced from excessive exhalation, whereby the air is disturbed and rarefied, and sets in motion the air in immediate contact with it. This movement of the air, however, is not everywhere of uniform velocity: it is more violent in the neighbourhood of the exhalation, where the motion began; fainter at a greater distance from it: just as heavy bodies, when rising, move more rapidly in the lower region where the propelling force is, and more slowly in the higher; and when the force which originally propelled them no longer acts upon them, they return to their natural position, that is, to the surface of the earth. If the propelling force continued to urge them onward with equal velocity, they would never have stopped; but now the force gradually ceases, being as it were expended, and the speed of the motion ceases with it.

Water, again, is transformed into an earthy substance: if we pour water into an earthy and hollow place, after a short time the water disappears, being absorbed by the earthy substance, so that it mingles with, and is actually transformed into, earth. And if any one says that it is not transformed or absorbed by the earth, but is drawn out by heat, either of the sun or some other body, he shall be shewn to be mistaken: for if the same water be put into a vessel of glass, or bronze, or any other solid material, and placed in the sun, for a considerable time it is not diminished except in a very small degree. Water, therefore, is transformed into an earthy substance: indeed, slime and mud are transformations of water into earth.

Moreover, the more subtle substance is transformed into the grosser; as in the case of the flame of a lamp dying out for want of oil,--we see it for a time borne upwards and, as it were, striving to reach its proper region, that is, the highest of all above the atmosphere, till, overpowered by the mass of intervening air, it no longer tends to its kindred place, but, as though mixed and interwoven with the particles of air, becomes air itself. The same may be observed with air. For, if a small vessel containing air and carefully closed be placed in water with the mouth uppermost, and then, the vessel being uncovered, the water be allowed to rush in, the air escapes from the vessel; but, being overpowered by the mass of water, it mingles with it again and is transformed so as to become water.

When, therefore, the air in the cupping glasses, being in like manner consumed and rarefied by fire, issues through the pores in the sides of the glass, the space within is exhausted and draws towards it the matter adjacent, of whatever kind it may be. But, if the cupping glass be slightly raised, the air will enter the exhausted space and no more matter will be drawn up.

They, then, who assert that there is absolutely no vacuum may invent many arguments on this subject, and perhaps seem to discourse most plausibly though they offer no tangible proof. If however, it be shewn by an appeal to sensible phenomena that there is such a thing as a continuous vacuum, but artificially produced; that a vacuum exists also naturally, but scattered in minute portions; and that by compression bodies fill up these scattered vacua, those who bring forward such plausible arguments in this matter will no longer be able to make good their ground.

Provide a spherical vessel, of the thickness of metal plate so as not to be easily crushed, containing about 8 cotylæ (2 quarts). When this has been tightly closed on every side, pierce a hole in it, and insert a siphon, or slender tube, of bronze, so as not to touch the part diametrically opposite to the point of performation, that a passage may be left for water. The other end of the siphon must project about 3 fingers' breadth (2 in.) above the globe, and the circumference of the aperture through which the siphon is inserted must be closed with tin applied both to the siphon and to the outer surface of the globe, so that when it is desired to breathe through the siphon no air may possibly escape from the vessel. Let us watch the result. The globe, like other vessels commonly said to be empty, contains air, and as this air fills all the space within it and presses uniformly against the inner surface of the vessel, if there is no vacuum, as some suppose, we can neither introduce water nor more air, unless the air contained before make way for it: and if by the application of force we make the attempt, the vessel, being full, will burst sooner than admit it. For the particles of air cannot be compression into which their bulk may become less; but this is not credible if there is no vacuum: nor again, as the particles press against one another throughout their whole surface and likewise against the sides of the vessel, can they be pushed away so as to make room if there is no vacuum. Thus in no way can anything from without be introduced into the globe unless some portion of the previously contained air escape; if, that is to say, the whole space is closely and uniformly filled, as the objectors suppose. And yet, if any one, inserting the siphon in his mouth, shall blow into the globe, he will introduce much wind without any of the previously contained air giving way. And, this being the uniform result, it is clearly shewn that a condensation takes place of the particles contained in the globe into the interspersed vacua. The condensation however is effected artificially by the forcible introduction of air. Now if, after blowing into the vessel, we bring the hand close to the mouth, and quickly cover the siphon with the finger, the air remains the whole time pent up in the globe; and on the removal of the finger the introduced air will rush out again with a loud noise, being thrust out, as we stated, by the expansion of the original air which takes place from its elasticity. Again, if we draw out the air in the globe by suction through the siphon, it will follow abundantly, though no other substance take its place in the vessel, as has been said in the case of the egg. By this experiment it is completely proved that an accumulation of vacuum goes on in the globe; for the particles of air left behind cannot grow larger in the interval so as to occupy the space left by the particles driven out. For if they increase in magnitude when no foreign substance can be added, it must be supposed that this increase arises from expansion, which is equivalent to a re-arrangement of the particles through the production of a vacuum. But it is maintained that there is no vacuum; the particles therefore will not become larger, for it is not possible to imagine for them any other mode of increase. It is clear, then, from what has been said that certain void spaces are interspersed between the particles of the air, into which, when force is applied, they fall contrary to their natural action.

The air contained in the vessel inverted in water does not undergo much compression, for the compressing force is not considerable, seeing that water, in its own nature, possesses neither weight nor power of excessive pressure. Whence it is that, though divers to the bottom of the sea support an immense weight of water on their backs, respiration is not compelled by the water, though the air contained in their nostrils is extremely little. It is worth while here to examine what reason is given why those who dive deep, supporting on their backs an immense weight of water, are not crushed. Some say that it is because water is of uniform weight: but these give no reason why divers are not crushed by the water above. The true reason may be shewn as follows. Let us imagine the column of liquid which is directly over the surface of the object under pressure, (in immediate contact with which the water is,) to be a body of the same weight and form as the superincumbent liquid, and that this is so placed in the water that i under surface coincides with the surface of the body pressed, resting upon it in the same manner as the previously superincumbent liquid, with which it exactly corresponds. It is clear, then, that this body does not project above the liquid in which it is immersed, and will not sink beneath its surface. For Archimedes has shewn, in his work on 'Floating Bodies,' that bodies of equal weight with any liquid, when immersed in it, will neither project above nor sink beneath its surface: therefore they will not exert pressure on objects beneath. Again, such a body, if all objects which exert pressure from above be removed, remains in the same place; how then can a body which has no tendency downward exert pressure? Similarly, the liquid displaced by the body will not exert pressure on objects beneath; for, as regards rest and motion, the body in question does [not] differ from the liquid which occupies the same space.

Again, that void spaces exist may be seen from the following considerations: for, if there were not such spaces, neither light, nor heat, nor any other material force could penetrate through water, or air, or any body whatever. How could the rays of the sun, for example, penetrate through water to the bottom of the vessel? If there were no pores in the fluid, and the rays thrust the water aside by force, the consequence would be that full vessels would overflow, which however does not take place. Again, if the rays thrust the water aside by force, it would not be found that some were reflected while others penetrated below; but now all those rays that impinge upon the particles of the water are driven back, as it were, and reflected, while those that come in contact with the void spaces, meeting with but few particles, penetrate to the bottom of the vessel. It is clear, too, that void spaces exist in water from this, that, when wine is poured into water, it is seen to spread itself through every part of the water, which it would not do if there were no vacua in the water. Again, one light traverses another; for, when several lamps are lighted, all objects are brilliantly illuminated, the rays passing in every direction through each other. And indeed it is possible to penetrate through bronze, iron, and all other bodies, as is seen in the instance of the marine torpedo.

That a continuous vacuum can be artificially produced has been shewn by the application of a light vessel to the mouth, and by the egg of physicians. With regard, then, to the nature of the vacuum, though other proofs exist, we deem those that have been given, and which are founded on sensible phenomena, to be sufficient. It may, therefore, be affirmed on this matter that every body is composed of minute particles, between which are empty spaces less than the particles of the body, (so that we erroneously say that there is no vacuum except by the application of force, and that every place is full either of air, or water, or some other substance), and, in proportion as any one of these particles recedes, some other follows it and fills the vacant space: that there is no continuous vacuum except by the application of some force: and again, that the absolute vacuum is never found, but is produced artificially.

These things having been clearly explained, let us treat of the theorems resulting from the combination of these principles; for, by means of them, many curious and astonishing kinds of motion may be discovered. After these preliminary considerations we will begin by treating of the bent siphon, which is most useful in many ways in Pneumatics.

4. Galenic Medicine

The Greek physician, Galen (ca. 131-201 A.D.), was the last great figure in ancient medicine. His extensive medical writings both summarized and extended the medical tradition of antiquity. Galen served as a physician to Roman aristocrats at a time when Rome was consolidating her control over the western world. In the selections that follow, Galen indicated his approach to medicine and his method of argument in physiology.

4.a. From *Galen on Medical Experience**

What is more manifold, more complicated, and more varied than disease? Or how does one discover that a disease is the same as another disease in all its characteristics? Is it by the number of the symptoms or by their strength and power? For if a thing be itself, then, in my opinion, it must be itself in all these characteristics, for if even one of them is lacking it is perverted and ceases to be itself, since it no longer possesses the quality lacking. We shall, however, concede them this point and allow that this disease which showed itself just now is, in all its characteristics, the same disease as before. In granting them this also, however, it can perhaps occur that this (disease) proves to be identical with the other two or three times but not very many times. Moreover, if it could happen very many times, no single individual could ever see it. Should he who sees it at this moment be other than the one who saw it at a different time, there is nothing to show that it was seen very many times; for the observer, and he who retains in his memory what was observed and remembered, must continually, perpetually, and uninterruptedly observe it. Again, what is regarded and observed must of necessity be observed by many people, since the case is as I have described it. How can a person determine whether what he sees at this moment is identical with that which someone has seen before or is something quite different, unless he himself has seen both? Now, lest they imagine that in pursuing our scrutiny and argument to these lengths we are injuring them and desirous of contending with them, we would for our part make also this concession and allow that it is indeed possible that a certain disease with all its symptoms is identical with another disease, and that one individual sees it very many times.

Further we must reflect at this point whether this is in any way advantageous to them; for my part, I think it is of no advantage to them at all. For if one were to be satisfied with mere observation of the number of symptoms by themselves without requiring to consider also their order, and which is first and second and third, some advantage might probably be derived therefrom. Now, however, it is found that by changing the order of

---

* *Galen on Medical Experience*, First Edition of the Arabic Version with English Translation and Notes by R. Walzer (London: Oxford University Press, 1944). Pp. 89-93; 98-103; 132-139.

some of the symptoms and by removing them from their places, or acting similarly in the case of some diseases, this disease is not only different from the foregoing one, but is frequently its reverse, because the similarity and consistency are void and perverted. What I am now going to explain to you shows best of all the correctness of our opinion: if, for example, convulsion follows fever, this is a sign of death, and if fever follows convulsion this is a sign of safety. So, too, when lethargy precedes trembling, it is not a sign of death, but if it follows trembling it is a very bad sign. Further, in regard to 'sour intestines', if this occurs after the disease known as 'slippery intestines' it is a good sign, but not if the reverse is the case. We know also that when a man is overtaken by the disease described as 'loss of memory', and on getting rid of it is immediately attacked by the disease known as 'phrenitis', this is better than if the man suffering from 'phrenitis' were afterwards to be attacked by 'loss of memory'. Again, if anyone requires a bandage and his intestines are full of the waste products of digestion, and one administers an enema first, and then bandages him, this is a great help to him, but if one treats him in the reverse order, no little harm can be done to him. In my opinion, too, the taking of nourishment after the application of ointment and bandages is frequently useful, but it is not good to apply ointment, to bandage, or to undertake any other manipulation after the patient has taken nourishment. It is not surprising that such changes in order and sequence among the sick are of great potency, since we find that bathing and gymnastic exercises immediately after meals are bad for healthy persons, but if they do the reverse and partake of food after these exercises, they derive great benefit therefrom. This is a fact, although there is a vast difference between a healthy person and a sick one, for the sick remain a shorter time in the same state and change more rapidly from one condition to the other, and are altogether more open to danger than are those who enjoy health. This, indeed, is so perfectly obvious that it hardly calls for argument. If then with a healthy person, who is nearly always more or less in the same condition, one cannot conjoin the things in which he is engaged absolutely and at haphazard, how much less possible is it to do so in the case of the sick? We ought not to strive after such foolishness. But I shall not desist even at this point, nor hold my peace. On the contrary, I shall concede this to them also and admit the veracity of those things which resemble the delusions of a madman, and are in very truth dreams and visions.

But now consider further, if this is in any way useful to them, or if they have not lost the whole of that which they are striving for. If anyone were to concede them all these things, numerous as they are, and should grant them all--and I should support them, if they conceded these things in friendly argument--they would (still) be as far from acquiring the knowledge they desire as I am from flying. For with respect to the salient causes of diseases they are exposed to greater doubt than in what was mentioned before. For someone may say: tell me, why is it that lassitude, burning caused by the sun, drunkenness, overeating, exposure to a cold atmosphere, overstepping the limits with regard to coition, and indigestion are things which must be remembered and inquired into, and to which reason must be applied, but other things, analogous to these, need not me made the subject of investigation? I mean by analogous things inquiring as to whether the sick man took a bath before the onset of his illness or not; whether he had lived in the town or in a village; whether he had stayed in a room or on a terrace and if he had slept or had lain awake, or if he had been depressed or had had worries, or if he had read some book. More remote from this would be the query as to whether he had worn a white garment before that time, or a red, or a black, or a crimson one. Furthermore, one might ask whether he had wrestled or had bathed with anyone, dined or slept with anyone. For all this and similar things, although there are others more remote than these, they must retain in their memories and investigate, when they have even once refused to disown the memorizing of what they see of the salient causes.

For if they would, like us, investigate these things, by way of determining the causes of diseases, they would very easily be able to distinguish and differentiate between them and the things which are not the causes of disease. Since, however, according to their own statement, they do not investigate these things by way of determining the causes of diseases, but as parts of the symptoms in their totality, how can they say that there are things which must be investigated and memorized as being single symptoms of the totality of symptoms, and other things which are not so? And it is just this very doubt and this very question to which they are exposed and constrained in regard to the remedies for diseases. For here, too, they are unable to differentiate between that which is ineffectual and harmful, and that which is useful and beneficial. For in the case of one particular sick person many things are found together: things which his body has assimilated and things which are evacuated, also things which externally affect the body. Since all this can have but one result, either improvement in the condition of the sick man or a turn for the worse, the Empiricists are quite unable to assure themselves as to which of these things must be made the cause of the sick man deriving benefit, when he is benefited, and which of them must be regarded as the cause of his being harmed, when he has been harmed. For because they only retain in their memories what comes at the end of the case, they can only have the knowledge that this has occurred very many times after such things have taken place. But that certain things are the cause of a sick man's recovery or death, and others are not, is a matter of which they are quite ignorant. This conclusion is borne in upon us in the most trivial and unimportant cases. Suppose that a man is attacked by cataract and he is loosened, and his eye is anointed, and he goes for a walk and reads, and his condition afterwards becomes worse, or if you prefer it improves, would the Empiricist be able to know which of these things was harmful and which was useful, if he did not observe the nature of each single one of them? What advantage has observation to him who knows nothing of this? But just because the number of concomitants of diseases is so great and there is such variety in what causes evacuation and what is vomited up and what is introduced into the organism, while those things that affect it from outside are still more numerous, the Empiricist is still less able to judge which of them are beneficial and which harmful. Let me say something which, in my opinion, is straightforward and most correct: I am sure that anyone who does not investigate things at the very outset and reflect upon them carefully is not capable at some later date even of beginning to memorize them, not to speak of anything more. And how can anyone do this who does not know from the very beginning what things have to be eliminated and disregarded as being superfluous and unnecessary, and what things have to be examined and to be judged carefully as to their usefulness and their necessity. However, on account of the Empiricists' negligence, which has overstepped all limit, I shall make a concession to them even here.

* * * * *

And the type of argument by which the first group of these three is characterized, is one which opposes the whole of the arts in general and, furthermore, rejects what is obvious to the eye, and contradicts all habits and customs of life adopted by mankind. And it also opposes him who speaks and him who argues with it. For they (the Empiricists) say: 'O you who reject experiences because they neglect inquiry into the nature of things, what think you of the *nautes*--i.e. he who steers a ship upon the ocean? Is he, until he has fathomed the logos of nature and discovered the elements of the whole, and examined the nature of the winds, unable to sail forward at a given moment, and to be aware of things before they happen--to know (e.g.) of the storm that is coming up on him, and can he not steer his ship after this has taken place until he reaches the place whither he wished to sail? And what think you, moreover, of the peasant? Is he, until he has learned from one of the philosophers something of the nature and substance of the soil, and what is the nature and substance of rain and wind, and how they come about, unable to know by experience what seeds to sow at certain times and on what soil, if they are to spring and flourish and attain completion and perfection? And what think you of the vine-grower? Must he, too, examine the nature of the vineyard? And do you think that the consumer of foods needs to draw inferences and to inquire into their nature and substance, and is not content to know of each one of them its action and effect upon the body (by experiencing) many times what results from it? And the agreement of mankind that at the time of the rising of the Pleiades harvest must start, and at the time of their setting ploughing should begin--do you hold that it is not sufficient to learn this by experience, but that this must be closely observed and attentively examined until the nature of the constellation of the Pleiades, and the nature of the Bear, of Sirius, and that of the other stars has been studied? And tell me, what about the shoemaker? Can he not know before ascertaining the nature of cattle and the nature of sheep, which skins are stronger, which more flexible? Is this not all absurd and ponderous and like the pastime of Sophists who abandon themselves to trivialities and idle talk? You know that men taken as a whole, of whatever type they may be, do not feel bound to examine into the nature of wine, but that they know perfectly well that too great indulgence in drinking wine is harmful. And so it is with mushrooms. One finds that the learned man who discourses on the natures of things, knows their nature. But if any mushrooms are placed before him, he does not know which are edible and which are not, whereas the country-dwellers can distinguish between them since they are familiar with them and see them constantly, and even the children know them, to say nothing of their elders. And likewise one finds that the baker knows which kind of wheat makes unadulterated bread and which does not, whereas you, O learned investigator of the nature of seeds, are ignorant in this respect. And in short, we find that of the bulk of mankind each individual by making use of his frequent observations gains knowledge not attained by another; for as Demokritos says, experience and vicissitudes have taught men this, and it is from their wealth of experience that men have learned to perform the things they do. Now since this is the case, what do you think about it? Is it logical to admit that in all other experiences, although the nature of the thing utilized is unknown, that is achieved which ought to be achieved, and to wrong medicine alone denying this to it--or do you say that the things which are known by other kinds of experience are stored up in the minds of those inhabitants of prosperous cities, who are possessed of insight and understanding, and those who in their nature are of a higher degree than the other people in these cities, but the things which are ascertained by medical experience, since they are inferior and lower, can only be memorized by simple-minded people like one Mammakythos or Meletides or others of those famed and known for their simplicity? But you know that this cannot be maintained, for I think that you too, who attack the method of experience, are agreed with us, that medicine is a thing which has passionately interested the best and most excellent of men. And the only difference between us is that you assert that these people did not deduce what they have deduced from experience, but by inferring what is concealed from what is manifest.

And again, I assert that what you have been striving to prove by your arguments is exceedingly bad and absurd. You reject, namely, the empirical because it aims to store up particular things, and for other reasons you praise and value the method of inference from the visible to the invisible, because in this way one learns in a general and comprehensive manner what one wishes to know. For instance, in the case of anyone wishing to treat a patient suffering from diarrhoea, it would be more useful and helpful to know that preparations conducive to constipation would benefit him. For knowledge of general things embraces both of these, and with them very many others, and comprises almost everything beneficial to the sufferer from diarrhoea. But the Empiricist, were he to mention and enumerate fifteen varieties of what would be helpful--to say nothing of his enumerating and mentioning only three or so--would not even then have come to an end of them, because those he has not mentioned are even more. And moreover, if one were to grant them that they were able to mention in their books everything that physicians could make use of for purposes of healing--although this is impossible--no one could remember all these things without having some generalization on which to rely, and without all these things being united by some single thing in which they are all alike. According to their argument, the characteristic of the logos is that everything it elucidates, it elucidates at once, and the characteristic of empiricism, that it elucidates little by little, gradually. And it is for them to tell us whether Hippocrates in his day--since they assert that the whole of medical knowledge was elucidated simultaneously--has at the very outset commanded the whole of medical science. Should they say that this is the case, then it must necessarily follow that Hippocrates' effort in setting down in his book *Epidemics* what he desired to be a memorial to his observation and memorizing was a vain and useless one. Or would they say that Hippocrates discovered much, and that those who followed after have not discovered less, and that one finds up to the present day that some things have already been discovered, and other things it is hoped to discover later. Should they say this, then the gradual discovery of a thing is more proper and more congenial to the empirical method than to the logos. And should this be the case--we believe, however, that it is not so--then not only is the view of those wrong who declare that nothing can be discovered by experience, but the view of those who say that everything is discovered by experience is certainly true. And beside the other points which the logic of the arguments forces upon the Dogmatists, there further follows of necessity for them that inquiry into the origin of medicine is a vain and superfluous thing. For you Dogmatists say that inquiry into that matter is only useful in so far as it was needed to discover what had not yet been discovered in the past, so that you can apply it, and by this means discover what you wish to discover.

But if everything is discovered by the logos, then it is no longer necessary for us to discover anything supplementary to what has already been found, and inquiry into how something that is used in medicine was discovered is useless and vain. And further the facts that you acknowledge and agree with us that up to the present much has not been discovered beyond what has already been discovered, and also that in the existing things we are forced to make a transference from one thing to another of a similar nature, prove clearly even to the unintelligent--to say nothing of the others--that matters concerning medicine are not to be discovered by the logos. And I do not know how it has happened that this argument about methods has led clearly to the possibility that by the logos which consists in inference from the visible to the invisible nothing has been discovered, although this was not our purpose of intention, but we desired rather to show that not everything can be discovered by this logos. And there are other arguments too, besides this one, which conform to this aim and tend in the same direction. For if nothing is discovered by means of the logos in conjunction with experience, then one 'who knows the natures' can do everything without the aid of experience, and achieve a healing of the body by means of that whereto the logos alone leads and directs him, which is not inferior to the healing of one who possesses a knowledge of both these things. And one who bases his method of healing only on that whereto experience alone leads him, cannot possibly know anything technically or accomplish anything that is technical. But this is not the case; on the contrary, if 'those who know the natures' were familiar with the discussion, argument, and logos in matters concerning medicine but lacked the knowledge gained by experience, they would never carry out any operation of medicine well, however small and trivial. And as for those who in the practice of medicine follow that whereto simple experience alone leads them, we frequently find very many of them who in the practice of medicine have attained a high measure of excellence. And from this it is seen that experience by no means requires the logos, and that the logos is of no use in the art of medicine. But too much time has been spent in speaking and arguing on this theme, and it has prepared the way for part of what we need for what we propose to go on to prove.

* * * * *

I think that it would be better and more fitting for me to explain the difference between the two methods of drawing a conclusion. I shall not content myself with explaining them by saying in general terms that what is known as epilogism is the conclusion pointing to visible things, and what is called analogism is the conclusion pointing to invisible things, but I shall show in detail in the case of single particular things how each of these methods is to be recognized.

I shall begin with the things wherein you agree with us in saying that he who discovers the categories of medical science discovers them and he who learns them learns them by explanations with commentary and summaries. I would say to you: You follow a path which is different from the path we are pursuing. You say first of all, it is necessary for the natural condition to be discovered, and he who does not know this will not succeed in recognizing the unnatural state of things. Then you inquire as to the manner in which man took his origin by the uniting of the elements which you claim to have discovered and found by first using the logos and investigation of the elements in order to discover this. Then you examine the functions and say this is of use in finding out and learning about the affected parts and the diseased organs of the body more easily and readily. For you assert that if one knows about the natural functions of a certain organ, it is easy, should that function be deranged, to understand something of what is necessary for the diseased organ. And should he know this, and know the salient cause, then there is no further difficulty; on the contrary, it is easy and a simple thing to find the method of healing which will eliminate this cause. I, for my part, think that if you proceed in this fashion, you are fittingly plunged into doubts and contradictions by inquiry into the elements, and also that you must inevitably hold different opinions as to the natural functions, upon which there is no unanimity and agreement. Likewise too, there will be diversity of opinions with regard to diseases in addition to (diversity of) opinion about functions. Each one of you affirms a doctrine which is different from the doctrine of the others, just because none of you are satisfied with one single universal doctrine. Respecting the inference known as epilogism it is, as we say, directed towards visible things, and is an inference common and universally used by the whole of mankind, and wherein men are unanimous, and where there is no such thing as schism and diversity of opinion. This is very fit and proper, since it has been well tested and rectified, because visible things testify to its correctness. Never at any time can it be divergent or confused or combine two contradictory things. Concerning the conclusion, however, which is called analogism, because the invisible things cannot be perceived by the senses, the really sound argument does not become credible and the weak and mendacious argument cannot be shown up and destroyed. For this reason therefore, when differences of opinion arise with regard to an abscess in the bladder even before it becomes visible, a decision can be reached between them. For if we see an abscess appear after lancing with a lancet, then its appearance puts to shame him who says there is no abscess in the bladder, and proves his view to be wrong, and furnishes evidence that the opinion of the other people is correct; but if on lancing no abscess is to be seen, then the reverse is the case. In the same way stones in the bladder are tested empirically. Whether, however, the burning inflammation arising from the blood results from a hot substance which flows into the organ or from blood falling from the arteries and veins, or from things which cause violent heat and swelling, or that the atoms--these are parts which cannot be divided further--remain in the pores between the veins, and whether the disease known as phrenitis arises from lesions of the brain itself, or from lesions of the membranes surrounding it, or from the integument; all these are instances of things which cannot possibly be proved to be true or wrong by means of any visible symptom. For this reason it is possible in the case of the one to arrive at a decision and to distinguish between the diversity of opinions, but not in the case of the other. And if you wish to know this, then consider how it is possible for us to decide the differences of opinion between these men, whether by perception of the senses--but how could this be possible since these are things which cannot be perceived by the senses--or by the logos and convincing words, for this is certainly better. But 'convincing' is only a relative conception and differs in the case of each individual, representing something that is non-specific with regard to the nature of the thing itself; but is specific with regard to the destruction and mischief in which people who adhere to theories are involved. When, therefore, anyone attempts to decide between people who hold diverse opinions with regard to invisible things, only two possibilities are open to him: either he is totally unprejudiced and impartial so that he remains suspended, showing no inclination nor partisanship, or else he is one of those people who hold a decided opinion, and allows himself to be deceived by his own opinion, which inclines him to one of the opinions of those people who refer to him as umpire. Everyone who accepts the office of umpire inclines to something different from what the other inclines to, and in this way schism and separation occur amongst them. For there are some people amongst them, who are led to do so by their inclination to the sort of thing that would carry conviction to Erasistratos; and so they praise Erasistratos' view and reject the views of all other people, calling themselves for this reason Erasistrateans and band themselves together like capable soldiers who are led by a single leader. Other people, again, assert Praxagoras' view to be good and right; so you find that by their belief in him they are convinced by what carried conviction to Praxagoras. A fitting motto for these persons would be what Homer said about Odysseus: 'Greatly do we desire to be companies of Praxagoras, the noble, great-hearted.' Then you will find a third army, the disciples of Asclepiades, and you will find other people who have made Herophilos their leader, master, and director in all their affairs, others again accord Hippocrates this position. I am sure you will have understood--unless you are utterly ignorant and superficial--that it is the conclusion and the logos known as epilogism if it is a logos universally known and used, and a logos which they all employ, and concerning which there is complete unanimity, and which refers to visible things alone. But if it is a conclusion and a logos which only some individuals employ and use, and which others regard as incorrect, and which refers to invisible things only, then it is the conclusion and logos which men call analogism.

Likewise in affirming what is necessitated by something that is said or done, you will find two kinds of affirmation, one after the manner of the logos known as epilogism, concerning which there is unanimity, and the other after the manner of the logos known as analogism concerning which there is no unanimity.

Asclepiades, for instance, says it is not necessary and indeed not advisable to apply blood-letting to one suffering from phrenitis. On being asked the reason for this view, he says: 'Because this disease is due to the atoms not being found in their proper places in the pores of the cerebral membrane, and if you empty out the blood from the veins, it would not be of use in this disease, but would only weaken and diminish the strength (of the sick person).' Now when Asclepiades says this, I hear him make mention of the atoms and pores and of position in the cerebral membrane. This, however, is a view concerning invisible things, so his statement is one peculiar to himself, and is accepted and maintained by none but himself. Since this is the case with regard to his opinion, I must regard it as an analogism. Then another comes along and says: 'I do not say that I know, nor that I reject or deny anything of that which this man says, because he speaks of things which are highly invisible, and if you wish to hear what in this case has been evident to the eye, not once, nor twice, but very many times, I shall describe it to you. For I have seen very many sufferers from phrenitis who were treated by blood-letting. Those of them who were young and strong benefited greatly therefrom, but the others derived but small benefit. Now if you were not to admit in your own mind that I and the other physicians are correct, then question them about it.' The Empiricist would say: 'Anyone hearing this opinion would recognize it at once as a statement concerning visible things, containing nothing peculiar to one person rather than another, and having nothing to do with invisible things.' Should he then go to the other physicians, and find that this is something wherein they all agree, then I do not doubt but that he will be led thereby to consider as correct the conclusion known as epilogism which refers to visible things, and that he will prefer it to the conclusion known as analogism which refers to invisible things.

Similarly, one of the physicians may say: 'A person suffering from the disease known as loss of memory (stupor) must not be spoken to, since his disease is due to inflammation of the ceregral membrane, and motion is not good for any inflamed organ.' This is a statement which belongs to the method known as analogism since it deals with invisible things, and is a view which is asserted only by those who follow this method, and concerning which men are not all unanimous, and think the same about it. Then another comes and says: 'I have often observed that in every case when we sat by the bedside of a person sick of this disease which had him completely in his power and controlled him, if we did not rouse him and keep him awake, he was worse.' This is a statement which belongs to the method known as epilogism. On the whole the conclusion known as epilogism prescribes the doing of what should be done on the basis of the good or evil which is inherent in the thing and accompanies it, whereas the conclusion known as analogism prescribes action on the basis of the natures of things. If someone were to ask, for instance, what is the reason for not allowing the stretching of a luxation which is accompanied by a wound (? ulcer), the physician using the method known as analogism would base his answer on an inquiry into the nature of the joints and sinews, and the substance of each one of them, as well as into the nature of this malady, and would then construct his argument as to what action and treatment he considered necessary on the basis of this investigation. As for the physician who uses the method known as epilogism, he would say: The luxation which is accompanied by a wound must not be stretched, for were we to do so, the result would be convulsions and death. If anyone were to say to him: and why is this the case, his opinion would be that investigation into the causes of this is an unnecessary superfluity. Likewise anyone asking: why is dropsy--which is the gathering of water resulting from feverish complaints--such a serious disease, the Dogmatist would thereupon inquire into the nature and substance of fever and of the disease known as dropsy, and how it is originated in feverish diseases, and the reason for its being a serious complaint. The Empiricist, however, demands only a partial cause, and a relation of the symptoms which this disease brings in its train, and says: 'This kind of dropsy becomes serious because the fever does not leave the person suffering from it, besides the disease causes him to feel great pain, and torments him extremely.' Likewise you will find that in speaking of the bladder the Empiricist says: 'when the bladder is hard, and painful as well, this is a serious thing at any time, but it is most tormenting when combined with fever.' On his being asked for the reason, he produces a partial cause, and says: 'for in the pains arising in the bladder there is such severity that he suffers torments, and in addition to this the sick person is prone to be constipated when attacked by this disease.' The Dogmatist in a case of this kind will inquire into the functions and nature of the organ, and frames his statement as to the cause of this in accordance with these inquiries.

You will find, too, that the supporter of 'memory and observation' says: 'if a patient is found uncovering his feet--his feet not being very warm--and if he throws about his hands and feet, and puts them down aimlessly, this is a bad sign.' Now were he to be asked for the reason of this, he would say: 'Because this points to nervous irritation'. But the Dogmatist, on the other hand, would again commit himself to lengthy babble and useless theories, because he is not satisfied with plain observation, but must needs inquire into the substance and nature of the disease. Now, if you consider the question asked about a person who suffers from sleeplessness, what is the reason why insomnia and perpetual sleeplessness become so serious and severe that one is unable to sleep either by night or by day--you will find that the Dogmatist sets to work to consider the nature of sleeping and waking, and to find out what happens to the pneuma within the body so that it is affected by each of these things. But you will find that the supporter of memory and observation in saying: 'if one cannot sleep either by day or by night, it is a very bad sign' makes an obvious thing the cause and says: 'because this man's sleeplessness arises either from pain and fatigue, or is a sign that he is suffering from phrenitis'. Since this is how matters stand, it is perfectly clear and obvious that a difference exists between each logos and conclusion used by the Dogmatists, and the logos and conclusion known as epilogism, which is universally used by everybody, namely that epilogism seeks the guidance of visible things--and it is from those that it seeks confirmation of its truth and rightness--whereas the conclusion called analogism, avoids visible things and arrives at an invisible foundation and root, which owing to its invisibility is peculiar to some people and not shared by others, namely the elements and functions. For if the dogmatic physician wishes to explain the cause of sleep or fever, or the burning inflammation arising from the blood, or pleurisy or phrenitis, or indeed any of those effects caused by nature of of the ailments arising from opposition to it, then since he has received many diverse views on the matter he must inevitably discover some special view of his own out of this diversity of views which does not command universal acceptance, nor conform to the method known as epilogism. This is the reason why those who do not accept his conclusion and do not agree with him upon it are very numerous.

4.b. Galen on the Natural Faculties*

XIII

Now the extent of exactitude and truth in the doctrines of Hippocrates may be gauged, not merely from the way in which his opponents are at variance with obvious facts, but also from the various subjects of natural research themselves--the functions of animals, and the rest. For those people who do not believe that there exists in any part of the animal a faculty for attracting *its own special quality* are compelled repeatedly to deny obvious facts. For instance, Asclepiades, the physician did this in the case of the kidneys. That these are organs for secreting [separating out] the urine, was the belief not only of Hippocrates, Diocles, Erasistratus, Praxagoras, and all other physicians of eminence, but practically every butcher is aware of this, from the fact that he daily observes both the position of the kidneys and the duct (termed the ureter) which runs from each kidney into the bladder, and from this arrangement he infers their characteristic use and faculty. But, even leaving the butchers aside, all people who suffer either from frequent dysuria or from retention of urine call themselves 'Nephritics," when they feel pain in the loins and pass sandy matter in their water.

I do not suppose that Asclepiades ever saw a stone which had been passed by one of these sufferers, or observed that this was preceded by a sharp pain in the region between kidneys and bladder as the stone traversed the ureter, or that, when the stone was passed, both the pain and the retention at once ceased. It is worth while, then, learning how his theory accounts for the presence of urine in the bladder, and one is forced to marvel at the ingenuity of a man who puts aside these broad, clearly visible routes, and postulates others which are narrow, invisible--indeed, entirely imperceptible. His view, in fact, is that the fluid which we drink passes into the bladder by being resolved into vapours, and that, when these have been again condensed, it thus regains its previous form, and turns from vapour into fluid. He simply looks upon the bladder as a sponge or a piece of wool, and not as the perfectly compact and impervious body that it is, with two very strong coats. For if we say that the vapours pass through these coats, why should they not pass through the peritoneum and the diaphragm, thus filling the whole abdominal cavity and thorax with water? "But," says he, "of course the peritoneal coat is more impervious than the bladder, and this is why it keeps out the vapours, while the bladder admits them." Yet if he had ever practised anatomy, he might have known that the outer coat of the bladder springs from the peritoneum and is essentially the same as it, and that the inner coat, which is peculiar to the bladder, is more than twice as thick as the former.

---

* Reprinted by permission of the publishers and the Loeb Classical Library from Arthur John Brock, translator, Galen, *On the Natural Faculties* (Cambridge, Mass.: Harvard University Press).

Perhaps, however, it is not the thickness or thinness of the coats, but the *situation* of the bladder, which is the reason for the vapours being carried into it? On the contrary, even if it were probable for every other reason that the vapours accumulate there, yet the situation of the bladder would be enough in itself to prevent this. For the bladder is situated below, whereas vapours have a natural tendency to rise upwards; thus they would fill all the region of the thorax and lungs long before they came to the bladder.

But why do I mention the situation of the bladder, peritoneum, and thorax? For surely, when the vapours have passed through the coats of the stomach and intestines, it is in the space between these and the peritoneum that they will collect and become liquefied (just as in dropsical subjects it is in this region that most of the water gathers). Otherwise the vapours must necessarily pass straight forward through everything which in any way comes in contact with them, and will never come to a standstill. But, if this be assumed, then they will traverse not merely the peritoneum but also the epigastrium, and will become dispersed into the surrounding air; otherwise they will certainly collect under the skin.

Even these considerations, however, our present-day Ascelpiadeans attempt to answer, despite the fact that they always get soundly laughed at by all who happen to be present at their disputations on these subjects--so difficult an evil to get rid of is this sectarian partizanship, so excessively resistant to all cleansing processes, harder to heal than any itch!

Thus, one of our Sophists who is a thoroughly hardened disputer and as skilful a master of language as there ever was, once got into a discussion with me on this subject; so far from being put out of countenance by any of the above-mentioned considerations, he even expressed his surprise that I should try to overturn obvious facts by ridiculous arguments! "For," said he, "one may clearly observe any day in the case of any bladder, that, if one fills it with water or air and then ties up its neck and squeezes it all round, it does not let anything out at any point, but accurately retains all its contents. And surely," said he, "if there were any large and perceptible channels coming into it from the kidneys the liquid would run out through these when the bladder was squeezed, in the same way that it entered?" Having abruptly made these and similar remarks in precise and clear tones, he concluded by jumping up and departing--leaving me as though I were quite incapable of finding any plausible answer!

The fact is that those who are enslaved to their sects are not merely devoid of all sound knowledge, but they will not even stop to learn! Instead of listening, as they ought, to the reason why liquid can enter the bladder through the ureters, but is unable to go back again the same way,--instead of admiring Nature's artistic skill--they refuse to learn; they even go so far as to scoff, and maintain that the kidneys, as well as many other things, have been made by Nature *for no purpose!* And some of them who had allowed themselves to be shown the ureters coming from the kidneys and becoming implanted in the bladder, even had the audacity to say that these also existed for no purpose; and others said that they were spermatic ducts, and that this was why they were inserted into the neck of the bladder and not into its cavity. When, therefore, we had demonstrated to them the real spermatic ducts entering the neck of the bladder lower down than the ureters, we supposed that, if we had not done so before, we would now at least draw them away from their false assumptions, and convert them forthwith to the opposite view. But even this they presumed to dispute, and said that it was not to be wondered at that the semen should remain longer in these latter ducts, these being more constricted, and that it should flow quickly down the ducts which came from the kidneys, seeing that these were well dilated. We were, therefore, further compelled to show them in a still living animal, the urine plainly running out through the ureters into the bladder; even thus we hardly hoped to check their nonsensical talk.

Now the method of demonstration is as follows. One has to divide the peritoneum in front of the ureters, then secure these with ligatures, and next, having bandaged up the animal, let him go (for he will not continue to urinate). After this one loosens the external bandages and shows the bladder empty and the ureters quite full and distended--in fact almost on the point of rupturing; on removing the ligature from them, one then plainly sees the bladder becoming filled with urine.

When this has been made quite clear, then, before the animal urinates, one has to tie a ligature round his penis and then to squeeze the bladder all over; still nothing goes back through the ureters to the kidneys. Here, then, it becomes obvious that not only in a dead animal, but in one which is still living, the ureters are prevented from receiving back the urine from the bladder. These observations having been made, one now loosens the ligature from the animal's penis and allows him to urinate, then again ligatures one of the ureters and leaves the other to discharge into the bladder. Allowing, then, some time to elapse, one now demonstrates that the ureter which was ligatured is obviously full and distended on the side next to the kidnesy, while the other one--that from which the ligature had been taken--is itself flaccid, but has filled the bladder with urine. Then, again, one must divide the full ureter, and demonstrate how the urine spurts out of it, like blood in the operation of venesection; and after this one cuts through the other also, and both being thus divided, one bandages up the animal externally. Then when enough time seems to have elapsed, one takes off the bandages; the bladder will now be found empty, and the whole region between the intestines and the peritoneum full of urine, as if the animal were suffering from dropsy. Now, if anyone will but test this for himself on an animal, I think he will strongly condemn the rashness of Asclepiades, and if he also learns the reason why nothing regurgitates from the bladder into the ureters, I think he will be persuaded by this also of the forethought and art shown by Nature in relation to animals.

CHAPTER TWO

THE TRANSMISSION OF ANCIENT SCIENCE

I. Narrative

A. The Byzantine Tradition

The great scientific works of antiquity were preserved by a series of accidents that border on the incredible. The wonder is not that we have lost so much but that anything at all survived to influence the growth of science in the west. A brief glance at the physical and social conditions surrounding the transmission of works of ancient science will prove instructive.

It is worth underlining the point that all the scientific treatises of real worth were written in Greek. This meant that they were inaccessible to the vast majority of people in the Latin West from the very beginning of Roman dominance. There were, of course, men like Scipio Africanus, Cicero and Seneca who learned Greek and fully appreciated the Greek heritage. The situation here may be compared with the modern one in which knowledge of Russian might be considered to be of importance to an intellectual in the West. This analogy points up one further obstacle in the way of the Latin assimilation of Greek science. The modern western scientist knows that his Russian counterpart is doing work of first-rate quality and he wishes to know of it. Hence the flourishing of professional scientific translators. By and large, the Roman aristocrat found Greek science irrelevant to his major concern which was the intellectual basis for morality or politics. The Greek scientific achievement tended to be ignored or, as we shall see, adulterated and diluted by Rome.

The materials and techniques used for the preservation of Greek scientific ideas made it extremely probable that they would not survive. Papyrus and even parchment are excellent materials for recording thoughts in the short term. They do, however, deteriorate with time and climate is crucial for their preservation. In the dry climate of North Africa and the Middle East, parchment and papyrus can survive for centuries. In the dampness of western Europe, with its extremes of heat and cold, papyrus and parchment soon mold, crumble and rot. Unless, of course, manuscripts are periodically copied or carefully cherished. To do either, one must be interested in their contents and this interest was lacking in Rome.

To the ravages of nature must be added the barbarity of man. The ancient world was attacked from two sides in the early centuries of the Christian era. From the north came the Gauls and Goths; from the south came the Arabs. We should not exaggerate the extent of their barbarism. Both groups had lived adjacent to the civilizations of Greece and Rome for centuries. Their leaders fully recognized the value of civilization, if only as it could be applied to heighten their own political power. Nevertheless, the barbarian incursions necessarily destroyed much of ancient culture. The sacking of cities inevitably destroyed manuscripts and military commanders were not always alert to the value of the contents of buildings they put to the torch. The Arab general who reportedly burned the books of the Museum of Alexandria in 640 to heat baths for his soldiers, undoubtedly felt that he was merely rewarding his troops for their valor in taking the city.

The fate of the scientific works that survived was three-fold. In the Eastern Empire which was able successfully to resist both Northern barbarians and Arabs, the Greek tradition and manuscripts survived at Byzantium. The level of original thought was low, but the heritage was preserved. The fall of Constantinople in 1453 led to a massive injection of Classical Greek culture into the West at a crucial point in European history The Arab conquests were so rapid and the Arab thirst for culture so avid that the Islamic explosion only momentarily affected the ancient corpus of learning. Some treasures were lost, but others were cherished and rapidly incorporated into the Islamic intellectual structure. It was through the Arabs that medieval man was introduced to the full flood of ancient science. It was in the Latin West that the heritage of ancient science was smallest. From the fall of Rome (traditionally dated 476 A.D. with the deposition of the last Roman Emperor), until the twelfth century when translations from the Arabic came into Europe, the medieval intellectual had to rely on meagre pickings from the ancient scientific corpus. This three-fold fate of ancient science is worth looking at in some detail.

In Byzantium, there was a continuity of the ancient tradition. Latin had never displaced Greek as the common language of intellectual discourse, so there was no problem of translation. The original manuscripts were copied and circulated, although interest in them was confined to a very narrow circle of intellectuals concentrated at Constantinople. The works of Aristotle, Galen, Euclid and Ptolemy were preserved and read. The more philosophical writers, particularly Plato and Aristotle, were intensely studied for the intellectual vigor of Byzantium was concentrated and focused upon theological questions which, it was hoped, could be illuminated by philosophical enlightenment. Pure and detailed scientific works might be studied for the mental discipline they created (Euclid's geometry, for example) but only rarely were the scientific results of antiquity criticized or questioned. The great exception is to be found in the writings of John Philoponus who flourished at the end of the fifth and beginning of the sixth century. Philoponus took serious exception to the Aristotelian doctrine of violent motion. The medium through which a projectile moves cannot serve to preserve the motion of the body. Rather, he insisted, the medium acts merely to resist the motion. This viewpoint forced Philoponus to face squarely the philosophical problem raised by the persistence of an effect (motion of a projectile) after the cause (the act of throwing) had ceased to act. Cause must equal effect yet, in purely temporal terms, here seemed to be a case where this philosophical axiom appeared to be violated. One way out of this dilemma was to invent a cause which did persist after the impelling force was removed. Such a cause could still be conceived in Aristotelean terms as a *form* which the act of throwing impressed upon the projectile, much as the placing of an iron ball near a fire impressed the form of heat in the ball. When the ball was removed from the fire, it retained its heat for some time, the form of heat being dissipated only gradually in a cooler atmosphere. So, too, the act of throwing gave an *impetus* to a body which kept it in motion after the withdrawal of the impelling force. The theory of impetus was to be important in the discussions of dynamics which occurred in the fourteenth century. [Readings, Medieval Science, Chapter Three, p. 316]. Philoponus' work however was not known in the West until late.

B. The Place of Science in Islam

The creation and expansion of Islam created quite different conditions for the preservation and transmission of ancient science. Here was no antiquarian attempt to preserve a heritage but a vital assimilation of ancient science to serve a vigorous new culture. Islam was no mere episode but an integral and major development in world history. Islamic science was more than Greek science in Arabic translation. The philosophers of Islam eagerly learned from their Greek predecessors but they transmuted this heritage as well as transmitted it. What they passed on to the Latin West in the eleventh, twelfth and thirteenth centuries was Greek science with a definite and often important Islamic flavor.

The culture of Islam is dominated by the life and work of Mohammed. Mohammed was born in Mecca about the year 570 A.D. His father died before he was born and his mother died while he was still a child. He was raised by a grandfather and an uncle and, as a youth, traveled widely on business for them. At 25, he married a wealthy widow fifteen years his senior and took over the administration of her business interests. Mohammed came from the commercial class of Arabia that lived from the profits of the caravan trade of the Middle East. Mecca and Medina, the two Arabian cities of central importance to early Islamic development, were commercial centers in which the tribal structure of the desert Arab culture was undergoing severe strain. New commercial and political interests were forcing the realignment of loyalties which threatened the old tribal basis of society. These strains were reflected in religion where the old pagan gods came under attack. Mohammed was not the first Arab trader to be exposed to the doctrines of the Jews or the Christians, both of whom insisted upon their devotion to one god, not many. The effect of this contact on Mohammed, however, was deep and permanent. He clearly felt dissatisfaction with the pagan gods of Mecca but was not prepared to deny his Arab blood and accept the monotheism of Jew or Christian. One night in the Arab month of Ramadan, 610 A.D., he received a revelation in which the angel Gabriel appeared to him and commanded him to "Recite" and who then proceeded to dispense verses to him. The *Koran* means *The Recital* in Arabic and this holiest of Islamic books contains the verses which were revealed to Mohammed from 610 to his death on

June 8, 632.

Armed with his vision, Mohammed went forth to convert his fellows to Islam--literally, the surrender to God. Progress was slow and the circle of converts only gradually grew beyond Mohammed's household. When his doctrine did reach out to attract others, it also generated opposition and on July 16, 622 Mohammed and his disciples felt it wise to leave Mecca and flee to Medina. This migration, known as the Hegira or Hijrah, marks the beginning of Islamic chronology. Muslims date historical events from this move in which Mohammed separated himself and his followers from paganism and set up Islam as a separate community. The new religion met with hard times but continued to grow under the wise leadership of Mohammed. By 629, Mohammed was able to lead a pilgrimage back to Mecca where the old pagan site of the Kaaba was recognized as a holy place in the new religion. In 632, Mohammed could insist that only Muslims be allowed at the holy places. By his death, the conversion of the entire Arab people was well under way. With this conversion, the Arabs burst upon a surprised world. Within less than a century, the warriors of Islam had penetrated as far West as the Atlantic, North beyond the Pyrenees until hurled back by Charles Martel at Poitiers and Eastwards to India. The primary instrument was the sword and so long as the Arabs conquered, they needed no further arguments. It was only when they settled down to enjoy the fruits of their victories that they ran into troubles. They had no desire to exterminate the peoples whom they had conquered. Indeed, Christians and Jews--the People of the Book--with whom Islam shared the earlier revelations of the Old and New Testaments were treated with respect and permitted to practice their religions freely. Intellectual interchange became both possible and probable. With it were created new demands upon Islam. The conqueror's sword was to no avail against the keen edge of logic wielded by a Christian theologian or a Talmudic scholar. The embattled Arab intellectual had to fall back upon his revelation, the Koran. As the most important work in Islam, the Koran is worthy of some attention here for it served both as stimulus and ultimate barrier to the progress of Islamic science.

The Koran is unlike either the Old or the New Testaments. It is neither the story of Mohammed and his relations with Allah, nor the history of the Arab people, but a series of revelations. It consists of 114 chapters, called *surahs* made up of 6,236 verses. During Mohammed's lifetime, these *surahs* were committed to memory by professional remembrancers but some were already being written down on palm-leaves, stones and any other material available. There is a unity about the Koran that is lacking in Scripture, undoubtedly due to the fact that the Islamic revelation came through one man in one place, while Jewish and Christian accounts are the products of many different men writing at different times in different places. There are a series of themes that run through the Koran. The primary one is the oneness of God. The religion of Islam is an uncompromising monotheism in which all knowledge and all power is located in Allah. Allah created the universe, populated it with his creatures to whom he gave their natures and crowned his creation with man. Man's primary duty is to submit himself to the will of Allah. Those who do, will find eternal life in a paradise in which streams run with wine, fruits are for the plucking and eating, and virgins serve the faithful. Those who defy Allah or refuse to accept his word as revealed in the Koran, will be subjected to the pains of eternal damnation. Man's first duty, therefore, is to recognize Allah. From this internal act come external actions pleasing to Allah. Kindness to orphans and charity to all are good works of which Allah approves. There follow further dietary and religious rules, all intended to glorify Allah and preserve human purity. There are also legal principles which are based upon the practical realities of Arabic life. There is little of the sexual puritanism to be found in the New Testament. Where Jesus found a man guilty of adultery if he lusted after a woman in his mind, the Koran recognizes and legalizes both polygamy and carnal usage of slave women.

What is striking to the Westerner is the repetition of the basic theme that Allah is all powerful and that disobedience to his will brings catastrophe. The stories of Moses and Pharaoh, of Lot and the cities of the plain, of the destruction of the Arabic tribes of Aad and Thamoud on account of their sins, are told and re-told to emphasize Allah's power. There are no subtle shadings or finely spun metaphysics--only the simple but overpowering command, "Submit." It was obedience to this command that led the Arabs to the conquest of most of the Mediterranean world. The problem which faced the rulers of the Islamic world was whether submission to the will of Allah as prescribed by the Koran would suffice to consolidate and preserve the Islamic empire. In some areas, the answer clearly was yes. Islamic law and the principles of administration could be firmly based on the Koran and the Mohammedan revelation became the keystone of Islamic thought in these areas. In other fields, the answer was not so easy to discern. Could the subtle thrusts of Christian and Hebrew theologians be parried by mere recitation of selected *surahs*? Could the practical problems of navigation, geography, the calendar and agriculture be attacked through revelation or should experience and the ancients be invoked? Was the nature of Allah's creation of any interest or importance to the true Believer or was it enough to know Allah's will and obey? These were some of the questions that were raised once the initial energy of the expansion of Islam had spent itself. They are clearly relevant to the history of science in Islam. Before considering the Islamic response to them in detail, it will be useful first to sketch out briefly the main outlines of the history of the contact between Islamic intellectuals and antiquity, on the one hand, and the cosmos on the other.

The conquering Arabs who overran the Middle East in the seventh and eighth centuries traveled with negligible intellectual baggage. The story of the burning of the books of the Library at Alexandria in 640, although challenged by some historians, probably contains a kernel of truth. Literacy was not widespread in Islam and books must have seemed trifles if not positively dangerous to those who could not read them. The stimulus to literacy came with the establishing of the written text of the Koran in the early years of Islamic expansion. The desire to explore the literature beyond the Koran grew out of contact with the literate peoples of the conquered territories of the East. The critical date here is 750 A.D. when the followers of Abu al-Abbas took Damascus and founded the Abbasid empire with its center in Persia. Abu al-Abbas' successor as Caliph (from Khalifat Rasul Allah--Successor of the Apostle of God) was al-Mansur who built his capital at Baghdad which rapidly became the center of the Eastern Islamic Empire. In the West, Islamic civilization flowered in Spain under the Ummayads, the sworn enemies of the Abbasids. In both areas, contact with non-Islamic peoples led to the first intellectual surge of Islam.

The Islamic fascination with Greek thought appears to have two sources. Al-Mansur and his successors were intent upon turning Baghdad into the center of the world. The splendor of the Abbasid court was to reflect the splendor of the Caliph and in their efforts to prove to the world that they were not illiterate barbarians, the Caliphs surrounded themselves with poets, artists and learned men. The Baghdad of Harun al-Rashid (reigned 786-809) is depicted in *The Arabian Nights* and its wealth, power and culture was meant to impress rulers as far away as Charlemagne. Constant contact with Byzantium through diplomatic envoys revealed to the Court the treasures of Greek thought. The presence in Persia of Persian scholars, Nestorian Christians and a famous medical school at Jundishapur all served to stimulate the translation of Greek works into Arabic. Further attention was focused upon the Greek heritage by the contact between Islamic and Christian theologians. There was an important colony of Nestorian Christians in Persia who were trained in the use of Greek philosophy for theological purposes and who were clearly better equipped than their Islamic conquerors to argue the fine points of the attributes of God. The Islamic intellectual found himself in much the same position as the early Christian Fathers of the West. Greek philosophy was both pagan and abominable but knowledge of it was absolutely essential if the true faith were to be preserved and defended. Thus, in the eighth century, there was an irresistible drive to assimilate Greek learning. The desire for theological support guaranteed a broad base; the princely ambitions and vanities of the Caliphs provided the necessary financial support. The result was the relatively rapid transmission of Greek science and philosophy to the Arab world for the translations made in Persia traveled almost immediately to the intellectual centers of Islam at Cairo in Egypt and Cordova in Spain. The result was not always everything to be desired. In the process of translation from Greek into Syriac and from thence into Arabic, the chances for clerical errors or honest mistakes were legion. The further transmission from Arabic into Latin multiplied the opportunities for error and the resultant works in the Latin West were often so distorted that their original authors would have been hard put to recognize them.

The "Age of Translation" extended through the tenth century, during which time most of the works of Greek science which have survived were turned into Arabic. The very availability of translations served as a stimulus for further inquiry. An important element in the growth of science has been the way in which men have carried on a dialogue with one another as well as with Nature. Such was the case in Islam. For example, the translation of the medical works of Galen was undertaken by Hunayn ibn Ishāq (d. ca. 873 or 877), the greatest of the translators, who was himself a physician. While he fully respected the greatness of Galen, he did not hesitate to criticize, modify and add to his teachings in original treatises of his own. Similarly, Arabic geographers appreciated the skill of their Greek predecessors but felt free to correct them when later observations proved the earlier ones false. Even in philosophy, the greater Arab commentators such as Ibn Sina (Avicenna) and Ibn Rushd (Averroes) disputed in print with their masters, Aristotle and Plato, and pointed out inconsistencies in logic or errors in observations of nature.

The demands made upon the Arabs by the practice of empire was a third source of stimulus to the study of Greek science. Geography has already been mentioned and its utility is obvious. Any administrator wishes to know the extent of the territory he administers as precisely as possible. The military aspects of empire demand an accurate knowledge of terrain. Commercial interests were concerned with the problems of navigation and the course of sea and land routes for commercial purposes. Finally, the leisure class which the exploitation of empire created was an eager audience for tales of the far-away and the picturesque. All these interests were served by the writings of a man such as al-Biruni (973-1051) whose work on India is a model of its kind. He was a keen observer trained in mathematics and astronomy who was able to describe what he saw with precision and accuracy. The expansion of Empire also accounts for another important aspect of Arabic science, namely its eclecticism. The primary element, as we have stressed, was Greek but the conquest of the Middle East brought the Arabs into contact with non-Greek sources of science as well. Particularly important was the influence of India whose medical, astronomical and mathematical heritage was absorbed into Islam. Non-Greek sources often served to stimulate criticism of Greek ideas as when Indian atomistic concepts collided with Greek ideas of the plenum. The so-called Arabic numerals are of Indian origin and their eager acceptance by Arab mathematicians gave a significant impulsion to the development of Arab mathematics.

Finally, there was the stimulus to knowledge of nature provided by the religion of Islam itself. This influence is a complex one for it worked both for and against the study of nature. Mohammed, himself, according to tradition, had praised the study of medicine. Astronomy was necessary for the correct practice of the Muslim rites. The believer faces Mecca when he prays; religious times of the years, particularly the holy month of Ramadan must be determined astronomically; and even the times when the faithful should pray during the day require astronomical aid in the absence of mechanical clocks. The Koran exhorts the faithful to the study of Allah's creation. "Can you not see how He created the seven heavens one above the other, placing in them the moon for a light and the sign for a lantern?" asks Noah in one Surah. Another clearly directs men to the contemplation of the Heavens.

> It was He that gave the sun his brightness and the moon her light, ordaining her phases that you may learn to compute the seasons and the years. He created them only to manifest the truth. He makes plain His revelations to men of understanding.
>
> In the alternation of night and day, and in all that Allah has created in the heavens and the earth, there are signs for righteous men.

The signs of Allah were not confined to the heavens. In a description of the silkworm, an Arabic author explained: "This worm is a mighty example of the manifestation of the power of the Artificer with whom none may be compared, . . . the Creator of 'Be, and it was,' who from the shine of such an insignificant worm produces such elegant garments."* From this "sign" one could read the glory and greatness of Allah. Other "signs" were less easily interpreted. "Allah coins metaphors for men. He has knowledge of all things," states the Koran. To understand the divine metaphors is to understand Allah and draw closer to Him. Thus it was possible to approach the natural world as an expression of the Divine will, rather than simply as a cosmic order. Natural phenomena, then, were not simply phenomena but metaphors which concealed a higher and divine meaning. If one could only discover the key to the metaphor of nature, then knowledge of the *true* meaning of the divine creation could be made available to man. It is this line of thought that led some Arabic scientists along the mystical way to science. Pythagorean number theory lay ready to hand and numerology was to flourish in Islam. Ptolemy's *Tetrabiblos* on astrology provided another cipher, once translated, for the reading of the heavenly metaphors. Astrology flourished at the courts of Baghdad and Cordova. The mystical art of alchemy, outlined in manuscripts from Alexandria, offered still another path to the comprehension of the Divine plan. In all these cases, the basic drive was theological rather than philosophical or scientific but numerology, astrology and alchemy were to remain part of the scientific scene until early modern times. Their effects on the evolution of truly scientific thought was generally baneful but certain beneficial aspects deserve notice. Numerology not only bred nonsense but also the faith that Truth was to be found in numbers, that the universe was basically mathematical, and that the Divine metaphor was ultimately expressible in numerical ratios. This was the faith that sustained a Johann Kepler as well as the hosts of numerologists of the Latin Middle Ages and the Renaissance. Astrology led to the creation of more accurate stellar and planetary tables as well as to the perfection, if not the invention, of such a fundamental astronomical instruments as the astrolabe and the armillary sphere. Alchemy generated more than

---

* Quoted in G. E. von Gruenbaum, *Islam, Essays in the Nature and Growth of a Cultural Tradition*, New York, 1961, p. 122, note 9.

its fair share of gibberish, but it also produced some of the basic chemical techniques upon which a more rational and empirical chemistry could be built.

The attempt to decipher the Divine metaphor exposed the deep anti-intellectual streak in Islam. Mohammed could urge everyone to "Seek knowledge from the cradle to the tomb, even as far as China," but the knowledge to be sought was carefully circumscribed. It was useful knowledge and utility was defined in terms of religious orthodoxy. "Knowledge is obligatory only in so far as is requisite for acting rightly," wrote an Islamic theologian. The pursuit of science may simply be a waste of time or even positively dangerous if it should lead a man to wrong ideas about Allah, his creation and/or man's obligations to Allah and his fellows. Knowledge of the laws of nature might lead to a weakening of one's faith in the omnipotence of Allah. The subtleties of philosophy might seduce one away from the true faith. In the last analysis, revelation was all one needed to know; the rest was superficial or dangerous. The anti-scientific attitude was clearly expressed by al-Ghazzali, the greatest of the orthodox Islamic philosophers. A science is to be considered blameworthy, according to al-Ghazzali, when

> delving into it does not benefit one with knowledge. . . . It is like investigating the mysteries of divinity which the philosophers and theologians have attempted without success. No one has been able to comprehend these mysteries . . . except the prophets and saints. One must forbid men to look for these mysteries and must turn then to the pronouncements of religious law, wherein there is sufficient proof for the believer to be content with. How many men have embarked on these sciences and harmed themselves, and would have been better off in religion had they not done so! . . . Many a person benefits by his ignorance of some matters.*

Islam, it may be recalled, means submission to God, not the active search for his attributes. Better to save one's soul than decipher the mysteries of the cosmos. It is no coincidence that al-Ghazzali lived (1058-1111) at the point in time when Arabic science began to decline. Science and philosophy were dangers to faith. The pursuit of the one threatened the purity of the other and one or the other must disappear. It is of some historical interest that Islam made the conscious choice of faith over science. From the twelfth century on, Islamic science was doomed but before it died, it was passed on to the Latin West. It is now time to look at this legacy in some detail, field by field. The catalogue that follows can only serve to give a slight idea of the full impact of Islamic learning upon Latin Christendom.

1. Institutions of Learning

The religion of Islam led rapidly to the creation of educational institutions for its preservation and dissemination.

---

* Quoted in Grunebaum, *op. cit.*, 118.

The first place in which learning was served in Islam was the mosque and educational institutions have traditionally been connected with the mosque and supported by religious endowments. Under the second caliph, Umar, the mosque began to serve as a school wherein the Koran was recited and the prophetic tradition was passed on. To this rudimentary instruction soon was added the teaching of Arabic grammar and literature. This teaching formed the nucleus for both the elementary school, open to both boys and girls, and the advanced centers of learning which were to become the first universities of the Middle Ages. The University at Cairo was to emerge as particularly important in the preservation of Islamic faith and orthodoxy. By and large, these institutions were not vital scientific centers for their devotion to orthodoxy led them to approach the Greek scientific heritage with caution, if not suspicion.

Institutions of scientific learning and research tended to form around the courts, rather than the mosques. The founding of Baghdad in 762 by al-Mansur created a natural center for science in the East, while Cordova in the West became the cultural capital of the Ummayads. It was to these centers that scholars and translators flocked, assured of royal support and favor.

The assimilation of ancient learning was rapid. It is worth here simply listing the ancient authors whose works were translated and made available to Islamic savants.

In mathematics, the philosophical influence of the Pythagoreans, Plato, and the Neo-Platonists was early felt for obvious reasons. The number mysticism and general other-worldliness of these philosophies had penetrated Persian learned circles long before the Arab conquest and was, therefore, ready at hand for those Arab intellectuals who were curious about the beliefs of their newly conquered peoples. This fact undoubtedly influenced the choice of early translators from the Greek who were eager to explore the mathematical and astronomical worlds of the Greeks. The *Elements* of Euclid were translated about 827, as was the *Syntaxis mathematekeis* of Claudius Ptolemy. It was at this time that this latter work was dubbed al-megiste--the greatest--by its Arab translator, from which comes the Latin title, the *Almagest*. Ptolemy's great work on astrology, the *Tetrabiblos*, was also turned into Arabic in the early ninth century. These basic treatises permitted Islamic scholars to undertake original investigations which, in turn, created new needs to be satisfied by further translations. The higher mathematics of Apollonios of Perga (conic sections), Archimedes and Diophantos (algebra) were made available to Arabic mathematicians in the ninth and early tenth centuries.

In astronomy, Ptolemy reigned supreme from the earliest years of Islamic astronomical interest. A rival was introduced with the translation of the astronomical works of Aristotle by Hunayn ibn Ishq and his school. As we shall see, the physical scheme of Aristotelian homocentric spheres was wedded to the mathematical hypothesis of Ptolemy to create a rather clumsy physico-mathematical model of the cosmos.

Next to astronomy and mathematics, medicine was the science which most intensely attracted the attention of the Islamic world. Here again Hunyan ibn Ishaq was the key figure. He personally translated some eighteen Galenic works and from his school came the translations of the works of Hippocrates as well. By the middle of the ninth century or thereabouts, the complete curriculum of the ancient medical school of Alexandria was available to Arab students of medicine. The *materia medica* had obvious connections with medicine and the great pharmacological works of Crateus and Dioscorides were translated in this period.

Works on natural history, geography and cosmology followed as the business of translation was organized. Here the caliph al-Mamun played a major role by founding the "house of Wisdom" at Baghdad and placing Hunayn ibn Ishaq in charge. Emissaries were sent to Constantinople in search of manuscripts and alumni from the school at Jundishapur were pressed into service. By the end of the tenth century, most of the Greek texts which we have today had been translated into Arabic.

The organization of translation was accompanied by the founding of special institutions for the study of specific sciences. We owe the creation of astronomical observatories as places of observation and centers of astronomical instruction to Islam. The first Islamic observatory was built by al-Mamun in Baghdad around 828 and was headed by two famous astronomers, al-Naubakht and al-Khwarazmi. Other observatories were built at Raqqa, Shiraz, Hamadan, Toledo and Seville. Some of these institutions were impressive centers of learning and received royal support from the rulers of Islam. The observatory at Maragha was begun in 1261 by order of Hulagu, the grandson of Genghis Khan and had a library of some 400,000 books associated with it. Its instruments were of excellent quality, to be surpassed only by those built especially for Tycho Brahe in the sixteenth century. The "professors" were all notable philosophers and astronomers. There was even a Chinese savant on the staff who passed Chinese astronomical ideas on to his associates.

The finest observatory in Islam was that built in the fifteenth century at Samarkand by Ulugh Beg, the grandson of Tamerlane. It was this observatory, together with the one at Istanbul, which served as the models for observatories in the West. The activities at such centers are vivdly described in the letter from the mathematician Ghiyath al-Din al-Kashami to his father which follows.*

> We now come to the subject of the Observatory. His Majesty, may God keep his realm and preserve *his* sovereignty, had seen the constructions at the Marāgha observatory in his childhood, but he had said that he had not seen them with a discerning eye. Before the arrival of this servant they had told His Majesty that the observatory was the place underneath the top (of the observatory hill) where people live (sit).

**Science and Civilization in Islam* by Seyyed Hossein Nasr, with a Preface by Giorgio De Santillana (Cambridge, Mass.: Harvard Univ. Press, 1968), pp. 81-87.

Two brass rings of six *gaz* diameter had been cast, for the measurement of the obliquity and solar observations, in accordance with Ptolemy's directions, unaware of the fact that, as that instrument was not free from defects, astronomers had brought about many refinements after Ptolemy's time and that they had deviated from the ring constructed by him.

No one knew either what the *geometrical pulpit* standing in the middle of the building (or, constructions) of the Marāgha Observatory was and for what purpose it was constructed. This servant brought the matter to His Majesty's knowledge and explained the divergences which may arise from their above-mentioned instrument. I also pointed out that in Adud al Dawla's time a ring was constructed the diameter of which was ten *gaz* and that the present one was smaller than that ring, adding that at the Marāgha Observatory they had constructed a *geometrical pulpit* instead, which is called *suds-i Fakhrī*, and that this had a diameter of six *gaz*.

His Majesty ordered the ring to be broken, and they made it into another instrument which this obedient servant had described. The construction of the building of the observatory too was ordered to be carried out in accordance with the explanations given by this servant. All these circumstances and other similar matters were made known to the notables of the country.

In like manner, every day and every week something new comes up, and through the felicity of your Lordship's magnanimity, this servant extracts it from the sphere of difficulty, with the mallet of preparedness, with the greatest ease.

One day His Majesty, may God preserve his realm and sovereignty, was busy studying, and Qāḍīzāda-i Rūmī was among those present. A proof had been referred to [al-Bīrūnī's] *Qānūn-i Mas ūdī*, and the *Qānūn* had been made ready. As the required proof could not be ascertained at the meeting, however. Qāḍīzāda had taken the *Qānūn* to his lodge in order to study it. After two days he brought it back and said that in the passage in question there was a lacuna. He believed this to be the reason why the problem could not be clarified and said that another copy of the book should be found for comparison. This servant had not left his house during the previous two days because of feverish lassitude and had at this juncture joined the meeting. Qāḍīzāda was still there. His Majesty chanced to look at this servant, and he said "Let our Mawlā solve this problem," passing the *Qānūn-i Mas ūdī* on to me. As soon as this servant read through five or six lines from that problem, he explained the whole matter, and the particular copy contained no lacunas.

Such things have happened many times since my arrival here. It will take too long to relate them all. Suffice it to say that in such a gathering and in the presence of so many authorities, one's knowledge is appraised neither through reliance upon other people's opinions nor merely on the basis of the claims made by that person himself.

Shortly after the arrival of this servant here and in a meeting in which His Majesty took part, this servant was speaking about a few problems on which there was agreement between the *Tuḥfa* [*Present*], the *Nihāya al Idrāk* [*On the Highest Understanding*], Mawlānā Niẓām al Dīn-i Nīshābūrī's *Commentary of the Tadhkira*, as well as the commentary of the *Tadhkira* [*Treasury*] by Sayyid Sharīf, May God bless his soul, but which were nevertheless wrong. My contention reached the ears of all the learned people by word of mouth. They were excited and busy speaking behind my back. "When a person objects to a thing on which so many authorities are in agreement," they declared, "he should prove his statement."

One day, at a gathering where the majority was present, I spoke on one of these controversial topics which I have thoroughly investigated, and I explained it both in a descriptive way and by geometrical proof in such a manner that it was accepted unanimously. As His Majesty is a scientist himself and well-versed in the subject, and as scientists are present here in large numbers, when a question becomes settled, no one who has previously spoken in another vein can demur, pretending to find faults, so as to make those who are not familiar with the topic believe in him. For the most distinguished scientists are present here.

One of the problems in question is this. It has been said that the maximum equation for the moon's anomaly on its epicycle takes place at a point of the eccentric region such that when this point is joined to the prosneusis center, the line joining these two points will be perpendicular to the diameter passing through the apogee. This is the assertion made in all the books written on the subject up to our day, but it is wrong. For if the line in question passes through a point seven degrees and fifty seconds underneath the prosneusis center it is perpendicular and otherwise not. The same sort of mistake has been made in the case of the planets also, and the source of the error of them all is that in the case of the sun the point of maximum equation occurs at a place such that when a line is drawn from it to the center of the universe the line is perpendicular to the said diameter. Ptolemy has given the proof for this in the *Almagest* and has referred to this proof in the cases of the moon and other planets. People have never realized that the cases of these latter cannot be referred to that of the sun. . . .

As to the inquiry of those who ask why observations are not completed in one year but require ten or fifteen years, the situation is such that there are certain conditions suited to the determination of matters pertaining to the planets, and it is necessary to observe them when these conditions obtain. It is necessary, e.g., to have two eclipses in both of which the eclipsed parts are equal and to the same side, and both these eclipses have to take place near the same node. Likewise, another pair of eclipses conforming to other specifications is needed, and still other cases of a similar nature are required. It is necessary to observe Mercury at a time when it is at its maximum morning elongation and once at its evening elongation, with the addition of certain other conditions, and a similar situation exists for the other planets.

Now, all these circumstances do not obtain within a single year, so that observations cannot be made in one year. It is necessary to wait until the required circumstances obtain and then if there is cloud at the awaited time, the opportunity will be lost and gone for another year or two until the like of it occurs once more. In this manner, there is need for ten or fifteen years.

Those people who do not know the nature of this activity and who have not witnessed others do it, are surprised when they see anyone occupy himself with it. But when someone knows how to do a thing, it becomes easy. It is to be hoped that God, he is exalted and high, will grant long life and give his help, so that with the felicity of the King of Islam, may God preserve his realm and sovereignty, this activity of observation will reach the stage of completion in a happy and successful manner.

At the present the greater part of the observatory building has been constructed. Nearly five hundred *tūmāns* worth of brick and lime have been used; one armillary sphere has been completed and another one is in the process of construction. Still other instruments, such as azimuthal quadrant and the instrument with movable sights and others, are being attended to and have been half constructed.

As to your query concerning whether the task to be accomplished at the observatory is entrusted to this servant or whether he has a partner for the work, it is a strange coincidence that your Lordship should ask this question after my achieving such fame here. The situation is that although people who are conversant with the mathematical sciences exist in large numbers here, none of them is such that he is acquainted with both the theoretical ("scientific") and applied ("practical") sides of observations (of the work done in an observatory). For none of them knows the *Almagest*.

One of them is Qāḍizāda who possesses the theoretical knowledge contained in the *Almagest* but not its applied side. He has not done anything that pertains to the practical. He is the most learned among them, but even he is only a beginner in theoretical astronomy. For every topic which is put forward by His Majesty, this servant finds the correct approach and supplies the well-rounded and complete answer, as was previously mentioned on the occasion of the problem connected with the *Qānūn-i Mas ūdī* and the like; and I am skilled in all aspects of the applied branch of this science.

Applied astronomy too is divided into scientific and practical branches. The practical branch of applied astronomy may be illustrated with the following example. Suppose, e.g., that two stars have reached the first vertical at a certain condition. Elevation is measured with an instrument, and the longitude and latitude of one of these stars is known. It is required to derive the longitude and latitude of the other from these data. The knowledge of how to derive these, i.e., to know to multiply which quantity with which and to divide by what, and how to proceed in order to obtain the desired result, constitutes the scientific side of this operation (the scientific side of applied astronomy). The scientific side of theoretical astronomy ("the absolutely scientific") is the knowledge of the science itself.

The absolutely practical side of such a problem is the carrying out of the multiplications and divisions and the calculation of the longitudes of celestial bodies in terms of signs, degrees, and minutes, and the determination of their latitudes, giving their actual numerical values.

Qāḍīzāda is weak in the scientific side of applied astronomy, and he cannot point out what pertains to the absolutely practical (the practical side of applied astronomy) except by performing multiplications and divisions with the help of the lattices of multiplication and division. And this is such that when he wishes to set up a lattice, he cannot do it without consulting a book. They read line by line and complete the operation step by step with the help of instructions. If something unusual is being sought this is not of much use (?).

I am not boasting. Your Lordship himself knows that with God's assistance I have confidence in myself to accomplish the purely theoretical, the applied side of the theoretical, and the scientific side of the practical as well as the purely practical, without consulting a book, so that if I were without any books at the observatory I could do everything necessary from the beginning of the period of work to the end and produce the astronomical tables. The only exception would occur in dealing with the results obtained concerning mean positions in previous observations performed on a given date, which is a matter pertaining to the factual realm, as well as the date of the given day. In observational work there is need for such data. For the difference between the mean positions resulting from the present observations and those of the earlier date is found and is divided by the time between the two observations so as to obtain the quantity of motion. All these calculations can be done on two sheets of paper.

Let your Lordship keep his blessed mind at ease. For

recourse to books for such an investigation is not indicative of a serious shortcoming and is not the same as the kind of recourse to books practiced at the present by others.

What I have related concerning Qāḍīzāda should not make people think that there is ill-will and lack of understanding between the two of us. There is a strong feeling of friendship and attachment between Qāḍīzāda and myself, and he acknowledges my superiority. He is not of such a disposition as to deny what is true or to be unfair. He himself asserts in the presence of others what this obedient servant has just said concerning him. He speaks and says so when he knows a thing, and he readily confesses it when he does not know.

The developments to date in the activity pertaining to the observatory have been in accordance with what this servant proposed to His Majesty, may God preserve his realm and sovereignty. This was what happened, e.g., in the case of the nature of the observatory building and the nature of each instrument. His Majesty reflected upon the recommendations with lucid mind and prompt understanding. Whatever he approved he ordered to be carried out, and as to other cases, he enriched them with new ideas and inferences and ordered the adoption of the modified versions.

The truth is that his inferences are very apt and do not contain the slightest error. If in certain cases there happens to be anything concerning which we, his servants, have some doubt, the point is discussed; and no matter from what side the clarification of the mistake comes, His Majesty will at once accept it without the least hesitation. For it is his aim to see that everything is thoroughly investigated and to have the work at the observatory accomplished in the best possible manner.

Your Lordship may infer herefrom the degree of liberality and benevolence of that personage. And there is no need to expand upon this matter. He is, indeed, good-natured to the utmost degree of kindness and charity, so that, at times, there goes on, at the madrasa, between His Majesty and the students of the seekers of knowledge so much arguing back and forth on problems pertaining to any of the sciences that it would be difficult to describe it. He has ordered, in fact, that this should be the procedure, and he has allowed that in scientific questions there should be no agreeing until the matter is thoroughly understood and that people should not pretend to understand in order to be pleasing. Occasionally, when someone assented to His Majesty's view out of submission to his authority, His Majesty reprimanded him by saying "you are imputing ignorance to me." He also poses a false question, so that if anyone accepts it out of politeness he will reintroduce the matter and put the man to shame.

When the said instrument (armillary sphere?) was completed it was brought to the side of the observatory. Every once in a while, when there is something to be done at the site of the observatory, such as the determination of the meridian line, Qāḍīzāda too comes there. If there is any problem, he too speaks in an approving or disapproving manner, as mentioned earlier apropos of the leveling of the observatory grounds wherein they disapproved, and I explained the matter to him.

The rest of the professors too present themselves to the observatory grounds and try to be obliging. The time for the difficult parts of the work has not come yet. For at the present the building is being constructed. When it is brought to completion and the instruments are completed and set up in their places, then observation, which consists of watching the stellar bodies through sights, will be made and measurements will be ascertained, and after that the eccentricities, the radii of epicycles, the degrees of inclination of the apse lines, the mean motions, and the distances of centers of constant speed to centers of eccentricity, etc., will have to be determined from these observations. It is then that work really starts.

It is not appropriate to be too lengthy. May your exalted shadow be unceasing and perpetual.

The least of your slaves,
Ghiyāth

The central institution for the teaching of practical (i.e., clinical) medicine was the hospital. The great hospital at Jundishapur served as the model for the first Islamic hospital created by the Ummayud caliph, Abd al-Malik in Damascus in 707. Under the Abbasid caliphs, medical education was well organized. The medical student was given a thorough grounding in "theoretical" medicine by the study of translations of Greek texts, particularly Galen. He also took his clinical training in a hospital, if possible, and wrote a treatise, like a modern thesis, based upon his medical experience. Acceptance of the thesis permitted him to practice. Many of the great Arab physicians remained associated with a hospital. Rhazes, for example, ran a large hospital in which he worked and which served also as an instructional center.

2. Mathematics and astronomy

The most famous mathematician of early Islam was Muhammad ibn Musa al-Khwarazmi (d. ca. 863) whose studies of both Greek and Indian mathematics permitted him to surpass his masters in mathematical achievement. His most famous work was *The Book of Summary in the Process of Calculation for Compulsion and Equation* which was translated several times into Latin with the title *Liber Algorismi*. It is from this title that the word algorism comes. The Arabic word, al-jabr, meaning compulsion or restoration, is the source of the English algebra. It indicated the following operation (using modern notation).

Given the equation: $5x^2 - 6x + 2 = 4x^2 + 7$

the Jabr given: $5x^2 + 2 = 4x^2 + 6x + 7$

and further simplification: $x^2 = 6x + 5$

Al-jabr is, then, the elimination of negative quantities by restoring a positive to the other side of the equation. The following extract from the Latin edition (translated into English) by Robert of Chester will give some idea of the nature of al-Khwarazmi's work.*

THE BOOK OF ALGEBRA AND ALMUCABOLA

Containing Demonstrations of the Rules of the Equations of Algebra

The Book of Albegra and Almucabola, concerning arithmetical and geometrical problems.

In the name of God, tender and compassionate, begins the book of Restoration and Opposition of number put forth by Mohammed Al-Khowarizmi, the son of Moses. Mohammed said, Praise God the creator who has bestowed upon man the power to discover the significance of numbers. Indeed, reflecting that all things which men need require computation, I discovered that all things involve number and I discovered that number is nothing other than that which is composed of units. Unity therefore is implied in every number. Moreover I discovered all numbers to be so arranged that they proceed from unity up to ten. The number ten is treated in the same manner as the unit, and for this reason doubled and tripled just as in the case of unity. Out of its duplication arises 20, and from its triplication 30. And so multiplying the number ten you arrive at one-hundred. Again the number one-hundred is doubled and tripled like the number ten. So by doubling and tripling etc. the number one-hundred grows to one-thousand. In this way multiplying the number one-thousand according to the various denominations of numbers you come even to the investigation of number in infinity.

Furthermore I discovered that the numbers of restoration and opposition are domposed of these three kinds: namely, roots, squares and numbers. However number alone is connected neither with roots nor with squares by any ratio. Of these then the root is anything composed of units which can be multiplied by itself, or any number greater than unity multiplied by itself: or that which is found to be diminished below unity when multiplied by itself. The square is that which results from the multiplication of a root by itself.

Of these three forms, then, two may be equal to each other, as for example:

**Robert of Chester's Latin Translation of the Algebra of Al-Khowarizmi* with an Introduction, Critical Notes and an English Version by Louis Charles Karpinski (New York: The Macmillan Company, 1915), pp. 67, 69, 71, 75.

Squares equal to roots,
Squares equal to numbers, and
Roots equal to numbers.

Chapter I

Concerning squares equal to roots

The following is an example of squares equal to roots: a square is equal to 5 roots. The root of the square then is 5, and 25 forms its square which, of course, equals five of its roots.

Another example: the third part of a square equals four roots. Then the root of the square is 12 and 144 designates its square. And similarly, five squares equal 10 roots. Therefore one square equals two roots and the root of the square is 2. Four represents the square.

In the same manner then that which involves more than one square, or is less than one, is reduced to one square. Likewise you perform the same operation upon the roots which accompany the squares.

Chapter II

Concerning squares equal to numbers

Squares equal to numbers are illustrated in the following manner: a square is equal to nine. Then nine measures the square of which three represents one root.

Whether there are many or few squares they will have to be reduced in the same manner to the form of one square. That is to say, if there are two or three or four squares, or even more, the equation formed by them with their roots is to be reduced to the form of one square with its root. Further if there be less than one square, that is if a third or a fourth or a fifth part of a square or root is proposed, this is treated in the same manner.

For example, five squares equal 80. Therefore one square equals the fifth part of the number 80 which, of course, is 16. Or, to take another example, half of a square equals 18. This square therefore equals 36. In like manner all squares, however many, are reduced to one square, or what is less than one is reduced to one square. The same operation must be performed upon the numbers which accompany the squares.

Chapter III

Concerning roots equal to numbers

The following is an example of roots equal to numbers: a root is equal to 3. Therefore nine is the square of this root.

Another example: four roots equal 20. Therefore one root of this square is 5. Still another example: half a root is equal to ten. The whole root therefore equals 20, of which, of course, 400 represents the square.

Therefore roots and squares and pure numbers are, as we have shown, distinguished from one another. Whence also from these three kinds which we have just explained, three distinct types of equations are formed involving three elements, as

A square and roots equal to numbers,

A square and numbers equal to roots, and

Roots and numbers equal to a square.

* * * * *

Chapter V

Concerning squares and numbers equal to roots

The following is an illustration of this type: a square and 21 units equal 10 roots. The rule for the investigation of this type of equation is as follows: what is the square which is such that when you add 21 units the sum total equals 10 roots of that square? The solution of this type of problem is obtained in the following manner. You take first one-half of the roots, giving in this instance 5, which multiplied by itself gives 25. From 25 subtract the 21 units to which we have just referred in connection with the squares. This gives 4, of which you extract the square root, which is 2. From the half of the roots, or 5, you take 2 away, and 3 remains, constituting one root of this square which itself is, of course, 9.

If you wish you may add to the half of the roots, namely 5, the same 2 which you have just subtracted from the half of the roots. This give 7, which stands for one root of the square, and 49 completes the square. Therefore when any problem of this type is proposed to you, try the solution of it by addition as we have said. If you do not solve it by addition, without doubt you will find it by subtraction. And indeed this type alone requires both addition and subtraction, and this you do not find at all in the preceding types.

Al-Khwarazmi's mathematics is hard-headed and restricted to the properties of numbers and the various operations these properties permit. In startling contrast, stands the work of a group who flourished in the tenth century, known as the Brethren of Purity. They produced one of the earliest encyclopedias of knowledge in fifty-two epistles. Their writings were extremely popular and they were one of the main sources for the mystic numerology of the Middle Ages. Their influence was primarily felt in Islam, but it spilled over, through other Arabic writers, into the Latin West. The idea that number is basic to physical reality, that the properties of things are to be found in the properties of numbers, is an idea which intoxicated some Western thinkers in the Renaissance and which fed directly into the Scientific Revolution of the seventeenth century. Its origin is

Greek, but it was sustained and transmitted through Islam.

The work of al-Khwarazmi began the algebraic tradition in Islam. Commentators such as al-Kindi (813-80) further developed algebraic techniques until, by the twelfth century, the Persian, Omar Khayyam (ca. 1038-ca. 1123), most noted for his poetry, could attack the problem of quadratic and cubic equations with fair success.

The Arabs served as more than mere transmitters in mathematics. The introduction of "Arabic" numbers and the techniques of algebra offered the West a new and potentially powerful mathematical tool to be used in conjunction with the geometrical methods of Euclid and Apollonius.

The contribution of the Arabs to astronomy was even greater than it was to mathematics. Scholars turned Greek, Indian and Persian treatises into Arabic, the observatories carefully checked and revised the astronomical observations of antiquity and mathematicians and astronomers discussed, criticized and modified their astronomical heritage.

The major influence on Arabic astronomy was Ptolemy's *Almagest*. This was one of the earliest works translated and the whole of Islamic astronomy was couched in its terms. With amazing rapidity, at least as compared with the Latin West, the astronomers of Islam mastered its mathematical techniques and even improved upon them. Where Ptolemy had been forced to work with tables of chords, Arabic mathematicians soon provided more sophisticated mathematical instruments. Al-Khwarazmi compiled trigonometric tables as early as the middle of the ninth century. In the late tenth century, spherical trigonometry was intensively investigated by Abul-Wafa (940-990) who was able to use the results of his predecessors. From Indian mathematics came the sine and the cosine. By the time of Abul-Wafa, tangents, cotangents, secants and cosecants were all known, as were the fundamental relations between them. The art of astronomical calculation in Islam in the tenth and eleventh century went far beyond what Ptolemy and the Greeks had had at their disposal.

The creation of observatories for geodetic, calendrical and astrological purposes offered the opportunity for accurate stellar observations. Once again, the Islamic heritage was an extraordinarily rich one. There was not only the *Almagest*, but also the Persian *Tables of the King*, compiled around 555 and Indian *Siddhantas* to provide basic astronomical data. The astronomical tables of Islam and the observations of the heavens improved greatly in accuracy. Al-Battani (Albategnias) who flourished in the second half of the ninth century was one of the most accurate of Islamic observers and may serve as an example of the state of the art. His observations revealed to him the increase of the sun's apogee since the time of Ptolemy which, in turn, led him to the discovery of the motion of the solar apsides. He determined the precession of the equinoxes as 54.5" per year and measured the inclination of the ecliptic as 23°35'. His major work, *On the Science of Stars*, which also contained a set of tables, was so useful that it was consulted in the West until the Renaissance.

Arabic astronomers also invented or perfected the observational tools basic to astronomy until the introduction of the telescope as a precision instrument in the eighteenth century. Hulagu's observatory at Maragha contained a mural quadrant with a radius of more than twelve feet, armillary spheres and instruments for accurate measurement of azimuths and altitudes. The astrolabe, a stereographic planar projection of the heavens at a specific latitude, was an Arab invention which greatly facilitated astronomical calculations.

The result of astronomical observations was the creation of stellar tables which were to provide a basic astronomical and geodetic framework until after the time of Copernicus. Whatever navigation there was across the open sea was done with these tables as guides. The measurement of the dimensions of the earth, accomplished especially by al-Biruni (973-1051), one of the foremost Muslim scientists, depended upon accurate astronomical determinations.

Accuracy of observation also suggested new paths in theoretical astronomy. It was early noted, for example, that the orbit of Venus, in relation to the observer on the earth, could always be represented as an epicycle whose center was the Sun. No one, however, seriously suggested that Venus was truly a solar satellite. Similarly, it is probable that al-Biruni knew of the possibility of the motion of the earth around the sun and even that this path might be elliptical. But, significantly, accurate observations could not provide the necessary thrust to break basically with Ptolemaic ideas. The closed geocentric universe of the *Almagest* was too important to Islam to be lightly discarded.

The major modifications made in the Ptolemaic system owed little to observation. The most important was the materialization of the Ptolemaic orbits. Ptolemy, it will be remembered, had put forward his system as a purely mathematical model merely to "save the phenomena." This was far too abstract for his Arabic followers to whom such mathematical playing with the cosmos made little sense. In the ninth century Thabit ibn Qurra (ca. 826-901) solidified the Ptolemaic orbits and filled the spaces between the orbs and their eccentrics with a compressible fluid. He also added a ninth orb to account for what he called the trepidation or oscillatory motion of the equinoxes superadded to the precession. This physical model was accepted by al-Haitham (c. 965-1039), the Latin Alhazen, and transmitted to the West. It is, with some modifications, the plan of the heavens which Copernicus overturned in the sixteenth century. The way in which this cosmos worked is described rather clearly by Alhazen:

> The movements of circles, and the fictitious point which Ptolemy has considered in a wholly abstract manner, we transfer to plane or spherical surfaces, which will be animated by the same movement. This is in fact a more exact representation: at the same time, it is more comprehensible to the intelligence. . . . Our demonstrations will be shorter than those in which use is made only of that ideal point and those fictitious cir-

---

* Nasr, *op. cit.*, pp. 177-8.

cles. . . . We have examined the diverse movements produced within the heavens in such a way as to make each of these movements correspond to the simple, continuous and unending movement of a spherical body. All these bodies, assigned thus to each of these movements, can be put into action simultaneously, without this action being contrary to their given position and without their encountering anything against which they could strike or which they could compress or shatter in any way. Moreover, these bodies in their motion will remain continuous with the interposed substance . . .

In describing the heavens, Alhazen writes that, at the extremity of the Universe, there is

the really supreme heaven, which envelops all things and which is immediately contiguous with the sphere of fixed stars. On its own poles, which are the poles of the world, it turns rapidly from East to West carrying with it, by its motion, all the heavens of the different stars. . . . It is itself starless.

As for the heaven of the fixed stars, it is

a round globe, enclosed within two spherical surfaces, whose center is the center of this globe and of the world. The external surface of this globe is contiguous with the largest of the heavens, the one which encloses all the moving heavens, and involves them in its rapid movement; the internal surface of the same globe touches the orbit of Saturn. This heaven [of the fixed stars] turns from the West to the East, according to the order of the signs on two fixed poles. Its movement is slow: during each hundred years it moves only one degree, while the whole circle is divided into three hundred and sixty degrees. The poles of this heaven are also the poles of the heaven of the signs [of the Zodiac], which the Sun traverses; Ptolemy, who discovered this by means of observations of the ancients and of his own, also mentions it. All the fixed stars are set in this heaven, and never change the position they occupy therein. Their mutual distances do not undergo any variations; rather, they always move together, according to the order of the signs and in accordance with the slow movement of their heavens. . . .

The spheres of the three upper planets--i.e., Saturn, Jupiter and Mars--are absolutely alike, both with regard to the number of heavens of which they are composed, and the nature of the movement which animates them. . . . Each of these planets has its own sphere, which is determined by two spherical surfaces, parallel to each other, whose common center is the center of the world; each sphere embraces the sphere immediately following it. The first heaven is that of Saturn, whose external surface is

> bounded by the sphere of the fixed stars, its internal surface by the sphere of Jupiter. Furthermore, the upper surface of the sphere of Jupiter touches the orb of Saturn; its inferior surface, the orb of Mars. Finally, the external surface of the sphere of Mars is contiguous with the sphere of Jupiter, while its internal surface touches the orbit of the Sun. Each of these heavens moves with the same slow movement around poles placed on the same axis as the poles of the heaven of the signs.
>
> In each heaven there is contained an eccentric sphere, encompassed by two surfaces with the same center as this sphere, which turns with a regular movement around two fixed poles in the direction in which the signs follow one another. This sphere is called the *deferent orb*.
>
> Between the two surfaces which form the boundary of this orb, there is enclosed a sphere . . . ; this sphere is named, in the case of each planet, for the epicycle of that planet. It moves in a circular path around its own center and two particular poles.
>
> Finally, the substance of each of the three upper planets is set in the substance of its epicycle, and moves with its motion. When the deferent orb is in its motion, the sphere of the epicycle moves at the same time, and its center describes a fictitious circle, which also bears the name of deferent.

Islamic astronomy, in this form, was easily united with cosmology and theology on the one hand and astrology on the other. The cosmos was created by Allah as stated repeatedly in the Koran. There, too, Allah is described as the First and the Last, the Hidden and the Manifested. From this, the physical cosmos could be and was suffused with spiritual significance. As First, God encompasses the universe, the outermost globe, if you will, of a series of concentric spheres descending both in size and in significance to our own corrupt earthly abode. Thus the material spheres of the Islamic cosmos are not merely astronomical realities, but represent states of being and purity rising to God in the highest. Allah as Last or Hidden can be interpreted as being at the center, as well as the periphery and may be connected to man, the microcosm, whose physical being is manifest while his spiritual essence is hidden. Thus man is not only *in* the cosmos but *of* it and the whole holds together with beauty, economy and divine symmetry. To break this cosmos is to shatter Islam and it is worth noticing that Islam, unlike the West, chose to ignore the Copernican revolution precisely because of its revolutionary implications.

The astrological element is clear. Since the basic principle of the cosmos is unity, then all aspects of the universe react upon one another. Furthermore, all is ordained by Allah and one can hope, perhaps, then to discern one's fate in the stars. The stars are both active agents and divine signs. To be able to "read" them means the possibility of discovering the future, if not controlling it. This astrological aspect is by no means negligible for it provided a powerful stimulus in Islam to close astronomical observation and the perfection of calculation techniques. In the West, it was one of the mainsprings behind the drive to assimilate Arabic astronomy through translation and self-education. It should not be forgotten that astrology remained a respectable profession until at least the time of Kepler who earned his living at it.

3. Medicine

Medicine held one of the highest places in the values of Islam. The wise man whose life and teachings were held up for general emulation was almost always a physician. Many of the best known philosophers and scientists of Islam were also physicians who earned their livelihood through the medical art. Avicenna and Averroes were both medical doctors, as was the great Jewish sage, Maimonides.

Arab medicine, unlike the other sciences in Islam, continued a living tradition rather than reviving a dead one. Jundishapur in Persia was a vital medical center and it was from Jundishapur that Arabic medicine took life. The Greek tradition had already been assimilated into Persian practice, and the influence of India soon made itself felt hard upon the heels of the Arabic conquests. The distance from Jundishapur to Baghdad was not far and the influence of the physicians of Jundishapur at the Abbasid court was felt early. Al-Mansur, the founder of Baghdad, suffered from dyspepsia and sought the aid of Persian and Syriac physicians. Their presence created the necessary environment for the translations of Hunain ibn Ishaq and his school. By the end of the ninth century, there were Greek, Persian and Indian medical traditions fully available to the Muslim medical student. The result was the immediate flowering of Arabic medicine.

Two Arabic physicians stand out. Muhammad ibn Zakariya al-Razi (ca. 865-925), known to the Latin West as Rhazes was the director of the Hospital at Baghdad to which students came from far and wide. Abu Ali al-Husain ibn Sina (980-1037), the Latin Avicenna, was probably the greatest scientist of Islam. He served as a physician to the Buwayhid princes who ruled Persia and, at one point in his life, even served as vizier until political circumstances forced his resignation. These two men may be used to epitomize Arabic medicine at its best.

Rhazes, according to al-Biruni who made a special study of his life and works, was the author of at least 184 major works. His great strength was clinical medicine for he was a master of close and accurate observation. His masterpiece was his *Treatise on Smallpox and Measles* which provided such good clinical descriptions of these diseases that it was used in the West until the nineteenth century. Rhazes' skill as a practical physician is revealed in the following account of one of his cases.

---

*Nasr, pp. 196-7.

Abdu'llāh ibn Sawāda used to suffer from attacks of mixed fever, sometimes quotidian, sometimes tertian, sometimes quartan, and sometimes recurring once in six days. These attacks were preceded by a slight rigor, and micturition was very frequent. I gave it as my opinion that either these accesses of fever would turn into quartan, or that there was ulceration of the kidneys. Only a short time elapsed ere the patient passed pus in his urine. I thereupon informed him that these feverish attacks would not recur, and so it was.

The only thing which prevented me at first from giving it as my definite opinion that the patient was suffering from ulceration of the kidneys was that he had previously suffered from tertian and other mixed types of fever, and this to some extent confirmed my suspicion that this mixed fever might be from inflammatory processes which would tend to become quartan when they waxed stronger.

Moreover the patient did not complain to me that his loins felt like a weight depending from him when he stood up; and I neglected to ask him about this. The frequent micturition also should have strengthened my suspicion of ulceration of the kidneys, but I did not know that his father suffered from weakness of the bladder and was subject to this complaint, and it used likewise to come upon him when he was healthy, and it ought not to be the case henceforth, till the end of his life, if God will.

So when he passed the pus I administered to him diuretics until the urine became free from pus, after which I treated him with terra sigillata, *Boswellia thurifera*, and Dragon's Blood, and his sickness departed from him, and he was quickly and completely cured in about two months. That the ulceration was slight was indicated to me by the fact that he did not complain to me at first of weight in the loins. After he had passed pus, however, I enquired of him whether he had experienced this symptom, and he replied in the affirmative. Had the ulceration been extensive, he would of his own accord have complained of this symptom. And that the pus was evacuated quickly indicated a limited ulceration. The other physicians whom he consulted besides myself, however, did not understand the case at all, even after the patient had passed pus in his urine.

Rhazes also was well-versed in anatomy, although here he was forced by religious circumstances to rely upon tradition, particularly Galen, rather than upon first-hand observation. Dissection of cadavers was forbidden by Islamic law. Thus, the treatises by Rhazes and other Islamic physicians did little more than echo their Greek predecessors. The same is true of physiology in which Galen was the dominant figure. Rhazes recognized his dependence upon Galen for theoretical knowledge. It was as a practical physician that Rhazes compiled his *Kitab al Hawi*, known in Latin as *Continens*, in which he summed up the practical medical learning of his day. It is a large, unorganized compendium of clinical medicine in which no attention is paid to the humours, the elements, anatomy, physiology or surgery. Except for the latter, these "theoretical" subjects were of little real use to the practicing physician and so Rhazes simply ignored them.

Rhazes' contributions to medicine were many. He was the first to identify a number of diseases and to suggest successful treatments for them. He recognized the value of alcohol as an antiseptic and he was the discoverer of the purgative qualities of calomel or mercurous chloride. His medical views were the foundation upon which the medical art in the West was built in the twelfth and later centuries.

Avicenna's mind was of a more philosophical cast than Rhazes. He took all the sciences for his province and made significant contributions to a number of them. His first love was philosophy and it is as a transmitter of Aristotelianism to the West that he is best known. His love of philosophy did not lessen his ability as a physician for it enabled him to generalize and synthesize where men like Rhazes had only been able to describe and enumerate.

Avicenna's great work was his *Canon of Medicine* which is the most widely read and best known Arabic work of medicine. In its five books, Avicenna summarized and systematized the knowledge of general medical principles, simple drugs, diseases of particular organs, diseases, like fever, that may have local origins but which are general in effect, and compound drugs. The *Canon* was *the* medical textbook of both East and West for centuries. The *Canon* of Avicenna, with the works of Rhazes, the anatomical and physiological writings of Galen, and the *Aphorisms* of Hippocrates were the bases of medical education until the eighteenth century.

4. Optics and Mechanics

Closely allied to both medicine and astronomy was the study of optics. Physicians in the Near East were particularly concerned with diseases of the eye which led them necessarily to consider the eye as an optical instrument. Similarly, the study of astronomy necessarily forced one to consider optical problems such as atmospheric refraction. As in other sciences, the starting point for optical investigations was the writings of the Greeks, particularly Euclid and Ptolemy.

The greatest Arabic investigator of optics was Ibn al-Haitham or Alhazen. His research was founded on the study of Euclid, Ptolemy, Archimedes, Hero of Alexandria and the work of Anthenios on curved mirrors. The eye as an optical instrument had been studied by Hunain ibn Ishaq and Rhazes. The *Conics* of Apollonius provided the sophisticated mathematics with which a thorough physico-mathematical optics could be created.

Alhazen parted with tradition at the very beginning of his optical studies by insisting that in vision light traveled from the object to the eye, rather than from the eye to the object. This permitted him to recognize the lens of the eye for what it was and to study it as part of an optical system. He was also able to do simple experiments to determine the rectilinear propagation of light, the properties of shadows and the result of the interposition of lenses on a ray of light. He was also the first person to analyze the *camera obscura* mathematically.

His most notable work was on reflection--that branch of optics denominated as catoptrics by the Greeks. He experimented with spherical and parabolic mirrors, recognizing and studying spherical aberration. He knew that a parabolical mirror concentrated all the incident parallel rays at a point so that it makes the best kind of burning mirror.

He studied refraction by experimenting with a graduated cylinder in water and carefully measuring both the angle of incidence and the angle of refraction. He came within a hair of discovering Snell's law but was able to discern a relation only at very small angles where the angle itself approximates its sine. His studies of refraction led him to understand and measure atmospheric refraction. His influence on the West was narrow but important. He stands prominently in the optical tradition that leads from Euclid and Ptolemy to Kepler and Newton. Some appreciation of his method of attack may be had from the following brief excerpt from his "Discourse on the Concave Spherical Mirror."*

A Discourse by Al-Hasan Bin Al-Hasan Bin Al-Haitham on Burning Mirrors of Circular Shape

The sun's rays proceed from the sun along straight lines and are reflected from every polished object at equal angles, i.e. the reflected ray subtends, together with the line tangential to the polished object which is in the plane of the reflected ray, two equal angles. Hence it follows that the ray reflected from the spherical surface, together with the circumference of the circle which is in the plane of the ray, subtends two equal angles. From this it also follows that the reflected ray, together with the diameter of the circle, subtends two equal angles. And every ray which is reflected from a polished object to a point produces a certain heating at that point, so that if numerous rays are collected at one point, the heating at that point is multiplied: and if the number of rays increases, the effect of the heat increases accordingly.

(a) In the case of every concave mirror of spherical concavity, which is less than a hemisphere, placed opposite to the sun so that its axis if produced would end at the body of the sun, the rays which proceed from the body of the sun along lines parallel to the axis of the mirror are reflected from the surface of the mirror ot its axis. And the axis of the mirror is the diameter of the sphere, which (diameter) is at right angles to the diameter of the base of the mirror.

Given a concave spherical mirror, let its axis be DB and its centre (of curvature) D (Fig. 1). Let a point Z be on the surface of the mirror, and let the line HZ be one of the rays which proceeds from the sun and parallel to the axis. I state that the line HZ is reflected to the axis.

---

*Nasr, pp. 130-2.

Proof of that:--

Let us imagine the line DZ joining the points D and Z. The lines HZ, ZD, DB, lie in a plane surface. And let us imagine that that surface cuts the sphere, thus forming an arc in the surface of that mirror whose radius is DB and whose centre is D; let is be the arc ABG. We draw the line ZC at an angle equal to HZD, i.e. DZC.

Now since the arc ABG is less than a semicircle, the arc BZ is less than a quadrant. Thus ZDC < a right angle. The line HZ is parallel to the line DC. Therefore, HZD < a right angle. And DZC = HZD, and is therefore < a right angle. Similarly for ZDC. ∴ The line ZC meets the line DB. Let it meet it at the point C, and let the ray HZ be reflected from the surface of the mirror at equal angles. ∴ It is reflected along the line ZC, and meets the axis DB. Similarly every ray which proceeds parallel to the axis and ends at a point on the surface of the mirror is reflected to the axis, and this is what we wished to demonstrate.

If we keep the axis DB fixed and rotate the arc AB it generates the surface of the mirror. We draw through the point Z on the surface of the mirror a circle every point of which is equidistant from the point C. Thus the rays which proceed parallel to the axis and end at the circumference of this circle are all reflected to the point C, and so the relation of every point on the surface of the mirror, with respect to the point C on the axis, is the same as that of the whole circle which the point (Z)

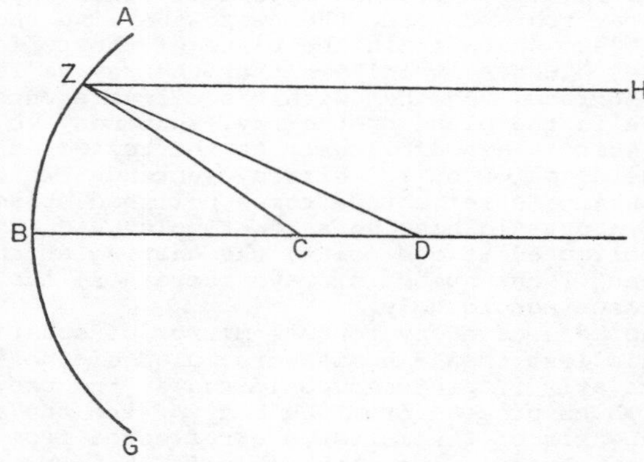

generates when the arc rotates. From what we have said it is clear that rays are not reflected, to a (particular) point (C) on the axis, from *within* the circumference of the circle in the surface of the mirror.

(b) If the rays from the circumference of a circle in the

surface of the sphere are reflected to a (particular) point on the axis of a concave spherical mirror no other rays are reflected to it from the surface of the sphere. Let there be a spherical concave mirror and let the arc which intersects its axis be the arc ABG, and let its axis be DB, and let rays be reflected to the axis from the circumference of one of the circles which fall within the sphere (i.e.) from the point Z. Accordingly, I say that no other ray is reflected from the point Z except the rays which are reflected from that circle.

The science of Mechanics in Islam was heavily influenced by the Peripatetic philosophy of Aristotle and his followers. Few dared to question the basic framework of Aristotelian physics and perhaps the greatest service done by Islam for mechanics was the transmission of Aristotle to the West. There were, however, some who found the Aristotelian system less than satisfying. The earliest of these anti-Peripatetics was al-Biruni who based his opposition on philosophical, rather than empirical, objections. We are fortunate in having a number of letters that al-Biruni addressed to Avicenna in which he suggested that Aristotle might not be the last word on such fundamental things as the doctrine of natural places and the necessity of celestial circular motion. A selection from this correspondence reveals al-Biruni's independence of mind.*

Questions Asked of Avicenna by Al-Biruni

Question 1. On the possible gravity of the heavens, their circular motion and the denial of the natural place of things.

Since the heavens have no motion toward or away from the center, Aristotle has not accepted the idea of the gravity of the heavens. However, such reasoning by Aristotle does not really aim at the desired end. It is possible to imagine that the heavens do possess a gravity which, however, does not cause them to move toward the center, in so far as each part of the heavens is like every other part. Having hypothesized their gravity, one may then say that, whenever by nature they are moved toward the center, their connected forms prevent them from moving so. It is because of their forms, therefore, that they remain stationary about the center. It is also conceivable that the heavens should possess levity, and that the levity could not cause them, nevertheless, to move away from the center, because motion could only take place when the parts of the heavens became separated from each other, or when a vacuum existed outside the heavens, so that the parts either moved or became fixed in that vacuum. Because it has been ascertained and proven that the dispersing of the parts of the heavens is impossible and the existence of a vacuum absurd, it follows that the heavens are themselves a hot fire assembled and confined in a place from which departure is impossible. Consequently, the levity or gravity of the heavens is not dependent upon the absurd ideas of [Aristotle].

---

*Nasr, p. 133-4.

As to only circular motion being possible for the heavens, it may be that the heavens are by essence and nature the source of rectilinear motion, and only by force and accident the source of circular motion, as is the case with the stars, which move by nature from East to West, and by force from West to East.

The presence of each element in its natural place is not certain. The natural place of gravity (i.e., the downward direction) is at the center, and the natural place of levity (i.e., the upward direction) is at the circumference. Yet the center is nothing but a point; and a part of the earth, no matter how small we conceive it to be, cannot fit at the center. As for the circumference, neither can it hold any body in such a way that a light body may ascend to it, since it is an imagined surface area. Furthermore, if we allow water to flow freely, taking away any obstacles in its path, undoubtedly it will reach the center; therefore, the assertion that the natural place of water is above the earth is without any basis. Consequently, there is no "natural place" for any body. On such a basis, he who says that the heavens are indeed heavy, but that it is their being attached that prevents their falling does not appear absurd.

* * * * *

Question 4. On the continuity and discontinuity of matter and space.

Why has Aristotle rejected the assertion of the theologians that a body consists of indivisible parts, and why has he chosen instead the assertion of the philosophers that bodies are infinitely divisible, even though the wickedness of the philosophers' beliefs is greater than the disgracefulness of the theologians' opinions? According to the philosophers, who consider bodies to be connected and infinitely divisible, it is necessary that a rapidly moving body not touch a preceding but more slowly moving body. The touching of a preceding body by a succeeding one is inevitable, if the succeeding body traverses the intermediate distance, but the traversing of that distance requires the traversing of its parts. Since the parts of that distance are infinite in number, how can one imagine that the distance can be crossed? Therefore, no succeeding body can reach a preceding one. It is necessary to give an example to prove this point. If there is a definite distance assumed between the Moon and the Sun, and both bodies are moving at that distance, it should be impossible for the Moon to reach the Sun, even though the motion of the Moon is much faster than that of the Sun. However, such is not the case; by observation it is found that the Moon does in fact overtake the Sun, though such an event brings disgrace and shame upon those who hold to the view of infinite divisibility so well-known and well-established among the geometers. What happens to the philosophers is thus more disgraceful than what happens to the theologians. How then can one escape what has befallen these two groups?

As mentioned earlier, al-Biruni even entertained the possibility of the motion of the earth around the sun, emphasizing that this was a problem for physics, not astronomy. The problem was to account for the physics of terrestrial motion in a circle around the sun--precisely the physical problem with which Copernicus and Galileo were to wrestle some centuries later.

The Aristotelian theory of projectile motion was another "soft spot" in Peripatetic physics. John Philoponos' ideas were known to Arabic scientists; the germ of the theory of impetus was to be found in Islamic commentators on Aristotle's physics. It should be emphasized that it was only the germ of the theory: its full development had to wait until the fourteenth century when Jean Buridan and Nicole Oresme in Paris carried the idea to the level of respectable scientific theory.

Criticism of Aristotle did not depend upon philosophy. It could be carried out simply by preserving and commenting upon the non-Aristotelian traditions inherited from the Greeks. Among such works were Hero of Alexandria's *On the Lifting of Heavy Things* and the mechanical works of Archimedes. No evidence is yet available to prove the direct translation of such Archimedean works as his *Equilibrium of Planes*, but we do know that there was a vigorous Archimedean tradition in the Islamic Middle Ages. Out of this tradition came the perfection of the most accurate scientific instrument of the Middle Ages--the balance--and, perhaps more importantly, the idea that the accurate measure of a quantitative aspect of a body such as weight or specific gravity could provide important clues to underlying real distinctions. Al-Biruni determined the specific gravity of a number of substances--Gold, Mercury, Copper, Brass, Iron, Lead, Sapphire, Ruby, Emerald, Pearl--seemingly following the Archimedean example set by the assay of Hero's crown. Had these accurate determinations been followed up, some of the fuzziness and nonsense of medieval alchemy might have been avoided. As it was, alchemy had at its disposal in the balance an instrument which it never exploited.

5. Alchemy

We have already glanced at the mystical and theological appeal of alchemy. We need only add greed to complete the motives for the pursuit of the philosopher's stone. The attempt to create gold drew upon Aristotle for its theoretical justification. Gold, as an inert substance and as a symbol of wealth, represented the perfect metal toward which all other metals strove. The task of the alchemist was merely to hurry the process along. The natural process took place deep in the matrix of the earth. The alchemist's dream was to realize this maturation in the laboratory. The process seemed feasible theoretically. Aristotelian physics was essentially qualitative and the process of transmutation simply required qualitative changes. The underlying substance--the *materia prima*--could be impressed with qualitative forms and thus undergo major change. In this view, gold could be defined as a heavy, yellow metal. To transform a base metal into gold, all that was necessary was to add the qualities of heaviness and yellowness to it. The process could be simplified by starting with a heavy metal such as lead or mercury and coloring it. All this had been worked out in Alexandria before the Islamic conquest. It was eagerly seized upon by the Arabs. To the search for gold, the Arabs added the quest for the elixir of life--this latter apparently a result of contact with China. Add now mysticism, the search for union with God and a sincere belief that one could gain real insights into the divine plan through alchemy, and one has the necessary framework for the creation of an almost incomprehensible body of mystical, metaphorical, cryptological nonsense. Such, in the main, was Arab alchemy.

The earliest Arab alchemist was Jabir ibn Hayyan who, until very recently, was considered to be a mythological personage. It seems certain now that he was a historical person who can be dated roughly 720-815. He was an Arab and a member of the Shiite sect which leaned toward mysticism as the way to God. The number of works attributed to him is enormous and it is probable that this corpus is the product of Jabir (Latin Geber), his disciples and those who followed his doctrines. In these works, cosmology, astrology, music, numerology and alchemy are all blended to yield a strange, but clearly Hermetic and mystical "science." The treatises describe various operations, often in highly symbolic and even incomprehensible terms which are supposed to lead the adept to ultimate perfection. The art-form of alchemical literature was set here and followed in later treatises, both in Islam and the Latin West. It is difficult to disentangle aspects of the real world from psychological or metaphysical fantasies from these treatises. Jabir's "system" recognized three classes of materials with which alchemy deals. These are "spirits" which are volatilized by fire; "metallic bodies" which are malleable, have luster, and ring when struck; "bodies" which shatter when struck. The spirits are sulfur, arsenic, mercury, sal ammoniac and camphor; the metals are obvious, and the "bodies" are minerals. It is possible from the many things which Jabir does with this classification to select parts which have a real, albeit elementary, chemical meaning but this would ignore completely the spirit behind Jabir's "research." His legacy was less chemical than theosophical and those who followed him sought salvation not scientific knowledge. The two are not mutually exclusive, but the alchemical path was not the broadest one available, even in the Middle Ages, to an umderstanding of the cosmos as a physical entity.

There were later Arab alchemists who recognized alchemy as a means of approaching Nature, not God. Primary among these was Rhazes who was, in fact, an accomplished alchemist before he turned to medicine. He rejected both the theosophical and symbolic dimensions of alchemy and sincerely tried to approach alchemy as a science of matter and material processes. His *Secret of Secrets* is actually a chemistry textbook which preserves the language of alchemy but tries to get to some of the problems of chemistry. It describes chemical apparatus such as beakers, flasks, smelting furnaces, alembics and mortars and instructs the reader in their proper use. His descriptions are relatively straightforward. If followed, they yield the results described by Rhazes and the *Secret of Secrets*, like many modern chemical texts, is of the cookbook type. Rhazes provided recipes which is about all the chemistry of his day could do. Rhazes believed in transmutation but his recipes make little or no use of this theory.

Both the traditions of Rhazes and Jabir were eagerly swallowed by the West. Alchemy became the source of both symbolic fantasies and increasingly sophisticated chemical technology in Western Europe. Both fantasies and technology contributed, as we shall see, to the birth of a reasonably "scientific" chemistry in the seventeenth and eighteenth centuries.

6. Natural History

The descriptive sciences throve in Islam. The Arabs showed themselves to be keen observers, unintimidated by their Greek predecessors. The inheritance, again, was impressive and some of it was not surpassed. Aristotle's works on the parts and generation of animals, for example, was assimilated but unchallenged by Arabic commentators. Only in such areas as falconry was the description of the generation, development and habits of animals, in this case hunting birds, carried to the same heights as those scaled by Aristotle. In general, where new species of plants or animals were encountered, as was often the case, they were accurately described and note taken of their uses, if any. The fabulous was not excluded. The giraffe, for example, was considered by some to be the offspring of a wild she-camel and an hyena while it was supposed by others to be the result of the mating of a camel and a panther. Entirely imaginary beasts such as the Roc that carried off Sinbad, appealed strongly to the Islamic sense of both the marvelous and the creativity of Allah.

Substances which contributed to the *materia medica* were sought out and their properties carefully examined. Pharmacology was undoubtedly enriched, as was the variety of poisons made available for public or private use.

Geography was of considerable interest to Islamic scholars. It had an obvious political and military use and so was supported by some of the royal regimes. It also had a clear appeal to the literate public interest in the strange customs of the many and various peoples conquered by or neighbors of the Muslims. The classic of this genre is al-Biruni's description of India. He notes and accurately describes physical features and social customs. He speculates shrewdly on the geological formation of certain geographical features such as the Ganges Basin as follows:*

One of these plains is India, limited in the south by the above-mentioned Indian Ocean, and on all three other sides by the lofty mountains, the waters of which flow down to it. But if you have seen the soil of India with your own eyes and meditate on its nature--if you consider the rounded stones found in the earth

---

*Nasr, p. 114.

however deeply you dig, stones that are huge near the mountains and where the rivers have a violent current; stones that are of smaller size at greater distance from the mountains, and where the streams flow more slowly; stones that appear pulverised in the shape of sand where the streams begin to stagnate near their mouths and near the sea--if you consider all this, you could scarcely help thinking that India has once been a sea which by degrees has been filled up by the alluvium of the streams.

* * * * *

In a similar way, sea has turned into land and land into sea; which changes, if they happened before the existence of man, are not known and if they took place later they are not remembered because with the length of time the record of events breaks off especially if this happens gradually. This only a few can realize.

This steppe of Arabia was at one time sea, then was upturned so that the traces are still visible when wells or ponds are dug; for they begin with layers of dust, sand and pebbles, then there are found in the soil shells, glass and bones which cannot possibly be said to have been buried there on purpose. Nay, even stones are brought up in which are embedded shells, cowries and what is called "fish-ears," sometimes well-preserved or the hollows are there of their shape while the animal has decayed. The same are found at the Bāb al-Abwāb on the shores of the Caspian Sea. But there is no memory of a known time nor any history about it for the Arabs have inhabited the land since their ancestor Yoqtān. Of course, they may have lived in the mountains of Yaman while the lowland was sea. These were the Arab al-Ariba of antiquity. They cultivated the land from a spring between two mountains, the waters rising to the top, and two gardens flourished right and left till the dam break of al- Arim ruined them because the water sank and cultivation ceased and in place of the two gardens there were two waste lands with bitter herbs, tamarisks, and a few willows.

In all, he set a standard not to be matched in the West until the great voyages of discovery of the fifteenth and sixteenth century and only rarely then.

7. Philosophy

The most dangerous of the legacies of Greek antiquity was Greek philosophy. Its very existence smelled of *hubris* for it implied the ability of the unaided human reason to rise to knowledge of Truth. To admit this premise endangered the sacredness of revelation and, thereby, threatened the very foundations of Islamic civilization. More specifically, Greek philosophy was heretical and, therefore, doubly dangerous. Aristotle taught that the world was eternal whereas the pivot of the Koran was the creation of the world and everything in it by Allah. Philosophy, then, was viewed with deep and justifiable suspicion by the orthodox and was, eventually, vanquished by them. The successful career of al-Ghazzali was devoted to the destruction of Greek philosophy.

Yet, before al-Ghazzali's death in 1111, enough philosophy had flowed into Islam to become a steady stream which debouched in the West in the twelfth century. The logical works of Aristotle were translated into Arabic and commented on by generations of Arabic scholars. The transmission of this intellectual organon to the West was enough, in itself, to set off a major intellectual revolution. But there was more. The great scientists from Rhazes to Avicenna had been philosophers as well. Their scientific works had been inseparable from their philosophical coloring. The very questions that one could ask of nature were influenced by the philosophical framework in which the questions had been raised. Not the least of the services of Islam, then, was the preservation and transmission of the philosophical tradition of antiquity.

This was not all. Philosophy came into the West, not in the guise of an obsequious beggar, but proudly, even arrogantly. The last great philosopher of Islam in the Greek tradition was Abul-Walid Muhammad ibn Rushd (1126-1198) known as Averroes to the Latins. Averroes was the greatest Islamic commentator on Aristotle and he passed this torch on to St. Thomas Aquinas. Averroes met the problem of the reconciliation of faith and reason head on. Allah created man with reason and Averroes insisted that man use it to the utmost. From reason came philosophical truth. If philosophical truth conflicted with Revelation directly and unquestionably, then philosophical truth must bow to Revelation. Otherwise, philosophy was to be considered a legitimate and valid guide and where there only "appeared" to be a contradiction then the philosopher could hold both deduced and revealed Truth at the same time. Averroes and his followers skated dangerously close to heresy. It was asserted, for example, that philosophical investigation led inexorably to the conclusion that the world was eternal. Averroes would yield (grudgingly) to Revelation and the Creation. But he saw no reason why one should not teach the philosophical arguments for the eternity of the world. Averroism was defeated in Islam, but it fell on fertile ground in Western Christendom. The warfare of science and theology, which is such an important element of the history of Western science, has at least part of its origin in Islam. This is not the least of the West's debt to the Arabs for this conflict was to stimulate the growth of both science and theology.

C. The Latin Heritage

1. The Roman Encyclopedists

The process of the direct transmission of Greek science to the Latin West began long before the fall of Rome. The injection of Greek thought into Roman civilization was coeval with the rise of Rome as the dominant Mediterranean power. The particular circumstances of the meeting of the Greek East with the Latin West greatly influenced the way in which Rome assimilated Greek learning. The Romans came to Greece and Asia Minors first as mediators, then as conquerors. Greek learning came to Rome through Greek captives who served as tutors to Roman youth. From the beginning of Greco-Roman contact on a large scale, the Romans found themselves in a somewhat ambiguous position. There could be no doubt of the superiority of Greek thought in almost every intellectual area. Philosophy was a Greek monopoly, physical speculation, theory and even practice went far beyond anything the Romans had devised and Greek medicine, with its recognition of the complexities of clinical symptoms, its anatomy and physiology, far out-distanced the simple reliance on cabbage and onions as panaceas which characterized the medical learning of a Cato the Elder. Those who took the trouble to learn Greek and explore the world opened up by the Greeks, were filled with awe and respect. Yet, above all, the Romans were a practical people and constantly before their eyes was the simple and brutal fact that, for all their cleverness, the Greek states were Rome's vassals and Greek citizens were Roman slaves. Of what use was philosophy and/or physics in a world dominated by military power? The Aristotelian Unmoved Mover might regulate the cosmos in Greek thought but Caesar ruled the world in Roman reality. Greek learning, therefore, never occupied the center of the Roman world nor stirred Roman hearts as it had those of Hellas. It was, by and large, an ornament, a mark of the educated Roman who, in his leisure time, would be moved by a Platonic dialogue or a Pindaric ode or abstractedly appreciate a Euclidean proof. Only in the stern morality of the Stoic philosophy or in the refined alienation of Epicureanism was his soul touched and these philosophies flourished in Rome. Otherwise, the Greek heritage was pushed aside to make way for the more Roman intellectual achievements. Law, administration, war and politics were what occupied the Roman aristocrat. Caesar's *Gallic Wars* and Cicero's orations before the Senate or the courts are the typical Roman products of the mind.

Science did not suffer a complete eclipse, although its light was dimmed. Its character, however, was completely transmuted. There is no Roman Archimedes who followed a difficult train of abstract mathematical thought for the sheer joy of it. There were Roman commentators on Greek science who culled useful and entertaining information from the more severe Greek treatment. For some writers, such as Celsus, it was the utility of their subject which induced them to study, summarize and organize their Greek sources; for others, such as Pliny the Elder, it was the pleasure of viewing the wonders of the world which drove him to authorship. Or, the Greek discovery and analysis of Nature might lead, as it did with Seneca, to the illustration of morality drawn from natural law.

Cornelius Celsus (first century A.D.) wrote prolifically on a number of subjects--agriculture, oratory, jurisprudence and the miliatry arts--but is most famous for his encyclopedia of medicine. His *De Medicina* (*On Medicine*) is a classic combining the purest Latinity with excellence of arrangement and intelligence in the selection of both sources and arguments. In these qualities it is a typically Roman work and one of the best of its kind. It is entirely derivative. Although there is still controversy on the point, there is little doubt among modern scholars that Celsus was not, himself, a physician. What he was was a highly intelligent scholar who had read deeply in the medical writings of Greece, was able to appreciate what he had read and, most importantly, was able to organize his materials so well that the treatise served as the basic medical textbook of Western Europe for centuries.

Like Celsus, Pliny the Elder (A.D. 23/24-79) cast his net widely, setting for himself no less a task than a description of the whole of natural history. His *Historia Naturalia* was completed in thirty-seven books. Like Celsus, Pliny was a compiler and organizer, not an original thinker or keen observer. Pliny was a very busy man, having a large law practice, holding high position in government and serving in the unofficial post of advisor to emperors. He was the author of treatises on javelin throwing from horseback, a history of the wars between the Romans and the Germans, a manual of oratory and books on grammar and Latin usage. He was able to complete his *Natural History* only by making the most efficient use of his time. He slept little, arising at 1 or 2 A.M. to begin his scholarly researches. Before noon he had completed his official duties and could turn to his scholarly pursuits. No moment was wasted. If he took a rest after lunch, a book was read to him. A slave accompanied him to his bath and read to him while he bathed. During dinner, he listened while a book was read. A secretary was constantly present to take notes and copy passages. He never walked but, if possible, was carried in a sedan chair so that he could read. A secretary walked by his side, even in winter, to take notes. The result of this constant effort was a prodigious acquaintanceship with the learning of the ancient world. What Pliny did with this learning was typically Roman. There is no semblance of originality in what he wrote. Rather, the *Natural History* is the product of thousands of notes and excerpts from other works, arranged and organized by Pliny. What fascinates him is the curious, the bizarre and the entertaining. He has no interest in discovering principles or laws or in any way finding some unifying thread that ties his material together. It is, rather, the very richness of detail, the multitude of individual and unconnected observations that he revels in. Presumably, his reader was expected to find equal enjoyment in the contemplation of the variety, oddity and even absurdities of nature. Since everything was grist for Pliny's mill, everything under the sun appears in the *Natural History*. A brief summary will serve to acquaint the reader with the work.

Book I contains Pliny's bibliography and indexes. The work properly begins in Book II with a discussion of cosmography and here it is worth noting Pliny's method. He cites Greek sources but modern scholarship has shown that he rarely, if ever, read them. His standard practice was to cite the Greek but use a Latin compiler who mentions, summarizes or quotes the Greek sources. Thus, in his cosmography, he cites Posidonius, a Greek geographer, but is actually copying from another Roman encyclopedist, Varro. After cosmic description, comes a consideration of the workings of the universe. It is spherical, revolves in 24 hours and contains planets. There are four elements, of which the earth alone is motionless. The Sun ahd the planets are discussed and here Pliny gives us his opinions as well as "facts" he has collected. Since Jupiter lies between the extreme cold of Saturn and the great heat of Mars, it must have a temperate climate. Venus, we are told, emits a dew which stimulates conception in plants and animals on earth. Each of the planets has its peculiarities which Pliny lovingly details. When his sources contradict one another, as often happens, Pliny allows the contradictions to stand without comment.

The section on eclipses is particularly revealing of the quality of Pliny's mind and the standards of Roman science. Not for him was the patient unravelling of astronomical observations or the laborious calculations necessary for the prediction of future eclipses. Instead, he is content to wonder at the whole process and give a qualitiative description of the event.

The description of the earth follows the Greek geographers closely in some places but in others he simply does not understand what he has read. His account of latitude and longitude is hopelessly confused. His estimate of terrestrial distances is often off because the figures he uses to describe intermediate distances have not been added correctly. It is possible that these are copyists' errors but, if not, they are quite consistent with the work as a whole. Pliny does not intend it to be accurate, only entertaining. When he comes to regional geography, there is little more than a jumble of place names by the thousands. He does interrupt this catalogue and monument to dogged, pedantic persistence to give asides of local color. It is here that we meet the fabulous creatures of Africa who fascinated Pliny's medieval readers. There are men without heads, others with different numbers of eyes or various other anatomical peculiarities.

When Pliny gets close to home, his geography improves noticeably. As an administrator of the Empire, he had gotten about in it and he is able to describe what he has seen.

The approach of the early books is followed in the later ones devoted to the plant, animal and mineral kingdoms. It would be tedious to follow him in detail. What he offers is a catalogue and a description of everything he has read about with an occasional remark drawn from personal knowledge.

It must be realized that the *Historia Naturalia* was, for centuries, *the* authoritative work on the world. The worship of authorities, the blind copying of earlier works and the sheer joy in the contemplation of the odd, the bizarre and the unusual are commonly associated with the medieval scholastics of the twelfth and thirteenth centuries. Such qualities, it might be noted, were inherited from Rome and did not spring entirely from barbarian naivete and backwardness. In all fairness to Pliny, however, we should not leave him surrounded by an aura of bookish credulity. He did have at least one characteristic of the scientist, a truly burning curiosity and he met his death as a result of it. When Vesuvius erupted in 79 A.D., Pliny was serving as admiral of the Western fleet stationed in the Bay of Naples. Not content with the view from afar, he sailed into the storm of pumice and ashes, dictating all the way. He died the next day, some say of apoplexy caused by the excitement of his day of volcanic observation.

There is a more sombre tone in the works of Pliny's older contemporary, Seneca (ca. 4 B.C. - 65 A.D.). Seneca was a philosopher and moralist who had found intellectual solace in Stoicism. He served as tutor to Nero and committed suicide at this Emperor's command. His basic interest was in morality, not science, and it is not surprising to find, therefore, that his work on science is suffused with questions of morality. His *Natural Questions* reflects his Stoicism. There is a natural order in the universe resulting from the diffusion through the universe of Spirit or pneuma. The presence of Spirit is what brings natural order out of Chaos. Scientific laws are merely the phenomenal manifestation of Spirit. More important than scientific law, however, is the existence of moral law. That moral law exists can be presumed from the existence of natural law and science, therefore, can be used to illustrate both the existence and the content of the moral law which also finds its origin in Spirit. Such is the aim of the *Natural Questions*. In the course of drawing morals from nature, Seneca here draws heavily upon Aristotle and served to transmit some Aristotelian ideas to the Dark Ages. Like Pliny's work, the *Natural Questions* was available after the fall of Rome and served as an authority to generations of medieval philosophers.

The works of Celsus, Pliny and Seneca represent the high point of Roman science and are characteristic of it. At its best, as in Celsus, Roman Science served to transmit some accurate observations and provide a few guidelines to further advances. At its worst, as in parts of Pliny and the lesser encyclopedists, it perpetuated the fancies and folk-lore of antiquity under the guise of and with the high reputation of Greek learning. It is less surprising that the medieval scholastics swallowed these tales whole than that they were ultimately able to view them semi-critically and begin to doubt their validity. In this sense, the Dark Ages were the darkness that precedes the dawn.

2. The Transmitters

Pliny, Celsus and Seneca wrote for an audience that wished to be instructed or entertained and did not particularly care whether the authors had transmitted Greek learning accurately or fully. The *De Medicina*, *Historia Naturalia* and *Quaestiones Naturales* stand on their own as encyclopedias or moral tracts to be read by those who are interested. As the centuries passed, a sense of decay and doom began to pervade the works of Roman intellectuals. Although Rome did not fall with a thud on a given day, by the fourth and fifth centuries it was perfectly clear to all who would look that the culture of antiquity was in a serious decline. Pliny could lightly mess up an astronomical account without worrying too much about it, secure in the knowledge that it wasn't important to get it right because, in the long run, it didn't really matter. What really mattered was the power, law and administration of Rome. By the fourth and fifth centuries, this confidence in Rome had disappeared and the thin edge of panic had begun to creep into the works of the encyclopedists. They, too, made egregious blunders but, unlike Pliny, they often tried to cover them up in a fog of rhetoric or with a battalion of cited authorities whom they had never read. As the twilight of the Empire came, there was also introduced a sense of shipwreck. Perhaps something could be saved. The purpose for which treatises were written changed. Entertainment and instruction became subsidiary to preservation of the ancient heritage. A man like Boethius saw his mission clearly as one of the conservation of as much of the intellectual achievement of antiquity as possible.

The second stage of the Latin transmission of Greek science, then,involved a two-fold movement. There was, first of all, the further degradation of the Roman encyclopedic tradition and then the conscious effort to save what could be saved before the night fell. Both are important, for the later encyclopedias enjoyed considerable popularity and influence in the Dark Ages, and the works of men such as Boethius set the intellectual stage for centuries to come.

The direction of Latin encyclopedic thought was significantly changed in the fourth century by the development of neo-Platonism. The neo-Platonic philosophy was largely the work of three thinkers, Plotinus (204-270), Porphyry (ca. 232-304) and Iamblichus (ca. 250-326) who rang a series of changes upon the Platonic view of the cosmos. For our purposes, we need only note their acceptance of the basic dichotomy of spirit and matter, the creative intercession of the Platonic demiurge or demiurges, and the acceptance of the transcendant and essentially mathematical nature of the Godhead. None of these philosophers were scientists or interested in nature *per se*, but they did create an intellectual atmosphere which stimulated encyclopedic writers to focus upon different aspects of the Greek inheritance from their predecessors. The most obvious new center of interest was Plato and, particularly, his cosmological, cosmogonical and cosmographical treatise, the *Timaeus*. As we have seen, the *Timaeus* was a work of extraordinary difficulty and it had been accompanied by commentaries almost from the time of its appearance. Cicero had felt it important enough to attempt a free translation of it but it was not through Cicero that the Platonic influence was to be felt in the Middle Ages. It was, rather, through the encyclopedic work of an obscure scholar, Chalcidius, that Platonic and neo-Platonic physical and mathematical ideas, together with a good deal of sheer nonsense, were injected into medieval thought.

Little is known of Chalcidius. He may have been a Christian and he appears to have flourished ca. 325 A.D. His commentary on the *Timeaus* was far more than an account and attempted explanation of this dialogue. The *Timeaus* served merely as the starting point for an encyclopedic tour of astronomy and cosmology. The first impression is that one is in the presence of a powerful and keen scientific mind as Chalcidius launches into a lengthy treatment of planetary and stellar motions. This impression is dispelled when Chalcidius contradicts himself or falls into simple errors. In fact, Chalcidius is merely a channel for earlier thought. Thus the astronomical exegesis is taken from Theon of Smyrna's *Manual of Mathematical Knowledge Useful for an Understanding of Plato*, probably written in the second century A.D. That Chalcidius could understand Theon well enough to translate him, speaks well for Chalcidius and puts him on a higher intellectural level than most of his contemporaries. One illustration may suffice. In Chapter 5, Chalcidius discusses the order of the planets and reports on the various textbook traditions. The Pythagoreans, for example, had assumed the order, moon, Mercury, Venus, sun, Mars, Jupiter, and Saturn. Eratosthenes had placed the sun immediately above the moon which would also accord with the stoic doctrine that the sun was the heart of the universe. Later, Chalcidius introduces the idea that Venus and, presumably, Mercury revolve about the sun. As a history of doctrines, this is acceptable, but as an account of actual order in the heavens, it could not help but confuse later readers. Nevertheless, the influence of Chalcidius was considerable and his work was one of the more advanced treatises on astronomy available to medieval thinkers.

In the fifth century, the Platonic cosmography was given extended treatment by two other commentators, Macrobius and Martianus Capella. Macrobius, who flourished in the first two decades of the fifth century, was a high official in the Roman state. His most important work in science is his *Commentary on the Dream of Scipio*, the Dream being a work by Cicero. It is not, however, a commentary, but a treatise of neo-platonic philosophy in which Macrobius can give free rein to numerological and cosmographical speculation. Book I, for example, contains a long digression on numbers and their properties. Eight, being the first cubical number (2x2x2) is called a solid or full number. It represents the number of revolving spheres in the cosmos and, beyond this, it is also the sum of the two important numbers, 1 and 7. The number 7 has so many attributes that it takes Macrobius eighteen pages to deal with them all. Nearly half the *Commentary* was devoted to cosmography and this section, often circulated as a separate treatise during the Middle Ages, was considered authoritative. Macrobius was here closely following an earlier commentary on the *Timaeus* by Porphyry but just how much of Porphyry he really understood is difficult to tell. At one point, for example, he becomes hopelessly confused about planetary velocities. The result is both contradictory and irreconcilable. We can dismiss it as ignorance or ineptitude but we must consider the effects of such accounts on medieval readers of the treatise. As an "authority" whose importance is guaranteed by his antiquity, Macrobius was to be studied and taken seriously. It was difficult, if not impossible, to believe that Macrobius simply did not know what he was talking about. And so great ingenuity had to be exercised to reconcile the irreconcilable and make sense out of nonsense. It took generations for medieval men to have the self-confidence to reject nonsense, regardless of its source.

In spite of such errors, Macrobius did pass on a considerable amount of Platonic and neo-Platonic astronomical lore to later generations. Besides the standard discussions of the order of the heavenly bodies (in which Macrobius again gets mixed up and presents conflicting accounts), he also dealt with the dimensions of the universe thereby permitting the introduction of numerological relationships. Thus, the sun is twice the distance of the moon from the earth, Venus three times the sun's distance, Mercury four times Venus' distance, Mars nine times Mercury's distance, Jupiter eight times Mars' distance and Saturn twenty-seven times Jupiter's distance. It is no coincidence that these numbers all correspond to proportions of the Neo-Platonic World Soul and that their ratios provide the mathematical basis for the harmony of the spheres.

Macrobius was no less influential as a geographer than as a cosmographer. Here, again, he relied upon an earlier compiler, Crates of Mallos (fl. 160 B.C.) who had divided the globe into four inhabited quarters separated from one another by two intersecting oceans. The inhabitants of the quarter directly opposite the known world were the antipodeans about whose presumed existence there was to be much discussion in the ensuing centuries. The tides were supposed to be the result of the collision of the opposing oceans at the poles, a belief which was shared by few of his contemporaries. The Macrobian view of the earth may have been the source for the rather bizarre geographical concepts of Isidore of Seville (Readings, Chapter Three, II, Ab) who confused Macrobius' quarters of spheres with quarters of circles.

It should be noted that Macrobius' commentary is a sizable step down from that of Chalcidius'. Chalcidius had written for the learned; Macrobius merely for the literate. This probably helps to account for the fact that Macrobius was more widely read than Chalcidius in the Middle Ages. He was, quite simply, easier to read, requiring little previous knowledge or technical preparation. Another step down into the Dark Ages was provided by Martianus Capella whose allegory of the marriage of Mercury and Philology provided the foundation of medieval education.

Martianus Capella was a Carthaginian lawyer who flourished ca. 410-439 A.D. His *Marriage of Mercury and Philology* is a fanciful and rather clumsy encyclopedia organized around the seven liberal arts. Capella's division of educational subjects into the trivium and quadrivium became the basic educational divisions for the Middle Ages. The trivium was made up of grammar, rhetoric and dialectic. The quadrivium contained the mathematical sciences--geometry, arithmetica, astronomy and music. The presentation of these seven liberal arts is puerile. The linguistic arts are described in barbarous and florid Latin while the mathematical subjects deal with only the most elementary aspects of their respective arts. Capella presents with pride the solution of the problem of constructing an equilateral triangle on a given straight line. Since this is Euclid's first proposition, it is hardly an example of deep geometric thought. *Arithmetica* is given little better shrift. He classifies numbers into even times even, odd times even, even times odd, and odd times odd. He then goes on to discourse on the different properties of numbers. All this is a rehash of earlier works with a little garbled Euclid thrown in for good measure. With astronomy, Capella is on a little firmer ground. Here, at least, he seems actually to be following his source faithfully and this section has been described as the most orderly and comprehensive treatment of astronomy by any Latin author whose work has survived. There are errors, but these are more than compensated for by the extent and relative accuracy of his description. It is in this section, for example, that is to be found the clearest account in Latin of the Heraclidean theory that Venus and Mercury go around the sun rather than around the earth. This does not prevent Capella, however, from reverting to the standard handbook practice of giving relative orders to the planets, a classification which makes little sense if the earth is not the center of all the orbits of the heavenly bodies.

Chalcidius, Macrobius and Martianus Capella, for all their faults, were precious legacies to the Middle Ages. In the absence of more profound or more detailed treatises, which would probably have been incomprehensible to the Christian monks and priests who would have used them, they kept alive the dim spark of ancient learning. Refracted through their errors, confusions and over-simplifications, there was still perceptible the ragged outlines of what the Greeks had achieved scientifically. This distorted view was to suffice for centuries. It did serve as a stimulus to learning even when it could hardly serve as a guide. The long road up from darkness was to be traveled swiftly only after the light from Islam shone upon the West in the twelfth century renaissance. During the Dark Ages proper, the only candle of method by which the encyclopedic tradition could be examined was that provided by two Christian scholars of the fifth and sixth centuries, Boethius and Cassiodorus.

Boethius was born about 480 into an illustrious and wealthy family. His father served as a Consul of the Empire and Boethius received the best education available. He, himself, served the Ostrogothic king, Theodoric, until he fell into disgrace, was imprisoned and put to death. Boethius, unlike his predecessors, recognized the parlous state into which learning had fallen in his own day and conceived a grandiose project to halt this decay. He set out to do nothing less than to provide textbooks, translations and commentaries which would permit the full understanding of the philosophies of Plato and Aristotle. Only a small part of this ambitious program was carried out, but even this small part was of fundamental importance for the Middle Ages.

Boethius' earliest work was a small treatise *On Arithmetic* which, as he frankly admitted, was a rather free version of Nicomachus' *Introduction to Arithmetic* which had first appeared in the first century. Unlike other compilers, Boethius seems to have understood the work which he was translating and presented its material clearly. This text was to be the basic text in arithmetic for almost a thousand years. His text *On Music* was even more successful. It was used as a basic work at Oxford, for example, until the eighteenth century. It was, of course a work of mathematical theory not of musical practice and reflected clearly the Pythagorean sources from which it was drawn. According to Cassiodorus, Boethius translated Euclid into Latin but we have no such extensive treatise to hand. What Boethius probably wrote was a manual of geometry, incorporating a few Euclidean theorems and proofs, but falling far short of the original. In order to complete his survey of the mathematical sciences, Boethius ought to have written a treatise on astronomy but if he did, there is no trace of it to be found.

After having provided a foundation for the study of the quadrivium, Boethius somehow found the time to write a number of works on logic. These took the form primarily of commentaries on Aristotle's logical works, as well as upon lesser logicians such as Porphyry and Cicero. It was through Boethius that knowledge of the syllogism as a logical instrument passed to the medieval West. When it is realized that this was the major logical tool until the recovery of the *Posterior Analytics* of Aristotle in the late twelfth century, then Boethius' contribution can be seen to be a major one. It was upon the foundations that Boethius provided that Peter Abelard later created his intellectual revolution.

Cassiodorus, like Boethius, came from a distinguished Roman family. Born sometime near the end of the fifth century, he early became enmeshed in the high administration of the Ostrogothic kingdom of Italy. After Theodoric's death and the "reconquest" of Italy by Justinian, Cassiodorus returned to his birthplace in southern Iatly and founded a monastery. He had long been concerned over the destruction of manuscripts and the gradual irreparable loss of the learning of antiquity that this entailed. He was also concerned, as a devout Christian, by the fact that there were few institutions where aspirants to the priesthood could receive a good education. At his monastery at Scyllacium, Cassiodorus gathered together a number of monks devoted to the copying and translating of manuscripts. The basis of all education, he maintained, was the Bible and he placed heavy emphasis upon Biblical scholarship. Secular knowledge, however, was essential to a proper understanding of Scripture and it was for this reason that Cassiodorus cast his educational net widely. His major work as a pedagogue was *On Training in Sacred and Profane Literature* which was an encyclopedia of sacred and profane learning. It is suffused with Christian piety and symbolism. Book I, on sacred literature, for example, contains thirty-three chapters to correspond with the age of Christ at his crucifixion. Book II makes the transition to the profane arts while retaining a Christian aura. The seven liberal arts reflect David's praise of the Lord seven times each day, the Solomonian house of wisdom supported by seven pillars, and the Book of Revelation's mention of seven churches and seven Spirits. Arithmetic is justified by the citation of the Lord's comment: "But the very hairs of your head are all numbered." Thus this treatise successfully healed the breach between the sacred and the profane and provided a justification for later scholars to continue to study the literature of antiquity. By making profane studies respectable, Cassiodorus countered the recurrent reaction in the Church against the works of pagan antiquity. Implicit in this work is the view that study of the world is but another path to God. After all, is not the world His creation?

and will not knowledge of the creation lead one to know and love the Creator? Since the philosophers of antiquity had progressed farther than any others in the understanding of the world, study of their writings was not to be shunned but pursued. Cassiodorus added little if anything to the content of this study. What he did provide was a rationale for the proper Christian who was fascinated by the ancients and wished to know them in their writings. He set the example of copying and annotating ancient manuscripts which preserved the ancient works and kept the spark of ancient culture alive through the grim centuries of the Dark Ages.

CHAPTER III

MEDIEVAL SCIENCE

A. The Dark Ages

The scientific heritage of classical antiquity underwent a final transformation in the last years of the ancient world. Its final refraction was through the culture of nascent Christianity. We have already witnessed the degradation of ancient science in a Roman setting. We must now ask what relevance Christianity found in the works of pagan philosophers and how much of pagan learning did they wish to preserve? The answers to these questions are surprisingly complex. We might expect, for example, that Christianity's focus upon the next world and the path to it might lead Christian thinkers to the rejection of this world and all knowledge of it. To such a Christian philosopher, science ought to be the supreme irrelevancy for what could be less valuable than knowledge of this world in which we spend such a short, and generally miserable, time? There were such men and we can hear an echo of their voices in Gregory the Great's admonitions on the study of grammar [Readings, p. 263]. Scripture, it could be argued, contained all that was necessary for a man to know. Thus writes an early missionary:

> But avoid all books of the heathen. For what hast thou to do with strange sayings or laws or lying prophecies which also turn away from the faith them that are young? What is lacking to thee in the word of God, that thou shouldst cast thyself upon these fables of the heathen? If thou wouldst read historical narratives, thou hast the Book of Kings; but if philosophers and wise men, thou hast the Prophets, wherein thou shalt find wisdom and understanding more than that of the wise men and philosophers. And if thou wish for song, thou hast the Psalms of David; but if thou wouldst read of the beginning of the world, thou hast the Genesis of the great Moses; and if laws and commandments, thou hast the glorious Law of the Lord God. All strange writings therefore which are contrary to these wholly eschew.*

The other-worldly strain in medieval thought should never be underestimated. Those to whom faith in Christ and hope for heaven sufficed never took kindly to the men who insisted upon reason and understanding in their search for God.

A Christian distaste for worldly studies however was counter-balanced by the political necessity of converting the pagans and defending the faith against pagan philosophers. The sublime character of the Gospels might be sufficient evidence of

---

*As quoted in M. L. W. Laistner, *Christianity and Pagan Culture*, Ithaca, N. Y., 1951, p. 50.

this truth to the believer, but only arguments could convince the skeptic. And arguments, even in late antiquity, were a classical art form which had to be mastered by a thorough study of the masters of the art. Thus even the most anti-intellectual of the Church Fathers had to know enough classical philosophy to be able to use it in the service of Christ. Scholasticism, the typical form of medieval intellectual discourse, thus has its origins in the early Christian battle for intellectual supremacy in the Roman Empire.

Not all Christians were hostile to classical learning or even to the classical ideal of understanding the cosmos. Particularly among the Greek fathers, there was the attempt to place classical science within a Christian framework. We can oppose to the previous quotation on the all sufficiency of Scripture, a citation from Gregory of Nazianus which puts pagan learning in a somewhat different light.

> I take it as admitted by men of sense, that the first of our advantages is education; and not only this our more noble form of it, which disregards rhetorical ornaments and glory, and holds to salvation and beauty in the objects of our contemplation; but even that pagan culture which many Christians spit upon, as treacherous and dangerous, and keeping us afar from God. For as we ought not to neglect the heavens, and earth, and air, and all such things, because some have wrongly seized upon them, and honour God's works instead of God; but to reap what advantage we can from them for our life and enjoyment, while we avoid their dangers; not raising creation, as foolish men do, in revolt against the Creator, but from the works of nature apprehending the Worker (Romans 1, 20 and 25) and, as the divine apostle says (II Corinthians 10, 4), bringing into captivity every thought to Christ: and again as we know that neither fire, nor food, nor iron, nor any other of the elements, is of itself most useful or most harmful, except according to the will of those who use it; and as we have compounded healthful drugs from certain of the reptiles; so from secular literature we have received principles of inquiry and speculation, while we have rejected their idolatry, terror, and pit of destruction. Nay, even those who have aided us in our religion, by our perception of the contrast between what is worse and what is better, and by gaining strength for our doctrine for the weakness of theirs. We must not then dishonour education because some men are pleased to do so, but rather suppose such men to be boorish and uneducated, desiring all men to be as they themselves are, in order to hide what is appropriate to them among the common mass and escape the detection of their want of culture.*

The goal of apprehending the Worker from the contemplation of His works was, as we shall see, one eagerly pursued for centuries. Certainly this argument sppeared to justify the study of Nature

---

*Quoted in *ibid.*, p. 55.

and could be used to make science respectable within a Christian context. But, in the Middle Ages, it provided only one pole of the possible attitudes to learning and the medieval intellectual was constantly torn by the conflict between this view and that expressed in the earlier citation. For every Peter Abelard who insisted that reason was the proper guide to Truth, there was a Bernard de Clairvaux who was equally adamant in his view that faith was above reason and that the path of reason could lead to perdition rather than Paradise.

This conflict, in part, determined the fate of many of the ancient classics. Had the anti-pagan forces been dominant, much more would have been lost and it is to the lingering respect for learning and the nostalgia for the greatness of antiquity that the medieval world owes what little survived the barbarian invasions and the collapse of Rome. The work of Martianus Capella and Boethius was picked up and continued by such Christian scholars as Cassiodorus. The institution of the Scriptorium in monasteries guaranteed that some, at least, of the ancient legacy would be transmitted to later ages.

What was transmitted, as we have seen, was pitifully little. Intellectually, the period from the end of the fifth century to the Renaissance of the twelfth century was a real Dark Ages in which the level of learning and thought was extremely low. There are a few "peaks" but these are heights only in relative terms. If thinkers such as Isidore of Seville, the Venerable Bede, John Scot Erigena and Gerbert are compared with any of the natural philosophers of Greece, the result can only be embarrassing.

The conditions for the flowering of the intellect were hardly favorable during these dark centuries. The collapse of Roman political power led to the disintegration of Roman society. The cities which had been the vital centers of Roman activity throughout the Empire were depopulated and survived only if they were important to the Church and the new barbarian conquerors. Schools disappeared and literacy became increasingly rare. The barbarians who now occupied the outlying provinces of the Empire--Vandals and Ostrogoths, Franks, Visigoths and Lombards--sometimes did what they could for learning and learned men, but their primary concern was often for survival rather than philosophy. With Saracens to the South, Huns to the East and Vikings to the North, it was difficult, if not impossible, to concentrate upon the life of the mind. It is only in those periods of relative peace that we find even the semblance of learning. Isidore of Seville (560-636) [Readings, p. 264] flourished in the brief twilight that preceded the conquest of Spain by Islam. The Venerable Bede (ca. 672-735) lived during a period of relative tranquillity in the British Isles. John Scot Erigena (ca. 830-880) thought and wrote at the Court of Charles the Bold immediately before the Norsemen devastated Gaul and Gerbert (940-1003) studied and wrote in the peaceful dawn of the late tenth century when the Vikings finally settled down to enjoy their conquests. Mention should also be made of the years of peace and order guaranteed by the military and administrative genius of Charlemagne but it should also be noted that the so-called Carolingian Renaissance stimulated little in the way of natural philosophy.

Isidore of Seville marks the end of the encyclopedic tradition of antiquity. Isidore could read and write but he had great difficulty in understanding what he read. His *Etymologies* is a half-digested compendium freely plagiarized from earlier authors with a Christian patina added. Isidore never misses an opportunity to point a moral and thereby illustrates one important function of natural philosophy in the Middle Ages. When a natural phenomenon can be used to illustrate a point of Christian doctrine, it is eagerly seized and used, with little regard for its accuracy or even existence. Isidore also illustrates well the tendency of the newly literate to treat words with awe. Such tendencies were enhanced by the Christian regard for the Word for, as the Gospel of St. John puts it so forcefully, "In the beginning was the Word, and the Word was with God, and the Word was God." Isidore's *Etymologies* was an attempt to penetrate the mysteries of the creation by discovering what words really meant. Thus, for example, he derives the Latin word for man, *homo*, from *humo*, dust and thereby reveals man's origins (And the Lord God formed man of the dust of the ground), his nature and ultimate physical destination (Dust thou art and unto dust thou shalt return). The result of this linguistic activity is literally fantastic but the *Etymologies* was to remain an authoritative work well into the late Middle Ages.

The Venerable Bede represents another aspect of scientific learning in the Dark Ages. Although he too, like Isidore, wrote a cosmology which was, incidentally, superior to Isidore's, he was also interested in certain specific problems that required some knowledge of science. Computing the date of Easter was one of these. The Christian calendar was based upon the Roman Julian calendar which depended upon the sun, whereas the fixing of Easter depended upon the Hebrew lunar calendar. To calculate the proper date for Easter, the most important religious festival in the Christian year, required the correlation of the solar year with the lunar month but such a correlation is impossible since the lengths of the solar year, the lunar month and the day are incommensurable. Hence it is necessary in constructing a Christian calendar to make specific arbitrary adjustments which will, however, follow some definite cycle. In a series of treatises, Bede was able to introduce some order into the confusion which had accumulated by the eighth century. With data provided from Irish sources, themselves based upon Continental writings, he reduced the problem to the rather simple use of a 19 year cycle permitting the calculation of Easter for years in the future. He also discussed such related areas as time measurement, arithmetical computation, chronology and astronomical observations. He often repeated from literary sources, but he also used his own ideas and constantly tried to get at scientific laws through reason and experience. His work on tides which made up Chapter 29 of his treatise *De Temporum Ratione* (725) was clearly the result of observation and clear thinking. From his literary sources, he learned that tides follow the phases of the moon and armed with this information he described some of the specific peculiarities of the tides and lunar positions. He discussed spring and neap tides* and also noted how tides lag behind the moon by definite intervals which may not be the same at all points on the same shore. For every port, therefore, it may be necessary to construct a specific tide table rather than to rely on a general one calculated solely from lunar positions. Such attention to specifics was rare in Bede's time and his works mark the high tide of learning in the Dark Ages.

Bede's treatises and the tradition he established spilled over onto the continent. When Charlemagne sought a scholar who could rejuvenate learning in the kingdom of the Franks, he could find no one better suited to the task than Alcuin of York (ca. 735-804) who counted himself a follower of the Venerable Bede. Under Alcuin's leadership, a school was founded at Charles' court in Aachen (Aix-la-Chapelle) and Charlemagne sought out the best scholars of the day to staff it. The result was the Carolingian Renaissance. The term is somewhat of an exaggeration for only a small part of the classical heritage was re-born and this infant legacy died with Charlemagne. Under Alcuin's tutelage, the court scholars studied and improved their Latin. It was the Trivium rather than the Quadrivium that engaged their attention. The result was a modest revival of linguistic purity, an attempt to emulate classical Latin authors as in Einhard's biography of Charlemagne modeled on Suetonius' lives of the Caesars, and a notable improvement in handwriting. The level of philosophizing was not affected and science remained on the level at which Isidore had left it.

The one truly surprising figure of the Dark Ages is John Scot Erigena. He is surprising because he flourishes in a time of troubles and because he violates the orthodoxy within which previous thinkers had been content to work. We know little enough about him. He was an Irishman who knew Greek and worked at the court of Charles the Bold to which he had been invited by the king himself. Until his views became too unorthodox, he was the head of the Palace school.

Erigena's doctrines were based on a faith in reason which sometimes shaded off into intellectual arrogance. "We learn that reason is prior by nature," he wrote, "but authority prior in time. For although nature was created at the same moment with time, authority did not begin with the beginning of time and nature." And further: "Reason itself teaches this. Authority sometimes proceeds from reason; but reason never from authority. For all authority which is not approved by true reason seems weak. But true reason, since it is established in its own strength, needs to be strengthened by the assent of no authority."

This declaration of intellectual independence was formulated by a wide-ranging intellect which viewed the Christian world from a rather unique perspective for the ninth century. Erigena was a neo-Platonist heavily influenced by Saint Augustine and the pagan neo-Platonists. Some of the penetration and subtlety of Greek philosophy was re-introduced into Latin theology, with a heavy emphasis on pre-destination that reflected the Augustinian influ-

---

*A neap tide occurs shortly after the first and third quarters of the moon. The high-water level is then at its lowest point.

ence. There was similar heterodoxy in his cosmological writings. Not only does Erigena retain the spherical earth (as opposed to Isidore's flat one), but he retains as well the idea that Mercury and Venus go around the sun which, in turn, circles the earth. More importantly, Erigena preserved the neo-Platonic doctrine of substance which was later to play an important part in the development of medieval optics. For the neo-Platonist, substance was pure potentiality determined by spatial dimensions and this meant that it was capable of being treated mathematically. Erigena did not so treat it, but he kept alive the basic notion with which later philosophers worked.

With Gerbert, we come to the end of the Dark Ages. It is not so much that Gerbert is much more advanced than Isidore or Bede, but that one senses a new eagerness and confidence in his approach to learning. Earlier scholars were eager to preserve a pitifully meagre inheritance; Gerbert actively seeks out new treasures and is led by his search to what will serve as the intellectual fountain of youth for Medieval Europe, namely, the acquaintance with Islamic culture.

Gerbert was born in Aquitaine in southern France around the year 950. His ancestry was so humble that we know neither the exact date nor place of his birth. He was educated at the Benedictine monastery of St. Geraldus at Aurillac in Auvergne. As a youth, he traveled to Spain under a Spanish duke's protection and studied mathematics there. The local Bishop later took him to Rome where he began to teach mathematics. There also he came to the attention of both the Papacy and the Emperor, Otto II. The rest of his life was spent under Imperial sponsorship which made him successively Abbot and Count of Bobbio, Archbishop of Ravenna and, finally, Pope Sylvestre II.

The combination of learning and imperial favor made Gerbert a focal point for younger scholars who flocked to him. From him can be dated the tradition which, through his disciples at Rheims and Chartres, led ultimately to the creation of the University of Paris in the twelfth century. He was, almost singlehandedly, the instrument for the purification of Latin letters in the tenth century. He was also a natural philosopher, interested particularly in logic, mathematics and astronomy. In both these fields his contributions were modest but they clearly foreshadow what is to come. In logic, he exploited the Boethian treatises fully and prepared the way for the assimilation of Aristotle's later logical treatises when they became available in translations from the Arabic. In mathematics, he improved means of computation in arithmetic--an important service before the introduction of Arabic numbers--and brought together the extant geometrical knowledge of his time. In astronomy, he constructed spheres and other astronomical models and probably was responsible for the introduction of the astrolabe into the Latin West. Too much should not be made of all this. Arithmetical computations still remained difficult and beyond the reach of most people; geometry was rudimentary, it still being considered evidence of true mathematical ability to prove that the opposite interior angles of an isosceles triangle are equal. Astronomy was no more advanced than it had been in Bede's time, although armillary spheres and astrolabes offered the possibility of greater clarity in presentation and greater precision in measurement. As a famous scholar and as a Pope, Gerbert served to "popularize" such studies and create a thirst for more knowledge. This thirst was to be quenched in the twelfth century when the expansion of Christendom in Spain and in Sicily brought the West into intimate contact with Islam. As had been the case in the east, conquest fostered curiosity and curiosity was satisfied only ty the translation and assimilation of Islamic learning. It was in this fashion that the knowledge of Greek science finally reached the West. The result was the Renaissance of the twelfth century and the flowering of medieval science.

B. The Renaissance of the Twelfth Century

During the tenth and eleventh centuries, Western Europe gradually grew more peaceful and stable. In 911, the Norsemen received the Duchy of Normandy from Charles the Simple of France. In 987, Hugh Capet was elected King of France, thus beginning a dynasty which was to consolidate and strengthen France throughout the ensuing centuries. In the eleventh century, the mountainous kingdom of northern Spain was won back from Islam. Toledo fell in 1085 and Saragossa in 1118. In 1060, a group of free lance younger sons of Norman nobles embarked on an adventure in southern Italy which led to the conquest of Sicily and the establishment of a Christian kingdom in an area heavily influenced by Islam. In 1066, Duke William of Normandy invaded and conquered England, imposed a feudal government upon the conquered territories, and once and for all secured England against the incursions of the Danes who had harried the land for generations. The First Crusade was launched in 1095.

The offensive of Western Christendom against internal disorder and external enemies created new needs and new directions in Western society. Feudal government had evolved from the simple mutual bond of German warriors pledged to fight for one another, into an increasingly complex system of administration. The feudal army was still bound to the king by personal oaths of allegiance, but the services a vassal was expected to perform became increasingly complicated with time. The great nobles were to be consulted in matters of grand policy; the petty noble was delighted to be relieved of some of his more onerous burdens by whatever means and this usually meant payment of a money tax. Institutions had to be devised for these new functions. A King's Council or Court formalized the king's relations with his barons; judicial courts under the royal aegis began to bring royal, and therefore impersonal, justice to remote corners of the realm; a treasury evolved from a mere treasure chest kept under the king's bed to an Exchequer in which accounts were kept, receipts issued and tax delinquents pursued.

As feudal governments expanded and differentiated into specialized branches, the medieval Church underwent a similar transformation. Great princes in the Church had participated in affairs of state since the collapse of Roman administration left the Church's organization as the sole bureaucratic institution in Western Europe. The new conquests and the new confidence which accompanied them meant new opportunities and new dangers for the Church. There were heathens to be converted in Spain and Sicily, pagans to be saved in Poland and the Eastern Marches, and new wealth and ideas to be assimilated within the body of Holy Church. There were also problems to be faced. Every high Churchman who plunged whole-heartedly into the problems of secular administration created by the new vigor of the Western monarchies left a spiritual void behind him into which heterodoxy, skepticism or heresy might move. The pursuit of worldly goods and ambitions could and did lead men away from God and the Church had to find ways to reform itself to prevent complete secularization. The early response was the foundation of the Cluniac and Cistercian orders of monks whose reforming zeal in the tenth and eleventh centuries kept pace with the material conquests of the secular arm. A more subtle danger arose from the contact with non-Christian lands, particularly Islam. It was one thing to launch a crusade to conquer Spain or the Holy Lands and quite another to win the minds and faith of those that had been conquered. The monk or priest, armed only with Holy Scripture, some St. Augustine and Boethius was no match for the overwhelming power in the hands of those who commanded the ancient instruments of logic, philosophy and science. If Christian theology were to survive, it had to meet the enemy on his ground. Ancient learning might be dangerous to the faith, but ignorance of it appeared fatal in those areas where Islam and Christianity confronted one another. Nor were the reasons for the exploration of the ancient heritage purely theological. The Church, like the State, was becoming increasingly complex in its organization and desperately needed the guidance which the experience of antiquity offered. Rome, after all, had been a universal state as the Church was the Church universal (or catholic). The principles of organization and administration devised by the ancient political philosophers, lawyers and administrators certainly should prove relevant to the new Church militant.

The new conditions and the new aspirations of the Latin kingdoms placed extraordinary demands on the old institutions which they were not always able to meet. The result was new ones intended to solve the problem that arose. Some of these institutions evolved slowly and were shaped by the practical circumstances that gave them birth. Such, for example, was the English parliament which grew out of the needs for a royal court, a tax assessment bureau for the realm, and a center for petitioning the king. Others arose more suddenly and seemed to respond more directly to immediate stimuli. Such were the medieval universities which made their appearance at the end of the twelfth century. The universities were an institutional response to a two-fold need: the necessity of assimilating and "purifying" the knowledge suddenly made available by contact with Islam, and the need for providing lawyers and administrators for both Church and state. It was in the twelfth century that the Latin West was exposed to the full power of ancient thought and, through the universities, began the process of bending this thought to the service of orthodoxy and political administration.

The major point of intellectual contact between Christendom and Islam was Spain. With the fall of Toledo in 1085, Western scholars, for the first time, could examine the legacy of antiquity as it had been preserved by Arabic scholars. The road to knowledge was not an easy one for few Latin scholars knew Arabic and even fewer Arabic scholars felt the urge to learn Latin. The usual practice was translation from Arabic into the current Spanish vernacular, usually done by a Christianized Jew, and from thence into Latin by a Latin Christian scholar. There were exceptions to this rule. The most industrious and prolific of all the twelfth century translators was Gerard of Cremona who learned Arabic in order to translate Ptolemy's *Almagest*. The translators came from all over Western Eruope, their origins reflected in their names. There were Adelard of Bath, Plato of Tivoli, Robert of Chester, Hermann of Carinthia, Rudolf of Bruges, Hugh of Santella and John of Seville, to mention only the more prominent. By the middle of the thirteenth century they had rendered into Latin the vast majority of the treatises of ancient science which have survived. Gerard of Cremona had translated the *Almagest* by 1175, together with Aristotle's *Posterior Analytics*, Euclid's *Elements*, a tract of Archimedes and various other treatises on geometry, algebra and optics. He was also responsible for making the writings of Galen and Hippocrates available in Latin. Other translators completed the rendering of the Aristotelian corpus into Latin. The Latin West received more than the scientific works of antiquity, however, for the translators also were intrigued with the Arabic commentaries on these works. Thus along with Aristotle came Averroes and Avicenna and with Euclid came al-Khwarizmi. The twelfth century scholar was thereby presented with both the legacy of antiquity and the legacy of Islam. It was almost too rich a feast and it caused serious intellectual indigestion until the major organ of assimilation--the university--could undertake the task.*

The university is uniquely a Western medieval institution. Nothing like it had existed in antiquity and it clearly reflects its medieval origins. The word *university* originally meant a corporation or a guild and only gradually did its meaning become narrowed to denote a learned corporation or society of masters and scholars. The earliest universities grew up around teachers active at Salerno and Bologna in Italy and Paris in France. Salerno's origins are lost in the mists of time. There appears to have been some kind of a medical school there as early as the ninth century, but its fame did not become widespread enough to attract students from the rest of Europe until the twelfth century. The University of Bologna is traditionally associated with the name of Irnerius and the revival of Roman Law. Peter Abelard (1079-1142) at Paris attracted so many students that regulations had to be created to control them. These regulations provide our

---

* The appended table taken from A. C. Crombie, *Medieval and Early Modern Science*, 2 vols., Doubleday & Co., Garden City, N.Y., 1959, vol. 1, 37-47, lists the works translated in this period.

THE PRINCIPAL SOURCES OF ANCIENT SCIENCE IN

WESTERN CHRISTENDOM BETWEEN 500 AND 1300 A.D.

Author	Work	Latin translator and language of original of translation	Place and date of Latin translation
(1) *Early Greek and Latin Sources*			
Plato (428-347 B.C.)	*Timæus* (first 53 chapters)	Chalcidius from Greek	4th century
Aristotle (384-22 B.C.)	Some logical works (*logica vetus)*	Boethius from Greek	Italy 6th century
Dioscorides (1st century A.D.)	*Materia Medica*	from Greek	by 6th century
Anon.	*Physiologus* (2nd century A.D. Alexandria)	from Greek	5th century
Anon.	Various technical *Compositiones*	from Greek sources	earliest MSS 8th century
Lucretius (c. 95-55 B.C.)	*De Rerum Natura* (known in excerpts from 9th century; full text recovered 1417)		
Vitruvius (1st century B.C.)	*De Architectura* (known in 12th century)		
Seneca (4 B.C.-65 A.C.)	*Quæstiones Naturales*		
Pliny (23-79 A.D.)	*Historia Naturalis*		
Macrobius (fl. 395-423)	*In Somnium Scipionis*		

Martianus Capella (5th century)	*Satyricon, sive De Nuptiis Philologiæ et Mercurii et de Septem Artibus Liberalibus*		
Boethius (480-524)	Works on the liberal arts, particularly mathematics and astronomy, and commentaries on the logic of Aristotle and Porphyry		
Cassiodorus (c. 490-580)	Works on the liberal arts		
Isidore of Seville (560-636)	*Etymologiarum sive Originum* *De Natura Rerum*		
Bede (673-735)	*De Natura Rerum* *De Temporum Ratione*		

(2) Arabic Sources from c. 1000

Jabir ibn Hayyan corpus (written 9th-10th century)	Various chemical works	from Arabic	12th and 13th centuries
Al-Khwarizmi (9th century)	*Liber Ysagogarum Alchorismi* (arithmetic)	Adelard of Bath from Arabic	early 12th century
	Astronomical tables (trigonometry)	Adelard of Bath from Arabic	1126
	Algebra	Robert of Chester from Arabic	Segovia 1145
Alkindi (d. c. 873)	*De Aspectibus; De Umbris et de Diversitate Aspectum*	Gerard of Cremona from Arabic	Toledo 12th century

Thabit ibn Qurra (d. 901)	*Liber Charastonis* (on the Roman balance)	Gerard of Cremona from Arabic	Toledo 12th century
Rhazes (d. c. 924)	*De Aluminibus et Salibus* (chemical work)	Gerard of Cremona from Arabic	Toledo 12th century
	Liber Continens (medical encyclopædia)	Moses Farachi from Arabic	Sicily 1279
	Liber Almansoris (medical compilation based on Greek sources)	Gerard of Cremona from Arabic	Toledo 12th century
Alfarabi (d. 950)	*Distinctio super Librum Aristotelis de Naturali Auditu*	Gerard of Cremona from Arabic	Toledo 12th century
Haly Abbas (d. 994)	Part of *Liber Regalis* (medical encyclopædia)	Constantine the African (d. 1087) and John the Saracen from Arabic	South Italy 11th century
	Liber Regalis	Stephen of Antioch from Arabic	c. 1127
pseudo-Aristotle	*De Proprietatibus Elementorum* (Arabic work on geology)	Gerard of Cremona from Arabic	Toledo 12th century
Alhazen (c. 965-1039)	*Opticæ Thesaurus*	from Arabic	end of 12th century
Avicenna (980-1037)	Physical and philosophical part of *Kitab al-Shifa* (commentary on Aristotle)	Dominicus Gundissalinus John of Seville, abbreviated from Arabic	Toledo 12th century
	De Mineralibus (geological and alchemical part of *Kitab al-Shifa*)	Alfred of Sareshel from Arabic	Spain c. 1200
	Canon (medical encyclopædia)	Gerard of Cremona from Arabic	Toledo 12th century

Alpetragius (12th century)	*Liber Astronomiæ* (Aristotelian concentric system)	Michael Scot from Arabic	Toledo 1217
Averroës (1126-98)	Commentaries on *Physica, De Cælo et Mundo, De Anima* and other works of Aristotle	Michael Scot from Arabic	early 13th century
Leonardo Fibonacci of Pisa	*Liber Abaci* (first complete account of Hindu numerals)	using Arabic knowledge	1202

(3) *Greek Sources from c. 1100*

Hippocrates and school (5th, 4th centuries B.C.)	*Aphorisms*	Burgundio of Pisa from Greek	12th century
	Various treatises	Gerard of Cremona and others from Arabic	Toledo 12th century
		William of Moerbeke from Greek	after 1260
Aristotle (384-22 B.C.)	*Posterior Analytics* (part of *logica nova*)	Two versions from Greek	12th century
		from Arabic	Toledo 12th century
	Meteorologica (Book 4)	Henricus Aristippus from Greek	Sicily c. 1156
	Physica, De Generatione et Corruptione, Parva Naturalia, Metaphysica (1st 4 books), *De Anima*	from Greek	12th century
	Meteorologica (Books 1-3), *Physica, De Cælo et Mundo, De Generatione et Corruptione*	Gerard of Cremona from Arabic	Toledo 12th century

Aristotle (384-22 B.C.)	*De Animalibus (Historia animalium, De partibus animalium, De generatione animalium* trans. into Arabic in 19 books by el-Batric, 9th century)	Michael Scot from Arabic	Spain c. 1217-20
	Almost complete works	William of Moerbeke, new or revised translations from Greek	c. 1260-71
Euclid (c. 330-260 B.C.)	*Elements* (15 books, 13 genuine)	Adelard of Bath from Arabic	early 12th century
		Hermann of Carinthia from Arabic	12th century
		Gerard of Cremona from Arabic	Toledo 12th century
		several revisions; revision of Adelard's version by John Campanus of Novara	c. 1254
	Optica and *Catoptrica*	from Greek	probably Sicily
	Optica	from Arabic	
	Data	from Greek	
Apollonius (3rd century B.C.)	*Conica*	perhaps Gerard of Cremona from Arabic (of this translation only a short fragment of Book 1 is now extant, as the introduction to Alhazen's *De Speculis Comburentibus*; but Book 2 was known to Witelo in the 13th century)	12th century
Archimedes (287-12 B.C.)	*De Mensura Circuli*	Gerard of Cremona from Arabic	Toledo 12th century

Archimedes (287-12 B.C.)	Complete works (except for the *Sandreckoner*, the *Lemmata*, and the *Method*)	William of Moerbeke from Greek	1269
Diocles (2nd century B.C.)	*De Speculis Comburentibus*	Gerard of Cremona from Arabic	Toledo 12th century
Hero of Alexandria (1st century B.C.?)	*Pneumatica*	from Greek	Sicily 12th century
	Catoptrica (attributed to Ptolemy in Middle Ages)	William of Moerbeke from Greek	after 1260
pseudo-Aristotle	*Mechanica (Mechanical Problems)*	from Greek	early 13th century
	Problemata	Bartholomew of Messina from Greek	Sicily c. 1260
	De Plantis or *De Vegetabilibus* (now attributed to Nicholas of Damascus, 1st century B.C.)	Alfred of Sareshel from Arabic	Spain, probably before 1200
pseudo-Euclid	*Liber Euclidis de Ponderoso et Levi* (statics)	from Arabic	12th century
Galen (129-200 A.D.)	Various treatises	Burgundio of Pisa from Greek	c. 1185.
	Various treatises	Gerard of Cremona and others from Arabic	Toledo 12th century
	Various treatises	William of Moerbeke from Greek	1277
	Anatomical treatises	from Greek	14th century
Ptolemy (2nd century A.D.)	*Almagest*	from Greek	Sicily c. 1160
		Gerard of Cremona from Arabic	Toledo 1175
	Optica	Eugenius of Palermo from Arabic	c. 1154

Alexander of Aphrodisias (fl. 193-217 A.D.)	Commentary on the *Meteorologica*	William of Moerbeke from Greek	13th century
	De Motu et Tempore	Gerard of Cremona from Arabic	Toledo 12th century
Simplicius (6th century A.D.)	Part of commentary on *De Cælo et Mundo*	Robert Grosseteste from Greek	13th century
	Commentary on *Physica*	from Greek	13th century
	Commentary on *De Cælo et Mundo*	William of Moerbeke from Greek	1271
Proclus (410-85 A.D.)	*Physica Elementa (De motu)*	from Greek	Sicily 12th century

first glimpse of the University of Paris. Perhaps some comfort can be drawn from the fact that the University makes its initial appearance on the historical scene in a student riot, bloodily repressed by the Provost of Paris.

Abelard is the central figure for an understanding of the intellectual milieu into which the legacy of antiquity was injected. Abelard is the contemporary of the great translators but he worked and thought without the benefit of most of the translated works. It was he, however, who set the pace and created the framework for the assimilation of ancient learning.

Abelard was the eldest son of a Breton noble who chose to follow the career of learning rather than that of arms. He carried over into the intellectual realm some of the arrogance and boldness of the feudal noble and introduced a new note of belligerence into Western thought. For Abelard, reason was a God-given faculty that God expected man to use. But, reason was to be used in the service of religion and it was toward the knowledge of God that Abelard directed his mental powers. It was in the works of Abelard that one of the great differences between Islam and Christianity was revealed. As we have already noted, the Koran was the product of one man's experience with God whereas Christian Scripture had been written down over the course of centuries. Christian Scripture, therefore, contained contradictions and obscurities not found in the Koran and Christian commentators somehow had to come to grips with these textual difficulties. Abelard grasped this nettle firmly and laid down both a program and method for further study. There was no sense ignoring these problems in Abelard's view. Far better to expose them to the light of reason and attempt, through reason, to solve them. His great work, *Sic et Non* (*Yes and No*), did exactly this. It offered citations from Scripture and the Church Fathers which contradicted one another and Abelard challenged his colleagues to reconcile these apparent contradictions. He offered some help in this task by suggesting that some of the contradictions were the result of textual corruptions, scribal errors due to copying or misunderstandings, or the failure to realize that particular passages should not be read literally. Clearly, before the contradictions could be removed, the passages had to be understood and this required close attention to language. Clear definition of terms must precede analysis of content. Further understanding would result by the application of logic to the disputed passages. A thesis could be stated and supported by authorities; counter-theses with counter-authorities would sharpen the argument and from this intellectual joust, Truth would emerge. There were those, like St. Bernard de Clairvaux, Abelard's arch-enemy, who suspected that arguments over faith would only serve to weaken it but Abelard won the day, at least in the Universities. His method grew into Scholasticism and it was through the scholastic philosophers that ancient learning was worked into medieval thought. St. Thomas Aquinas used the same method in his attack on an Aristotelian text as he did when explaining St. Augustine or Scripture itself. Terms are defined (sometimes fancifully), theses stated, arguments both pro and con are presented, and conclusions finally drawn. The emphasis is upon words and logic, not things and processes. Logical coherence and generality are more important than factual detail or specific validity. And all learning, it must be emphasized again, was at the service of faith. A fact, in and of itself, was relatively uninteresting. It was only when a fact illuminated the path to God or salvation that it became of preeminent worth. And no fact, by and of itself, could be expected to destroy the grand synthesis of ancient learning and Christian faith that was created in the thirteenth century by men such as Albertus Magnus and St. Thomas Aquinas. It was in the universities that this synthesis was achieved and it was in the universities that medieval science developed.

There are a number of stages in the evolution of medieval science. In the first, there is the introduction to the legacy of antiquity as presented by the translators. The immediate result was two-fold; indigestion and fear for the purity of the faith. The indigestion is most clearly illustrated by the reception of Ptolemy's *Almagest*. After Gerard of Cremona had translated it, no one knew what to do with it. Parts of it could be understood but the mathematics was difficult and beyond the comprehension of most Western scholars. The true level of mathematical learning is revealed in a treatise by John of Holywood (fl. 1200) or Sacrobosco in Latinized form. The *Sphere* of Sacrobosco is an elementary work on spherical geometry with only the rudiments of trigonometry. It was completely inadequate as an introduction to the *Almagest*, yet it served as an advanced and popular textbook for generations. It was not, in fact, until the fourteenth century that the *Almagest* could be completely understood and its mathematical methods actually applied consistently to the computational problems of astronomy.

The threat to faith was present in the works of Aristotle whose doctrines flatly contradicted fundamental articles of Christian doctrine. The most obvious case was the conflict between Aristotle's clearly reasoned conclusion that the world was eternal and *Genesis*' account of the creation. More importantly, Aristotle and the Arabic commentators who accompanied him into the West, tended to bring all theology under the dominance of reason. The Arab-Aristotelian system was strictly deterministic, leaving no scope for free will either on the Divine or human scale. Aristotle himself had insisted that the unaided human reason could rise to the comprehension of God and, from thence, deduce the nature of the World. There was no room here for individual responsibility, individual salvation or mystery. Yet medieval Christianity was a mystery religion based upon such incomprehensible doctrines as the Trinity and the ultimate free will of every individual Christian. This was no laughing matter for one had to consider seriously whether the new learning was worth the price of possible damnation. It should not be forgotten that it was not only philosophy and science that were pouring into Western Europe at this time. There were, as well, religious doctrines such as Manichaeanism, which led to the Albigensian heresy in southern France. If Aristotle were to be accepted, he must be "cleaned up" and made acceptable to orthodox Christians. The Church, therefore, moved swiftly. As early as 1210, the study of Aristotle was forbidden at Paris. In 1231, Pope Gregory IX modified this ruling and set up a commission to examine the controversial works, but there is no evidence that the commission ever carried out this work. By 1255, all Aristotle's scientific works, unchanged, were being taught at Paris and, although the Papal ban was renewed in 1263, there was no effective way of enforcing the prohibition. The job of making Aristotle acceptable could not be accomplished by Papal fiat but had to be left to the patient labor of a generation of scholars. We need not pause here to examine the various schools of Aristotelian scholarship that grew up but we should note that this scholarship developed within a controversial, theological framework. Thus, the achievement of St. Thomas Aquinas who was able most successfully to reconcile Aristotelian science with Christian doctrine was essentially a theological victory. Aquinas succeeded in making Aristotle acceptable, some would say essential, to Christian theology but in the process he gave a theological dimension to science which made it possible in later centuries to confuse scientific innovation with religious heterodoxy. The result could only be detrimental to both science and religion.

The initial phase of assimilation and "purification" of Greek science was followed by a second phase which appears to contain contradictory opposites. On the one hand, the acceptance of Greek science, particularly Aristotle in natural philosophy and Galen in medicine, led to scientific dogmatism. On the other hand, acquaintance with certain aspects of Greek science such as natural history, optics and dynamics led to intense and intensive criticism of the ancient legacy. The contradiction is only apparent, not real, for the subject matter tended to determine the treatment of ancient science. Aristotle's cosmology and general theory of natural philosophy suited the requirements of medieval intellectuals admirably. The Aristotelian cosmos was hierarchical in nature, as was the medieval Christian world. To question seriously the Aristotelian hierarchy from formless *materia prima*, through the great chain of being to the intelligences that moved the planets and finally to the Unmoved Mover upon which all motion and form ultimately depended was both to discard the most comprehensive system of the world then available and to tear at the very fabric of society with its hierarchy of serf, bourgeois, noble, king, angel and Christ. The system was all of a piece and, *as a system*, it was to be contemplated and appreciated, not attacked or chipped at. We shall see later the intellectual trauma that resulted from the destruction of the Aristotelian cosmos.

The respect for Galen is somewhat more difficult to understand. What was at stake was not the intellectual foundations of medieval society, but the privileges and prerogatives of the medical profession. It was in the Middle Ages that the physician became a doctor whose medical degree attested to his learning, which might or might not aid him in his treatment of illness. To be a doctor meant to be learned in Galen, to have read the Galenic treatises and the Arabic commentaries upon them, and to have disputed various medical points. The dignity of the profession was based upon this learning so it is not surprising to find the Galenic medical system (if one can call it that) protected and supported against all criticism. One does not wish, after all, to have to learn new things after one has been certified a doctor! If Galen had been good enough for the ancients and for the Arabs, then surely he was good enough for medieval man. Then, too, there were not very many opportunities to challenge Galen. To be sure, adherence to Galenic prescriptions did not always effect a cure, but then medicine was an art, not a science, and one should not expect miracles. Clinical observations, which Galen and Hippocrates had used to such advantage, could not be expected to carry sufficient weight to overturn the massive authority of the master. Even the teaching of medicine was conducted in such a way as to minimize the possibility of criticism. The teacher, himself a doctor, read the works of Galen while seated in his professorial chair. Students took notes on the reading or lecture. In the early days, that was it and there was nothing upon which the student could base any criticism whatsoever. In the fourteenth century in Italy, the lecture was accompanied by dissection of a cadaver, but even here the opportunities for criticism were minimal. The professor, being a learned man, could not be expected to undertake the actual dissection himself. The students, being potential learned men, also could not be expected to involve themselves in this rather messy job. The task was, therefore, relegated to a menial who carved away under the physician's direction. Armed with a long pointer, the professor would then illustrate his reading of Galen by pointing distastefully to the appropriate organ laid bare by the dissector's knife. The student often observed from a distance and was literally in no position to see enough to question the text being read to him. It was only when physicians undertook the dissecting themselves that they were able to discover the discrepancies between what Galen said was there and what could actually be discerned by the medically trained eye.

The criticism of ancient science took place, not surprisingly, in those areas in which medieval men were able to detect flaws easily and which were also of no fundamental importance for the total structure of medieval thought. Thus, for example, a false observation by Aristotle in natural history, or an erroneous account of the rainbow or an insufficient explanation of the fall of a stone could be handled dispassionately without fear of destroying one's own intellectual orientation. No man, after all, is perfect and that Aristotle or some other ancient erred *in matters of detail* was only to be expected. So, hand in hand with the deepest respect for ancient authority in matters of cosmic importance, there developed, in the thirteenth and fourteenth centuries, an intensely critical tradition which saw nothing wrong with simply calling any ancient authority wrong in matters of fact.

1. Natural History

The focus on the philosophical tradition of the Middle Ages, with its emphases upon definition, logic and disputation over words has often obscured the fact that medieval men were close to nature and excellent observers of it. The sculpture adorning the portals of the great medieval cathedrals abound with examples of plants and animals so lifelike that they are easily identifiable. Many medieval intellectuals traversed Europe on foot on pilgrimage or bent on an ecclesiastical mission. Those with sharp eyes carefully noted the flora and fauna of the countries through which they passed. Such a one was Albertus Magnus who, as a leading member of the Dominican Order, traveled extensively throughout the West. Even the nobility who generally found little disadvantage in illiteracy were keenly interested in the hunt and in the habits of both game and the birds and animals used in chase. It was a most exceptional member of this class who wrote one of the finest and most critical works on natural history during the Middle Ages. Frederick II Hohenstaufen (1194-1250) was no ordinary medieval prince. As Holy Roman Emperor, he commanded unusual resources which he fully exploited. He kept a personal zoo which accompanied him on his travels in Italy and Germany. It included elephants, camels, panthers, lions, leopards, monkeys and the first giraffe ever seen in Europe. His motives appear simple--he enjoyed looking at strange beasts. He also enjoyed hunting, particularly with falcons. His curiosity here led him to explore the literary accounts and to make simple experiments. The result was his *De Arte Venandi cum Avibus* (*The Art of Hunting with Birds*) which is both an exhaustive treatise on falconry and a critical examination of the natural history of various birds. His treatment of literary sources is delightfully frank. When he read palpable nonsense, he had no hesitation in labeling the passage "lying and inadequate" even if the author were Aristotle himself. The pictures of birds, of which there are some 900, are drawn from life; the depiction of birds in flight are clearly based on close and accurate observation. Frederick II settled the question of whether vultures were attracted to carrion by sight of smell by the simple expedient of sewing their eyelids shut so they could not see. Without sight, a vulture cannot find its food. Similarly, he exploded the myth that barnacle geese were hatched from barnacles on trees by procuring barnacles, opening them, and announcing that there was nothing inside that vaguely resembled a bird. He concluded that the story had grown up because no one had ever actually observed the hatching of barnacle geese. He dissected birds and described the air cavities in their bones, the structure of their lungs and other hitherto unnoted aspects of avian anatomy.

His curiosity, skepticism in the face of authority and use of simple experiments led him to undertake some investigations whose results were less spectacular than those recorded in the *De Arte Verandi*. It had been argued, for example, that Hebrew must have been man's "natural" tongue from the time of the Creation. Frederick II "tested" this by attempting to raise two infants in isolation from human speech and record their first words. The experiment failed when the children died. Another "experiment" was tried to determine when the soul left the body. A convict was sealed in a trunk until he died. Then, in the presence of the Imperial court, the lid was lifted but no one could say for sure that he had seen the dead man's soul fly out. These failures of the "experimental method" should warn us that the use of experiment was no guarantee of scientific progress.

The existence of a Frederick II or an Albertus Magnus should also not blind us to the fact that there were credulous naturalists in the Middle Ages as well as skeptical and critical ones. The influence of Pliny was pervasive and there was always the temptation to pass on fabulous tales if only because they were so entertaining. The writings of a man such as Bartholomew the Englishman, Frederick's contemporary, which abounded in fanciful descriptions and wonderful accounts of mythical beasts were popular for centuries. Shakespeare drew heavily upon Bartholomew, not Frederick or Albertus Magnus.

2. The Rainbow

We move more surely into science with the medieval discussions of the rainbow. The rainbow had intrigued men for centuries and Aristotle had provided an explanation which had satisfied the ancients. He had suggested that it was produced by reflection from raindrops. Since the light is reflected, the rainbow always appears to the viewer opposite the sun. Since reflection from a dark substance such as water produces color, particularly red, the rainbow is a red bow; the other colors are produced by the weakening of our sight by distance. A series of medieval scholars laid siege to this theory and substituted for it one that agrees much more closely with observation. The first shot was fired by Robert Grosseteste (ca. 1168-1253) who felt that the rainbow was the result of the refraction, rather than the reflection, of light. This refraction was produced by a cloud acting like a lens and he tried to demonstrate this process by the use of a spherical lens. This work, indicentally, led Grosseteste to a detailed consideration of refraction including the attempt to formulate a mathematical law. Soon after, spectacles were invented in northern Italy, an early technological "spin-off" from pure scientific research.

Grosseteste's interest in the rainbow was continued by a number of followers. His disciple, Roger Bacon (? 1219-92) made careful observations with an astrolabe to show that the bow was always opposite the sun and that the center of the bow, the observer and the sun were always in a straight line. He also showed that the angle made by the rays coming from the bow to the observer with the rays from the sun was always 42°. It followed from these data that each observer saw a different rainbow and this he confirmed by showing that the bow moved with him when he changed position. The careful observations led him nowhere, however, when it came to the question of the origin of the colors of the bow. Later investigators came a little closer to an answer but the value of their work lies more in their method than in their results. The Silesian writer Witelo (born ca. 1230) measured angles of refraction in an attempt to discover the mathematical connection between incident and refracted ray suggested by Grosseteste. It is interesting to note that many of Witelo's "measurements" were actually figures deduced from what he thought to be obvious. Thus, it never occurred to Witelo that there might be an angle at which *no* refraction took place but at which all the light was reflected. The mental process is worth underlining. A series of measurements establish an empirical regularity that seems to justify extrapolation. The existence of a critical angle cannot be deduced; it must be observed. It was to take centuries for men to realize that nature can *never* be taken for granted. Obvious deductions *always* have to be checked. Experiment is a critical tool, as well as an instrument of discovery.

Witelo's quantitative investigation of refraction led him to the discovery that refraction through an hexagonal prism produced the colored spectrum. Thus Grosseteste's suggestion that the rainbow was caused by refraction appeared to be verified, but Witelo was at a loss to explain the spectrum. Nevertheless, the explanation had progressed one significant step.

The final medieval attack on the problem was made by Theodoric of Freiburg (died 1371). It is difficult to make precise, detailed observations on the individual drops of rain in a rainbow. Theodoric took the significant step of arguing from an analogy which permitted him to experiment with and observe the equivalent of an individual drop. Theodoric worked with a spherical glass vessel filled with water and with a crystal ball. It is by no means obvious that either of these objects ought to act precisely like a raindrop. Both are far larger and both contain a foreign element not present in rain. Yet, Theodoric was able to argue that, for his purpose, the analogy was sufficiently exact to permit him to substitute these artificial "drops" for real ones. Light ought to act similarly in both cases. This methodological assumption permitted Theodoric to transform a problem in natural history into one in experimental physics. The difference is an important one. In natural history one must rest content with observation and, perhaps, measurement. In experimental physics, one can alter the conditions and vary them in such ways as to extract correlations never revealed by observation. In this way, Theodoric was able to suggest the actual path of the incident light ray as being an initial refraction into the raindrop, internal reflection, and refraction out again. The observed secondary bow could be accounted for by multiple internal reflection before the second refraction. Using his crystal balls and spherical glass vessels he was also able to produce the colors of the rainbow and the close observation of his laboratory analogies led him to realize that the colors were produced by the first refraction. Beyond this he could not go and, for theory, had to fall back upon a theory of color proposed by Averroes in his commentaries on Aristotle. Once again we should note that experiment, alone, can go only so far in the solution of a specific scientific problem. It may be a necessary condition for its ultimate resolution, but it does not appear to be sufficient in and of itself.

II. Readings on Medieval Science

A. The Nature of Science in the Middle Ages

The phrase "The Dark Ages" was once considered to be both self-explanatory and true. The period from the end of the Roman Empire to the rebirth of letters in the Italian Renaissance was supposed to have been one of almost unrelieved night in which the mind of Western man stagnated. The uncovering of beautiful *objets d'art*, the contemplation of the great medieval cathedrals and the appreciation of the literature of the Middle Ages served to challenge this view and to suggest that the civilization of medieval Europe was only different, not inferior, to that which preceded and followed it. But what of science? Was it possible to argue that an Isidore of Seville was merely looking for different things than an Archimedes or is it necessary to admit a scientific Dark Ages? In the selections that follow, a number of modern authors discuss the nature and environment of science in the Middle Ages and the level of science is then illustrated by selections from contemporary authors.

1. Charles Singer on the Dark Ages*

Charles Singer was one of the pioneers in the history of science. He was particularly interested in the history of biology and medicine.

The Dark Ages! The phrase conjures up a picture of disorder, of ineptitude, of coarse decadent art, of a childish form of piety. As the men of the Empire in its decline had chewed the cud of the past that had been Greece and Rome, its savour turned into that of sand and sawdust. For many the crazy cults of the Orient yielded still a lurid interest to life. For some the inevitable determination of man's fate provided by Epicurean materialism or astrological rule gave that certainty in which some yet find solace. Very few were they who could recite with the philosopher emperor "At all times and in all places it is my charge to rest content with my lot, to deal justly with my neighbours, and above all to guard my heart, that nothing unverified may creep therein!" Yet fewer could dwell serene with the Antonine on Olympus' height in that deep brooding melodious melancholy which felt neither pain nor pleasure, nor joy nor woe nor anger. And so it was that the might of Rome was brought to nought.

On that hard Pagan world disgust
    And secret loathing fell.
Deep weariness and sated lust
    Made human life a hell.

---

*Charles Singer, "The Dark Age of Science," in *The Realist*, vol. 2 (1929), pp. 281-295.

She veil'd her eagles, snapp'd her sword,
And laid her sceptre down;
Her stately purple she abhorr'd
And her imperial crown.

She broke her flutes, she stopp'd her sports,
Her artists could not please;
She tore her books, she shut her courts,
She fled her palaces.
(Matthew Arnold, *Obermann once more*.)

Such was the end of the science of antiquity. When books are torn, courts are shut and palaces are fled, literature and art change their forms. They become barbarous. But as for science--she does not languish only, but she dies. For science, unlike literature and art, is a process, and is conditioned by time. Like most processes, it can be reversed. Science is the making of knowledge, and knowledge can not only be made but also unmade.

The burden of that unmaking cannot be laid upon the faith that was to replace the systems of the older pagan world. When Christianity appeared upon the horizon, as a cloud no bigger than a man's hand, the unmaking had already gone far. Ancient science had already raised a motiveless machine of a universe, a machine that worked by pitiless mathematical rule, grinding all men to their doom. From such an horror men turned in fear, preferring the poor assurances, only half believed, held out to them by Mithra, Cybele, Isis and the rest. It was to these and to all manner of magic folly that they fled. The early fathers of the Church were less in disaccord with the spirit of the older philosophy than were these cults. For them the orderliness of nature was no mechanical tyranny, since it reflected the orderliness of the mind of God. Thus Clement (about A.D. 100) called "from the Church of God that sojourneth at Rome to the Church of God that sojourneth at Corinth" to remember that "sun and moon and the companies of the stars roll on in harmony in their appointed courses according to His will, and swerve not at all therefrom. The earth teemeth at her proper season and all the things thereon obey a rule, for there is no change in His decrees. The impassable ocean and the worlds beyond are governed by the same laws. The seasons give way to one another in peace, according as He hath ordained." Early Christian thought was certainly not more out of tune than the other religions of the Empire with the older physical philosophy.

The Church has sometimes been accused of the destruction of ancient science. So far as the studies of the writer of this article entitle him to express a judgment, the charge is groundless. Science was in headlong decay long before Christianity began to shape the characteristic interests of Europe. At a later date--in the thirteenth century and after--and especially with the intellectual conflicts of the sixteenth and seventeenth centuries, the Church certainly set herself against independent thought. But in the "Dark Ages" before the scientific movement arose, this could hardly be. It was inward decay and not attacks from without that destroyed ancient science. It was Science's own dogmas that removed from her the motive for further research. The Science of the declining Empire was of a piece with her times. The late pagan world was without causes, without enthusiasms. Christianity at last brought a cause, but by then Science had already long been lifeless.

> Lust of the eye and pride of life
> She left it all behind,
> And hurried, torn with inward strife,
> The wilderness to find.
>
> Tears wash'd the trouble from her face!
> She changed into a child!
> 'Mid weeds and wrecks she stood--a place
> Of ruin--but she smiled!

For various reasons, and at various times, men have exalted the thought and the life of the Middle Ages that stand between antiquity and modernity. Mediaeval religion, mediaeval art, and a supposed mediaeval harmony of life, have been and still are held by some to have surpassed anything that we now know. Into this discussion we shall not enter here, for we are dealing with science, and few have been found to exalt the science of the Middle Ages. Even the adherents of the philosophy which is called Neo-scholasticism are apologetic in their explanation of the value of the scholastic method for science.

Of late there has arisen a school that denies the existence of a true "Dark Age." It is pointed out that the lives of saints such as Benedict (died 544), of men of literary genius such as Bede (died 735), of philosophers and scholars such as John the Scot (died 880), could not be the products of mere barbarism. Their works, however, are individual creations, while science--quite contrary to a commonly expressed opinion--demands for its development a continuous and unbroken tradition. For the painting of the Dark Ages of science no colours can be too dark.

So far as science is concerned the whole course of history presents no more clear division than that between the earlier Middle Ages or "Dark Age" and the later Middle Ages or "Scholastic Age." The critical event is the arrival of the Arabian influence. Those not accustomed to deal with mediaeval documents may not be aware of the tremendous revolution in thought produced during the twelfth and thirteenth centuries by the arrival in Europe of a number of Latin translations of Arabic works. We may bestow, for a few moments, some attention to that phenomenon.

The two centuries that preceded the twelfth were the golden period of Islamic culture. The great works of science and philosophy left by the Greeks had already been translated into Arabic. Moreover, the relation between East and West was very different from that which we now know. From the confines of China to the Atlantic, in Spain and Sicily, in Asia Minor, Egypt, Morocco and Mesopotamia, there was stable and civilised Moslem rule. The language of the Koran was spoken and read, for trade as for law and philosophy, throughout this vast territory. Culture had reached a high standard. Greek thought was familiar in an extensive literature translated into Arabic. Academies had been established. Learning was widely diffused. And now Islam, with a population, a wealth and a unity far exceeding that of Christendom, turned to develop this material. The product was portentous.

In the twelfth century the Arabian writings began to be accessible to Christendom in Latin translations. The stream of these gathered force for some three hundred years. This impact of Arabian literature upon Latin Europe precipitated an intellectual revolution fairly comparable in extent and character to that produced by modern science. The results and character of this revolution we need not now attempt to trace. What concerns us for our present theme is that it cuts off the earlier Dark Age from the later scholastic centuries of Arabian influence as clearly as one period in the history of thought has ever been cut off from another. When in contact with a new mediaeval document the first and most elementary question that the historian of science asks himself is always: "Can I discern Arabian influence here?" If the Arabian element is present, the document is placed in the "Scholastic" category, if absent, in the "Dark Age" category.

We may turn now to consider the characteristics of these Dark Age documents, of which a good example lies before us at this moment. The *Handboc* of the monk Byrhtferth of the monastery of Ramsey has long been a stumbling block to students of Anglo-Saxon. It was the one literary monument in that language that continued inaccessible. Now the *Handboc* has at last been most ably edited and translated by Mr. S. J. Crawford of Southampton. Mr. Crawford's work is wholly admirable. It exhibits the results of deep and varied learning presented with irreproachable clarity. The *Handboc* itself, as a specimen of Dark Age science, opens a new world to the English reader.

It was written half a century before the Norman Conquest. The *Handboc* of Byrhtferth is a compendium of the physical knowledge of its day, and yields a vivid picture of the degradation of the contemporary intellect. It is interesting as the earliest work on "science" written in English. It is even more interesting as an exemplar of the fate of the human mind should knowledge cease to grow, should men cease to be critical, should philosophy cease to be coherent. Skilled writers who are gifted with anthropological learning have enabled us to enter into the mind of the savage. There is room for a scholar who can introduce us to the sophisticated childishness, the inane learning, and the humourless edificatory imbecility of the men of the Dark Age. Brother Byrhtferth presents these undesirable qualities neither in greater nor less degree than most of his contemporaries. He is a good average "Dark Age" writer, and he is worth perusal by those who dwell in the light that science has since shed.

Byrhtferth opens with an elaborate discussion of the Calendar, of how the year is divided, of how to reckon dates, and how to calculate the festivals of the Church. This topic, known throughout the Middle Ages as *Computus*, occupies the leading place in all early works on general science. It is difficult nowadays to understand this insatiable interest in what is, to most of us, a very arid theme. But in Byrhtferth's world communications were difficult and often interrupted, the only industry was agriculture or was linked with agriculture, books were few and costly, literacy was rare. The very existence of that continuity necessary for the preservation of the last remains of civilisation hung by a slender thread. Differences in the dates of Church festivals, incident on different methods of calendar reckoning, could utterly divide neighbouring communities. Such differences had already caused the widest rifts in Christendom, both East and West. Moreover, the men of the "Dark Age" felt their darkness. The one thing certain, in their gloomy and uncertain world, was the regular succession of the seasons and the stars. Thus such education as survived was almost necessarily based on the *Computus*. Nor was the task quite as simple as might be thought, for the mode of reckoning was confused, then as now, by the two incommensurables, the lunar and the solar year.

As one surveys a work of this kind, the impression conveyed to the mind is less of simplicity than of a feeble sophistication. The world is in its second childhood. There is such immense stress laid on names, such slavish reliance on older writings, such a display of learning which is never real. Byrhtferth assures his pupil that:

> "We know of a surety that there are very many rustic clerks who do not know how many kinds of years there are; but I am willing to show myself indulgent to their slothfulness, supported as I am by the protection of the Fathers, with whose dogs I am not worthy to lie down.
>
> "The first and chief year is the solar year, because, as Cicero says, the sun is the 'leader and prince and governor of all the other lights'; Heraclitus the sophist calls it a fountain of celestial light. It is called the leader therefore, because it surpasses all in the majesty of its light; the prince, because it so far excels that, because it appears as the only one of its kind it is called 'sol.'"

In all this rigmarole there is not a genuine sentence of his own. He had never read Cicero. The works of Heraclitus were no more accessible to him than they are to us. The ridiculous derivation of *sol* from *solus* (alone) was copied verbally from the same work from which he got his neighbouring quotations!

In considering the Middle Ages, and still more the Dark Age, it is necessary always to remember that the knowledge of the day was not only corrupted in quality but also extremely small in quantity. Strange as it may seem, it is just this latter element that gives its main interest to mediaeval literary studies. Our civilisation is nowadays so complex, and all parts of our world so interdependent that it would be extremely difficult to trace the sources of any modern writer and to provide any exact demonstration of the degree to which he is original. With mediaeval writers, and especially with those of the Dark Age, the case is different. With them originality was not esteemed a virtue and every statement had to be given on authority. Furthermore, even the most learned of these mediaeval writers knows so piteously little compared to a modern scholar that it is possible, with sufficient application, to trace all the sources of his information. It is this fact which makes mediaeval literature valuable as a medium for demonstrating cultural movements. There is no idea, and there is hardly a phrase, in Byrhtferth that a well-equipped scholar, such as Mr. Crawford, cannot trace to its sources.

Next in importance after the Calendar, in the estimate of our author and of his contemporaries, stands the understanding of the nature of numbers. Our use of numerals seems so natural and obvious that we are liable to consider it as a normal development of thinking about number. It has become a part of our consciousness. Thus it may be a surprise to some that not only is our method modern and exotic in origin, but that, even when introduced, it took centuries to assert its supremacy over an older and clumsier system. All of us find the alternative use of *Roman* numerals an occasional convenience, and may forget that these represent a more ancient and less perfect mode of reckoning than the usual *Arabic* figures, in which the digit depends for its value on its position.

No department reveals so surely as mathematics the mental condition of a society. The peoples of Europe started their careers in a mentally incoherent condition. Devoid of philosophy, with no knowledge of the principles of language, with the arts in a vestigial state, they succeeded in remaining just above the barbarian level through such bare elements of culture as they had salved from the ruins of the Roman Empire. In the remains of the civilisation of antiquity they were to quarry for centuries. Mathematics, among these folk, was as decayed as other departments of mental activity. Such mathematical skill as is to be found among them, when not directed to the calendar, was devoted to the equally arid topic of the most elementary properties--real or imagined--of numbers. The world of thought was so limited and narrowed that it was in such discussion alone that the cramped intellects of men found any space to move.

All Dark Age writers who deal with numbers exhibit Pythagorean tendencies, that is, they treat numbers as though they had a real existence and ascribe physical and moral qualities to them. We are accustomed to our own time to be amused by the foolish notion that thirteen is an "unlucky number." But we can hardly think ourselves into a world in which a recognised instructor of young men in a recently "reformed" school could write, as Byrhtferth wrote, that:

> "The number four is a perfect number, and it is adorned with four virtues--righteousness, temperance, fortitude, and prudence. The number is also crowned with the four seasons of the year, whose names are: spring, summer, autumn, and winter. It is also adorned with the doctrines of the four Evangelists, who are said to be the four animals in

> the Book of Ezekiel, the famous prophet. The number four is reverently upheld by the four letters in the name of God, that is to say, D, E, U, S, and likewise by the name of the first created man, namely, ADAM. Fittingly it has an attraction which I do not think ought to be passed over in silence--I mean the fact that there are two equinoxes and two solstices. There are indeed four principal winds, whose names are these: the east, west, north, and south winds. There are four elements: air, fire, water, and earth: there are four regions of the world, viz. east, west, north, and south. If these parts are carefully studied, they will be found in the name of ADAM according to Greek numeration. For the Greeks term the east *Anatole*, and the west *Dysis*, and the north *Arktos*, and the south *Mesembrion*."

This passage is extremely characteristic of the thought of the time. To men of the Dark Age there was no real distinction between physical events, mental abstractions, and moral truths. It is a view which our children share with them. The hurt child slaps the offending object and says that is has stumbled over a "naughty stone."

The mental process by which the men of the Dark Age attained to a similar standpoint presents a striking and not uninteresting contrast to what we nowadays regard as science. The essential difference lies in the use of *analogy* as an intellectual weapon. A modern man of science habitually employs analogy as a means of attaining truth through the suggestion of lines of experiment, but he never adduces an analogy to demonstrate his conclusions. In setting forth his results, indeed, he usually emphasises his inductive proofs, and thus conceals, along with his abandoned "working hypotheses," the memory of the analogical processes that suggested them. This was far from the case with the mediaeval thinker. He started with the idea that the universe was built on a systematic plan or pattern. The broad outlines of this he believed had been revealed to the fathers of old, a small part of whose wisdom had come down to him. Therefore the investigation of the rest of the pattern, on an analogical basis, should yield results similar to the pattern already known. Research was undreamed of by the Dark Age thinker and would not have appealed to him as either necessary or desirable, since the world, both physical and moral, could be explored by playing the much easier game of analogy.

The effect of this view in the theological field is well known. Every event in nature was given a moral significance. The rain did *not* descend indifferently upon the field of the just and the unjust. On the contrary, Nature in every aspect and exhibition, had a meaning and a purpose.

The department which we are discussing was developed upon this assumption and the instrument of development was analogy. To Byrhtferth and his contemporaries had been handed down the tradition that there were four elements in the outer world, the macrocosm, namely earth, air, fire, and water, corresponding to four humours in the inner world, man's body, the microcosm. What more reasonable than to suppose that there were four principal organs or parts of the body? There are four seasons of the year in the macrocosm. Must there not be then four ages of man in the microcosm? Again, the twelve signs of the zodiac were held from of old to influence the parts of man's body. Did not the twelve signs arrange themselves in four groups corresponding to the four quarters of heaven to correspond to the four principal organs of the body?

Thus arose a whole mass of beliefs linked and interlinked round the number four. The "lore of the fours," which Byrhtferth develops along the lines we have indicated, is a quite characteristic product of mediaeval thought. It is but one of innumerable results that might be adduced of the excessive use of analogy.

We turn now from these relatively complex conceptions of number to the practical manipulation of the numerals themselves. The process of reckoning was much less easy for the men of the Dark Age than it is for us. They were ignorant of our modern system in which the value of a digit depends upon its position. An instrument for reckoning, known as the Abacus, had been employed in ancient Rome. In the centuries following the break-up of the Empire the use of the Abacus had been almost forgotten in the West. At the time that Byrhtferth was writing, a knowledge of it was coming back again, and its use is discussed in certain contemporary works which bear a strong resemblance to his. A description of the Abacus was even perhaps included in the missing portion of his *Handboc*.

Once the Abacus regained its popularity it remained in use for centuries. It is indeed extraordinary how the Roman numerals, and their instrument the Abacus, withstood the introduction of the far superior method of reckoning to which we are accustomed to-day. As late as the middle of the sixteenth century a work on the Abacus appeared in English. The Abacus has in fact certain special advantages in the keeping of accounts by those who have not fully mastered the art of writing. For this reason it has remained in use in the East to this very day.

Calendrical material and a bare modicum of astronomy, together with such very elementary mathematical material, make up the whole sum of positive "science" in the Dark Age. There was no trace of biological knowledge, or even of curiosity as to the structure of living things. Geography was so corrupted and misinterpreted as to be scarce worthy of the name. Medicine, so far as it existed, was contracted to drug lists or foolish discussion about imaginary humours in imaginary organs. History was in no better plight and was represented either by bare annals or by a series of legendary statements, of well-known origin, concerning the "Ages of the World."

Even in setting forth this degraded material every statement needed to be covered by authority. It is of course a commonplace that in the Middle Age the authority of antiquity, and especially of Biblical antiquity, was given much greater weight than with us. But we do not believe that this statement carries with it an adequate appreciation of the paralysis thus induced into the most elementary forms of thought. The very multiplication table itself was, at each step, submitted to the test of authority! This is what Byrhtferth says on the point:

> "It is my pleasure to give you a brief extract from the account of the number ten given by Abbo, of worthy memory, the splendid worth of whose life is attested by miracles after his death. For he was skilled in the art of teaching and proficient in learning. For he used to say: 'If you multiply a single number by ten, you will give ten to each unit and one hundred to each ten. If you multiply ten by a single number, you will give to each unit ten, and to every ten one hundred. If you multiply ten by ten, you will give to each unit one hundred, and to every ten one thousand.'
>
> "Having explained these matters in accordance with the principles of our teacher and Christ's martyr, let us proceed to other things. The number one thousand is a perfect number, as we have mentioned before; but we think it will be fitting to sum up in a clear account the gist of what ancient authorities have said on this subject. For there are six ages of the world. The first was from Adam to Noah, the second from Noah to Abraham, the third from Abraham to David, the fourth from David to the removal (to Babylon), the fifth from the removal (to Babylon) to the Advent of Christ, the sixth from the Advent of Christ to His second Advent."

The Abbo in question was Abbo of Fleury (died 1004), an older contemporary of Byrhtferth. Abbo had spent two years in England, assisting Archbishop Oswald of York in reforming and restoring the monastic system that had fallen into decay during the tenth century, after the Danish troubles. Abbo had himself been Abbot of Byrhtferth's monastery of Ramsey. He met his death in France while quelling a monkish revolt.

Byrhtferth comes just at the period when the human intellect had touched its nadir. The knowledge that survived from antiquity was now at its lowest ebb, and nothing had been added. Until Abbo, no attempt had been made, in this country at least, to introduce order and coherence into a chaotic mass. Abbo, however, brought with him from France the tradition of the "liberal" arts. This phrase, in the French schools of this and the following periods, was no mere generality, as it is now, for the things of the mind. The seven *artes liberales* represent a first attempt to organise profane knowledge. They were divided into the *trivium*, providing the elements of linguistic knowledge classified under the three heads "grammar, rhetoric, and dialectic," a group that we might perhaps class together as "philology"--and the *quadrivium*--the sciences proper--classified under the four heads "geometry, arithmetic, astronomy, and music." In what has gone before we have seen something of Byrhtferth's interpretation of the *quadrivium*. Before we leave him we may glance at his version of the trivium--a term, by the way, that has given rise to our modern word "trivial."

Throughout the Dark Age, and indeed well into the Scholastic Age, there was nothing of what we should now call a "science of language." Languages during the Middle Ages, with the sole exception of Latin, were never acquired save by the spoken word. Thus the grammatical knowledge of any language save Latin was practically absent during this whole stretch of time. Such gleanings of Hebrew or Greek as were picked up by a few scholars hardly ever show any conception of the structure of the language. The neglect of linguistics is the more remarkable when we recall the extreme importance of the Greek and Hebrew scriptures in the lives of these people and their extraordinary reverence for the written word. This reverence betrayed itself in the conception that exotic phrases had some special force which was often given magical value. Hence writers of the time were only too ready to introduce foreign and mysterious words. A quotation from Byrhtferth will suffice to emphasise this point, and will also give some insight into Byrhtferth's attitude to the trivium.

> "*Paronomasia* [in Greek], that is *denominatio* in Latin. This figure is employed in various senses, as in the following example which I give: *Amans* and *amens*, and *semens* and *sementis* and *seminarium*. *Amans homo* is a loving man and *amens* is a mad man, and *semens* is sowing and *sementis* is one of sowing, and *seminarium* is [a nursery]. The prophet Isaiah made a graceful use of this figure when he sang and spoke thus: *Expectaui ut faceret judicium et ecce iniquitas: et iustitiam, et ecce clamor* (Isaiah v. 7, 'I looked for judgment, but behold oppression; for righteousness, but behold a cry'). There is a very beautiful congruity between these words in the Hebrew language, as we will here demonstrate to the reader. The Latin *iudicium* is judgment in English and *mesapháát* in Hebrew: the Latin *iustitia* is righteousness in English and *sadaca* in Hebrew: the Latin *iniquitas* is termed unrighteousness in English, and *mesaphàá* in Hebrew: the Latin *clamor* is interpreted loudness in English and *suaca* in Hebrew. He arranged the parallels between the nouns beautifully. *Iudicium* he called *mesapháát*, and *iniquitas mesaphàá*, and *iustitia sadaca*, and *clamor suaca*."

It must not be thought for a moment that our author exhibits here any knowledge of Greek, of Hebrew, or of Latin etymology. It is purely copied material and the foreign words, being mysterious, have a special value for his readers.

We have trailed enough of Byrhtferth before the reader to give him an idea of the mental incoherence that was characteristic of his time. The writer of this article is not so simple as to suppose that the readers of THE REALIST need any warning against mediaeval methods of study. Nevertheless, he believes that the age in which Byrhtferth lived has been sufficiently misrepresented by able modern writers for it to be worth while to put the other side, and that it is further worth while to examine into the cause of such mental degradation.

A thing that separates our age from Byrhtferth is our forward way of looking. The men of that time--and for five centuries after--had their gaze ever riveted upon the past. Just about the period of Byrhtferth the lowest pitch of mental deterioration was reached, and after him intellectual competence tended again upward. At last, in the thirteenth and fourteenth centuries, we begin to encounter a very small but appreciable extension of natural knowledge. There was even then, however, no widespread acceptance of the ancient view that had been last voiced in antiquity by the philosopher Seneca (died A.D. 65) that knowledge may be indefinitely extended. That view appears to be an essential element in any effective doctrine of progress, which is itself, in the writer's opinion, fundamental for the development of science. When we reach the fifteenth century and the full influence of Humanism we encounter a few forward-looking thinkers, but they are still isolated. Not until the sixteenth century is there any effort, at once organised and conscious, to translate into action this new-born hope in the future. Only with the seventeenth century does the hope obtain formal philosophical expression once more, with Francis Bacon (died 1626) and René Descartes (died 1650).

The question of what induced this belief in progress, this habit of looking forward to the future rather than backward to the past for a golden age, has often been discussed. Many solutions have been proposed. To the writer it seems intimately linked with the process now called "science." Science, of its nature, demands a conception of progress. But progress implies not merely an advance but also some method of preserving the advance; in other words it implies a record. This, in its turn, implies the belief that the progress will continue.

Thus the manifestation of a care for the record is an essential expression of the idea of progress. We can understand the lonely hermit or the inhabitant of the desert island who investigates nature from curiosity, but we do not understand his painfully recording his experiences unless he thinks that some one will use the record. It is extremely important to remember that the record is as essential a factor in the progress of science as the process of investigation itself. Unless the investigator has the record of those who have gone before him, each investigator must start again at the beginning. Thus the record is fundamental for the development of the idea of progress, and the idea of progress is fundamental for science. Science is a clock; the idea of progress, that is investigation, is the mainspring; the record is the escapement; neither mainspring nor escapement can function without the other.

What, then, was it that happened in the sixteenth century that started science on her way? Why and how and where do men get the idea of progress in that age? How is it that they became shut off, in their way of thinking, from the Middle Ages? The writer believes that the answer is not as far to seek as some have thought. Throughout the Middle Ages, of which we have taken Byrhtferth as our exemplar, men insisted on seeing the universe as a finite and limited existence. It had known boundaries, known dimensions, and a known form. Its parts went through a known series of movements around their known centre, the earth. The general pattern or outline was thus confidently held to be known. Was it greatly worth investigating this scheme further?

The task was, at best, only a rather difficult jigsaw puzzle. Science, even had it developed as a separate discipline, must have taken a low rank beside the infinite possibilities of Theology and later of Philosophy. In practice it was not developed at all.

But in the fifteenth and sixteenth centuries a series of philosophers, beginning with Nicholas of Cusa (died 1464), continuing through Copernicus (died 1543) to Giordano Bruno (died 1600), contributed to the formulation of the conception of an *infinite* universe which was set off against the finite universe of the mediaevals. With an infinite universe the whole conception of the office of science changes completely. It is no longer a process of fitting missing pieces into a known pattern. It becomes instead a voyage of exploration, a great adventure toward an unknown goal. It is a boundless ocean on which the man of science now embarks. Who can say what unheard-of lands he may encounter? How different is his task from that of poor Byrhtferth. It is the infinity of the universe that marks off the modern from the mediaeval thinker.

And lastly a word on the reactions of this new method on the older system of thought. It is sometimes proclaimed that ecclesiastical anger with Copernicus, with Giordano, with Galileo, was due to their view that set the sun rather than the earth in the centre of the universe. That was, to some extent, the ostensible cause, but there was something at stake far deeper and more fundamental. The conception of "creation in time" of the universe and of all within it, was basic for the theologico-political system of the Middle Ages. That conception must fall if the universe be thought of as infinite. "Creation" was and is, doubtless, still susceptible of metaphysical distinction, but the world could no longer be looked upon as a "fabrica," a piece of workmanship. Thus the new infringement extended beyond the letter and beyond the meaning, even to the very spirit of scripture. To changes in letter and meaning the Church was practised in accommodating herself. Had she not, for instance, freely adopted Aristotle's world scheme? The trouble was and is far, far deeper. St. Thomas (died 1274) had long ago foreseen that "creation in time" was an integral part of the Church's view of existence. That now was threatened. Giordano Bruno saw this in all its clearness, as he uttered those memorable words "Perchance you who condemn are in greater fear than I who am condemned." It was an ember from the fire in which he perished that lit the torch of modern science.

Unduped of fancy, henceforth man
   Must labour!--must resign
His all too human creeds, and scan
   Simply the way divine!

But now the old is out of date,
   The new is not yet born,
And who can be *alone* elate,
While the world lies forlorn?

2. Alistaire Crombie on the 12th Century Renaissance*

Alistaire Crombie of All Souls College, Oxford, is one of the leading modern historians of medieval science.

Science in Western Christendom Until The Twelfth-Century Renaissance

The contrast between the scientific ideas of the early Middle Ages, that is from about the 5th to the early 12th century, and those of the later Middle Ages, can best be seen in a conversation which is supposed to have taken place between the widely travelled 12th-century scholar and cleric Adelard of Bath and his stay-at-home nephew. Adelard's contribution to the discussion introduces the newly-recovered ideas of the ancient Greeks and the Arabs; that of his nephew represents the traditional view of Greek ideas as they had been preserved in Western Christendom since the fall of the Roman Empire.

The conversation is recorded in Adelard's *Quæstiones Naturales*, written, probably, after he had studied some Arabic science but before he had achieved the familiarity with it which is shown in his later translations, such as those of the Arabic text of Euclid's *Elements* and the astronomical tables of al-Khwarizmi. The topics covered range from meteorology to the

---

*A. C. Crombie, *Medieval and Early Modern Science*, Volume I: *Science in the Middle Ages, V-XIII Centuries*. Cambridge, Mass.: Harvard University Press, Copyright, 1952, 1959, 1961 by A. C. Crombie. Reprinted by permission of the Harvard University Press and William Heinemann Ltd., London. Pp. 9-25.

transmission of light and sound, from the growth of plants to the cause of the tears which the nephew shed for joy at the safe return of his uncle.

> When not long ago, while Henry, son of William [Henry I, 1100-35], was on the throne, I returned to England after my long period of study abroad, it was very agreeable to meet my friends again. After we had met and made the usual enquiries about one another's health and that of friends, I wanted to know something about the morals of our nation. . . After this exchange, as we had most of the day before us and so lacked no time for conversation, a nephew of mine who was with the others--he was interested rather than expert in natural science--urged me to disclose something new from my Arab studies. To this, when the rest had agreed, I delivered myself as in the tract that follows.

The nephew declared himself delighted at such an opportunity of showing that he had kept his youthful promise to work hard at philosophy, by disputing the new ideas with his uncle, and declared:

> if I were only to listen to you expounding a lot of Saracen theories, and many of them seemed to me to be foolish enough, I would get a little restless, and while you are explaining them I will oppose you wherever it seems fit. I am sure you praise them shamelessly and are too keen to point out our ignorance. So for you it will be the fruit of your labour if you acquit yourself well, while for me, if I oppose you plausibly, it will mean that I have kept my promise.

The scientific inheritance of the Latin West, represented by the nephew's contribution to the dialogue, was limited almost exclusively to fragments of Greco-Roman learning such as had been preserved in the compilations of the Latin encyclopædists. The Romans themselves had made hardly any original contributions to science. The emphasis of their education was upon oratory. But some of them were sufficiently interested in trying to understand the world of nature to make careful compilations of the learning and observations of Greek scholars. One of the most influential of these compilations, which survived throughout the early Middle Ages as a text-book, was the *Natural History* of Pliny (23-79 A.D.) which Gibbon described as an immense register in which the author has 'deposited the discoveries, the arts, and the errors of mankind.' It cited nearly 500 authorities. Beginning with the general system of cosmology it passed to geography, anthropology, physiology and zoology, botany, agriculture and horticulture, medicine, mineralogy and the fine arts. Until the 12th century, when translations of Greek and Arab works began to come into Western Europe, Pliny's was the largest known collection of natural facts, and it was drawn on by a succession of later writers.

The mathematics and logic of the Latin West rested on the work of the 6th-century Boethius, who did for those studies what Pliny had done for natural history. Not only did he compile elementary treatises on geometry, arithmetic, astronomy and music, based respectively on the work of Euclid, Nicomachus and Ptolemy, but he also translated the logical works of Aristotle into Latin. Of these translations only the *Categories* and the *De Interpretatione* were widely known before the 12th century, but until that time the translations and commentaries of Boethius were the main source for the study of logic as of mathematics. Knowledge of mathematics was largely confined to arithmetic. The only mathematical treatise remaining intact, the so-called 'Geometry of Boethius,' which dates from no earlier than the 9th century, contained only fragments of Euclid and was concerned mostly with such practical operations as surveying. Cassiodorus (c. 490-580), in his popular writings on the liberal arts, gave only a very elementary treatment of mathematics.

Another of the compilers of the early Middle Ages who helped to keep alive the scientific learning of the Greeks in the Latin West was the Visigothic bishop, Isidore of Seville (560-636). His *Etymologies*, based on often fantastic derivations of various technical terms, remained popular for many centuries as a source of knowledge of all kinds from astronomy to medicine. For Isidore the universe was limited in size,* only a few thousand years old and soon to perish. The earth, he thought, was shaped like a wheel with its boundaries encircled by the ocean. Round the earth were the concentric spheres bearing the planets and stars, and beyond the last sphere was highest heaven, the abode of the blessed.

From the 7th century onwards the Latin West had to rely almost exclusively for scientific knowledge on these compilations, to which were added those of the Venerable Bede (673-735), Alcuin of York (735-804), and the German Hrabanus Maurus (776-856), each of whom borrowed freely from his predecessors.

The gradual penetration of the barbarians into the Western Roman Empire from the 4th century had caused some material destruction and eventually serious political instability, but it was the eruption of the Mohammedan invaders into the Eastern Empire in the 7th century that gave the most serious blow to learning in Western Christendom. The conquest of much of the territory of the Eastern Empire by the Arabs meant that the main reservoir of Greek learning was cut off from Western scholars for centuries by the intolerance and mutual suspicion of opposing creeds, and by the dragon wing of the Mediterranean. In this intellectual isolation Western Christendom could hardly have been

---

* The littleness of man in the universe was, however, a familiar theme for reflection and this passage from Boethius' *De Consolatione Philosophiæ* (II, vii) was well known throughout the Middle Ages: 'Thou hast learnt from astronomical proofs that the whole earth compared with the universe is not greater than a point, that is, compared with the sphere of the heavens, it may be thought of as having no size at all. Then, of this tiny corner, it is only one-quarter that, according to Ptolemy, is habitable to living things. Take away from this quarter the seas, marshes, and other desert places, and the space left for man hardly deserves the name of infinitesimal.'

expected to make many original contributions to man's knowledge of material universe. All the West was able to do was to preserve the collection of facts and interpretations already made by the encyclopædists. That so much was preserved in spite of the gradual collapse of Roman political organisation and social structure under the impact, first, of Goths, Vandals and Franks, and then, in the 9th century, of Norsemen, was due to the appearance of monasteries with their attendant schools which began in Western Europe after the foundation of Monte Cassino by St. Benedict in 529. The existence of such centres made possible the temporary revivals of learning in Ireland in the 6th and 7th centuries, in Northumbria in the time of Bede, and in Charlemagne's empire in the 9th century. Charlemagne invited Alcuin from Northumbria to become his minister of education, and one of Alcuin's essential reforms was to establish schools associated with the more important cathedrals. It was in such a school, at Laon, that the nephew of Adelard received his education in the 12th century, when the curriculum was still based on the work of the encyclopædists. Studies were limited to the seven liberal arts as defined by Varro in the first century B.C. and by Martianus Capella six hundred years later. Grammar, logic and rhetoric made up the first stage or *trivium*, and geometry, arithmetic, astronomy and music made up the more advanced *quadrivium*. The texts used were the works of Pliny, Boethius, Cassiodorus and Isidore.

One development of importance which had taken place in the studies of the Latin West between the days of Pliny and the time when Adelard's nephew pursued his studies at Laon was the assimilation of Neoplatonism. This was of cardinal importance for it determined men's views of cosmology until the second half of the 12th century. St. Augustine (354-430) was the principal channel through which the traditions of Greek thought passed into the reflections of Latin Christianity, and St. Augustine came profoundly under the influence of Plato and of Neoplatonists such as Plotinus (c. 203-80 A.D.). The chief aim of Augustine was to find a certain basis for knowledge and this he found in the conception of eternal ideas as expounded by the Neoplatonists and in the Pythagorean allegory, the *Timæus*, by Plato himself. According to this school of thought, eternal forms or ideas existed quite apart from any material object. The human mind was one of these eternal essences and had been formed to know the others if it would. In the process of knowing, the sense organs merely provided a stimulus spurring on the mind to grasp the universal forms which constituted the essence of the universe. An important class of such universal forms was mathematics. 'If I have perceived numbers by the sense of the body,' Augustine said in *De Libero Arbitrio* (book 2, chapter 8, section 21),

> I have not thereby been able by the sense of the body to perceive also the nature of the separation and combination of numbers . . . And I do not know how long anything I touch by a bodily sense will persist, as, for instance, this sky and this land, and whatever other bodies I perceive in them. But seven and three are ten and not only now but always;

> nor have seven and three in any way at any time not been ten, nor will seven and three at any time not be ten. I have said, therefore, that this incorruptible truth of number is common to me and anyone at all who reasons.

In the 9th century such scholars as John Scot Erigena (d. 877) re-emphasised the importance of Plato. In addition to the work of the Latin encyclopædists and others, he began to use some original Greek works, some of the most important being the 4th-century translation by Chalcidius of Plato's *Timæus* and commentary by Macrobius, and the 5th-century commentary by Martianus Capella. Erigena himself showed little interest in the natural world and seems to have relied for his facts almost entirely on literary sources, but the fact that among his sources he included Plato, for whom St. Augustine had also had so marked a preference, gave to men's interpretations of the universe a Platonic or Neoplatonic character for about 400 years, though it was not till the development of the school of Chartres in the 12th century that the more scientific parts of the *Timæus* were particularly emphasized.

In general the learning of Western Christendom as represented by the views of Adelard's nephew, the Latin encyclopædists, and the cathedral and the monastic schools was predominantly theological and moral. Even in classical times there had been very little attempt to pursue scientific inquiry for 'fruit,' as Francis Bacon called the improvement of the material conditions of life. The object of Greek science had been understanding, and under the influence of later classical philosophers such as the Stoics, Epicureans and Neoplatonists natural curiosity had given way almost entirely to the desire for the untroubled peace which could only be won by a mind lifted above dependence on matter and the flesh. These pagan philosophers had asked the question: What is worth knowing and doing? To this Christian teachers also had an answer: That is worth knowing and doing which conduces to the love of God. The early Christians continued their neglect of natural curiosity and at first also tended to disparage the study of philosophy itself as likely to distract men from a life pleasing to God. St. Clement of Alexandria in the 3rd century poked fun at this fear of pagan philosophy, which he compared to a child's fear of goblins. Both he and his pupil Origen claimed that all knowledge was good since it was perfection of mind and that the study of philosophy and of natural science was in no way incompatible with a Christian life. St. Augustine himself in his searching and comprehensive philosophical inquiries had invited men to examine the rational basis of their faith. But in spite of these writers natural knowledge continued to be considered of very secondary importance during the early Middle Ages. The primary interest in natural facts was to find illustrations for the truths of morality and religion. The study of nature was not expected to lead to hypotheses and generalisations of science but to provide vivid symbols of moral realities. The Moon was the image of the Church reflecting the divine light, the wind an image of the spirit, the sapphire bore a resemblance to divine contemplation, and the number eleven, which 'transgressed' ten, representing the commandments, stood itself for sin.

This preoccupation with symbols is shown clearly in the bestiaries. Since the time of Aesop stories about animals had been used to illustrate various human virtues and vices. This tradition was continued in the 1st century A.D. by Seneca in his *Quæstiones Naturales*, and by later Greek works, culminating in the 2nd century with a work of Alexandrian origin known as the *Physiologus*, which was the model for all the medieval moralising bestiaries. In these works facts of natural history collected from Pliny were mixed with entirely mythical legends to illustrate some point of Christian teaching. The phoenix was the symbol of the risen Christ. The ant-lion, born of the lion and the ant, had two natures and so was unable to eat either meat or seeds and perished miserably like every double-minded man who tried to follow both God and the Devil. The *Physiologus* had enormous popularity. It was translated into Latin in the 5th century and into many other languages, from Anglo-Saxon to Ethiopian. In the 4th century, when St. Ambrose wrote a commentary on the Bible, he made liberal use of animals as moral symbols. As late as the early years of the 13th century Alexander Neckam could claim in his *De Naturis Rerum*, in which he showed very considerable interest in scientific fact, that he had written the book for purposes of moral instruction. In the 12th century there were many signs, as, for instance, in the illustrations to certain manuscripts and the descriptions of wild life by Giraldus Cambrensis (c. 1147-1223) and other travellers, that men were capable of observing nature very clearly, but their observations were usually simply interpolations in the course of a symbolic allegory which to their minds was all important. In the 13th century this passion for pointing out moral symbolism invaded even the lapidaries, which in the Ancient World, as represented in the works of Theophrastus (c. 372-288 B.C.), Dioscorides (1st century A.D.) and Pliny and even in the Christian works of 7th-century Isidore or 12th-century Marbode, Bishop of Rennes, had been concerned with the medical value of stones or with their magical properties.

This preoccupation with the magical and astrological properties of natural objects was, with the search for moral symbols, the chief characteristic of the scientific outlook of Western Christendom before the 13th century. There was a wealth of magic in the works of Pliny and one of its characteristic ideas, the doctrine of signatures according to which each animal, plant or mineral had some mark indicating its hidden virtues or uses, had a profound effect on popular natural history. St. Augustine had to bring all the skill of his dialectic against the denial of free will which astrology implied, but had not been able to defeat this superstition. Isidore of Seville admitted that there were magical forces in nature, and though he distinguished between the part of astrology which was natural, since it led man to study the courses of the heavenly bodies, and the superstitious part which was concerned with horoscopes, he yet admitted that these heavenly bodies had an astrological influence on the human body and advised doctros to study the influence of the moon on plant and animal life. It was a very general belief during the whole of the Middle Ages and even into the 17th century that there was a close correspondence between the course of a disease and the phases of the moon and movements of other heavenly bodies, although throughout that time certain writers, as, for instance, the 14th-century Nicole Oresme and the 15th-century Pierre d'Ailly, had made fun of astrology and had limited celestial influence to heat, light and mechanical action. Indeed, medical and astronomical studies came to be closely associated.* Salerno and later Montpellier were famous for both and in a later age Padua welcomed both Galileo and Harvey.

An example of this astrological interpretation of the world of nature as a whole is the conception of the correspondence between the universe, or Macrocosm, and the individual man, or Microcosm. This theory had been expressed in the *Timæus* and had been elaborated in relation to astrology by the Stoics. The classical medieval expression of the belief was given in the 12th century by Hildegard of Bingen, who thought that various parts of the human body were linked with special parts of the Macrocosm so that the 'humours' were determined by the movements of the heavenly bodies.

Gilson has said of the world of the early Middle Ages, typified by the nephew of Adelard: 'To understand and explain anything consisted for a thinker of this time in showing that it was not what it appeared to be, but that it was the symbol or sign of a more profound reality, that it proclaimed or signified something else.' But this exclusively theological interest in the natural world had already begun to be modified even before the writings of the Greek and Arab natural philosophers became more fully and widely known in Western Christendom, as a result of increasing intellectual contact with the Arab and Byzantine worlds. One aspect of this change in outlook is to be seen in the increasing activity of the computists, doctors and writers of purely technical treatises of which there had been a continuous tradition throughout the early Middle Ages. In the 6th century Cassiodorus, when making arrangements for an infirmary in his monastery,** had in his *Institutio Divinarum Litterarum*, book 1,

---

* Cf. the Prologue to Chaucer's *Canterbury Tales* (11.411 *et seq.*):
'With us ther was a Doctour of Phisyk;
In al this world ne was ther noon hym lyk,
To speke of phisik and of surgerye;
For he was grounded in astronomye.
He kepte his pacient a ful greet del
In houres, by his magik naturel.
Wel coude he fortunen the ascendent
Of his images for his pacient.
He knew the cause of everich maladye,
Were it of hoot or cold, or moiste, or drye,
And where engendred, and of what humour;
He was a verrey parfit practisour.'

** At Monte Cassino St. Benedict had also established an infirmary. The care of the sick was regarded as a Christian duty for all such foundations.

chapter 31, given some very precise and practical advice on the medical use of herbs:

> Learn, therefore, the nature of herbs, and study diligently the way to combine various species . . . and if you are not able to read Greek, read above all translations of the *Herbarium* of Dioscorides, who described and drew the herbs of the field with wonderful exactness. After this, read translations of Hippocrates and Galen, especially the *Therapeutics* . . . and Aurelius Celsus' *De Medicina* and Hippocrates' *De Herbis et Curis*, and divers other books written on the art of medicine, which by God's help I have been able to provide for you in our library.

A good example of the influence of practical problems in preserving the habit of observation, and a good illustration of the state of Latin scientific knowledge before the translations from Greek and Arabic, is provided by the writings of Bede. The main sources of Bede's ideas about the natural world were the Fathers, especially St. Ambrose, St. Augustine, St. Basil the Great and St. Gregory the Great; and Pliny, Isidore and some Latin writings on the calendar. Although he knew Greek, it was on Latin sources that he almost entirely drew. Based on these sources, Bede's writings on scientific subjects fall into two main classes: a largely derivative account of general cosmology, and a more independent treatment of some specific practical problems, in particular those connected with the calendar.

Bede's cosmology is interesting for showing how an educated person of the 8th century pictured the universe. He set out his views in *De Rerum Natura*, based largely on Isidore's book of the same title but also on Pliny's *Natural History*, which Isidore had not known. It was largely because of his knowledge of Pliny, as well as his more critical mind, that made Bede's book so greatly superior to Isidore's. Bede's universe is one ordered by ascertainable cause and effect. Whereas Isidore had thought the earth shaped like a wheel, Bede held that it was a static sphere, with five zones, of which only the two temperate were habitable and only that in the northern hemisphere actually inhabited. Surrounding the earth were seven heavens: air, ether, Olympus, fiery space, the firmament with the heavenly bodies, the heaven of the angels, and the heaven of the Trinity. The waters of the firmament separated the corporeal from the spiritual creation. The corporeal world was composed of the four elements, earth, water, air and fire, arranged in order of heaviness and lightness. At the creation these four elements, together with light and man's soul, were made by God *ex nihilo*; all other phenomena in the corporeal world were combinations. From Pliny, Bede got a much more detailed knowledge of Greek understanding of the daily and annual movements of the heavenly bodies than had been available to Isidore. He held that the firmament of stars revolved round the earth, and that within the firmament the planets circled in a system of epicycles. He gave clear accounts of the phases of the moon and of eclipses.

The problem of the calendar had been brought to Northumbria along with Christianity by the monks of Iona, but long before that time methods of computing the date of Easter had formed part of the school science of *computus*, which provided the first exercises of early medieval science.

The main problem connected with the Christian calendar arose from the fact that it was a combination of the Roman Julian calendar, based on the annual movement of the earth relative to the sun, and Hebrew calendar, based on the monthly phases of the moon. The year and its divisions into months, weeks, and days belonged to the Julian solar calendar; but Easter was determined in the same way as the Hebrew Passover by the phases of the moon, and its date in the Julian year varied, within definite limits, from one year to the next. In order to calculate the date of Easter it was necessary to combine the length of the solar year with that of the lunar month. The basic difficulty in these calculations was that the lengths of the solar year, the lunar month and the day are incommensurable. No number of days can make an exact number of lunar months or solar years, and no number of lunar months can make an exact number of solar years. So, in order to relate the phases of the moon accurately to the solar year in terms of whole days, it is necessary, in constructing a calendar to make use of a system of *ad hoc* adjustments, following some definite cycle.

From as early as the 2nd century A.D. different dates of Easter, resulting from different methods of making the calculations, had given rise to controversy and had become a chronic problem for successive Councils. Various cycles relating the lunar month to the solar year were tried at different times and places, until in the 4th century a 19-year cycle, according to which 19 solar years were considered equal to 235 lunar months, came into general use. But there was still the possibility of differences in the manner in which this same cycle was used to determine the date of Easter, and even when there was uniformity at the centre, sheer difficulty of communication could and did result in such outlying provinces as Africa, Spain and Ireland celebrating Easter at different dates from Rome and Alexandria.

Shortly before Bede's birth Northumbria had, at the Synod of Whitby, given up many practices, including the dating of Easter, introduced by the Irish-trained monks of Iona, and had come into uniformity with Rome. But there was still much confusion, by no means confined to Britain, as to how the date of Easter was to be calculated. Bede's main contribution, expounded in several treatises, beginning with *De Temporibus* written in 703, for his pupils at Jarrow, was to reduce the whole subject to order. Using largely Irish sources, themselves based upon a good knowledge of earlier Continental writings, he not only showed how to use the 19-year cycle to calculate Easter Tables for the future, but also discussed general problems of time measurement, arithmetical computation, cosmological and historical chronology, and astronomical and related phenomena. Though often relying on literary sources when he could have observed with his own eyes--as, for example, in his account of the Roman Wall not ten miles from his monk's cell--Bede never copied without understanding. He tried to reduce all observed occurrences to general laws, and, within the limits of his knowledge, to build a consistent picture of the universe, tested against the evidence. His account of the tides in *De Temporum Ratione* (chapter xxix), completed in 725 and the most important of his scientific writings, not only shows the practical curiosity shared by him and his Northumbrian compatriots but also contained the basic elements of natural science.

From his sources Bede learned the fact that the tides follow the phases of the moon, and the theory that tides were caused by the moon attracting the ocean. He discussed spring and neap tides, and, turning to things which 'we know, who live on the shore of the sea divided by Britain,' he described how the wind could advance or retard a tide and enunciated for the first time the important principle now known as 'the establishment of a port.' This states that the tides lag begind the moon by definite intervals which may be different at different points on the same shore, so that tides must be tabulated for each port separately. Bede wrote: 'Those who live on the same shore as we do, but to the north, see the ebb and flow of the tide well before us, whereas those to the south see it well after us. In every region the moon always keeps the rule of association which she has accepted once and for all.' On the basis of this, Bede suggested that the tides at any port could be predicted by means of the 19-year cycle, which he substituted for Pliny's less accurate 8-year cycle. Tidal tables were frequently attached to *computi* written after Bede's time.

Against the background of its time Bede's science was a remarkable achievement. It contributed substantially to the Carolingian Renaissance on the Continent, and found its way into the educational tradition dating from the cathedral schools established for Charlemagne by Alcuin of York. Bede's treatises on the calendar remained standard text-books for five centuries, and were used even after the Gregorian reform of 1582; *De Temporum Ratione* is still one of the clearest expositions of the principles of the Christian calendar.

Besides in Northumbria, Anglo-Saxon England saw some scientific developments in Wessex. In the 7th century, astronomy and medicine were taught in Kent; there is evidence that surgery was practised; and Aldhelm, Abbot of Malmesbury, wrote metrical riddles about animals and plants. But the most notable contribution came in the first half of the 10th century in the *Leech Book* of Bald, who was evidently a physician living during or shortly after the reign of King Alfred, to whom the book contains allusions. The *Leech Book* gives a good picture of the state of medicine at the time. The first part is mainly therapeutical, containing herbal prescriptions, based on a wide knowledge of native plants and garden herbs, for a large number of diseases, working downwards from those of the head. Tertian, quartan and quotidian fevers are distinguished, and reference is made to 'flying venom' or 'air-borne contagion,' that is, epidemic diseases generally, and to smallpox, elephantiasis, probably bubonic plague, various mental ailments, and the use of the vapour bath for colds. The second part of the *Leech Book* is different in character, dealing mainly with internal diseases and going into symptoms and pathology. It seems to be a compilation of Greek medicine, perhaps mainly derived from the Latin translation of the writings of

Alexander of Tralles, together with some direct observation. A good example is the account of 'sore in the side,' or pleurisy, of which many of the 'tokens' or symptoms are described by Greek writers, but some are original. The Anglo-Saxon leech recognised the occurrence of traumatic pleurisy and the possibility of confusing it with the idiopathic disease, which the ancient writers did not. Treatment began with a mild vegetable laxative administered by mouth or enema, followed by a poultice applied to the painful spot, a cupping glass on the shoulders, and various herbs taken internally. Many other diseases are described, for example pulmonary consumption and abscesses on the liver, treatment here culminating in a surgical operation. But on the whole there is little evidence of clinical observation; no use was made of the pulse and little of the appearances of the urine, which were standard 'signs' for the Greeks and Romans. Anglo-Saxon surgery presents the same combination of empiricism with literary tradition as the medicine; treatments of broken limbs and dislocations, plastic surgery for harelip, and amputations for gangrene are described.

A remarkable work showing the intelligent interest of the Anglo-Saxon scholars in improving their knowledge of natural history in relation to medicine is the translation into Old English, probably made about 1000-50 A.D., of the Latin *Herbarium* attributed apocryphally to Apuleius Barbarus, or Platonicus. As in most early herbals the text is confined to the name, locality found, and medical uses of each herb; there are no descriptions for identification, which was to be made by means of diagrammatic paintings, copied from the manuscript source and not from nature. About 500 English names are used in this herbal, showing an extensive knowledge of plants, many of them native plants which could not have been known from the Latin sources.

There are many other examples of the influence of practical interests on the scientific outlook of scholars. In the 8th century appeared in Italy the earliest known Latin manuscript on the preparation of pigments, gold-making, and other practical problems which might confront the artist or illuminator; one of Adelard's writings was to be on this subject. In the field of medicine, the traditional literary advice on the treatment of disease came under some criticism in Charlemagne's cathedral schools, and much sharper criticism in the light of practical experience is found in the *Practica* of Petrocellus, of the famous medical school of Salerno. The computists likewise continued to collect a body of experience and elementary mathematical techniques in their work on the calendar. It was this problem of calculating the date of Easter that was chiefly responsible for the continuous interest in arithmetic, and various improvements in technique were attempted from the beginning of the 8th centurn, when Bede produced his chronology and 'finger reckoning,' to the end of the 10th century when the monk Helperic produced his text-book on arithmetic, and down to the 11th and 12th centuries when there appeared numerous manuscripts on this subject. The calculation of dates led also to an interest in astronomical observations, and more accurate observations became possible when knowledge of the astrolabe was obtained from the Arabs by Gerbert and other scholars of the 10th century. The chief scientific centre at that time was Lotharingia, and Canute and later Earl Harold and William the Conqueror all encouraged Lotharingian astronomers and mathematicians to come to England, where they were given ecclesiastical positions.

Besides this persistent concern with practical problems, another tendency that was equally important in substituting a different approach to the world of nature for that of moralising symbolism was a change in philosophical outlook, and especially that which is associated with the 11th-century nominalist, Roscelinus, and his pupil Peter Abelard (1079-1142). At the end of the 11th century the teaching of Roscelinus opened the great dispute over 'universals' which led men to take a greater interest in the individual, material object as such and not, as St. Augustine had done, to regard it as simply the shadow of an eternal idea. The debate began over some remarks of Boethius concerning the relation of universal ideas such as 'man,' 'rose' or 'seven' both to individual things and numbers and to the human minds that knew them. Did the universal 'rose' subsist with individual roses or as an eternal idea apart from physical things? Or had the universal no counterpart in the real world, was it mere abstraction? One of the most vigorous attacks on St. Augustine's point of view was made by Roscelinus' pupil Abelard, almost an exact contemporary of Adelard of Bath; his dialectical skill and violence won him the nickname of *Rhinocerus indomitus*. Abelard did not accept Roscelinus' view that universals were simply abstractions, mere names, but he pointed out that if the only reality were the eternal ideas then there could be no real difference between individual roses or men, so that in the end everything would be everything else. The outcome of this criticism of the extreme Augustinian view of the universal was to emphasise the importance of the individual, material thing and to encourage observation of the particular.

3. Pope Gregory the Great on secular knowledge*

One of the early problems faced by the Christian Church was the determination of the place (if any) of secular learning in a Christian world. Christ's Kingdom, after all, was not of this world and there were serious questions raised as to the worth of knowledge of this world. Would not secular learning, including science, tend to bind one too firmly to this world at the expense of the contemplation of the next? Yet, was not knowledge of this world necessary if one were to convert the heathen and bring them to Christ? The conflict can be seen in the following selection from the correspondence of Gregory the Great (ca. 540-604) who, as Pope, was faced with the administration of a secular realm, but who, as a devout Christian, desired to turn his gaze only on heaven.

To Desiderius, Bishop of Gaul

Gregory to Desiderius, &c.

Many good things having been reported to us with regard to your pursuits, such joy arose in our heart that we could not bear to refuse what your Fraternity had requested to have granted to you. But it afterwards came to our ears, what we cannot mention without shame, that thy Fraternity is in the habit of expounding grammar to certain persons. This thing we took so much amiss, and so strongly disapproved it, that we changed what had been said before into groaning and sadness, since the praises of Christ cannot find room in one mouth with the praises of Jupiter. And consider thyself what a grave and heinous offence it is for bishops to sing what is not becoming even for a religious layman. And, though our most beloved son Candidus the presbyter, having been, when he came to us, strictly examined on this matter, denied it, and endeavoured to excuse you, yet still the thought has not departed from our mind, that in proportion as it is execrable for such a thing to be related of a priest, it ought to be ascertained by strict and veracious evidence whether or not it be so. Whence, if hereafter what has been reported to us should prove evidently to be false, and it should be clear that you do not apply yourself to trifles and secular literature, we shall give thanks to our God, who has not permitted your heart to be stained with the blasphemous praises of the abominable; and we will treat without misgiving or hesitation concerning the granting of what you request.

We commend to you in all respects the monks whom together with our most beloved son Laurentius the presbyter and Mellitus the abbot we have sent to our most reverend brother and fellow-bishop Augustine, that, through the succour of your Fraternity, no delay may stop their onward progress.

---

* Gregory the Great, "To Desiderius, Bishop of Gaul," in *A Select Library of Nicene and Post-Nicene Fathers of the Christian Church*, Second Series. Volume XIII, Part II. Parker and Sons Ltd., Oxford, 1898. Pp. 69-70. Reprinted by permission of Parker and Sons Ltd.

4. Isidore, Bishop of Seville, an encyclopedist of the Dark Ages

Isidore, Bishop of Seville (ca. 570-636) was a prolific author. His most popular work was his Etymologia,* *an Encyclopedia based on the meanings and origins of words. It was to be a standard reference work throughout the Middle Ages and illustrates perfectly just how dark the Dark Ages were.*

On the Seven Liberal Arts

1. The disciplines belonging to the liberal arts are seven. First, grammar, that is, practical knowledge of speech. Second, rhetoric, which is considered especially necessary in civil causes because of the brilliancy and copiousness of its eloquence. Third, dialectic, called also logic, which separates truth from falsehood by the subtlest distinctions.

2. Fourth, arithmetic, which includes the significance and the divisions of numbers. Fifth, music, which consists of poems and songs.

3. Sixth, geometry, which embraces measurements and dimensions. Seventh, astronomy, which contains the law of the stars.

*   *   *   *   *

On the Four Mathematical Sciences

Preface. Mathematics is called in Latin *doctrinalis scientia*. It considers abstract quantity. For that is abstract quantity which we treat by reason alone, separating it by the intellect from the material or from other non-essentials, as for example, equal, unequal, or the like. And there are four sorts of mathematics, namely, arithmetic, geometry, music and astronomy. Arithmetic is the science of numerical quantity in itself. Geometry is the science of magnitude and forms. Music is the science that treats of numbers that are found in sounds. Astronomy is the science that contemplates the courses of the heavenly bodies and their figures, and all the phenomena of the stars. These sciences we shall next describe at a little greater length in order that their significance may be fully shown.

Chapter 1. On the name of the science of arithmetic.

1. Arithmetic is the science of numbers. For the Greeks call number ἀριθμός. The writers of secular literature have decided that it is first among the mathematical sciences since it needs no other science for its own existence.

2. But music and geometry and astronomy, which follow, need its aid in order to be and exist.

*   *   *   *   *

---

* Ernest Brehaut, *An Encyclopedist of the Dark Ages: Isidore of Seville* (New York: Columbia University Press, 1912). Pp. 96-98; 125-127; 133-134; 143-145; 147-148; 151-152; 51-52; 158-162; 193-194; 235-236.

Chapter 3. What number is.

1. Number is multitude made up of units. For one is the seed of number but not number. *Nummus* (coin) gave its name to *numerus* (number), and from being frequently used originated the word.

Chapter 4. What numbers signify.

1. The science of number must not be despised. For in many passages of the holy scriptures it is manifest what great mystery they contain. For it is not said in vain in the praises of God: "Omnia in mensura et numero et pondere fecisti." For the senarius, which is perfect in respect to its parts, declares the perfection of the universe by a certain meaning of its number. In like manner, too, the forty days which Moses and Elias and the Lord himself fasted, are not understood without an understanding of number.

3. So, too, other numbers appear in the holy scriptures whose natures none but experts in this art can wisely declare the meaning of. It is granted to us, too, to depend in some part upon the science of numbers, since we learn the hours by means of it, reckon the course of the months, and learn the time of the returning year. Through number, indeed, we are instructed in order not to be confounded. Take number from all things and all things perish. Take calculation from the world and all is enveloped in dark ignorance, nor can he who does not know the way to reckon be distinguished from the rest of the animals.

* * * * *

Chapter 11. On the four-fold division of geometry.

1. The four-fold division of geometry is into plane figures, numerical magnitude, rational magnitude, and solid figures.

2. Plane figures are those which are contained by length and breadth. Numerical magnitude is that which can be divided by the numbers of arithmetic.

3. Rational magnitudes are those whose measures we can know, and irrational, those the amount of whose measurement is not known.

4. Solid figures are those that are contained by length, breadth, and thickness, which are five in number, according to Plato.

Chapter 12. On the figures of geometry.

1. The first of the figures on a plane surface is the circle, a figure that is plane, and has a circumference, in the middle of which is a point upon which everything converges (*puncta convergunt*) which geometers call the center, and the Latins call the point of the circle.

2. A quadrilateral figure is one on a plane surface, and it is contained by four straight lines. . . .

3. A sphere is a figure of rounded form equal in all its parts.

A cube is a solid figure which is contained by length, breadth, and thickness.

5. A cone *(conon)* is a solid figure which narrows from a broad base like the right-angled triangle.

6. A pyramid is a solid figure which narrows to a point from a broad base like fire. For fire in Greek is called πυρ.

7. Just as all number is contained within ten so the outline of every figure is contained within the circle.

Chapter 13. On the first principle of geometry.

1. . . . A point is that which has no part. A line is length without breadth. A straight line is one which lies evenly in respect to its points. A superficies is that which has length and breadth alone.

Chapter 14. On the numbers of geometry.

1. You search into the numbers of geometry as follows: the extremes being multiplied, amount to as much as the means multiplied; as for example, VI and XII being multiplied, make LXXII; the means VIII and IX being multiplied amount to the same.

* * * * *

Chapter 28. On the subject-matter of astronomy.

1. The subject-matter of astronomy is made up of many kinds. For it defines what the universe is, what the heavens, what the position and movement of the sphere, what the axis of the heavens and the poles, what are the climates of the heavens, what the courses of the sun and moon and stars, and so forth.

Chapter 29. On the universe and its name.

1. *Mundus* (the universe) is that which is made up of the heavens and earth and the sea and all the heavenly bodies. And it is called *mundus* for the reason that it is always in *motion*. For no repose is granted to its elements.

Chapter 30. On the form of the universe.

1. The form of the universe is described as follows: as the universe rises toward the region of the north, so it slopes away toward the south; its head and face, as it were, is the east, and its back part the north.

Chapter 31. On the heavens and their name.

1. The philosophers have asserted that the heavens are round, in rapid motion, and made of fire, and that they are called by this name *(coelum)* because they have the forms of the stars fixed on them, like a dish with figures in relief *(coelatum)*.

2. For God decked them with bright lights, and filled them with the glowing circles of the sun and moon, and adorned them with the glittering images of flashing stars.

Chapter 32. On the situation of the celestial sphere.

1. The sphere of the heavens is rounded and its center is the earth, equally shut in on every side. This sphere, they say, has neither beginning nor end, for the reason that being rounded

like a circle it is not easily perceived where it begins or where it ends.

2. The philosophers have brought in the theory of seven heavens of the universe, that is, globes with planets moving harmoniously, and they assert that by their circles all things are bound together, and they think that these, being connected, and, as it were, fitted to one another, move backward and are borne with definite motions in contrary directions.

Chapter 33. On the motion of the same.

1. The sphere revolves on two axes, of which one is the northern, which never sets, and is called Boreas; the other is the southern, which is never seen, and is called Austronotius.

2. On these two poles the sphere of heaven moves, they say, and with its motion the stars fixed in it pass from the east all the way around to the west, the *septentriones* near the point of rest describing smaller circles.

Chapter 34. On the course of the same sphere.

1. The sphere of heaven, [moving] from the east towards the west, turns once in a day and night, in the space of twenty-four hours, within which the sun completes his swift revolving course over the lands and under the earth.

Chapter 35. On the swiftness of the heavens.

1. With such swiftness is the sphere of heaven said to run, that if the stars did not run against its headlong course in order to delay it, it would destroy the universe.

Chapter 36. On the axis of the heavens.

1. The axis is a straight line north, which passes through the center of the globe of the sphere, and is called axis because the sphere revolves on it like a wheel, or it may be because the Wain is there.

Chapter 37. On the poles of the heavens.

1. The poles are little circles which run on the axis. Of these one is the northern which never sets and is called Boreas; the other is the southern which is never seen, and is called Austronotius.

Chapter 38. On the *cardines* of the heavens.

1. The *cardines* of the heavens are the ends of the axis, and are called *cardines* (hinges) because the heavens turn on them, or because they turn like the heart *(cor)*.

Chapter 40. On the gates of the heavens.

1. There are two gates of the heavens, the east and the west. For by one the sun appears, by the other he retires.

* * * * *

Chapter 47. On the size of the sun.

1. The size of the sun is greater than that of the earth

and so from the moment when it rises it appears equally to east and west at the same time.* And as to its appearing to us about a cubit in width, it is necessary to reflect how far the sun is from the earth, which distance causes it to seem small to us.

Chapter 48. On the size of the moon.

1. The size of the moon also is said to be less than that of the sun. For since the sun is higher than the moon and still appears to us larger than the moon, if it should approach near to us it would be plainly seen to be much larger than the moon. Just as the sun is larger than the earth, so the earth is in some degree larger than the moon.

Chapter 49. On the nature of the sun.

1. The sun, being made of fire, heats to a whiter glow because of the excessive speed of its circular motion. And its fire, philosophers declare, is fed with water, and it receives the virtue of light and heat from an element opposed to it. Whence we see that it is often wet and dewy.

Chapter 50. On the motion of the sun.

1. They say that the sun has a motion of its own and does not turn with the universe. For if it remained fixed in the heavens all days and nights would be equal, but since we see that it will set to-morrow in a different place from where it set yesterday, it is plain that it has a motion of its own and does not move with the universe. For it accomplishes its yearly orbits by varying courses, on account of the changes of the seasons.

2. For going further to the south it makes winter, in order that the land may be enriched by winter rains and frosts. Approaching the north it restores the summer, in order that fruits may mature, and what is green in the damp weather may ripen in the heat.

Chapter 51. What the sun does.

1. The rising sun brings the day, the setting sun the night; for day is the sun above the earth, night is the sun beneath the earth. From the sun come the hours; from the sun, when it rises, the day; from the sun, too, when it sets, the night; from the sun the months and years are numbered; from the sun come the changes of the seasons.

2. When it runs through the south it is nearer the earth; when it passes toward the north it is raised aloft. God has appointed for it different courses, places, and times for this reason, lest if it always remained in the same place all things should be consumed by its daily heat--just as Clement says: "It takes on different motions, by which the temperature of the air is moderated with a view to the seasons, and a regular order is observed in its seasonal changes and permutations. For when it ascends to the higher parts it tempers the spring, and when it

---

* This passage indicates Isidore's belief in a flat earth.

comes to the summit of heaven it kindles the summer heats; descending again, it gives autumn its temperature. And when it returns to the lower circle it leaves to us the rigor of winter cold from the icy quarter of the heavens."

Chapter 52. On the journey of the sun.

1. The eastern sun holds its way through the south, and after it comes to the west and has bathed itself in ocean, it passes by unknown ways beneath the earth, and again returns to the east.

* * * * *

Chapter 76. On the wandering stars.

1. Certain stars are called *planetae*, that is, wandering, because they hasten around through the whole universe with varying motions. . . .

Chapter 68.

1. *Praecedentia* or *antegradatio* of stars is when a star seems to be making its usual course and [really] is somewhat ahead of it.

Chapter 69.

1. *Remotio* or *retrogradatio* of stars is when a star, while moving on its regular orbit, seems at the same time to be moving backward.

Chapter 70.

1. The *status* of stars means that while a star is continuing its proper motion it nevertheless seems in some places to stand still.

Chapter 71. On the names of stars.

3. *Stellae* is derived from *stare*, because the stars always remain *(stant)* fixed in the heavens and do not fall. As to our seeing stars fall, as it were, from heaven, they are not stars but little bits of fire that have fallen from the ether, and this happens when the wind, blowing high, carries along with it fire from the ether, which as it is carried along gives the appearance of falling stars. For stars cannot fall; they are motionless (as has been said above) and are fixed in the heavens and carried around with them.

16. A comet is so-called because it spreads light from itself as if it were hair *(comas)*. And when this kind of star appears it indicates pestilence, famine, or war.

17. Comets are called in the Latin *crinitae* because they have a trail of flames resembling hair *(in modum crinium)*. The Stoics say there are over thirty of them, and certain astrologers have written down their names and qualities.

20. The planets are stars which are not fixed in the heavens like the rest, but move along in the air. . . . Sometimes they move towards the south, sometimes towards the north, generally in a direction opposite to that of the universe, sometimes

with it, and their Greek names are Phaeton, Phaenon, Pyrois, Hesperus, Stilbon.

21. To these the Romans have given the names of their gods, that is, of Jupiter, Saturn, Mars, Venus, Mercury. Deceiving themselves and wishing to deceive [others] into worship of these gods, who had bestowed upon them somewhat in accordance with the desire of the world, they pointed to the stars in heaven, saying that that was Jove's star, that Mercury's, and the empty idea arose. This erroneous belief the devil cherished, but Christ destroyed.

* * * * *

In describing the universe the philosophers mention five circles, which the Greeks call παράλληλοι, that is, zones, into which the circle of lands is divided. . . . Now let us imagine them after the manner of our right hand, so that the thumb may be called the Arctic circle, uninhabitable because of cold; the second, the summer circle, temperate, inhabitable; the middle (finger), the equinoctial (*Isemerinus*) circle, torrid, uninhabitable; the fourth, the winter circle, temperate, inhabitable; the fifth, the Antarctic circle, frigid, uninhabitable. The first of these is the northern, the second, the solstitial, the third, the equinoctial, the fourth, the winter circle, the fifth, the southern. . . . The following figure shows the divisions of these circles. (Fig. 1.) Now, the equinoctial circle is uninhabitable because the sun, speeding through the midst of the heaven, creates an excessive heat in these places, so that, on account of the parched earth, crops do not grow there, nor are men permitted to dwell there, because of the great heat. But, on the other hand, the northern and southern circles, *being adjacent to each other*, are not inhabited, for the reason that they are situated

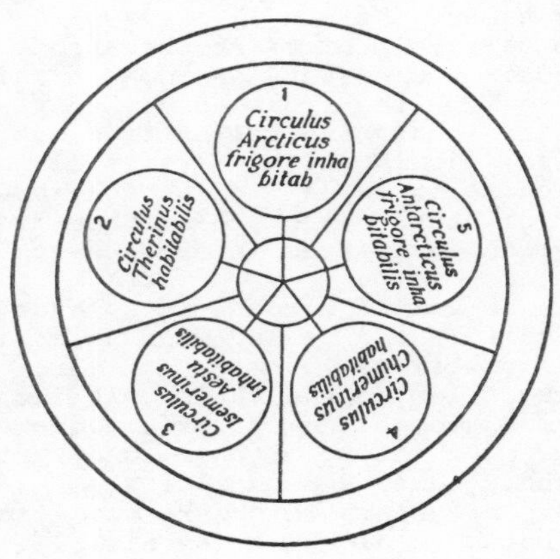

far from the sun's course, and are rendered waste by the great rigor of the climate and the icy blasts of the winds. But the circle of the summer solstice which is situated *in the east, between the northern circle and the circle of heat,* and the circle which is placed *in the west, between the circle of the heat and the southern circle,* are temperate for the reason that they derive cold from one circle, heat from the other. Of which Virgil [says]:

"Between these and the middle [zone] two are granted to wretched mortals by the gift of the gods."

Now, they who are next to the torrid circle are the Ethiopians, who are burnt by excessive heat.

* * * * *

Extracts

Chapter 1. On medicine.

1. Medicine is that which guards or restores the health of the body, and its subject-matter deals with diseases and wounds.

* * * * *

Chapter 5. On the four humors of the body.

1. Health is the integrity of the body and the compound *(temperantia)* made by nature from hot and moist which is the blood, whence also it has been named *sanitas*, as it were *sanguinis status* (state of the blood).

2. Under the general name of *morbus* (disease) all disorders of the body are embraced, to which the ancients gave the name of *morbus* in order to indicate by the very name the power of death *(mortis)* which arises from it. Between health and disease the mean is cure, and unless it harmonizes with the disease it does not lead to health.

3. All diseases arise from the four humors, that is, from blood, bile, black bile, and phlegm. Just as there are four elements so also there are four humors, and each humor imitates its element: blood, air; bile, fire; black bile, earth; phlegm, water. There are four humors, as four elements, which preserve our bodies.

* * * * *

17. Pestilence is a contagion, and when it seizes one it quickly passes to more. It is produced from a corruption of the air, and makes its way by penetrating into the inward parts. Although this is generally caused by the powers of the air, still it is certainly not caused against the will of Omnipotent God. . . . It is a disease so acute that it affords no time to hope for life or death, but a sudden weakness and death come at the same moment.

* * * * *

Chapter 8. On diseases that appear on the surface of the body.

11. Leprosy is a scaly roughness of the skin, like *lepidus* (pepper-wort), whence it took its name, and its color now turns to black, now to white, now to red. On the body of a man leprosy is diagnosed in this way, if a varied color appears here and there between sound parts of the skin, or if it spreads everywhere in such a way as to make all of one unnatural color. . . .

Chapter 9. On remedies and medicines.

1. The curative power of medicine must not be despised. For we remember that Isaiah sent something of medicinal nature to Hezekiah when he was sick, and Paul the apostle said a little wine was good for Timothy.

3. There are three kinds of cures in all. The first is the dietetic; the second, the pharmaceutical; the third, the surgical. Diet *(diaeta)* is the observance of the law of life. Pharmacy is curing by medicines. Surgery is cutting with the knife; for with the knife is cut away that which does not feel the healing of medicines. . . .

5. Every cure is wrought either by contraries or by likes. By contraries, as cold by warm and dry by moist, just as in man pride cannot be cured except by humility.

6. By likes, as a round bandage is put on a round wound, or an oblong one on an oblong wound. For the very bandage is not the same for all wounds, but like is fitted to like. . . .

7. *Antidotum* in the Greek means in the Latin *ex contrario datum.* For contraries are cured by contraries in the medical system. On the other hand likes are cured by likes, as for example, πικρὰ which means bitters because its taste is bitter. It received a suitable name because the bitterness of disease is dispelled by its bitterness.

* * * * *

Chapter 5. On angels.

2. The word angel is the name of a function, not of a nature; for they are always spirits, but are called angels when they are sent.

3. And the license of painters makes wings for them in order to denote their swift passage in every direction, just as also in the fables of the poets the winds are said to have wings on account of their velocity. . . .

4. The sacred writings testify that there are nine orders of angels, namely, angels, archangels, thrones, dominions, virtues, principalities, powers, cherubim and seraphim. And we shall explain by derivation why the names of these functions were so applied.

5. Angels are so called because they are sent down from heaven to carry messages to men. . . .

6. Archangels in the Greek tongue means *summi nuntii* in the Latin. For they who carry small or trifling messages are called angels; and they who announce the most important things are called archangels. . . . Archangels are so called because they hold the leadership among angels. . . . For they are leaders and

chiefs under whose control services are assigned to each and every angel.

17. Certain functions of angels by which signs and wonders are done in the world are called virtues, on account of which the virtues are named.

18. Those are powers to whom hostile virtues are subject, and they are called by the name of powers because evil spirits are constrained by their power not to harm the world as much as they desire.

19. Principalities are those who are in command of the hosts of the angels. And they have received the name of principality because they send the subordinate angels here and there to do the divine service. . . .

20. Dominions are they who are in charge even of the virtues and principalities, and they are called dominions because they rule the rest of the hosts of the angels.

21. Thrones are the hosts of angels who in the Latin are called *sedes*; and they are called thrones because the creator presides over them, and through them accomplishes his decisions.

22. Cherubim . . . are the higher hosts of angels who, being placed nearer, are fuller of the divine wisdom than the rest. . . .

24. The seraphim in like manner are a multitude of angels, and the word is translated from the Hebrew into the Latin as *ardentes* or *incendentes*, and they are called *ardentes* because between them and God no other angels stand, and therefore the nearer they stand in his presence the more they are lighted by the brightness of divine light.

25. And they veil the face and feet of God sitting on his throne, and therefore the rest of the throng of angels are not able to see fully the essence of God, since the seraphim cover him.

28. To each and every one, as has been said before, his proper duties are appointed, and it is agreed that they obtained these according to merit at the beginning of the world. That angels have charge over both places and men, an angel testifies through the prophet, saying: "Princeps regni Persarum mihi restitit" (Dan. x. 13).

* * * * *

On the atoms.

1. The philosophers call by the name of atoms certain parts of bodies in the universe so very minute that they do not appear to the sight, nor admit of τομή, that is, division, whence they are called atoms. These are said to flit through the void of the universe with restless motions, and to move hither and thither like the finest dust that is seen when the rays of the sun pour through the windows. From these certain philosophers of the heathen have thought that trees are produced, and herbs and all fruits, and fire and water, and all things are made out of them.

2. Atoms exist either in a body, or in time, or in number, or in the letters. In a body as a stone. You divide it into parts, and the parts themselves you divide into grains like the

sands, and again you divide the very grains of sand into the finest dust, until if you could, you would come to some little particle which is now [such] that it cannot be divided or cut. This is an atom in a body.

3. In time, the atom is thus understood: you divide a year, for example, into months, the months into days, the days into hours, the parts of the hours still admit of division, until you come to such an instant of time and fragment of a moment as it were, that it cannot be lengthened by any little bit and therefore it cannot be divided. This is the atom of time.

4. In numbers, as for example, eight is divided into fours, again four into twos, then two into ones. One is an atom because it is indivisible. So also in case of the letters. For you divide a speech into words, words into syllables, the syllable into letters. The letter, the smallest part, is the atom and cannot be divided. The atom is therefore what cannot be divided, like the point in geometry. . . .

B. THE 'FLOWERING' OF MEDIEVAL SCIENCE

1. Robert Grosseteste, From *On Light, or the Incoming of Forms**

The influence of Aristotle on the medieval mind was overpowering but not entirely overwhelming. The influence of Plato remained and was, indeed, strengthened by the Renaissance of the 12th century. The rivalry between Aristotelians and Platonists tended to be incorporated into the rivalry between the two great orders of the Dominicans and the Franciscans. Robert Grosseteste, Bishop of Lincoln (c. 1168-1253) was neither, but he was a teacher of the Franciscans and his doctrines had great weight with that order. His treatise, On Light, *provided some sound Platonic reasons for studying the optical aspects of the natural world and provided an alternative approach to that advocated by the enthusiastic disciples of Aristotle.*

The first bodily form *(forma)*, which some call corporeity, I judge to be light. For light *(lux)* of itself diffuses itself in every direction, so that a sphere of light as great as you please is engendered instantaneously *(subito)* from a point of light, unless something opaque stands in the way. But corporeity is that upon which of necessity there follows the extension of matter into three dimensions, although nevertheless each of them, namely corporeity and matter, is a substance which in itself is simple and has no dimensions at all. But it was impossible for form which in itself is simple and without dimensions to bring in everywhere dimensions into matter which is similarly simple and without dimensions, except by plurifying itself and by diffusing itself instantaneously in every direction and, in its diffusion of itself, extending matter, since form cannot abandon matter, because it (form) is not separable, and because matter cannot be emptied of form. Still, I have put forward light as being that which of itself has this operation, namely to plurify itself and to diffuse itself instantaneously in every direction. Therefore whatever does this work either is light itself or is a doer of this work insofar as it participates in light, which does this of itself. Therefore corporeity either is light itself or is the doer of the said work and the bringer of dimensions into matter, insofar as it (corporeity) participates in light itself and acts through the virtue of the light itself. But it is impossible for the first form to bring dimensions into matter through the virtue of a form which follows upon it (the first form). Therefore light is not a form which follows upon corpore-

---

* Robert Grosseteste, Bishop of Lincoln (1168-1253), *On Light, or The Incoming of Forms*, the first translation into this language of *De Luce Seu De Inchoatione Formarum*, Charles Glenn Wallis, Translator. The St. John's Bookstore, Annapolis, 1939.

ity, but is corporeity itself.

Further: men of good sense judge that the first bodily form is more worthy than all the later forms and of a more excellent and noble essence and more like the forms which stand separate. But light is of a more worthy and more noble and more excellent essence than all bodily things; and it is more like the forms which stand separate,--and they are the intelligences--, than all bodies are. Therefore light is the first bodily form.

Therefore as light, which is the first form created in first matter and which of itself plurifies itself everywhere infinitely and stretches out equally in every direction, could not abandon matter, it drew out matter, along with itself, into a mass as great as the world-machine *(machina mundi)* and in the beginning of time extended matter. Nor could the extension of matter occur through a finite plurification of light, because a simple which is plurified a finite number of times does not engender a quantum *(simplex finities replicatum quantum non generat)*, as Aristotle shows in the DE COELO ET MUNDO. But if a simple is plurified an infinite number of times, it necessarily engenders a finite quantum, because the product of the infinite plurification of something exceeds infinitely that by the plurification of which it was produced. Yet a simple is not exceeded infinitely by a simple, but a finite quantum alone exceeds a simple (thing) infinitely. For an infinite quantum exceeds a simple (thing) infinitely an infinite number of times. Therefore, if light, which in itself is simple, is plurified an infinite number of times, it necessarily extends matter, which is similarly simple, into dimensions of finite magnitude.

But it is possible that an infinite sum of number be related to an infinite sum (of number) in every numeric ratio and also in every non-numeric ratio. And there are infinites which are greater *(plura)* than other infinites; and infinites which are smaller *(pauciora)* than other infinites. For the sum of all numbers both even and odd is infinite; and so it is greater than the sum of all even numbers, which nevertheless is infinite. For (the sum of the even and off) exceeds the sum of the even by the sum of all the odd numbers. Moreover the sum of the numbers doubled continuously from unity is infinite; and similarly the sum of all the halves corresponding to these doubles is infinite. And the sum of these halves is necessarily half of the sum of their doubles. Similarly the sum of all numbers tripled from unity is three times the sum of all the thirds corresponding to the triples. And the same thing is clear in all species of numeric ratio, since the infinite can be proportioned to the infinite in any of these ratios.

But if there are posited the infinite sum of all the doubles continuously from unity and the infinite sum of all the halves corresponding to those doubles and if unity or any finite number you please be taken away from the sum of the halves; then, after the subtraction has been made, the ratio of two to one will no longer hold between the first sum and the remainder of the second sum. Nor does any numeric ratio hold any longer; because, if, in the case of numeric ratio after a subtraction has been made from the lesser sum, some other numeric ratio still holds, it is necessary that what has been substracted be an aliquot part or the aliquot parts of an aliquot part of that from which it has been substracted. But a finite number can not be an aliquot part or the aliquot parts of an aliquot part of an infinite number. Therefore, if a number is substracted from the infinite sum of halves, a numeric ratio no longer holds between the infinite sum of doubles and the remainder of the infinite sum of halves.

Therefore, since this is the case, it is manifest that light, by its infinite plurification, extends matter into lesser finite dimensions and into greater finite dimensions according to any ratios you please, that is, numeric and non-numeric ratios. For if light by an infinite plurification of itself extends matter to a dimension of two cubits, then by twice this same infinite plurification it extends matter to a dimension of four cubits, and by half of that same plurification it extends matter to the dimension of one cubit; and so on according to the other numeric and non-numeric ratios.

This, I presume, was the concept *(intellectus)* of the philsophers who lay down that all things are composed of atoms and who say that bodies are composed of surfaces, and surfaces of lines, and lines of points.--And this opinion does not contradict the one which lays down that magnitude is composed only of magnitudes; because 'whole' is said in as many senses as 'part' is. For in one sense 'half' is said to be 'part' of the 'whole', because, if taken twice, it gives the whole: and in another sense the side is part of the diameter, not because, if taken an aliquot number of times, it gives the diameter; but because, if taken an aliquot number of times, it is exceeded by the diameter. And in another sense the angle of tangency is said to be part of a right angle, into which it goes an infinite number of times, and nevertheless, if subtracted from it a finite number of times, lessens it; and in still another sense a point is part of a line, into which it goes an infinite number of times, and, if subtracted from it a finite number of times, does not lessen it.

Accordingly, returning to my discourse, I say that by the infinite plurification of itself equally in every direction light extends matter everywhere equally into the form of a sphere; and it follows of necessity that in this extension the outmost parts of matter are more extended and more rarefied than the inmost parts near the center. And since the outmost parts will have been rarefied to the utmost, the inner parts will still be susceptible of greater rarefaction.

Therefore light in the aforesaid way, extending matter into the form of a sphere and rarefying the outmost parts to the utmost, has in the farthest sphere fulfilled the possibility of matter and has not left matter susceptible of any further impression. And so the first body is perfected in the boundary of the sphere and is called the "firmament", having nothing in its composition except first matter and first form. And accordingly it is the most simple body as regards the parts constituting its essence and greatest quantity, and it does not differ from the genus body except that in it (the most simple body) matter has been fulfilled merely by the first form. But the genus body, which is in this and in other bodies and which has first matter and first form in its essence, abstracts from the fulfillment of matter by the first form and from the diminishing of matter by the first form.

An so, when the first body, which is the firmament, has been fulfilled in this way, it spreads out its lumière *(lumen)* from every part of itself to the center of the whole. For since light *(lux)* is the perfection of the first body and plurifies itself from the first body naturally, then of necessity light is diffused to the center of the whole. And since light is the whole which is not separable from matter in the diffusion of itself (light) from the first body, it extends the spirituality of the matter of the first body. And thus there proceeds from the first body "lumière", which is a spiritual body or, as you may prefer to say, bodily spirit. And this lumière in its passage does not divide the body through which it passes; and accordingly it passes instantaneously *(subito)* from the first body of the heavens down to the center. And its passage is not as if you were to understand that something one in number passes instantaneously from the heaven to the center,--for that is quite impossible; but its passage occurs through the infinite plurification of itself and the infinite engendering of lumière. Therefore the lumière itself, which has been spread out from the first body to the center and gathered together, has assembled the mass *(molem)* existing within the first body. And since the first body, as being fulfilled and invariable, could not now be diminished, and since no place could become void, it was necessary in the very assembling that the outmost parts of the mass should be extended and dispersed. And thus a greater density came about in the inmost parts of the said mass, and the rarity was increased in the outmost parts. And the power of the lumière which was doing the assembling and the power of the lumière which in the very assembling was doing the separating were so great that they subtilized and rarefied to the utmost the outmost parts of the mass contained within the first body. And so there came to be in the outmost parts of the said mass "the second sphere", which is fulfilled and not receptive of any further impression. And thus there is the fulfillment and perfection of the second sphere: for lumière is engendered from the first sphere, and light, which in the first sphere is simple, is twofold in the second sphere.

But just as the lumière engendered by the first body has fulfilled the second sphere and within the second sphere has left the mass denser, so the lumière engendered from the second sphere has perfected the "third sphere" and within the third sphere has left the mass still denser by the assembling. And this assembling which disperses *(congregatio disgregans)* proceeded in this order, until the "nine celestial spheres" were fulfilled, and until the most dense mass,--which was matter for the four elements, was assembled within the ninth and lowest sphere. But the lowest sphere, which is the sphere of the "moon", also engenders lumière from itself, and by its lumière it has assembled the mass contained within itself, and by this assembling it has subtilized and dispersed its outmost parts. Nevertheless the power of this lumière was not so great that by its assembling it dispersed its outmost parts to the utmost. On that account imperfection and the possibility of the reception of assembling and dispersal has remained in every part of this mass. And the highest part of this mass was not dispersed to the utmost but by its dispersal was made to be fire, and it still remained matter for the elements. And this element, engendering lumière from itself and assembling the mass contained within itself, has dispersed its outmost parts, but with a smaller dispersal of the fire itself; and thus it has brought forth "fire". But fire, engendering lumière from itself and assembling the mass contained within, has dispersed its outmost parts, but with a smaller dispersal of itself. And thus it has brought forth air. Air also, engendering from itself a spiritual body or bodily spirit and assembling that which is contained within itself and by this assembling that which is contained within itself and by this assembling dispersing its outer parts, has brought forth "water" and "earth". But because more of this assembling virtue than of the dispersing has remained in water, the water together with the earth has remained weighty.

So in this way the thirteen spheres of this sensible world were brought into being; namely the nine celestial, which cannot be altered, increased, generated, or corrupted, because fulfilled; and the four spheres which exist in the contrary manner and can be altered, increased, generated, and corrputed, because unfulfilled. And that is clear, since every higher body by reason of the lumière engendered from itself is the form *(species)* and perfection of the body following. And just as unity is potentially every number which follows, so the first body by the plurification of its own lumière is every body which follows.

The earth however is all the higher bodies because the higher lumières are summed up in itself; on that account the earth is called Pan by the poets,--that is, All; and it is named Cybele, as if *cubile*, from the cube, that is, from solidity; because the earth is the most greatly compressed of all bodies, that is, Cybele the mother of all the gods; because, though the higher lumières are gathered together in the earth, nevertheless they are not arisen in the earth by their own operations, but it is possible for the lumière of any sphere you please to be drawn forth from the earth into act and operation; and so whatever god you wish will be born of the earth as if of some mother. But the middle bodies have two relations. For indeed they are related to the lower bodies as the first heaven is to all the remaining; and to the higher bodies, as the earth is to all the other bodies. And thus in some certain modes all the remaining bodies are in any one of them.

And the form *(species)* and perfection of all bodies is light *(lux)*: but the light of the higher bodies is more spiritual and simple, while the light of the lower bodies is more bodily and plurified. Nor are all bodies of the same form or species, though they have originated from a simple or plurified light; just as all numbers are not of the same form or species, though nevertheless they are produced by the greater or lesser plurification from unity.

And in this discourse it is quite clear what the meaning is of those who say, "all things are one by the perfection of one light", and the meaning of those who say, "those things which are many are many by the diverse plurification of the very light".

But since the lower bodies participate in the form *(formam)* of the higher bodies, the lower body, but its participation in the same form as the higher body, is receptive of movement from the same bodiless motor virtue, by which motor virtue the higher body is moved. Wherefore the bodiless virtue of intelligence or soul, which moves the first and highest sphere by the daily movement, moves all the lower celestial spheres by the same daily movement. But insofar as they are lower, they receive this movement more weakly, because insofar as a sphere is lower, the first and bodily light in it is less pure and more weak.

But though the elements do participate in the form of the first heaven, nevertheless they are not moved in a daily movement by the mover of the first heaven. Although they participate in that first light, nevertheless they do not yield to the first motor virtue, since they have that light as impure, weak, and distant from its purity in the first body, and since they have density of matter too, which is the beginning *(principium)* of resistance and unyieldingness. Nevertheless some think that the sphere of fire wheels around in the daily movement, and they take the wheeling around of comets as a sign of that, and they say moreover that this movement continues as far as the waters of the sea, so that the tides of the sea may come from it. But nevertheless all who rightly philosophize say that the earth is exempt from this movement.

Moreover, in the same way because the spheres after the second sphere,--usually named the eighth in the upward reckoning--, participate in its form, all share in its movement which they have as their own in addition to the daily movement.

But because the celestial spheres are fulfilled and are not receptive of rarefaction or condensation, the light in them does not bend the parts of matter away from the center, in order to rarefy them, or towards the center, in order to condense them. And on that account the celestial spheres themselves are not receptive of movement upward or downward, but only of circular movement from the intellectual motor virtue, which turns back its glance towards itself in a bodily fashion *(in sese aspectum corporaliter reverberans)* and makes the spheres themselves resolve in a circular bodily movement. But because the elements themselves are unfulfilled, rarefiable, and condensable, the lumière which is in them either bends away from the center, in order to rarefy them, or towards the center in order to condense them. And on that account they are naturally movable either upward or downward.

But in the highest body, which is the most simple of bodies, there are four things to be found, namely, form, matter, composition, and the composite. Now the form, as being most simple, has the place of unity. But on account of the twofold power of the matter, namely its ability to receive impressions and to retain them, and also on account of density, which has its roots in matter,--and this twofold power belongs first principally to the number two--, matter is duly allotted the nature of the number two. But the composition holds the number three in itself, because in the composition there are evident the formed matter and the materialized form and the thing about the composition which is its very own *(proprietos)* and found in any composite whatever as a third thing other than the matter and the form. And that which besides these three is properly the composite is comprehended under the number four. Therefore the number four is in the first body, wherein all the other bodies are virtually; and accordingly at the roots *(radicaliter)* the number of the other bodies is not found to be beyond ten. For when the number one of the form, and the number two of the matter and the number three of the composition and the number four of the composite are added together, they make up the number ten. On this account ten is the number of the bodies of the spheres of the world, because, although the sphere of the elements is divided into four, nevertheless it is one by participation in the terrestrial and corruptible nature.

From this it is clear that ten is the full number of the universe, because every whole and perfect thing has something in itself like form and unity, and something like matter and the number two and something like composition and the number three, and something like the composite and the humber four. And it is not possible to add a fifth beyond these four. Wherefore every whole and perfect thing is a ten.

But from this it is evident that only the five ratios found between the four numbers one, two, three, and four, are fitted to the composition and to the concord which makes every composite steadfast. Wherefore only those five concordant ratios exist in musical measures, in dances, and in rhythmic times.

2. Roger Bacon, From *Opus Majus**

Roger Bacon (ca. 1219-1292) was the leading exponent of the experimental method in the Middle Ages. In his Opus Majus, *he spelled out the way in which this new method should be applied to the problem of unveiling the mysteries of Nature.*

Having laid down fundamental principles of the wisdom of the Latins so far as they are found in language, mathematics, and optics, I now wish to unfold the principles of experimental science, since without experience nothing can be sufficiently known. For there are two modes of acquiring knowledge, namely, by reasoning and experience. Reasoning draws a conclusion and makes us grant the conclusion, but does not make the conclusion certain, nor does it remove doubt so that the mind may rest on the intuition of truth, unless the mind discovers it by the path of experience; since many have the arguments relating to what can be known, but because they lack experience they neglect the arguments, and neither avoid what is harmful nor follow what is good. For if a man who has never seen fire should prove by adequate reasoning that fire burns and injures things and destroys them, his mind would not be satisfied thereby, nor would he avoid fire, until he placed his hand or some combustible substance in the fire, so that he might prove by experience that which reasoning taught. But when he has had actual experience of combustion his mind is made certain and rests in the full light of truth. Therefore reasoning does not suffice, but experience does.

This is also evident in mathematics, where proof is most convincing. But the mind of one who has the most convincing proof in regard to the equilateral triangle will never cleave to the conclusion without experience, nor will he heed it, but will disregard it until experience is offered him by the intersection of two circles, from either intersection of which two lines may be drawn to the extremities of the given line; but then the man accepts the conclusion without any question. Aristotle's statement, then, that proof is reasoning that causes us to know is to be understood with the proviso that the proof is accompanied by its appropriate experience, and is not to be understood of the bare proof. His statement also in the first book of the Metaphysics that those who understand the reason and the cause are wiser than those who have empiric knowledge of a fact, is spoken of such as know only the bare truth without the cause. But I am here speaking of the man who knows the reason and the cause through experience. These men are perfect in their wisdom, as Aristotle maintains in the sixth book of the Ethics, whose simple

---

* Roger Bacon, *The Opus Majus of Roger Bacon*, A Translation by Robert Belle Burke, Volume II, University of Pennsylvania Press, Philadelphia, 1928. Pp. 583-589; 615-616; 628-633. Reprinted by permission of the University of Pennsylvania Press.

statements must be accepted as if they offered proof, as he states in the same place.

He therefore who wishes to rejoice without doubt in regard to the truths underlying phenomena must know how to devote himself to the experiment. For authors write many statements, and people believe them through reasoning which they formulate without experience. Their reasoning is wholly false. For it is generally believed that the diamond cannot be broken except by goat's blood, and philosophers and theologians misuse this idea. But fracture by means of blood of this kind has never been verified, although the effort has been made; and without that blood it can be broken easily. For I have seen this with my own eyes, and this is necessary, because gems cannot be carved except by fragments of this stone. Similarly it is generally believed that the castors employed by physicians are the testicles of the male animal. But this is not true, because the beaver has these under its breast, and both the male and female produce testicles of this kind. Besides these castors the male beaver has its testicles in their natural place; and therefore what is subjoined is a dreadful lie, namely, that when the hunters pursue the beaver, he himself knowing what they are seeking cuts out with his teeth these glands. Moreover, it is generally believed that hot water freezes more quickly than cold water in vessels, and the argument in support of this is advanced that contrary is excited by contrary, just like enemies meeting each other. But it is certain that cold water freezes more quickly for any one who makes the experiment. People attribute this to Aristotle in the second book of the Meteorologics; but he certainly does not make this statement, but he does make one like it, by which they have been deceived, namely, that if cold water and hot water are poured on a cold place, as upon ice, the hot water freezes more quickly, and this is true. But if hot water and cold are placed in two vessels, the cold will freeze more quickly. Therefore all things must be verified by experience.

But experience is of two kinds; one is gained through our external senses, and in this way we gain our experience of those things that are in the heavens by instruments made for this purpose, and of those things here below by means attested by our vision. Things that do not belong in our part of the world we know through other scientists who have had experience of them. As, for example, Aristotle on the authority of Alexander sent two thousand men through different parts of the world to gain experimental knowledge of all things that are on the surface of the earth, as Pliny bears witness in his Natural History. This experience is both human and philosophical, as far as man can act in accordance with the grace given him; but this experience does not suffice him, because it does not give full attestation in regard to things corporeal owing to its difficulty, and does not touch at all on things spiritual. It is necessary, therefore, that the intellect of man should be otherwise aided, and for this reason the holy patriarchs and prophets, who first gave sciences to the world, received illumination within and were not dependent on sense alone. The same is true of many believers since the time of Christ. For the grace of faith illuminates greatly, as also do divine inspirations, not only in things spiritual, but in things corporeal and in the sciences of philosophy; as Ptolemy states in the Centilogium, namely, that there are two roads by which we arrive at the knowledge of facts, one through the experience of philosophy, the other through divine inspiration, which is far the better way, as he says.

* * * * *

Since this Experimental Science is wholly unknown to the rank and file of students, I am therefore unable to convince people of its utility unless at the same time I disclose its excellence and its proper signification. This science alone, therefore, knows how to test perfectly what can be done by nature, what by the effort of art, what by trickery, what the incantations, conjurations, invocations, deprecations, sacrifices, that belong to magic, mean and dream of, and what is in them, so that all falsity may be removed and the truth alone of art and nature may be retained. This science alone teaches us how to view the mad acts of magicians, that they may be not ratified but shunned, just as logic considers sophistical reasoning.

This science has three leading characteristics with respect to other sciences. The first is that it investigates by experiment the notable conclusions of all those sciences. For the other sciences know how to discover their principles by experiments, but their conclusions are reached by reasoning drawn from the principles discovered. But if they should have a particular and complete experience of their own conclusions, they must have it with the aid of this noble science. For it is true that mathematics has general experiments as regards its conclusions in its figures and calculations, which also are applied to all sciences and to this kind of experiment, because no science can be known without mathematics. But if we give our attention to particular and complete experiments and such as are attested wholly by the proper method, we must employ the principles of this science which is called experimental. I give as an example the rainbow and phenomena connected with it, of which nature are the circle around the sun and the stars, the streak [*virga*] also lying at the side of the sun or of a star, which is apparent to the eye in a straight line, and is called by Aristotle in the third book of the Meteorologics a perpendicular, but by Seneca a streak, and the circle is called a corona, phenomena which frequently have the colors of the rainbow. The natural philosopher discusses these phenomena, and the writer on Perspective has much to add pertaining to the mode of vision that is necessary in this case. But neither Aristotle nor Avicenna in their Natural Histories has given us a knowledge of phenomena of this kind, nor has Seneca, who composed a special book on them. But Experimental Science attests them.

Let the experimenter first, then, examine visible objects, in order that he may find colors arranged as in the phenomena mentioned above and also the same figure. For let him take hexagonal stones from Ireland or from India, which are called rainbows in Solinus on the Wonders of the World, and let him hold these in a solar ray falling through the window, so that he may find all the colors of the rainbow, arranged as in it, in the shadow near the ray. And further let the same experimental turn to a somewhat dark place and apply the stone to one of his eyes which is almost closed, and he will see the colors of the rainbow clearly arranged just as in the bow. And since many employing these stones think that the phenomenon is due to the special virtue of those stones and to their hexagonal shape, therefore let the experimenter proceed further, and he will find this same peculiarity in crystalline stones correctly shaped, and in other transparent stones. Moreover, he will find this not only in white stones like the Irish crystals, but also in black ones, as is evident in the dark crystal and in all stones of similar transparency. He will find it besides in crystals of a shape differing from the hexagonal, provided they have a roughened surface, like the Irish crystals, neither altogether smooth, nor rougher than they are. Nature produces some that have surfaces like the Irish crystals. For a difference in the corrugations causes a difference in the colors. And further let him observe rowers, and in the drops falling from the raised oars he finds the same colors when the solar rays penetrate drops of this kind. The same phenomenon is seen in water falling from the wheels of a mill; and likewise when one sees on a summer's morning the drops of dew on the grass in meadow or field, he will observe the colors. Likewise when it is raining, if he stands in a dark place and the rays beyond it pass through the falling rain, the colors will appear in the shadow near by; and frequently at night colors appear around a candle. Moreover, if a man in summer, when he rises from sleep and has his eyes only partly open, suddenly looks at a hole through which a ray of the sun enters, he will see colors. Moreover, if seated beyond the sun he draws his cap beyond his eyes, he will see colors; and similarly if he closes an eye the same thing happens under the shade of the eyebrows; and again the same phenomenon appears through a glass vessel filled with water and placed in the sun's rays. Or similarly if one having water in his mouth sprinkles it vigorously into the rays and stands at the side of the rays. So, too, if rays in the required position pass through an oil lamp hanging in the air so that the light falls on the surface of the oil, colors will be produced. Thus in an infinite number of ways colors of this kind appear, which the diligent experimenter knows how to discover.

* * * * *

Chapter on the Second Prerogative of Experimental Science

This mistress of the speculative sciences alone is able to give us important truths within the confines of the other sciences, which those sciences can learn in no other way. Hence these truths are not connected with the discussion of principles but are wholly outside of these, although they are within the confines of these sciences, since they are neither conclusions nor principles. Clear examples in regard to these matters can be

given; but in what follows the man without experience must not seek a reason in order that he may first understand, for he will never have this reason except after experiment. Hence in the first place there should be readiness to believe, until in the second place experiment follows, so that in the third reasoning may function. For if a man is without experience that a magnet attracts iron, and has not heard from others that it attracts, he will never discover this fact before an experiment. Therefore in the beginning he must believe those who have made the experiment, or who have reliable information from experimenters, nor should he reject the truth, because he is ignorant of it, and because he does not arrive at it by reasoning. I shall state, then, those things that I hold to have been proved by experiment.

Example I

Mathematical science can easily produce the spherical astrolabe, on which all astronomical phenomena necessary for man may be described, according to precise longitudes and latitudes. The device of Ptolemy in the eighth book of the Almagest is used with reference to circles as well as stars, as I have stated, by means of a certain similitude, but the subject is not fully explained by that device, for more work is necessary. But that this body so made should move naturally with the daily motion is not within the power of mathematical science. But the trained experimenter can consider the ways of this motion, aroused to consider them by many things which follow the celestial motion, as, for example, the three elements which rotate circularly through the celestial influence, as Alpetragius states in his book on Celestial Motions, and Averroës in the first book on the Heavens and the World; so also comets, the seas and flowing streams, marrows and brains and the substances composing diseases. Plants also in their parts open and close in accordance with the motion of the sun. And many like things are found which, according to a local motion of the whole or of parts, are moved by the motion of the sun. The scientist, therefore, is aroused by the consideration of things of this kind, a consideration similar in import to that in which he is interested, in order that at length he may arrive at his goal. This instrument would be worth the treasure of a king, and would supersede all other astronomical instruments and clocks, and would be a most wonderful instrument of science. But few would know how in a clear and useful manner to conceive of such a miracle and of similar ones within the confines of mathematical science.

* * * * *

Example III

In the third place, the dignity of this science can be exemplified in alchemy. For that whole art is scarcely so perfected that the greater metals may be produced from the lighter ones, as gold from lead, and silver from copper. But that art never suffices to show the natural and artificial grades of gold and the

modes of its grades. For experimental science has brought both to light, since it has discovered both the four natural grades and their seventeen modes and the artificials ones. By experiment it can be produced beyond twenty-four. Thus the vessel in which the liquor was contained, by means of which the ploughman became the messenger of the king, had a purity of gold far beyond the twenty-four, as its test and worth showed. But when those twenty-four degrees of gold and one part of silver or one degree, the gold is inferior to the former, and thus the diminution of the degrees of the gold goes as far as sixteen, so that there are eight grades of gold with an admixture of silver. But the mineral power in the belly of the earth is not able sometimes to digest matter into the nature of gold, and does what it can by digesting it into the form of silver. And that I am not led astray in this matter by my imagination is proved by the fact that men are found in several parts of the world who are clever at producing those sixteen modes, and have discovered pieces and masses of gold in those seventeen modes. They then made a mixture of silver and air with gold in the aforesaid modes, so that they might have seventeen lumps of gold made artificially, by means of which they might learn the natural modes of gold. Since this art is not known to the majority of those who are eager for gold, many frauds consequently are perpetrated in this world. The art of alchemy not only omits these modes, but this gold of twenty-four degrees is very rarely found, and with the greatest difficulty. There have always been a few who during their life have known this secret of alchemy; and this science does not go beyond that. But experimental science by means of Aristotle's Secrets of Secrets knows how to produce gold not only of twenty-four degrees but of thirty and forty degrees and of as many degrees as we desire. For this reason Aristotle said to Alexander, "I wish to disclose the greatest secret"; and it really is the greatest secret, for not only would it procure an advantage for the state and for every one his desire because of the sufficiency of gold, but what is infinitely more, it would prolong life. For that medicine which would remove all the impurities and corruptions of a baser metal, so that it should become silver adn purest gold, is thought by scientists to be able to remove the corruptions of the human body to such an extent that it would prolong life for many ages. This is the tempered body of elements, of which I spoke above.

Chapter on the Third Prerogative of the Dignity of the Experimental Art

But there is a third dignity of this science. It arises from those properties through which it has no connection with the other sciences, but by its own power investigates the secrets of nature. This consists in two things; namely, in the knowledge of the future, the past, and the present, and in wonderful works by which it excels in the power of forming judgments the ordinary astronomy dealing with judgments. For Ptolemy in the book introductory to the Almagest says that there is a more certain road than that through the ordinary astronomy, and this is the pathway

of experiment, which follows the course of nature, to which many of the philosophers who are believers are turning, just like Aristotle and a host of the authors of judgments formed from the stars, as he himself says, and as we know by proper practice, which cannot be gainsaid. This science was discovered as a complete remedy for human ignorance and inadvertence; for it is difficult to get accurate astronomical instruments, and it is more difficult to get verified tables, especially those in which the motion of the planets is equalized. The use, moreover, of these tables is difficult, but still more difficult is the use of the instruments. But this science has discovered the definitions and the means by which it can answer easily every question, as far as the power of a single branch of philosophy can do so, and by which it can show us the forms of the celestial forces, and the influences of the heavenly bodies on this world without the difficulty of the ordinary astronomy. This part of the science relating to judgments has four principal divisions or secret sciences.

Moreover, certain bear witness that activities of this science which display philosophy consist in changing the character of a region, so that the habits of its people are changed. One of such witnesses was Aristotle himself, the most learned of philosophers. When Alexander asked him in regard to the nations which he had discovered, whether he should exterminate them because of the ferocity of their character, or should permit them to live, he replied in the book of Secrets, "If you can alter the air of those nations, permit them to live; if you cannot, then kill them." For he maintained that the air of these nations could be changed advantageously, so that the complexions of their bodies would be changed, and then their minds influenced by their complexions would choose good morals in accordance with the freedom of the will. This is one of the secrets.

Moreover, certain assert that change is effected by the sun. There is, as an illustration, the example of Aristotle when he said to Alexander, "Give a hot drink from the seed of a plant to whomsoever you wish, and he will obey you for the rest of your life." Some maintain that an army may be stupefied and put to flight. Of this number is Aristotle, who says to Alexander, "Take such a stone, and every army will flee from you." They bear witness that these statements and innumerable others of this kind are true, not meaning that violence is done to the freedom of the will, since Aristotle, who maintains this view, says in the Ethics that the will cannot be coerced. The body, moreover, can be changed by the influence of things, and the minds of people are then aroused and influenced to desire voluntarily that to which they are directed; just as we see in the book of Medicine that through potions and many medicines people can be changed in body and in the passions of the soul and in the inclination of the will.

There are, moreover, other inventions belonging more to nature which do not have as their object a marvelous change in the will, and they are diversified in character. Some of these possess an excellence of wisdom with other advantages, as, for example, perpetual baths most suitable for human use that do not require any artificial renewal; and ever-burning lamps. For we see many things that cannot be impaired by fire, nay, that are purified by fire, like the skin of the salamander and many other things of this kind, which also can be so prepared that they are externally luminous of themselves, and retain the power of fire, adn give forth flame and light. Moreover, against foes of the state they have discovered important arts, so that without a sword or any weapon requiring physical contact they could destroy all who offer resistance. There are many kinds of these inventions. Some of these are perceived by no one of the senses, or by smell alone, and of these inventions Aristotle's book explains that of altering the air, but not those of which I spoke above. These are of a different character, since they act by means of an infection. There are others also that change some one of the senses, and they are diversified in accordance with all the senses.

Certain of these work a change by contact only and thus destroy life. For malta, which is a kind of bitumen and is plentiful in this world, when cast upon an armed man burns him up. The Romans suffered severe loss of life from this in their conquests, as Pliny states in the second book of the Natural History, and as the histories attest. Similarly yellow petroleum, that is, oil springing from the rock, burns up whatever it meets if it is properly prepared. For a consuming fire is produced by this which can be extinguished with difficulty; for water cannot put it out. Certain inventions disturb the hearing to such a degree that, if they are set off suddenly at night with sufficient skill, neither city nor army can endure them. No clap of thunder could compare with such noises. Certain of these strike such terror to the sight that the coruscations of the clouds disturb it incomparably less. Gideon is thought to have employed inventions similar to these in the camp of the Midianites. We have an example of this in that toy of children which is made in many parts of the world, namely, an instrument as large as the human thumb. From the force of the salt called salpeter so horrible a sound is produced at the bursting of so small a thing, namely, a small piece of parchment, that we perceive it exceeds the roar of sharp thunder, and the flash exceeds the greatest brilliancy of the lightning accompanying the thunder.

There are also very many things that slay every poisonous animal by the gentlest touch, and if a circle is made around these animals with things of this kind the animals cannot get out, but die, although they are not touched. But if a man is bitten by a poisonous animal, by the application of the powder of such things he can be healed, as Bede states in his Ecclesiastical History and as we know by experience. And thus there are innumerable things that have strange virtues, whose potencies we are ignorant of solely from our neglect of experiment.

But there are other inventions which do not possess such advantage for the state, but are to be looked upon as miracles of nature, such as experiments with the magnet, not only on iron, but on gold and other metals. Moreover, if the experiment on iron were not known, it would be viewed as a great miracle. And surely in respect to the action of the magnet on iron there are phenomena unknown to those who use the magnet which show in a wonderful way the dissolutions of nature. Just as also from these the faithful experimenter knows how to experiment on the mutual attraction of other things, as, for example, the stone that passes to the acid, and bitumen that ignites from fire placed at a distance from it, as Pliny states in the second book of the Natural History; and certain other things that are mutually attracted although locally separated. This is truly wonderful beyond all that I have seen and heard. For after I saw this, there has been nothing difficult for my intellect to believe, provided it had a trustworthy authority. And that this fact may not be hidden from your Reverence, this phenomenon occurs in the parts of plants divided and locally separated. For if a sapling of one year's growth is taken, which springs forth beside the roots of the hazel, and is divided longitudinally, and the divided parts separated by the space of a palm or four fingers, and one person holds on one side the extremities of the two parts, and another similarly on the other side, always with an equal and gentle grasp, so that the parts are kept opposite each other in the same position they had before the division, within the space of a half a mile* the parts of the twig begin to approach each other gradually, but with greater force at the end of the experiment, so that at length they meet and are united. The ends, however, remain apart, because they are prevented from meeting owing to the force exerted by those holding the parts. This is a very wonderful thing. For this reason magicians perform this experiment, repeating different incantations, and they believe that the phenomenon is caused by virtue of the incantations. I have disregarded the incantations and have discovered the wonderful action of nature, which is similar to that of the magnet on iron. For just as the one attracts the other because of the similar nature of the iron and the magnet, so do the parts in this case. Hence the natural force, which is similar in both parts of the twig, causes them to unite. If they were arranged in the required way, they would meet at the extremities just as in the middle and more quickly, as, for example, if the ends were minutely pierced and threads passed through the ends, so that they could be suspended in the air without hindrance. This is true not only of hazel saplings but of many others, as in the case of willows and perhaps in that of all saplings if they were arranged in the required manner. But since in such matters the mind thinks more aptly than the pen writes, I forbear for the present. I am here merely writing down the statements of scientists and noting their achievements. The genius of these men I admire more than I understand.

Concluding thus the subject of this science experimental without restriction, I shall now show its advantage to theology, as I have done similarly in the case of the other sciences. Since I have now shown the intrinsic nature of this science, it is evident to all that next to moral philosophy this science is the most useful, and it is so in the first place to theology itself in its unrestricted sense because of the literal and spir-

---

* Time taken to walk half a mile.

itual meaning in which it consists. For I showed above that the literal meaning consists in expressing the truth in regard to created things by means of their definitions and descriptions, and I likewise showed that reasoning does not arrive at this truth, but that experiment does. Wherefore this science next to moral philosophy will present the literal truth of Scripture most effectively, so that through suitable adaptations and similitudes the spiritual sense may be derived, owing to the peculiar nature of the sacred Scripture and in accordance with the methods employed by the sacred writers and by all sages.

Then this science as regards the commonwealth of believers is useful, as we saw in its special knowledge of the future, present, and past, and in its display of wonderful works on behalf of Church and state, so that all useful activities are promoted and the opposite are hindered both in the few and in the multitude, as was explained. And if we proceed to the conversion of unbelievers, it is evidently of service in two main ways with numerous subdivisions, since a plea for the faith can be effectively made through this science, not by arguments but by works, which is the more effective way. For to the man who denies the truth of the faith because he cannot understand it I shall state the mutual attraction of things in nature, just as I described it. Likewise I shall tell him that a jar may be broken without human force, and the wine contained in it remain motionless and without flow for three days; and that gold and silver in a pouch, and a sword in its scabbard may be consumed without injury to their containers, as Seneca states in the book of Natural Questions. I shall tell him, moreover, that the birds called kingfisher in the depth of winter compel the stormy sea to be calm and restrain itself until they have laid their eggs and similar ones ought to influence a man and urge him to accept the divine verities. Since if in the vilest creatures verities are found by which the pride of the human intellect ought to be subdued so that it may believe them although it does not understand them, conviction should follow, or injury will be done to infallible truth, since a man ought rather to humble his mind to the glorious truths of God. Surely there is no comparison.

But there is still another very useful way; since the formation of judgments, as I have said, is a function of this science, in regard to what can happen by nature or be effected in art, and what not. This science, moreover, knows how to separate the illusions of magic and to detect all their errors in incantations, invocations, conjurations, sacrifices, and cults. But unbelievers busy themselves in these mad acts and trust in them, and have believed that the Christians used such means in working their miracles. Wherefore this science is of the greatest advantage in persuading men to accept the faith, since this branch alone of philosophy happens to proceed in this way, because this is the only branch that considers matters of this kind, and is able to overcome all falsehood and superstition and error of unbelievers in regard to magic, such as incantations and the like already mentioned. How far, moreover, it may serve to reprobate obstinate unbelievers is already shown by the violent means that have just been touched upon, and therefore I pass on.

We must consider, however, that although other sciences do many wonders, as in the case of practical geometry, which produces mirrors that burn up every opposing object, and so too in the other sciences, yet all things of such wonderful utility in the state belong chiefly to this science. For this science has the same relation to the other sciences as the science of navigation to the carpenter's art and the military art to that of the engineer. For this science teaches how wonderful instruments may be made, and uses them when made, and also considers all secret things owing to the advantages they may possess for the state and for individuals; and it directs other sciences as its handmaids, and therefore the whole power of speculative science is attributed especially to this science. And now the wonderful advantage derived from these three sciences in this world on behalf of the Chruch of God against the enemies of the faith is manifest, who should be destroyed rather by the discoveries of science than by the warlike arms of combatants. Antichrist will use these means freely and effectively, in order that he may crush and confound the power of this world; and by these means tyrants in times past brought the world under their sway. This has been shown by examples without end.

3. Adelard of Bath, From *Quaestiones Naturales**

Ancient learning and medieval lore met in the twelfth century as Latin scholars confronted the heritage of antiquity passed on to them by Islam. One of the more prolific translators was Adelard of Bath who, as Crombie has pointed out (See p. 250), represents the learned man of the West attempting to assimilate the new ("old") science of the Greeks. His dialogue with his nephew reveals the blend of medieval lore with ancient science.

What Theory is to be Held Concerning Sight?

ADELARD: Many different views have been expressed about the nature of sight, and it will be perhaps convenient first to set them forth, and then enquire which of them is the most reasonable.

NEPHEW: Then, if you approve, it shall be my task to state these various theories, and yours to state any objections there are to them when I have done so.

ADELARD: Your suggestion is a reasonable one.

NEPHEW: The theories I have been able to collect in various quarters about sight fall into four different groups. Some say that the mind, sitting in the brain as its chief seat, and looking forth upon outer things through open windows, viz., the eyes, gets knowledge of the shapes of things, and when it has got knowledge of them, judges them; it being always understood that nothing from the mind passes to the outside, and nothing from the shapes outside makes its way to the mind. Others, again, maintain that sight takes place through the approach of shapes, saying that the shapes of things give shape to the air that intervenes between themselves and the eyes, and that in this way the materials for judgment pass to the mind. Very many also assert that something is sent forth by the mind, i.e., visible breath, and that the shapes of the things that are to be seen meet it in mid-air: having taken shape from these, the breath returns to its seat, and presents the shape to the mind for it to exercise judgment upon. A fourth party maintains that no shapes of objects approach the eye, but that something which they call "fiery force," and which is produced in the brain by means of concave sinews, passes first through the eyes, and then to the objects to be seen, and by returning to its point of origin brings back to the mind, with the same quickness as it went, the shape impressed upon it as though by a potter.

Let us deal first with the first theory. The use of all the senses belongs, as Boethius declares in his *"De musica,"* to all living creatures; but what is their strength, and what are the

---

* Adelard of Bath, *Quaestiones Naturales*, in *Dodi Ve-Nechdi (Uncle and Nephew), The work of Berachya Hanakdan*. Now edited from MSS at Munich and Oxford, with an English translation, introduction, etc., to which is added the first English Translation from the Latin of Adelard of Bath's *Questiones Naturales*, by Herman Gollancz. Oxford University Press, London, 1920. Pp. 114-118; 138-139; 140-141; 143-144; 157-161.

limits to their use, is not perfectly clear except to the intellect of the philosopher; for both the effects of things follow upon the antecedent causes according to a most subtle nexus, and causes along with their effects differ from one another by the most subtle differences, so that even philosophers themselves often fail in their understanding of nature. Thus in the present case, if they mean that the mind placed in the brain as a seat regards external objects through the windows of the eyes, then when they assert this they will either be attributing a sort of power to the windows of the eyes, or else assigning no means of contemplating external things to these windows. But by calling the eyes windows, they are attributing to them a certain faculty for seeing external objects: do they then mean that the mind is a corporeal thing? In that case it would require a free and unimpeded means of egress without risk of injuring itself by coming into contact with other things; or do they think that in that conception of shapes which we call sight, there is some corporeal power needed for the mind to prevent it itself from being checked by contact with any obstacle, and that hence windows are required? But neither the mind, nor its consideration of external things, are corporeal things, and therefore they need have no fear of contact with corporeal things, and consequently, so far as the things perceived by them are concerned, do not require any corporeal opening. The formula then of these people includes no force, nor do they assume any path for the mind through the windows of the eyes, since they do not require this. This being so, why do they say that it sees external things through the eyes, especially as the eyes too are not perforated, but are more solid than the other instruments of sense, so that if the mind required any corporeal power, the ears of the nostrils (which have passages through them) would supply it. Further if, as is asserted, the mind should see the shapes of things by looking at external things, how could the human mind, by regarding a mirror, see the shape of its own face? The mirror, being opposite to its windows, it would be able to see; but its own face, though opposite to it, could not be seen according to this idea. This theory therefore lacks consistency, and we must now discuss the second view previously stated.

ADELARD: By all means, nor do I see how the upholders of this first view are to get the better of your objections. It was on this account that a theory was propounded by the stoics, that external forms make their way to the mind itself, and that it is imprinted by them as wax might be. This it was that made Boethius in his *"de Consolatione"* say, "in bye-gone days the stoic school introduced us to a set of out-of-date old men who hold that perceptions and images are imprinted on our minds by external bodies, just as at times it is people's habit to make and leave marks on the smooth paper with a swift pen." Although Boethius in the same passage attacks this idea as being pointless, I should like to tell you my objections to it as follows:--The shapes of things to be seen approach the mind of the seer either in their own subject and along with it, or in another subject and along with that. Now it is impossible that it should do so in its own subject, and not along with it; nor does the body that is seen approach me: therefore it must be in another subject, and along with that.

NEPHEW: In air and with air. For the body, as they say, gives shape to air, and that air to other air, till it comes to that in the brain which acts upon the mind itself.

ADELARD: If approach to the mind therefore were to be by such a transmission of shapes how could this be accomplished should a glassy body be interposed? Would not the advance be prevented through such an obstacle? Would not the air in the neighbourhood of the glass be acted upon by it? Will it receive shape from that of the more distant and less splendid body? This is of course absurd, and absurd too is the theory we are discussing. However, let us, as Boethius says in the *"Topica,"* admit it for the sake of argument, that we may see what follows. Let us grant that the progression of shapes as far as the eye, is made by the eye even to the brain, or the air of the brain; but let us note that passage which they call a sort of potter's impression. If the air of the brain imprints its shape on the mind, it gives either that shape actually and essentially, or another like it. But that it should be the same is impossible, for no individual shape can pass from one subject to another, as in the passing the shape would be without a subject, which is impossible. On the other hand, if it imprints another shape, it will at once require local parts in the mind just as it had in the air, and not finding them in it, it will not be able by moulding to give shape to it. Since then this theory is obviously untenable, let us pass to the next. This one--the third--is held by those who grant that a visible truth issues from the brain, but most certainly does not go so far as the body, which is relatively very far from it, for the reason that it finds the shapes it seeks in the intervening air.

Hence it has no need to do more than this, and consequently having been impressed returns, bringing back the shape to the mind by which it was sent forth. Those who say this do not realise what is the necessary consequence of their words; for if, as they assert, between the seer and the things to be seen, the air, by reason of the progression of similar shapes, offers to the visible breath that of which it was in search, then let us assume, first, a man looking from the east westwards, with the object of discerning the shape of a white body (and this, they say, he will find in the intervening air); next, at the same moment, assume another looking from the west eastwards, in order to behold a black body; and let him consequently by the same progression find the shape of the black body in the same intervening air: from this it follows, that the same or indivisible air is the subject alike of blackness and whiteness. Thus two contrary things, acting in opposition, are found in the same subject. But this is impossible, and we are therefore bound to reject the views of those who assert it. Finally, and beyond doubt, there is another consideration which, even if we put other objections on one side, is sufficient to upset all the views we have mentioned. It is this: we are familiar enough with the sight of our own shapes in a mirror; but this, though its reality is established by everyday life, does not agree with the theories we have recounted. It will be better, therefore, to deal with the view of which philosophy approves, and dismissing other theories as lacking strength, put our faith in this academic truth. This theory is as follows: In the brain there is generated a certain air of the most subtle nature, and made of fire, and consequently exceedingly light: this makes its way from the mind along the nerves, whenever it so pleases, and necessity arises, to see things outside. Hence it is called by physicists "visible spirit": being a body, it naturally requires a local exit, which exit it finds through the different concave nerves, which the Greeks call "optic," extending from the brain to the eyes: then travelling to the body to be seen, it makes its way with wondrous speed, and being impressed with the shape of the body, it both receives and retains the impression, and then returning to its original position, it communicates the shape it has received. Now this spirit is called by philosophers "fiery force," and this force, when it finds a mirror opposite to it, or any other light-giving body, being reflected by it, returns as a result of the reflection to its own face, and still retaining the shape, when it enters, reveals it to the mind. You are not, however, to suppose that this fiery force found the shape of the face in the mirror; but, being reflected from the surface which is too smooth for it to abide there, received the shape while returning, and having received it, brought it back. This then is the divine theory which Plato has adopted, among other things, in his *"Timaeus."* "There are, in my opinion," says Plato, "two virtues in fire, one consuming and destructive, the other soothing and endowed with harmless light. With this one, therefore, in virtue of which light bringing in the day unfolds itself, the divine powers are in harmony, for it has been their pleasure that the intimate fire of our bodies, own brother of the fire which is a passing bright, clear, and purged fluid, should flow through the eyes, and issue from them in order that through the eyes, slight, cramped, and affrighted, as it were, by the stouter substance, but yet offering a narrow medium, the more subtle clear fire might flow down through the same medium. Hence when the light of day lends itself to the diffusion of sight, then no doubt the two like lights meeting in turn cohere into the appearance of a single body, in which the flashing brightness of the eyes meet, while the intimate brightness of the diffusion as it spreads is reflected by meeting with the image at close quarters. All this then goes through one and the same experience, and the result of that same experience, when either it touches something else, or is touched by it; moved by this contact, it spreads itself through the whole body, and making its way through that body to the mind and produces the sense which is called 'sight.'" Concerning mirrors and water, Plato says a little further on: "When both fires--the inner and the outer--fall together upon a light plane surface, they are formed into many different shapes, and the eidola rebound from the smooth surface." From these words of the philosopher you will see that just as truth, if never sought for, lay unnoticed, so also the false sometimes did not pass unnoticed: you will, I mean, understand how he says that the fiery breath emanates from the eyes, and is reflected from the object: nor does he forget to say that it suffers a similar experience, i.e., a similar shape, and that it spreads, when returning, through the body of the eye. Then he says that it proceeds to the mind, and that thus is sight effected: in the case of mirrors, he says also that the same thing happens as a consequence.

* * * * *

If a Hole Were Made Straight Through the Earth, In What Direction would a Stone Thrown into it Fall?

NEPHEW: My next question is in no wise contrary to what has gone before; I see that this results from the mere coherence of things. My difficulty is this: Supposing the earth to be pierced, so that there were a passage straight through, and a stone be thrown in, what would be the direction of its fall?

ADELARD: That which causes the stationary position of the earth, would produce equilibrium in the stone.

NEPHEW: The answer satisfies me; for I understand that it would come to rest at the central point.

ADELARD: There is a further point I should like to make clear to you: as all nature loves its like, so it shuns the contrary. Fire is opposed to earth in the effective power of its qualities, and hence it follows that earth shuns fire. The whole of the upper space environing the world is the home of fire, and this upper space with its fire is therefore necessarily to be shunned by earth: but whatever flees from the central point will come into collision with that which it wants to avoid: therefore that it may not in unfortunate flight come into collision with that which it avoids, the earth seeks that point which is on all sides equally distant from the upper spaces. This position then it holds for two reasons, (1) through its own weight it seeks that for which it has a fondness, (2) because it shuns that which it does not like.

NEPHEW: If then, as explained by you, the centre and the lowest point are the same thing in the frame-work of the universe, how is that Statius, the poet (in this point, Statius the philosopher) has contrasted them; for he says, "Either the lowest part of the earth or its centre, both adjoin the hidden universe"; by thus separating them, he has adjudged them to be opposites.

ADELARD: He has a two-fold object to gain: he is both hinting at the falsity of vulgar and self-contradictory belief, and openly setting forth a physical truth; for the common herd do not distinguish between circumference and containing plans. Consequently, with confused minds they wrongly trust the eye, and wrongly invent an hemispherical imperfection; and, therefore, from this stupid point of view the bottom of the earth will not be the centre. To right the mistake is, however, an easy task for the individual, and therefore outside the scope of the present treatise. It is now clear even to the unlearned that earth is both the bottom and the centre of this mundane mass.

* * * * *

The Cause of the Ebb and Flow of the Tides.

NEPHEW: Now that this has been settled, I think we might deal with another notorious difficulty--the ebb and flow of the tides, and whether the theory of some philosophers that they are due to a violent action, is to be accepted. These say, that the ocean proper flowing through hot channels causes streams of very great quantity to flow back from east and west into the Arctic and Ant-arctic regions. These flowing together with great violence produce, they say, the tides--the impact of conflict giving us the flow, and the recoil the ebb.

ADELARD: I would not dare to find fault with what philosophers say, but this much let me affirm confidently; that if, as they say, the waters in very big arms of the sea come together, when the waves are once mingled, there will be no second impact; for it is not possible that they should separate again; or at any rate, if they should a second time come into collision, the second one will be less than the first, and the third than the second, while later it will be very small, and finally nothing at all. I should like to know what answer your philosophers will make to this. Now let me briefly give my own explanation: I admit the recoils, and do not deny the meetings; but I do not admit (*condo*, in the original should be *concedo*, or its abbreviated form) that they flow together, or come into violent conflict. The reason for this I take to be the situation of the earth; for though the channels of the sea are fiercely eager to meet one another and flow together, yet it happens through the interposition of mountains and the somewhat elevated situation of the earth that on their ebb they are drawn back from that particular course. The result is that they are held back by their position from the point to which they are impelled by their natural and inherited movement. I am not ignorant that there are those who say that this movement goes on in one sea, the Caribbean; but if this were true, there would be similar violent movement of no less strength in those seas which are nearer the torrid zone; while, as a matter of fact, all those seas are free from any agitation of the sort, and for this reason,--that they are far removed from the cause we have previously mentioned.

*   *   *   *   *

Why the Inflow of the Rivers Does Not Increase the Size of the Ocean.

NEPHEW: Since it is agreed that nothing that is possible must be put aside, we must consider this next question. If, as the common herd declare, all rivers flow into the sea, it is strange, having regard to the great bulk of their waters, their constant flow, and their almost infinite number, that they do not swell the ocean's size.

ADELARD: If you follow the common herd you will tumble into a pit. They not only understand nature so badly as to be like men in a dream, but when they talk about her, positively snore. It is not true that all rivers run into the sea, though many do; and just as some run into it, so others rise out of it. Consequently, the sea gives as well as receives, and so gets no sensible increase. In the same way some people have raised the question why, seeing that many subterranean streams proceed from it, and the stars also drink up a great part of it, it does not decrease rather than increase. Hence we find in Statius, that Phoebus sings of "the spring that feeds the boundless main." As a matter of fact, the sea gives as much as it receives.

* * * * *

Why, if a Vessel Be Full and Its Lower Part Open, Water Will Not Flow From It Unless the Upper Lid Be First Removed.

NEPHEW: There is another point in which I am in doubt about the nature of water. As you know, some little time past we visited an old witch in order to study magic, and there attracted by her sense, or perhaps her nonsense, we spent some days. In the house was a vessel of remarkable powers, which was brought out at meal-times. Both at top and bottom it was pierced with many holes; and when water for washing the hands had been put into it, so long as the servant kept the upper holes closed by putting his thumb over them, no water came out of the lower holes: but as soon as he removed his thumb, there was at once an abundant flow of water for the benefit of us who were standing round. This seemed to me to be the effect of magic; and I said, "What wonder that the old woman is a sovereign enchantress, when her man-slave can work such wonders!" You, however, though according to your habit you paid great attention to enchantments, refused to regard this as magic. Now tell me what you think about this matter of the water: the lower holes were always open, and yet it was only at the water-carrier's will that water issued from them.

ADELARD: If it was magic, it was nature's rather than the servant's power. The body of this sensible universe is composed of four elements; they are so closely bound together by natural affection, that just as none of them would exist without the other, so no place either is, or could be, empty of them. Hence it happens, that as soon as one of them leaves its position, another immediately takes its place; nor is this again able to leave its position, until another which it regards with special affection is able to succeed it. When, therefore, the entrance is closed to that which is to come in, in vain will the exit be open for the departing element: thanks to this loving waiting, it will be all in vain that you open an exit for the water, unless you give an entrance to the air. These elements, as I have said, are not pure, and are so closely conjoined together, that they neither can nor will exist without one another. Hence it happens that if there be no opening in the upper part of the vessel, and an opening be made at the lower end, it is only after an interval, and with a sort of murmuring, that the liquid comes forth. The quantity of air which comes in is equal to that of the water which goes out; and the air finding the water porous, passes through it, thanks to its natural tenuity and lightness, and takes possession of the apparently empty upper part of the vessel.

*   *   *   *   *

Whether the Stars Are Animate.

NEPHEW: My question is answered; and now, calling my mind to order again, I want to hear about a subject on which you touched previously, for when you were talking of the moon, you spoke of it as animate. Now though I may be a fool, I am not a forgetful one, and consequently I come back to the point: Do you regard the stars as being animate, or inanimate?

ADELARD: The man who calls them inanimate is in my opinion without a mind *(anima)* himself. The reasons which make me think them animate I derive partly from their position, partly from their composition, and partly also from their action. If this world of ours with its storms of hail, its ugly clouds, and its teeming darkness, must needs, as having the power, maintain reason and foresight, how much more must the ethereal expanse, free as it is from all defilement, be obedient to mind and reason! Furthermore, if in this dark world of ours that spot abounds more in philosophers which is free of the denser pollution, and enjoys a certain serenity of climate, with what confidence can anyone, unless quite mad, assert that the expanse of the heavens, which is free from all stain, in proportion to its remoteness from us, is destitute of the motion which mind bestows? Again, if there is not, and could not be, anything better among created things than Mind, is mind to be buried in darkness, and the place fittest for it to be deprived of that which, through likeness of nature, it eagerly demands? If that is so, the order of nature is indeed inverted, for contraries are joined together, and like made to quarrel with like. It is only a fool who can set up a confusion of this sort, and the Orderer of the universe is all-wise, and therefore has no sort of wish or power to destroy the natural order of things, and it is therefore impossible that such an inversion should be. It is then out of all keeping that such an idea should come into the mind of a philosopher.

We must now consider the question of composition; for it is of no small importance in all reasoning to consider what is the nature of the thing under discussion. We have to take for granted, rather than explain, the action of the efficient cause; and putting that on one side, there is nothing which shows consequent effects more clearly than the composition of the particular essence. I am talking of composition both in material and shape. Let us then, first, discuss the question of material.

Now the bodies of stars are composed in such proportions, that although they contain all four elements, they have a more abundant share in what is most adapted for life and reason; for they are fiery rather than terrestrial; and this fire, as Cleantes proves, must be considered either destructive, like the fire of outer substances, or soothing and harmless, like the inner fire of our bodies. If, however, it were destructive, it would long ago have modified the shape of its subject, which would have become the cone-shape of external fire; but it does not act upon its subject, or produce a cone-shape, and is therefore not destructive but soothing and harmless: it is consequently obedient to sense and reason, and open to their action. As regards shape, what is there to say? Even the Latins realise that that of all shapes is best adapted to the action of mind, which the eye sees to be full and round. Next, we must take note of their action, in which we must accept not my view but Aristotle's, or rather what is my view because it is his.

Aristotle says, that whatever is in a state of motion is moved either by nature, by force, or by its own will. Now that which is moved by nature moves either upwards, as fire, or downwards as earth; but this is not the movement of the stars, which therefore are not moved by nature. Again, they are not moved by force, for what force could be greater than theirs? We must then put force on one side, and admit that they are moved spontaneously and voluntarily. But if they move spontaneously, it follows that they move with the motion of living beings--a view which I will prove against no matter what opposition, as follows:--If things which are in a state of motion sometimes come to rest, and at other times move, going sometimes backward and sometimes forward, then they are not moved by nature, for whatever is moved by nature neither comes to rest, nor changes its motion. It remains, therefore, that they are moved either by force or by will; now there is no force in nature more powerful than the turning force of the *aplanos*; but they are not moved by this, for they travel in the opposite direction. It follows, then, that they are moved by will, and the consequence of this is plain. Furthermore, if their action determines the life or death of the lower animals, there is only one view we can hold about them. When the Sun withdraws from Cancer and our region, vegetation withers, and the joy of springtide bows its head in mourning, and presently the trees are bereft of the glory of their leaves. Finally, it is well known that many living things, not only terrestrial but those of the air, also die naturally in winter, and come to life again in summer. We must admit then that it is impossible to imagine that what produced life in others is itself devoid of life; only an irresponsible jester could say so. Further, it is certain that whatever observes a determinate arrangement and a fixed principle in its movement must employ reason; and nothing can have a more definite arrangement, or a more absolute order, than the course of the stars. When have the planets gone outside the zodiac? The Sun, when he has reached the extremity of Capricorn, checks his course and returns to us, just as he never goes outside Cancer. The case is just the same with the other stars; and there is therefore no difference between them and other rational creatures. Give then your most earnest attention to what follows: when things which but a little while ago started off and hastened away at full speed to Capricorn, return from it without the application of external force, they either know, or do not know, that they must return from it. If they do not know that they must return from it, why do they not go further instead of returning with such exactitude? If, on the other hand, they know, then they are endowed with knowledge; but to have knowledge without also having mind is impossible; and the stars are therefore animate, and possessors of reason and knowledge.

Granted That the Stars Are Living Beings, On What Food Do They Live?

NEPHEW: Thus far you have been so busy in heaping up reasons that I have not been able to get in a word. Your breath ran short long before your subject-matter; and now while you are getting your breath back, I must get my pipe into order again. If what you say is true, another question arises: All living creatures require some sort of sustenance; and if, as you maintain, the stars are living beings, what food do you assign to them?

ADELARD: Very good. Just as the stars are more divine in position, composition, shape, and reason than the lower animals, so also they have both the need and the ability to live on purer food than we do. They are attracted to higher things; and they therefore enjoy the moisture of the earth and water at a great distance, but only in a rarified form; and while making use of them, are neither borne down by weight, nor dulled by them, to the loss of reason and foresight.

Ought We to Regard the *aplanos* as an Inanimate Body, or a Living Thing, or a God?

NEPHEW: You have now provided me with a definite opinion about those matters which, in regard to the stars, seemed doubtful. What then do you think is the right point of view in regard to the *aplanos*, containing in itself as it does the shapes of all things? I have read many writings of many philosophers, and found in them very different opinions about the sphere which contains the whole universe. As these are all quite different, I do not think they can all be true; in fact, I am prepared to swear that they are all false. Some have been bold enough to say that the *aplanos* is inanimate, while others have maintained that it is animate, but not in the same way as a rational living being; others again--possessed either of deeper understanding, or else quite mad--have dared to call it a god. Which of these explanations commends itself to you is what I am anxious to learn, as I sit here.

ADELARD: It is understanding rather than sitting that is wanted, if you are to get a right view of the sphere of which we are talking. Just as it is unfitting to go down to one division of nature, so it is impossible to go up to another. A man of education--I say nothing about one who is not--would be ashamed to say that the sphere is inanimate, when the fact that it is animate is proved by the beauty of its outward form and shape, by the subtlety of its elemental composition, by its naturally holding the highest and therefore the noblest imaginable position, and finally by the indefatigable vitality of its orbicular motion and the indescribable velocity of its revolution. To say, however that this same continent sphere is a god, is to speak in one way indeed as a philosopher, but in another as a madman. If we are speaking relatively to mere animal reason, then it must be granted that the *aplanos* is a god; but if relatively to God as the first cause, not made by hands, without form, unchangeable, and infinite, then to say that the outer sphere is a god is a profanation.

NEPHEW: Yes, to use the word in such connection certainly is so. We agreed, however, at the beginning of our discussion to follow reason rather than authority; and, as we have so far followed the plan of beginning with more trifling matters and working upwards, we have now reached a point at which it becomes necessary to speak about God as the efficient cause of everything, for my knowledge is nothing unless I know about Him. To come to the point then: some people assert the existence of a God, while others deny it altogether. Of those who maintain His existence, some say that He is material, others form, others the universe, others the *aplanos*, while some again say that the Sun is God. I am therefore particularly anxious to hear from you, with reason only as our guide, and no sort of deference to authority, whether God exists or does not exist, what He is, and what He does.

ADELARD: You are putting a difficult question to me: I find it easier to prove what He is not, than what He is. In such matters I find it less difficult to confute the false than to prove the true; for when we come to talk about God, we have to treat of mind (?), . . . of simple forms and elements in the pure state; and just as much as these by their innate simpleness transcend the nature of all compounds, so much discussion about them transcends all other discussion both in subtlety of understanding and difficulty of language. We have already spoken at some length about compounds; and now that the evening suggests sleep, let us refresh our minds with natural repose, and in the morning--if your will still holds good--let us meet again, and discuss the beginning or beginnings.

NEPHEW: Nothing could please me better. To instruct my mind about God, whom we acknowledge to be the glorious Father of all things, and to speak about Him wisely, is for me, who do not admit authority, most difficult. It will, therefore, be most useful to discuss this and the concomitant questions, in which the multitude of counsellors has produced much confusion. Gladly then shall I accept the refreshment of sleep, that we may come fresh to a fresh discussion.

Ended are the *Natural Questions* of Adelard of Bath.

Praise be to God and the Virgin Mary!

Let him who would of things the hidden causes know,
See me, who can with ease their interpretation show.

4. St. Thomas Aquinas, From *Commentary on Aristotle's Physics.**

The experimental method advocated by Roger Bacon was by no means the dominant method of scientific investigation in the Middle Ages. In the formal "Schools" of Paris, Oxford, Padua, etc., the student progressed from a study of ancient texts to disputations over their meaning. The greatest of the Schoolmen (or Scholastics) was St. Thomas Aquinas (1225-1274). His Commentary on Aristotle's Physics *illustrates his method well. He first cites the relevant passages in Aristotle's text, then points out what these mean, and then indicates how the Christian faith forces certain modifications in Aristotle's conclusions. The result is a "science" with a peculiarly medieval flavor.*

Lecture 2

Arguments for the Eternity of Motion

After he has raised the question of the eternity of motion, he intends here to show that motion is eternal.

This discussion is divided into two parts. First he proves his position. Secondly, where he says, 'The arguments that may . . .' (252 b 7), he answers possible objections to the contrary.

Concerning the first part he makes two points. First he gives arguments to prove the eternity of motion. Secondly, where he says, '. . . and cannot have existed . . .' (252 a 4), he gives arguments against the opinions of the philosophers who hold the contrary.

Concerning the first part he makes two points. First he shows that there has always been motion. Secondly, where he says, 'The same reasoning . . .' (251 b 29) he shows that there always will be motion.

Concerning the first part he makes two points. First he proves the proposition with an argument taken from motion. Secondly, where he says, 'Further, how can there be . . .' (251 a 17), he introduces the proof of the proposition. Thirdly, where he says, 'For some things cause . . .' (251 a 29), he shows the necessity of this proof.

He says, therefore, first that to prove the proposition, we ought to begin with those things which have already been determined in the *Physics*, so that we may use them as principles. By this he wants us to understand that the preceding books, in which he discussed motion in general and which are thus universally called *de Naturalibus*, are distinct from Book VIII, in which he begins to apply motion to things.

He assumes, therefore, what is said in *Physics*, III, namely,

---

* St. Thomas Aquinas, *Commentary on Aristotle's Physics*, Trans. by Richard J. Blackwell, Richard J. Spath and W. Edmund Thirlkel, Intro. by Vernon J. Bourke (London: Routledge, Kegan Paul, 1963). Pp. 474-479; 480-487.

that motion is the act of a mobile object insofar as it is mobile. It is apparent from this that in order for there to be motion, there must be things which can be moved by motion. For there cannot be act without a subject of act. Thus from the definition of motion it is clear that there must be a mobile subject in order for there to be motion.

But even apart from the definition of motion this is apparent in itself, as is clear from the common opinion of all men. For everyone admits that a thing is not moved unless it can be moved. This applies to every motion, for a thing is not altered unless it is alterable, and a thing is not changed in place unless it is mutable in respect to place.

And since a subject is naturally prior to that which is in the subject, we can conclude in regard to individual mutations, both from the standpoint of the mobile object and the mover, that a subject is burnable before it is burned, and a subject is a combustive, that is, able to burn, before it burns. I say 'before', not always in time, but in nature.

From this proof of Aristotle Averroes takes the opportunity of speaking contrary to what we hold about creation according to faith.

To come to be is to be changed in some way. Moreover, every mutation requires a subject, as Aristotle proves here. Hence it is necessary that everything which comes to be, comes to be from some subject. Therefore, it is impossible for a thing to come to be from nothing.

He adds to this a second argument. When it is said that black comes to be from white, this is not said to occur *per se* such that the white itself is converted into black. Rather this is said to occur *per accidens* because black takes the place of the receding white. Whatever is *per accidens*, however, is reduced to that which is *per se*. Moreover, that from which a thing comes to be *per se* is the subject, which enters into the substance of the thing made. Everything, therefore, which is said to come to be from its opposite comes to be from that opposite *per accidens*, but from the subject *per se*. It is not possible, therefore, for being to come to be from absolute non-being.

Thirdly, he adds to this the common opinion of all of the ancient physicists who hold that nothing comes to be from nothing.

Moreover, he gives two reasons why he thinks that the position that something comes to be from nothing has arisen.

The first is that the common man thinks that only those things exist which can be perceived by vision. Therefore, since the common man sees that something has been made visible which was not visible before, he thinks that it is possible for something to come to be from nothing.

The second reason is that the common man thinks that an agent needs matter in order to act because its power is diminished. This, however, is not due to the agent's lack of power, but to the very nature [*ratio*] of motion. Since, therefore, the first agent does not possess a power which is deficient in any way, it follows that this agent may act without a subject.

But if one thinks correctly, he would realize that Averroes has been deceived for a similar reason--the same one which is thought to have deceived us, namely, the consideration of particular beings.

For it is clear that the active potency of a particular agent presupposes a matter which a more universal agent makes, for example, an artist uses the matter which nature provides. Therefore, from the fact that every particular agent presupposes a matter which it does not make, it is not necessary to think that the first universal agent, which is the active power of the whole of being, presupposes something which, as it were, is not caused by it.

Moreover, this does not agree with Aristotle's intention. For he proves in *Metaphysics*, II, that that which is most true and most being is the cause of being for all existing things. Hence it follows that the very being in potency which primary matter has is derived from the first principle of being, which is the most being. Therefore, it is not necessary to presuppose something for its action which has not been produced by it.

And since every motion requires a subject, which Aristotle here proves and which is true, it follows that the universal production of being by God is neither motion nor mutation, but a certain simple emanation. And so 'to become' and 'to make' are used equivocally in reference to this universal production of things and in reference to other productions.

Therefore, if we were to think that the production of things by God is from eternity, as Aristotle and many Platonists held, it is not necessary, in fact it is impossible, that some non-produced subject be understood for this universal production. Moreover, if we hold according to the judgment of our faith that God did not produce things from eternity, but that He produced them after they were not, it is not necessary to posit some subject for this universal production.

It is clear, therefore, that what Aristotle proves here, namely, that every motion requires a mobile subject, is not contrary to the judgment of our faith. For it was said that the universal production of things, whether from eternity or not, is neither a motion nor a mutation. Motion or mutation requires that a thing be otherwise now than it was before, and so the thing would be previously existing. Consequently we are not now talking about the universal production of things.

Similarly, when he says that a thing is said to come to be from its opposite *per accidens* and from its subject *per se*, this is true of particular productions, according to which this or that being comes to be, for example a man or a dog. However, this is not true of the universal production of being.

This is clear from what the Philosopher has said in *Physics*, I. For he said there that if this animal comes to be insofar as it is this animal, it is not necessary that it comes to be from 'non-animal' but from 'this non-animal'. For example, man comes to be from non-man, or horse from non-horse. But if animal as animal comes to be, it must come to be from non-animal. If, therefore, some particular being comes to be, it does not come to be from absolute non-being. But if the whole of being comes to be, that is, if being as being comes to be, it must come to be from absolute non-being, if it can be said that it 'comes to be' (for 'comes to be' is used equivocally, as was said).

What he introduces concerning the opinions of the ancient philosophers is not applicable. For the ancient natural philosophers were unable to arrive at the first cause of the whole of being. Rather they considered the causes of particular mutations.

* * * * *

Therefore, it is clear that we are not moved to hold that something comes to be from nothing because we think that only visible things exist. Rather, on the contrary, we hold this because we do not consider only particular productions from particular causes, but the universal production of the whole of being from the first principle of being. Neither do we hold that a diminished power needs matter in order to act, as if it were deficient in natural power. Rather we say that this pertains to a particular power which does not have power over the whole of being, but which causes some being.

And so it can be said that a diminished power makes something from something, just as we might say that a particular power is less than a universal power.

Next where he says, 'Moreover, these things also . . .' (251 a 17), having shown that motion requires a mobile object and a motive power, he argues as follows.

If motion has not always existed, one must say either that mobile objects and motive powers were made at some time before which they were not, or else they are eternal. Therefore, if it is said that every mobile object has been made, one must say that before the mutation which is taken as the first, there was another mutation and motion, according to which was made the mobile object itself which can be moved and was moved. This inference depends on what has gone before. If it is granted that motion has not always existed, but rather there is some first mutation before which there was none, then it will follow that that first mutation had some mobile object, and that this mobile object was made, before which it was not. For it was granted that all mobile objects have been made. Everything which comes to be, before which it was not, comes to be through some motion or mutation. Moreover, the motion or mutation by which the mobile object comes to be is prior to the mutation by which the mobile object is moved. Therefore, before the mutation which was said to be first, there is another mutation, and so on to infinity.

If, however, it is said that mobile objects were always preexisting, even though no motion existed, this seems to be irrational and the words of those who are unlearned. For it is immediately apparent that if there are mobile objects, there must be motion. For natural mobile objects and movers exist together, as is clear from Book III. And when movers and natural mobile objects exist, there must be motion.

But in order to proceed more profoundly in search of the truth, we should say that this same thing must happen even if it is granted that movers and mobile objects always pre-exist before motion. This follows if it is granted that these have been made, that is, if prior to the mutation which is given as first, there was another mutation to infinity. This is clear as follows. Let it be granted that there are mobile objects and movers, and at some time the first mover began to move and something was moved by it, and before this nothing was moved, but there was rest. It is then necessary to say that another mutation occurred earlier in the mover or mobile object which the first mover begins to move. This is clear as follows.

Rest is the privation of motion. Privation, however, is not in that which is receptive of a habit or form except through some cause. There was, therefore, some cause either on the part of the mover or on the part of the mobile object which was the cause of rest. Therefore, while it endured, there was always rest. If, therefore, at some time the mover begins to move, this cause of rest must be removed. But it cannot be removed except through some motion or mutation. Therefore, it follows that before the mutation which was said to be first, there was another earlier mutation by which the cause of rest was removed.

Next where he says, 'For some things cause motion . . .' (251 a 29), he proves the necessity of the preceding argument.

One might say that it happens that a thing is at one time at rest and at another time in motion without any pre-existing cause of rest being removed. Hence he wishes to reject this.

Concerning this he makes two points. First he sets forth a certain thing which is necessary for his position. Secondly, where he says, 'But at any rate . . .' (251 b 1), he proves his position.

He says, therefore, first that some movers move singly, that is, in only one way, and others move in respect to contrary motions.

Things which move in only one way are natural. For example, fire always heats and never causes coldness. But intelligent agents move according to contrary motions, for contraries seem to be treated in one science. For example, medicine is the science of health and sickness. Hence it seems that a doctor by his own knowledge is able to move according to contrary motions.

He makes this distinction of movers because in regard to things which act through intelligence what he has said does not seem to be true, that is, it does not seem to be true that if a thing is moved after it was at rest, then the cause of that rest must first be removed.

For intelligent agents seem to be related to opposites without any mutation occurring in themselves. Hence it seems that they can move and not move without any mutation.

Therefore, lest this destroy his argument, he adds that his argument holds in a similar fashion for things which act through intellect and for things which act through nature.

Things which act through nature always move *per se* to one thing, but sometimes they move to the contrary *per accidens*. And for this accident to occur, there must be some mutation. For example, a cold thing always makes cold *per se*, but *per accidens* it heats.

It heats *per accidens* when it is changed in some way, either insofar as it is turned to another site so that it is related in another way to that which it now makes hot and which it previously made cold, or else insofar as it disappears entirely. For we say that the disappearance of cold causes heat just as a helmsman by his absence causes the sinking of a ship. In a similar way cold becomes the *per accidens* cause of heat either by a greater withdrawal or a greater nearness, just as in winter the inner parts of animals are warmer as the warmth withdraws farther inside because of the encompassing cold.

And the same applies to intelligent agents. For although there is one science of contraries, nevertheless there is not equal science of both. Rather it is principally of one. For example, medicine is ordained *per se* to produce health. If, therefore, it happens that a doctor uses his knowledge to induce illness, this will not be through his knowledge *per se* but *per accidens*, because of something else. And in order for that other to occur which before was not, some mutation is necessary.

Next where he says, 'But at any rate . . .' (251 b 1), he introduces the proof of his position.

He says, therefore, that since agents which act through nature and agents which act through intelligence are thus related in a similar way, we can say universally that whatever has the potency to do or to suffer or to move or to be moved cannot move or be moved in every disposition in which it is found. Rather this occurs insofar as such things exist in some determinate state and nearness to each other.

And he concludes this from the foregoing. For it has already been said that in both natural agents and voluntary agents there is not one cause of diverse things unless this cause exists in some other disposition. Therefore, whenever a mover and the moved approach each other with a suitable nearness, and likewise when they are in whatever disposition is required so that one moves and the other is moved, then the one must be moved and the other must move.

If, therefore, there has not always been motion, then it is clear that they did not exist in such a relation that one moves and the other is moved. Rather they existed in such a way that it was not possible for them to move and be moved. Afterwards, however, they do exist in such a relation that one moves and the other is moved. Therefore, one of them must have been changed.

In all things which are called relations we see that a new relation occurs only through a mutation of one or the other. For example, if a thing which before was not double is now made double, then if one of the extremes is not changed, at least the other must be changed. And so, if a new relation should occur so that the one thing moves and another is moved, one or the other must be moved first. Hence it follows that there is a certain mutation which is prior to the mutation which was said to be first.

Next where he says, 'Further, how can there be . . .' (251 b 10), he proves his position with an argument taken from time.

First he sets forth two things which are necessary for the following proof.

The first is that there cannot be a before and after unless there is time. For time is nothing other than the before and after according to which things are numbered.

The second is that there cannot be time unless there is motion. This is clear from the definition of time which he gave above in Book IV, saying that time is the number of motion in respect to before or after.

Secondly, where he says, 'If, then, time . . .' (251 b 11), he comes to a conditional conclusion from what was said in Book IV.

For he stated there, according to his opinion, that time is the number of motion. In the same place he said that other philosophers have held that time is a certain motion.

Whichever of these may be true, it follows that this condition is true: if time is eternal, then motion must be eternal.

Thirdly, where he says, 'But so far as time . . .' (251 b 13), he proves the antecedent of the above condition in two ways.

He does this first by means of the opinions of others. He says that all philosophers except one, namely Plato, seem to agree that time is ungenerated, that is, time did not begin to be after it previously was not. Hence even Democritus proves that it is impossible for all things to have been made as if they began anew, because it is impossible for time to have been so made that it began anew.

Only Plato 'generates time', that is, only he says that time was made anew. For Plato says that time was made together with the heavens. And he held that the heavens 'were made', that is, they have a beginning of duration, as Aristotle here imputes to him, according to which his words seem to sound superficial. The Platonists, however, say that Plato said that the heavens were made in the sense that they have an active principle of their being but not in the sense that they have a beginning of duration. Therefore, Plato alone seems to have understood that there is no time without motion. For he did not hold that time existed before the motion of the heavens.

Secondly, where he says, 'Now since time . . .' (251 b 19), he proves the same thing through reason. It is impossible to say or to think that there is time without the 'now', just as it is impossible for a line to exist without a point. Moreover, the 'now' is a certain intermediate, having such a nature [*ratio*] that it is both a beginning and an end, that is, the beginning of the future and the end of the past. From this it seems that time must be eternal. For whatever time is taken, its extreme on either side is a 'now'. This is clear because no part of time is in act except the 'now'. For what has passed has already gone, and what is future as yet is not. Moreover, the 'now' which is taken as the extremity of time is a beginning and an end, as was said. Therefore, on either side of any given time there must always be time. Otherwise the first 'now' would not be the end, and the last 'now' would not be a beginning.

From the statement that time is eternal, he concludes that motion must be eternal. And he gives the reason for this conclusion. Time is a certain property of motion, for it is its number, as was said.

It seems, however, that Aristotle's argument is not effective. For the 'now' is related to time as a point is related to a line, as was explained in Book VI. But the nature [*ratio*] of a point is not such that it is a middle. Rather there is a point which is only the beginning of a line and another point which is only an end. It would happen, however, that every point is a beginning and an end insofar as it is a part of an infinite line. It cannot be proven, therefore, that a line is infinite because every point is a beginning and an end. Rather, conversely, from the fact that a line is infinite, it can be proven that every point is a beginning and an end. Therefore, if it seems that every 'now' is a beginning and an end, this is not true unless it is granted that time is eternal. It seems, therefore, that in assuming this, Aristotle presupposes the eternity of time, which he ought to prove.

Averroes, however, wishing to save Aristotle's argument, says that the 'now' is always a beginning and an end insofar as time does not stand still, as does a line, but rather is in flux.

This clearly is not at all pertinent. For from the fact that time is flowing and not standing still, it follows that one 'now' cannot be taken twice as one point can be taken twice. But the flux of time has no bearing on the 'now' being both a beginning and an end. For the same nature [*ratio*] is found in the inception and termination of every continuum, whether permanent or in flux, as is clear from Book VI.

Therefore, we should re-interpret Aristotle's statement that every 'now' is a beginning and an end, which he wishes to derive from what he assumed first, namely, that there is no before and after unless there is time. He uses this assumed principle only to conclude that every 'now' is a beginning and an end. Let it be granted that some 'now' is the beginning of some time. It is clear, moreover, from the definition of 'beginning' that the beginning of time is that before which no time exists. Therefore, the 'now' which was given as the beginning of time is also an end of time. And in the same way, if a 'now' is an end of time, it follows that it is also a beginning, because it is the nature [*ratio*] of an end that after it there is nothing of it. But there is no after without time. It follows, therefore, that the 'now' which is an end is also a beginning of time.

Next where he says, 'The same reasoning . . .' (251 b 29), he shows that there will always be motion.

He proves this from motion. The argument given above which was taken from motion concluded only that motion never began. But the argument taken from time concluded both that motion never began and that it will never cease.

He says, therefore that the same argument which proves that motion never began can also be used to prove that motion is incorruptible, that is, that motion will never cease. For just as it follows, if there is a beginning of motion, that there was some mutation prior to the mutation given as first, so if it is held that motion at some time ceases, it will follow that there will be some mutation after the mutation which was given at last.

He explains how this follows by abridging what he has said more fully above about the beginning of motion. For he said that if motion begins, mobile objects and movers either began or always were. And a similar distinction can be made here, because if motion ceases, then mobile objects and movers will cease.

On this supposition he says that the actual motion and the mobile object do not cease at the same time. Rather, just as the generation of the mobile object is prior to its motion, so the corruption of the mobile object will be later than the cessation of its motion. And this is clear because it happens that a burnable object remains after the burning stops.

And the same thing may be said of the mover as was said of the mobile object. For the moving being in act and the moving being in potency do not stop together. Thus it is clear that if the mobile object itself is corrupted after the cessation of motion, then there must be a corruption of that mobile object.

Moreover, since it was granted that all movers and moved objects cease, then the thing which corrupts will necessarily be corrupted at a later time. And since corruption is a mutation, it follows that there are mutations after the last mutation. Since, therefore, this is impossible, it follows that motion endures forever.

These, then, are the arguments by which Aristotle intends to prove that motion always was and never ceases.

One part of his position, namely, that there was always motion, conflicts with our faith. For according to our faith nothing has always existed except God alone, Who is altogether immobile, unless one wishes to say that motion is divine understanding. But this meaning of motion is equivocal. For Aristotle does not here mean motion of this kind, but motion in its proper sense.

But the other part of his position is not altogether contrary to faith. For as was said above, Aristotle is not treating the motion of the heavens, but motion in general. But according to our faith we hold that the substance of the world at some time began to be but it will never cease to be. We hold also that some motions will always be, especially in men, who will always remain, living an uncorruptible life, either damned or blessed.

Indeed some, attempting in vain to show that Aristotle has not spoken contrary to faith, have said that Aristotle does not intend here to prove as a truth that motion is eternal, but to introduce arguments on both sides, as if for a point in doubt. But because of his method of procedure this appears to be nonsense. And besides, he uses the eternity of time and of motion as a principle to prove the existence of a first principle, both here in Book VIII and in *Metaphysics*, XII. Therefore it is clear that he assumes this as proven.

But if one correctly considers the arguments given here, the truth of faith cannot effectively be opposed to such arguments.

For arguments of this kind are effective in proving that motion did not begin by way of nature, as some have held. But it cannot be proven with these arguments that motion did not begin in the sense that things were produced anew by the first principle of things, as our faith holds. This is clear to one who considers the individual inferences which are given here.

For when one asks whether or not movers and mobile objects have always existed if there has not always been motion, one must answer that the first mover has always existed. All other things, whether they be movers or mobile objects, have not always existed but began to be from the universal cause of the whole of being. It was shown above, moreover, that the production of the whole of being by the first cause of being is not a motion, whether or not it is granted that this emanation of things is from eternity.

Thus, therefore, it does not follow that before the first mutation there is another mutation. However, this would follow if movers and mobile objects were newly produced in being by some particular agent which acts on some presupposed subject which is changed from non-being to being, or from privation to form. Aristotle's argument deals with this type of beginning.

But since we hold that at least the first mover has always existed, we still need to give an answer to his next deduction, in which he concludes that if motion begins to be anew when movers and mobile objects pre-exist, then movers and mobile objects must not previously have been in that disposition in which they are while there is motion. And thus some mutation must precede the first mutation.

If we speak about motion itself, the answer is easy. Mobile objects were not previously in the disposition in which they now are, because previously they did not exist. Hence they could not be moved. And as was said, existence is not acquired through a mutation or a motion, but through an emanation from the first principle of things. Thus it does not follow that there was a mutation before the first mutation.

But there remains a further question about the first production of things. If the first principle, which is God, is not related differently now than He was before, He does not produce things now rather than before. And if He were related differently, at least a mutation on His part will be prior to the mutation which is first.

Now if He were an agent only through nature, and not through will and intellect, this argument would conclude with necessity. But because He acts through His will, He is able through His eternal will to produce an effect which is not eternal, just as through His eternal intellect He can understand a thing which is not eternal. For a known thing is in a certain way the principle of action in agents who act through the will, just as a natural form is the principle of action in agents who act through nature.

Let us pursue this further. We do not see that the will puts off doing what it wishes unless something is expected in the future which does not yet exist in the present. For example, I do not wish to make a fire now but later in the future when I expect cold, which is the reason why I make the fire; or at least it is expected at the present time. Moreover, since time succeeds time, this cannot occur without motion. Therefore, a will, even if it is immutable, cannot put off doing what it wills except by some intervening motion. And so it is not possible for a new production of things to proceed from an eternal will unless intermediate motions succeed each other to infinity.

But such objectors do not see that this objection proceeds from an agent in time, that is, from an agent who acts in a presupposed time. For in an action of this kind which occurs in time, one must consider some determinate relation to this time or to those things which are in this time, so that it occurs at this time rather than at the other. But this argument has no application to a universal agent which produces even time itself together with the rest of things.

For when we say that things were not eternally produced by God, we do not mean that an infinite time has preceded in which God ceased from acting, and that after a determined time He began to act. Rather we mean that God produced time and things together in being after they were not. And so we need not consider that the divine will willed to make things not then, but afterwards, as if time already existed. Rather we need only consider that He willed that things and the time of their duration should begin to be after they were not.

If, however, one asks why He willed this, without doubt it must be said that He did this for His own sake. For just as He made things for His own sake so that a likeness of His goodness would be manifested in them, so He wills them not always to be so that His sufficiency would be manifested in this, that when all other things do not exist, He has within Himself every sufficiency of beatitude and of power for the production of things.

This indeed may be said insofar as human reason can understand divine things. Nevertheless, the secrets of divine wisdom, which cannot be comprehended by us, are preserved.

Since, therefore, the answer to this argument proceeds from the supposition that there has not always been time, it remains to answer the argument through which it seems to be shown that there was always time. Aristotle perhaps gives the argument concerning time after the argument concerning motion because he thought that the preceding argument concerning motion was not effective unless it is granted that time is eternal. Therefore he says that whenever there is time, it must be admitted unhesitatingly that there is a 'now'. That every 'now', however, is a beginning and an end of time cannot be conceded unless it is also granted that there has always been motion such that every indivisible that is taken in motion, which is called an 'impulse', is a beginning and an end of motion. For 'now' is related to 'impulse' as time is related to motion. If, therefore, we hold that there has not always been motion but that there is a first indivisible in motion before which there was no motion, then there will also be a 'now' in time before which there was no time.

We have already shown above, in explaining the text, that what Averroes says in confirmation of this argument is not effective.

And Aristotle's position that there is no before and after without time is also not effective.

For when we say that the beginning of time is that before which none of it is, it cannot be said on account of this that the 'now' which is the beginning of time is preceded by a time which is signified by 'before'. In the same way if in regard to magnitude I say that the beginning of a magnitude is that outside of which none of it is, it cannot be said that 'outside of that beginning' signifies a place existing in nature, but only an imaginary place. Otherwise one could posit a place outside the heavens whose magnitude is finite, having a beginning and an end.

In a similar way the first 'now' which is the beginning of time is not preceded by a time existing in nature, but only in our imagination. And this is the time which is designated when it is said that the first 'now' is a beginning of time 'before' which there is no time.

Or it can be said that when the beginning of time is said to be that before which there is no time, the word'before' does not remain affirmative, but becomes negative. Thus it is not necessary to posit a time before the beginning of time. With respect to things which are in time, it happens that some time pre-existed their beginning. For example, when it is said that the beginning of youth is that before which there is no youth, it is possible to understand the 'before' affirmatively, because youth is measured by time. Time, however, is not measured by time. Hence time did not pre-exist its beginning. And so the word 'before', which is used in the definition of the beginning of time, cannot remain affirmative, but becomes negative.

There is, however, a duration of time, namely, the eternity of God, which has no extension of either before or after, as does time, but is a simultaneous whole. This does not have the same nature [*ratio*] as time, just as divine magnitude is not the same as corporeal magnitude.

Thus when we say that outside the world nothing exists except God, we do not posit any dimension outside the world. In the same way when we say that before the world nothing was, we do not posit a successive duration before the world.

5. John Buridan (d. ca. 1358), *Questions on the Eight Books of the Physics of Aristotle**

It took a century for the philosophy of Aristotle to be fully absorbed into the intellectual culture of medieval Europe. By the middle of the fourteenth century, Aristotelian philosophy was so well known that philosophers could begin to criticize it on both philosophical and scientific, as well as on purely theological, grounds. Natural philosophers focused upon the Aristotelian doctrines of mechanics and directed their most intense criticism at the Aristotelian concept of force and motion.

John Buridan, rector of the University of Paris, was one of the most severe critics of Aristotelian concepts of motion. Buridan was concerned with the problem of how motion could sustain itself once the source of "pushing force," such as a bowstring, was removed from an object. To answer this and other problems, he devised his theory of impetus.

1. Book VIII, Question 12. It is sought whether a projectile after leaving the hand of the projector is moved by the air, or by what it is moved.

It is argued that it is not moved by the air; because the air seems rather to resist, since it is necessary that it be divided. Furthermore, if you say that the projector in the beginning moved the projectile and the ambient air along with it, and then that air, having been moved, moves the projectile further to such and such a distance, the doubt will return as to by what the air is moved after the projector ceases to move. For there is just as much difficulty regarding this (the air) as there is regarding the stone which is thrown.

Aristotle takes the opposite position in the eighth [book] of this work (the *Physics*) thus: "Projectiles are moved further after the projectors are no longer in contact with them, either by antiperistasis, as some say, or by the fact that the air having been pushed, pushes with a movement swifter than the movement of impulsion by which it (the body) is carried towards its own [natural] place." He determines the same thing in the seventh and eighth [books] of this work (the *Physics*) and in the third [book] of the *De caelo*.

2. This question I judge to be very difficult because Aristotle, as it seems to me, has not solved it well. For he touches on two opinions. The first one, which he calls "antiperistasis," holds that the projectile swiftly leaves the place in which it was, and nature, not permitting a vacuum, rapidly

---

* John Buridan, *Questions on the Eight Books of the Physics of Aristotle*, Document 8.2, in *The Science of Mechanics in the Middle Ages* by Marshall Clagett. The University of Wisconsin Press, Madison, Wisconsin, 1959. Pp. 532-538. Reprinted by permission of the University of Wisconsin Press and Marshall Clagett.

sends air in behind to fill up the vacuum. The air moved swiftly in this way and impinging upon the projectile impels it along further. This is repeated continually up to a certain distance. . . . But such a solution notwithstanding, it seems to me that this method of proceeding was without value because of many experiences (*experientie*).

The first experience concerns the top and the smith's mill (i.e. wheel) which are moved for a long time and yet do not leave their places. Hence, it is not necessary for the air to follow along to fill up the place of departure of a top of this kind and a smith's mill. So it cannot be said [that the top and the smith's mill are moved by the air] in this manner.

The second experience is this: A lance having a conical posterior as sharp as its anterior would be moved after projection just as swiftly as it would be without a sharp conical posterior. But surely the air following could not push a sharp end in this way, because the air would be easily divided by the sharpness.

The third experience is this: a ship drawn swiftly in the river even against the flow of the river, after the drawing has ceased, cannot be stopped quickly, but continues to move for a long time. And yet a sailor on deck does not feel any air from behind pushing him. He feels only the air from the front resisting [him]. Again, suppose that the said ship were loaded with grain or wood and a man were situated to the rear of the cargo. Then if the air were of such an impetus that it could push the ship along so strongly, the man would be pressed very violently between that cargo and the air following it. Experience shows this to be false. Or, at least, if the ship were loaded with grain or straw, the air following and pushing would fold over the stalks which were in the rear. This is all false.

3. Another opinion, which Aristotle seems to approve, is that the projector moves the air adjacent to the projectile [simultaneously] with the projectile and that air moved swiftly has the power of moving the projectile. He does not mean by this that the same air is moved from the place of projection to the place where the projectile stops, but rather that the air joined to the projector is moved by the projector and that air having been moved moves another part of the air next to it, and that [part] moves another (i.e., the next) up to a certain distance. Hence the first air moves the projectile into the second air, and the second [air moves it] into the third air, and so on. Aristotle says, therefore, that there is not one mover but many in turn. Hence he also concludes that the movement is not continuous but consists of succeeding or contiguous entities.

But this opinion and method certainly seems to me equally as impossible as the opinion and method of the preceding view. For this method cannot solve the problem of how the top or smith's mill is turned after the hand [which sets them into motion] has been removed. Because, if you cut off the air on all sides near the smith's mill by a cloth, the mill does not on this account stop but continues to move for a long time. Therefore it is not moved by the air.

Also a ship drawn swiftly is moved a long time after the

haulers have stopped pulling it. The surrounding air does not move it, because if it were covered by a cloth and the cloth with the ambient air were withdrawn, the ship would not stop its motion on this account. And even if the ship were loaded with grain or straw and were moved by the ambient air, then that air ought to blow exterior stalks toward the front. But the contrary is evident, for the stalks are blown rather to the rear because of the resisting ambient air.

Again, the air, regardless of how fast it moves, is easily divisible. Hence it is not evident as to how it would sustain a stone of weight of one thousand pounds projected in a sling or in a machine.

Furthermore, you could, by pushing your hand, move the adjacent air, if there is nothing in your hand, just as fast or faster than if you were holding in your hand a stone which you wish to project. If, therefore, that air by reason of the velocity of its motion is of a great enough impetus to move the stone swiftly, it seems that if I were to impel air toward you equally as fast, the air ought to push you impetuously and with sensible strength. [Yet] we would not perceive this.

Also, it follows that you would throw a feather farther than a stone and something less heavy farther than something heavier, assuming equal magnitudes and shapes. Experience shows this to be false. The consequence is manifest, for the air having been moved ought to sustain or carry or move a feather more easily than something heavier. . . .

4. Thus we can and ought to say that in the stone or other projectile there is impressed something which is the motive force *(virtus motiva)* of that projectile. And this is evidently better than falling back on the statement that the air continues to move that projectile. For the air appears rather to resist. Therefore, it seems to me that it ought to be said that the motor in moving a moving body impresses in it a certain impetus *(impetus)* or a certain motive force *(vis motiva)* of the moving body, [which impetus acts] in the direction toward which the mover was moving the moving body, either up or down, or laterally, or circularly. *And by the amount the motor moves that moving body more swiftly, by the same amount it will impress in it a stronger impetus.** It is by that impetus that the stone is moved after the projector ceases to move. But that impetus is continually decreased by the resisting air and by the gravity of the stone, which inclines it in a direction contrary to that in which the impetus was naturally predisposed to move it. Thus the movement of the stone continually becomes slower, and finally that impetus is so diminished or corrupted that the gravity of the stone wins out over it and moves the stone down to its natural place.

This method, it appears to me, ought to be supported because the other methods do not appear to be true and also because all the appearances are in harmony with this method.

5. For if anyone seeks why I project a stone farther than a feather, and iron or lead fitted to my hand farther than just as much wood, I answer that the cause of this is that the reception

* The italics here and elsewhere are Professor Clagett's.

of all forms and natural dispositions is in matter and by reason of matter. *Hence by the amount more there is of matter, by that amount can the body receive more of that impetus and more intensely. Now in a dense and heavy body, other things being equal, there is more of prime matter than in a rare and light one. Hence a dense and heavy body receives more of that impetus and more intensely, just as iron can receive more calidity than wood or water of the same quantity.* Moreover, a feather receives such an impetus so weakly that such an impetus is immediately destroyed by the resisting air. *And so also if light wood and heavy iron of the same volume and of the same shape are moved equally fast by a projector, the iron will be moved farther because there is impressed in it a more intense impetus, which is not so quickly corrupted as the lesser impetus would be corrupted. This also is the reason why it is more difficult to bring to rest a large smith's mill which is moving swiftly than a small one, evidently because in the large one, other things being equal, there is more impetus.* And for this reason you could throw a stone of one-half or one pound weight farther than you could a thousandth part of it. For the impetus in that thousandth part is so small that it is overcome immediately by the resisting air.

6. From this theory also appears the cause of why the natural motion of a heavy body downward is continually accelerated. For from the beginning only the gravity was moving it. Therefore, it moved more slowly, but in moving it impressed in the heavy body an impetus. This impetus now [acting] together with its gravity moves it. Therefore, the motion becomes faster; and by the amount it is faster, so the impetus becomes more intense. Therefore, the movement evidently becomes continually faster.

[The impetus then also explains why] one who wishes to jump a long distance drops back a way in order to run faster, so that by running he might acquire an impetus which would carry him a longer distance in the jump. Whence the person so running and jumping does not feel the air moving him, but [rather] feels the air in front strongly resisting him.

Also, since the Bible does not state that appropriate intelligences move the celestial bodies, it could be said that it does not appear necessary to posit intelligences of this kind, because it would be answered that God, when He created the world, moved each of the celestial orbs as He pleased, and in moving them He impressed in them impetuses which moved them without his having to move them any more except by the method of general influence whereby he concurs as a co-agent in all things which take place; "for thus on the seventh day He rested from all work which He had executed by committing to others the actions and the passions in turn." And these impetuses which He impressed in the celestial bodies were not decreased nor corrupted afterwards, because there was no resistance which would be corruptive or repressive of that impetus. But this I do not say assertively, but [rather tentatively] so that I might seek from the theological masters what they might teach me in these matters as to how these things take place. . . .

7. The first [conclusion] is that that impetus is not the

very local motion in which the projectile is moved, because that impetus moves the projectile and the mover produces motion. Therefore, the impetus produces that motion, and the same thing cannot produce itself. Therefore, etc.

Also since every motion arises from a motor being present and existing simultaneously with that which is moved, if the impetus were the motion, it would be necessary to assign some other motor from which that motion would arise. And the principal difficulty would return. Hence there would be no gain in positing such an impetus. But others cavil when they say that the prior part of the motion which produces the projection produces another part of the motion which is related successively and that produces another part and so on up to the cessation of the whole movement. But this is not probable, because the "producing something" ought to exist when the something is made, but the prior part of the motion does not exist when the posterior part exists, as was elsewhere stated. Hence, neither does the prior exist when the posterior is made. This consequence is obvious from this reasoning. For it was said elsewhere that motion is nothing else than "the very being produced" and the "very being corrupted". Hence motion does not result when it *has been* produced but when it *is being* produced.

8. The second conclusion is that that impetus is not a purely successive thing because motion is just such a thing and the definition of motion [as a successive thing] is fitting to it, as was stated elsewhere. And now it has just been affirmed that that impetus is not the local motion.

Also, since a purely successive thing is continually corrupted and produced, it continually demands a producer. But there cannot be assigned a producer of that impetus which would continue to be simultaneous with it.

9. The third conclusion is that that impetus is a thing of permanent nature, distinct from the local motion in which the projectile is moved. This is evident from the two aforesaid conclusions and from the preceding [statements]. And it is probable that that impetus is a quality naturally present and predisposed for moving a body in which it is impressed, just as it is said that a quality impressed in iron by a magnet moves the iron to the magnet. And it also is probable that just as that quality (the impetus) is impressed in the moving body along with the motion by the motor; so with the motion it is remitted, corrupted, or impeded by resistance or a contrary inclination.

10. And in the same way that a luminant generating light generates light reflexively because of an obstacle, so that impetus because of an obstacle acts reflexively. It is true, however, that other causes aptly concur with that impetus for greater or longer reflection. For example, the ball which we bounce with the palm in falling to earth is reflected higher than a stone, although the stone falls more swiftly and more impetuously to the earth. This is because many things are curvable or intracompressible by violence which are innately disposed to return swiftly and by themselves to their correct position or to the disposition natural to them. In thus returning, they can impetuously push or draw something conjunct to them, as is evident in the case of the

bow. Hence in this way the ball thrown to the hard ground is compressed into itself by the impetus of its motion; and immediately after striking, it returns swiftly to its sphericity by elevating itself upwards. From this elevation it acquires to itself an impetus which moves it upward a long distance.

Also, it is this way with a cither cord which, put under strong tension and percussion, remains a long time in a certain vibration from which its sound continues a notable time. And this takes place as follows: As a result of striking [the chord] swiftly, it is bent violently in one direction, and so it returns swiftly toward its normal straight position. But on account of the impetus, it crosses beyond the normal straight position in the contrary direction and then again returns. It does this many times. For a similar reason a bell, after the ringer ceases to draw [the chord], is moved a long time, first in one direction, now in another. And it cannot be easily and quickly brought to rest.

This, then, is the exposition of the question. I would be delighted if someone would discover a more probably way of answering it. And this is the end.

6. St. John of St. Amand on the Magnet*

John of St. Amand (flourished 1261-98) was a little known commentator on the mysterious action of the magnet. His work seems to have been neglected in favor of that of his more famous contemporaries, Petrus Peregrinus and Thomas Aquinas, but he offers some interesting and creative comments on both the magnet and the nature of magnetism.

But then there is the more difficult question how the magnet attracts iron, and also the magnet the magnet, since nothing can evaporate from it, since it is so hard that it can with difficulty be broken. I say that it does it by multiplying its like and, without any evaporation, exciting the active power which exists incomplete in iron, which is born to be completed by the form of the magnet, nay is moved towards it. Wherefore I say that in the magnet is a trace of the world, wherefore there is in it one part having in itself the property of the west, another of the east, another of the south, another of the north. And I say that in the direction north and south it attracts most strongly, little in the direction east and west. Wherefore the virtues of the poles are stronger in it, which is recognized by sailors, because it attracts, that they have a north or south wind.

But then how is it told whether it is south or north? I say in this way. An eggshell is taken full of water and is put in violent motion. Then the magnet is placed on the shell as it moves violently and the south part will be moved southward and the north northward. And sometimes it happens that the southern part attracts that which has the property and nature of the north, albeit they have the same specific form, and this is not except by some property existing more complete in the southern part which the northern part has potentially and thereby its potentiality is completed. Wherefore I say that the southern part never attracts the southern part nor the northern the northern, because there is not in the one anything that the other needs on account of which motion should be made, since they are of the same form and property.

By this is exposed the ignorance of some who say that sometimes the magnet drives away the magnet and the southern part the southern part, because this is false. It may seem to repel yet does not repel but attracts the northern part existing in one section of the magnet. And because in the opposite direction was the property as it were of the south, therefore in attracting the northern part to itself it seems to repel the southern part. For instance, take a magnet of which one part has the property of the south and the other of the north and put a needle above that stone so that it lies on the stone. Then one end of the needle touches one end of the magnet and the other the other, and there flows into the end of the needle the virtue of that part which it

---

* "John of St. Amand on the Magnet" by Lynn Thorndike. *ISIS*, Vol. XXXVI, Nos. 105 and 106, October 1946. Pp. 156-157.

touches, so that, if it touches the southern, the southern virtue flows in. Then let the needle be raised higher. Then, since there is a current from the magnet through the entire needle placed directly above it, that part of the needle in which at first there was southern virtue will become northern, as the current from the magnet flows through the whole needle. So that if we should suppose a dish full of water to be placed directly underneath the needle, the current would flow into the bottom of the dish. Similarly that part of the needle which first touched the southern part when it was rubbed against or lay on it, when that part is rubbed on that part directly, that part which at first possessed the southern property now has northern property. And then that which at first was southern, since it is now northern, is attracted by the southern part of the magnet, since it does not attract the southern, as has been said. And by the fact that one is attracted the other seems to be repelled. And so in this sort of phenomena like is not actually attracted by like but because it is possible that parts possessing the same form and species should have diverse properties, one being complete, the other incomplete, from which attraction results.

7. Peter of Limoges on the Comet of 1299*

Peter of Limoges, canon of Evreux, studied at the University of Paris and seems to have been dean of the medical faculty in 1270. He enjoyed a considerable scholarly reputation in the fields of theology, medicine, astronomy and astrology. His short commentary on the comet of 1299 is a mixture of observation, Aristotelian cosmology, and astrological prediction.

In the year of the Lord 1299, before the end of January and all through February and for some days in March, appeared a comet of moderate size with a long tail for the size of its body, of a color somewhat bordering on dark blue, from which I infer that it was the variety of comet known as Lord Ascone, which in Arabic and in Hebrew means the same as Lord of Death in Latin. For it appeared in the west, becoming visible in the evening, and when it first appeared its position as determined by a *turquetum* was in the 18th degree of Taurus on a circle passing through the poles of the zodiac. And it had a southern latitude to the ecliptic of more than 30 degress. But after the feast of St. Matthew its position was found to be the 14th degree of Taurus and its southern latitude 5 degrees. It still remained visible until the fifth day of March, much diminished in body and in tail, and it kept rising towards the Pleiades and Aldebaran to the north, so that its motion was always greater northward than westward with respect to the fixed stars. Therefore it was borne by varied motion and in manifold wise, for the place of its generation, which is the upper part of the air contiguous to the sphere of fire, was moved from east to west, for thus the superior elements are moved by the motion of the heavens. But since fire and the upper air are moved more slowly than the movement of the heavens, therefore if a comet generated in the upper air were moved westward by the motion of the heavens only, it would lag towards the east behind the fixed stars and so from mere retardation would seem to move in the opposite direction from the heavens, as is the case with certain planets. Now the fact that it was moved westward faster than the heavens was because it was very strongly drawn westward by its principal generating force, Mercury, which from the beginning of the comet's appearance was in trine aspect to it, and because Mercury was west of it in longitude and north of it in latitude. And so the traction of the sun (?) was moved northward and westward changing position with reference to the fixed stars.

Moreover, Mars was sharer with Mercury, which is shown from this, that the tail of the comet which, when it first appeared, was directed towards the lesser dog-star, gradually was raised to the north, while the body of the comet remained southward with reference to its tail, until the tail pointed to Mars in a straight line. This makes it clear how the comet moved more to

---

* "Peter of Limoges on the Comet of 1299," by Lynn Thorndike. *ISIS*, Vol. XXXVI, No. 103, October, 1945. Pp. 4-5.

the north than to the west with reference to the fixed stars, although it had a double motion by which it was drawn. Since in the westward movement of the comet Mercury alone was the cause which was west of it. But in the movement to the north Mars and Mercury were a cause simultaneously, since both were to the north of the comet.

These things being so, I say according to the doctrine of judicial astrology that a comet of this sort signifies wars, conflicts, future diseases or scab and itch, mortality of men and beasts from corruption of the air, many violent winds, great earthquakes in certain parts of the earth, excessive rains, vehement cold in winter time, failure and scarcity of victuals, rotting of crops and of the fruit of trees, and destruction of the same. And because the phenomenon has lasted for many days, it indicates that its sequels will be of long duration. But since in the conjunction preceding the vernal equinox the comet was within the rays of Venus and at about its finish was in close conjunction with her, since also when the comet first appeared Jupiter was in sextile aspect to it--these circumstances, I say, may mitigate the ill effects of the comet. Also by reason of some subsequent constellation the sequels of the comet may be either intensified or diminished.

This should be known and firmly believed, that divine power is not fettered by those petty signs, nay He absolutely is able to alter their power according to his good pleasure in whole or in part. Also it is to be hoped that He will change them, if we shall have lived aright. For our God is merciful who speaks through Jeremiah, Fear not those signs which the Gentiles fear. For the Gentiles, that is, those living a worldly life, may well fear them. But oft divine clemency on account of the merits of the just is wont to pity and spare the unjust.

So ends the judgment as to the comet star by master Peter of Limoges, canon of Evreux.

C. Marshall Clagett, "Medieval Mechanics in Retrospect"*

The achievement of the medieval natural philosophers in the area of mechanics has been summed up by Marshall Clagett, one of the foremost historians of medieval science.

As we close this volume one final task is left for us, to summarize in a single and coherent whole some of the principal medieval mechanical concepts which still circulated in the sixteenth century, either in printed editions of the works of medieval authors or in the works of sixteenth-century authors who still parroted the views and words of their predecessors. We shall not attempt in this summary to pay much attention to the order in which we have already presented these concepts in the previous chapters. Our hope here is more for coherence than for strict recapitulation.

In singling out and numbering the principal medieval concepts, we have sometimes quoted directly from the documents given in earlier chapters and at other times we have for the sake of economy contented ourselves with an accurate paraphrase. But in either case reference has been made to the appropriate documentary source and discussions already presented. Finally, it should be noticed that we make no attempt here to summarize the general Aristotelian framework assumed in medieval mechanics but only the distinctive and influential concepts taken up or invented by the medieval schoolmen.

At the heart of both ancient and modern systems of mechanics lie the nature, definition, and role of weight. All of the principal systems of mechanics from Aristotle to Newton accepted weight as a force. But the concept and definition of force changed from a *cause of motion* in ancient and medieval mechanics to a *cause of change of motion* in Newtonian mechanics. Among the most important distinctions with regard to weight that began to develop from the time of Aristotle was the distinction between gross weight and specific weight. This distinction, present in germinal form in the *De caelo* of Aristotle, was made more quantitatively precise in Archimedes' genuine work *On Floating Bodies*, and it proved to be of some importance for both the statics and dynamics of the Middle Ages. In Arabic treatises concerned with specific gravities, the distinction was sharpened beyond the statements found in Archimedes' work. Whether original with them or not, the Arabic precision was duplicated in at least one medieval Latin work which stemmed from the Arabic tradition, and we should like to single out as our first concept the definitions of gross and specific weight given in the pseudo-Archimedean *De insidentibus in humidum* of the thirteenth century:

---

* Marshall Clagett, *The Science of Mechanics in the Middle Ages*, The University of Wisconsin Press, Madison, 1959. Pp. 673-682.

1. *"One body is said to be heavier than another numerically if, when these bodies are suspended at the ends of the balance beam, its arm of the balance inclines downward; or, if its weight is equal to a greater number of calculi. . . . Of two bodies equal in volume, the one whose weight is equal to a greater number of calculi is of greater specific weight. Of two bodies of the same kind* (i.e., of the same specific gravity), *the proportion of volumes to weights is the same."*

Starting, then, with a distinction between gross weight and specific weight, many mechanicians accepted the following simple extension of the basic Aristotelian law relating force (and thus weight) to velocity:

2. *The force exerted by a heavy body is proportional to its weight, and thus for a given volume, force is proportional to density; the speed of a heavy body is proportional to the force it exerts, and so with a given volume assumed, the speed of fall is proportional to the density of the heavy body.*

This extension of the Peripatetic law was actually found in the *De caelo* of Aristotle and elaborated in the popular *Liber de ponderoso et levi* attributed to Euclid and composed in late antiquity. This work was translated from the Arabic and circulated widely in the thirteenth and fourteenth centuries. Its basic ideas were expressed by Johannes de Muris, Albert of Saxony, Blasius of Parma, and no doubt many others in the course of the fourteenth and fifteenth centuries. As we have seen in Chapter 11, Benedetti and Galileo (in his youth), both under the influence of Archimedes' hydrostatics, went one step further and singled out specific gravity, without regard for the volume or absolute weight involved, as the principal determiner of the velocity of fall--a uniform medium assumed. Now granting the importance of the motivating force--whether gross or specific weight--one still had to assess the role of the resisting medium. We find some tendency (starting in late antiquity) to refute the role assigned to the resisting medium by Aristotle. The tenor of this criticsm we can paraphrase as follows:

3. *The effect of the resistance of a medium is an effect to be subtracted from the original force of movement rather than one to be divided into the original force of movement.*

This view, also adopted by Benedetti and Galileo (in his early *De motu*), arose historically out of John Philoponus' criticism of Aristotle's "law" of dynamics in the sixth century A.D., although it was not precisely stated in this manner by Philoponus. From Philoponus the germ of this view was taken up by Avempace, and his views were known to the Latin West as the result of their criticism by Averroes. The first precise mathematics statement of this view was made in the fourteenth century by Bradwardine, who rejected it and attempted to save Aristotle with a new and quite different form of Aristotle's law, expressible as follows:

4. *Velocity follows the "geometric proportionality"* (i.e., is an exponential function) *of the ratio of the motive force to the resistance* (expressed in modern terminology as $V \propto \log F/R$).

This law of Bradwardine was very widely accepted by the schoolmen of the fourteenth and fifteenth centuries. It was particularly important for introducing exponential functions to represent physical occurrences. But even more important, it was a law which attempted to describe instantaneous changes in velocity rather than average velocity. Thus it foreshadowed the differential equation used so universally in modern mechanics. Bradwardine's law was, however, without adequate physical verification; and it passed out of vogue by the sixteenth century. Its great significance was that, being like a "differential" equation, it not only brought to a head the consideration of instantaneous velocity, but it had the most significant kinematic consequences at Merton College--consequences we shall summarize shortly.

Concerned so paramountly with weights, forces, and resistances, medieval mechanics from the thirteenth century occupied itself with problems of the equilibrium of forces and weights as represented by balances, levers and other statical situations. Heir of Hellenistic mechanics, the medieval mechanician sharpened the concept of virtual displacements, which had had its origin in the Pseudo-Aristotelian treatise *Mechanica*. The form of the principle of virtual displacements used by the thirteenth century mathematician Jordanus and expressed by one of his thirteenth- or fourteenth-century commentators (in the so-called *Aliud commentum* published in 1533 by Peter Apianus) was essentially of this form:

5. *What suffices to lift a weight W through a vertical distance will lift a weight kW through a vertical distance H/k or a weight W/k through a vertical distance kH.*

This principle was employed by Jordanus to prove the law of the lever as applied to both a straight and a bent lever. It was also used in the elegant proof of the proposition concerning the equilibrium of interconnected weights on oppositely inclined planes whose lengths vary directly as the weights. Furthermore, in the proposition concerning the bent lever, what is essentially the concept of static moment was conceived:

6. *The effective force of a weight on any lever arm, straight or bent, depends on both its weight and its horizontal distance from the vertical line passing through the fulcrum.*

Still another fertile statical concept was used by the author of the *De ratione ponderis*. This was the concept of positional gravity used to determine the component of natural gravity acting along an inclined plane. This concept can be expressed as follows:

7. *The ratio of the effective weight (positional gravity) of a body in the direction of the inclined plane on which it rests to the free natural gravity is equal to the ratio of the vertical component of any given potential trajectory along that plane to that trajectory.*

This concept is equivalent to the modern formulation $F = W \sin a$, where F is the force along the plane, W is the free weight and a is the angle of inclination of the plane. It was employed by the medieval author to establish the law of equilibrium of interconnected weights on oppositely inclined planes. This concept and its use marked an important step in the rise of a vectorial analysis of forces.

Fortunately the medieval mechanicians did not limit themselves to propositions concerning statics and dynamics but also pursued in an original manner some of the kinematic possibilities made pregnant by Bradwardine's discussions of dynamics. In this kinematic investigation they outstripped antique efforts. In the first place, the followers of Bradwardine at Merton College, Oxford, made more explicit the distinction between dynamics and kinematics already clear to William Ockham and Bradwardine himself. As Swineshead puts the distinction, it takes this form:

8. *In the first place the velocity in every successive movement is measured causally by the proportion of the motive force to the resisting force; while in the second place it is to be measured by its effects, i.e., by the distance traversed in comparison to the time.*

In pursuing the kinematic aspects of movement, the junior contemporaries of Bradwardine inherited from their thirteenth-century predecessor, Gerard of Brussels, this general kinematic statement:

9. *"The proportion of the movements* (i.e., speeds) *of points is that of the lines described in the same time."*

Furthermore, as the result of past kinematic statements, the Merton College kinematicists agreed on this precise definition of uniform speed:

10. *"Uniform local motion is one in which in every equal part of the time an equal distance is described."* (From Swineshead)

This Merton definition was precisely the definition adopted by Galileo later. Similarly, the masters of Merton were also agreed upon this general definition of acceleration later concurred in by Galileo:

11. *"Any motion whatever is uniformly accelerated if, in each of any equal parts of the time whatsoever, it acquires an equal increment of velocity."* (From Heytesbury's *Regule*)

Now in order to treat properly problems of acceleration, the Merton College kinematicists arrived at a concept of "qualitative" or "instantaneous" velocity. Such velocity had its measure in "degrees," as did any qualitative measure. For the practical determination of instantaneous velocity, the schoolmen were to anticipate almost exactly the words of Galileo. The Merton definition of the measure of instantaneous velocity was expressed in this way:

12. *"Instantaneous velocity is not measured by the distance traversed, but by the distance which would be traversed by such a point, if it were moved uniformly over such or such a period of time at that degree of velocity with which it is moved in that assigned instant."* (Heytesbury)

In their analysis of the many problems involved in acceleration and deceleration, the Merton schoolmen discovered the following form of the theorem describing uniform acceleration:

13. *"A moving body uniformly acquiring or losing that increment* (of speed) *will traverse in some given time a magnitude completely equal to that which it would traverse if it were moving continuously through the same time with the mean degree [of velocity]."* (Heytesbury [?])

This form of the acceleration theorem was proved in a number of ways in the course of the fourteenth and fifteenth centuries, the most important of which was employed by Oresme at Paris just after 1350. Using a graphing system, Oresme showed that a right triangle representing uniform acceleration (i.e., the distance traversed in some movement of uniform acceleration) is equal to the rectangle representing the distance traversed in a uniform movement, where the altitude of the rectangle (the altitude representing the uniform speed) is half the altitude of the triangle (this altitude representing the final speed in the movement of uniform acceleration).

Both the medieval acceleration theorem (in slightly modified form) and Oresme's (or Casali's) geometric type of proof were given by Galileo before he passed on to his well-known form: $S \propto t^2$. But note well that the Merton formula does not appear to have been applied in the fourteenth century to the problem of falling bodies, as of course it was later applied in the sixteenth century by Domingo de Soto and in the seventeenth by Galileo and Beeckman.

The schoolmen of the thirteenth and fourteenth century were actually much confused as to the measure of the spped of falling bodies. Jordanus in the thirteenth century seemed to accept the proportionality of speed and time in a germinal fashion, while Oresme accepted it somewhat more clearly. But his teacher, Buridan, at Paris appears to have held these two contradictory conclusions without realizing it:

14. *The speed of falling bodies increases directly with the distance of fall. The same speed increases directly with the time of fall.*

The same confusion is evident in the treatment of the problem by Albert of Saxony, who, when specifically talking about the measure of the speed of fall, says that it grows as the distance of fall. "When some space has been traversed by this [motion], it has a certain velocity, and when a double space has been traversed by it, it is twice as fast, and when a triple space... it is three times as fast, and so on." And yet, in the same question a little bit farther on, when Albert is talking about the cause of acceleration he seems to accept the direct proportionality of speed and time. A similar confusion plagued Leonardo da Vinci, Galileo in his earlier fragments, and Descartes.

Except for Oresme and Albert of Saxony, the authors at the University of Paris were somewhat less interested in kinematics than the English. Their glory lay in a new form of an earlier dynamics critical of Aristotle. This was the so-called impetus dynamics. The most original exponent of the impetus mechanics at Paris was John Buridan. In Buridan's scheme the continuance of projectile motion was no longer considered as resulting from the action of the surrounding air, as in the Aristotelian explanation; rather the following explanation was given:

15. *"The Motor in moving a moving body impresses in it a certain impetus or a certain motive force of the moving body, [which impetus acts] in the direction toward which the mover was moving the moving body, either up or down, or laterally or circularly."* (Buridan)

The impetus then appears to be some kind of intrinsic mover impressed in the projectile by the projector. So far, this is the same explanation as that offered by John Philoponus in the sixth century A.D. But the originality of Buridan's discussion of the impetus lies in the measure he assigns the impetus:

16. *"By the amount the motor moves that moving body more swiftly, by the same amount it will impress in it a stronger impetus."*

Hence for Buridan the impetus varies directly as the speed impressed in the moving body by the original mover. But it is also measured by the amount of prime matter in the body:

17. *"By the amount more there is of matter, by that amount can the body receive more of that impetus and more intensely. Now in a dense and heavy body, other things being equal, there is more of prime matter than in a rare and light one. Hence a dense and heavy body receives more of that impetus and more intensely. . . . And so also if light wood and heavy iron of the same volume and of the same shape are moved equally fast by a projector, the iron will be moved father because there is impressed in it a more intense impetus, which is not so quickly corrupted as the lesser impetus."*

The two factors taken conjointly of which impetus is a function, for Buridan, are clearly velocity and prime matter, and so using medieval "proportional" expressions, we can write the following relationships between the impetus *(I)*, the velocity *(V)* and the quantity of matter *(m)*:

$$I_1 : I_2 :: V_1 : V_2 \text{ when } m_1 = m_2,$$
$$I_1 : I_2 :: m_1 : m_2 \text{ when } V_1 = V_2.$$

Taken conjointly, these expressions are equivalent to this modern metric definition: $I = mV$. The resemblance to the modern definition of momentum is evident.

One other extremely important feature of Buridan's impetus was that it was considered as something of permanent nature, not self-corrupting. Its destruction was accomplished by the resistance of the medium and the weight or contrary inclination of the body:

18. *The "impetus is a thing of permanent nature, distinct from the local motion in which the projectile is moved. . . . [It] is a quality naturally present and predisposed for moving a body in which it is impressed. . . . [It] is impressed in the moving body along with the motion by the motor; so with the motion it is remitted, corrupted, or impeded by resistance or a contrary inclination." The impetus would last indefinitely if it were not diminished by a contrary resistance or by an inclination to a contrary motion."*

With impetus considered as tending toward permanence, it is not surprising that Buridan should suggest that the everlasting movement of the heavens might be explained by the impression of impetus by God; the impetus being thought of as lasting indefinitely, since in the heavenly regions it would be without resistance. Thus Buridan thought it possible to impress circular motion and circularly acting impetus in something of the same way as rectilinear motion and impetus. It was not until Benedetti that a freely moving body under the influence of impetus was thought to move only in a straight line.

Of the numerous applications of the impetus theory to phenomena, none was more fertile than Buridan's use of the theory to explain the acceleration of falling bodies, which he stated as follows:

19. *"A heavy body not only acquires motion unto itself from its principal mover, i.e., its gravity, but it also acquires unto itself a certain impetus with that motion. This impetus has the power of moving the heavy body in conjunction with the permanent natural gravity . . . . from the beginning the heavy body is moved by its natural gravity only; hence it is moved slowly. Afterwards it is moved by that same gravity and by the impetus acquired at the same time; consequently, it is moved more swiftly. And because the movement becomes swifter, therefore the impetus also becomes greater and stronger, and thus the heavy body is moved by its natural gravity and by that greater impetus simultaneously, and so it again will be moved faster; and thus it will always and continually be accelerated to the end."*

Buridan's application of the impetus theory to the acceleration of falling bodies was essentially the same as that of Abū 'l-Barakāt earlier. Buridan's somewhat clumsy expression of the impetus explanation of acceleration was sharpened by later authors, for example by Benedetti, who said that "if a body is moved naturally, it will always increase its velocity, since the impression and impetus in it would always be increased. This is so because it has contact with the motive power perpetually."

The Buridan doctrine, then, by the sixteenth century had clearly become the following: Continually acting gravity (the primary force) impresses continually increasing impetus (the intermediary force) in the falling body which results in continually increasing velocity. Now, when in modern mechanics impetus is conceived as an *effect* rather than a *cause*, impetus loses its position as an intermediary force, and we are left with the familiar Newtonian doctrine, a continually acting force results in acceleration. And furthermore, there is evidence that some of the adherents to the impetus mechanics were tending toward the conversion of impetus into an effect in the sixteenth and early seventeenth centuries. Finally, the impetus analysis of fall was of importance in stressing the continuous action of gravity and impetus *in time*, thus bringing to the fore time of fall rather than distance of fall as the direct measure of the speed of fall.

Not all of the medieval schoolmen who accepted the impetus mechanics accepted Buridan's "inertial" impetus. Many of his successors returned to an old-fashioned "self-expending" impetus. Furthermore, Buridan's principal successor at Paris, Oresme, conceived of impetus as being produced by the *acceleration* of a body and in turn producing further acceleration. With this interpretation of impetus he also returned to a peculiar antique theory that projectiles "accelerated" at the beginning of their flight.

The same Parisian masters who developed the theory of the impetus, and particularly John Buridan and Nicole Oresme, also considered seriously the possibility of the earth's rotation on its axis. In so arguing this, these men advanced and developed important mechanical concepts, not the least of which was their use of an older idea of the complete relativity of the detection of motion. In the words of Oresme we are told:

20. *"Local motion can be sensibly perceived only in so far as one may perceive one body differently disposed with respect to another."*

The example of this doctrine used by the medieval and the early modern authors was that of observers on ships who are able only to detect their movement relative to each other (so that if both were moving at the same speed in the same direction it would seem "that neither ship is moving"). The observer on the earth is in precisely the same boat, so far as detecting the movement of the heavenly bodies, as the observer on one ship trying to decide, as the distance to another ship varies, which of the ships is moving. He cannot tell whether in fact the heavens move in diurnal rotation and the earth is at rest or vice versa.

Furthermore, Oresme came particularly close in the discussion of this problem to the concept of a closed mechanical system. An arrow shot from a moving earth would share the same horizontal velocity as the earth, and hence only *its motion relative to the earth*, i.e., its vertical rectilinear path, could be detected by an observer on the earth, and he would be unable to say anything about its absolute movement. The analogy given by Oresme to illustrate this idea is the observer on a ship which is moving eastward rapidly. He draws his hand down the mast of the ship, and "it would seem to him that his hand was moved with rectilinear movement only. According to this opinion, it seems to us in the same way that an arrow descends or ascends in a straight line."

We have, then, come to the end of our review of some significant medieval mechanical doctrines. Admittedly, most of these concepts we have singled out as important were formed within the Aristotelian framework of mechanics. But these medieval doctrines contained within them the seeds of a critical refutation of that mechanics. The medieval mechanicians, as they propagated these concepts, were attempting to amend the system at the very points it was weakest, and in so doing they focused attention on those weaknesses, at the same time making preliminary and not completely unsuccessful efforts to solve the crucial problems--the problems arising from considering the balance and the lever in operation, the stone in its fall, and the arrow in its flight.

INDEX

Abelard, Peter (1079-1142), 214, 218, 224, 232-33, 262
Abul-Wata (940-90), 190
Adelard of Bath (ca. 1090-ca. 1150), 251, (Readings, pp. 293)
Aesculapius, 28
Al-Battani (Albategnias) (fl. ca. 850), 190-191
Albert of Saxony (ca. 1316-90), 330
Al-Biruni (973-1051), 191, 199-201, 203-204
Albertus Magnus (1206-80), 236, 237
Alcmaeon of Croton (ca. 500 B.C.), 29-30
Alciun of York (ca. 735-804), 220, 254
Al-Ghazzali (1058-1111), 177, 205
Al-Haitham (Alhazen) (ca. 965-1039), 191-193
Alhazen (965-1038), 196-199
Al-Khwarazmi (d. ca. 863), 186-190
Al-Kindi (813-80), 190
Anaxagoras of Clazomenae (ca. 500-428B.C.), 10-11
Anaximander (ca. 600-545 B.C.), 7-8, 16
Anaximenes (ca. 585-525), 7-8
Angels, 272
Appolonius of Perga (fl. 285 B.C.), 24, 196
Archimedes (287-212 B.C.), 9, 24, 27-28, (Readings, pp. 144), 326
Aristarchus of Samos (fl. ca. 281 B.C.), 25
Aristotle (384-322 B.C.), 13-21, (Readings: pp. 61, 113, 123), 233-35, 326-27
Atoms, 273
Averroës (1126-98), 205, 238, 311
Avicenna (980-1037), 175, 194-195, 199-201
Babylonians, 1, 2, (Readings: pp. 35, 41, 50), 4
Bacon, Roger (ca. 1212-92), 237, (Readings, pp. 282)
Bradwardine, Thomas (ca. 1295-1349), 329
Byrhtferth (fl. ca. 970), 242-49
Bartholomew the Englishman (ca. 1260), 237
Bede (672-735), 218, 219-220, 258-60
Bible, 7
Boethius (480-524), 210, 213-214, 252-53
Buridan, John (d.ca. 1358), (Readings, pp. 316), 330-33
Carolingian Renaissance, 220, 254
Cassiodorus (490-585), 214-215, 253
Celsus (ca. A.D. 30), 206-207, 209
Chalcidius (fl. ca. 325 A.D.), 210-211, 213
Crateus (fl. 80 B.C.), 33, 180
Cuneiform tablets, 2
Democritus of Abdera (fl. ca. 430 B.C.), 11, 29
Dioscorides (1st cent. A.D.), 33, 180
Egyptians, 3, 4, 6, (Readings, pp. 38)
Empedocles (fl. ca. 450 B.C.), 10
Erasistratus (fl. 260 B.C.), 30-31
Euclid (fl. ca. 300 B.C.), 23, 179
Eudoxus (ca. 408-355 B.C.), 13, 14 Fig. 1, 22
Four Humors, 271
Frederick II Hohenstanfen (1194-1250), 236-37
Four Causes, 16

ılen (A.D. 131-201), 21, 31-33, (Readings: pp. 156, 167), 196, 234-35
erald of Brussels (fl. ca. 1200), 329
erard of Cremona (114-87), 224, 233
erbert (940-1003), 218, 221-222
'egory the Great, 216, (Readings, pp. 263)
'osseteste, Robert (ca. 1168-1253), 237-38, (Readings, pp. 274)
eracleides of Pontus (ca. 388-310 B.C.), 24-25
eraclitus of Ephesus (fl. 501 B.C.), 8
erbals, 260-61
ero of Alexandria (ca. A.D. 62), 27, (Readings, pp. 150), 201
erophilus (fl. 290 B.C.), 30-31
.pparchus of Nicaea (ca. 190-120 B.C.), 24
.ppocrates of Cos (ca. 460-350 B.C.), 29-30, (Readings, pp. 85), 196
omer, 3-5
amblichus (ca. 250-326), 210
sidore of Seville (560-636), 218, 219, 253, (Readings, pp. 264), 256
abir ibn Hayyan (Gerber) (ca. 720-815), 202-203
ohn of Hollywood (Sacrobosco) (fl. 1200), 233
ohn of St. Amand (fl. 1261-98), (Readings, pp. 322)
ohn Scot Erigena (ca. 830-880), 218, 220-221, 255
oran, 172-73
eucippus (fl. ca. 440 B.C.), 11
acrobius (395-423), 211-212
artianus Capella (fl. ca. 410-439), 211-213, 254
ohammed (A.D. 570-632), 171-72
useum of Alexandria, 21, 170
eo-Platonism, 210-212
mar Khayyan (ca. 1038-ca. 1123), 190
resme, Nicole (d. 1382), 330, 332-33
armenides of Elea (fl. 475 B.C.), 8-9
eter of Limoges (fl. 1270-99), (Readings, pp. 324)
hiloponus, John (ca. A.D. 500), 171-72, 201, 327
lato (427-347 B.C.), 12-13, 17, (Readings: pp. 55, 96), 254
lotinus (204-270), 210, 254
liny the Elder (A.D. 23-79), 207-209, 252
orphyry (ca. 232-304), 210
re-Socratic philosophers, 5-11
tolmeny of Alexandria (fl. ca. A D. 150), 2, 13, 25, (Readings, pp. 126), 176, 179
ythagorus (fl. 530 B.C.), 9-10, 22
hazes (ca. 865-925), 194-196, 203
chliemann, Heinrich, 3
eneca (ca. 4 B.C.) - 65 A.D.), 209, 249
ocrates (470-399 B.C.), 11-12
t. Augustine (354-430), 254
trato of Lampsacus (fl. ca. 270 B.C.), 26, (Readings, pp. 150)
t. Thomas of Aquinas (1227-74), (Readings, pp. 304)
umerians, 1
wineshead, Richard (fl. ca. 1344-54), 329

Thales of Miletus (fl. ca. 584 B.C.), 6-7
Theodoric of Freiburg (d. 1371), 238
Theophrastus (372-288 B.C.), 33
William of Heytesbury (ca. 1313-72), 329
Witelo (fl. 1270), 237-38
Xenophanes of Colophon (ca. 570-475 B.C.), 5
Zodiac, 2

INDEX

Alchemy, 2-3
Appolonius of Perga (fl. 285 B.C.), 8
Archimedes (287-212 B.C.), 2, 7, 63
Aristotle (384-322 B.C.), 1, 2, 45-46, 53
Aristotelian philosophy, 5, 8-9, 17-18, 24-25, (Readings: p. 49-63; Readings: p. 64-79)
Astrology, 3, 9-10

Bacon, Francis (1561-1626), 64, (Readings: p. 80-108, 317-321)
Borelli, Giovanni (1608-1679), 38, 44-45
Boyle, Robert (1627-1691), (Readings: p. 274-283)
Brahe, Tycho (1546-1601), 20-23
Bruno, Giordano (c. 1548-1600), 19-20, 319-320

Cardan, Jerome (1501-76), 32
Columbus, Realdus (1516-59), 41
Copernicus, Nicholas (1473-1543), 1, 2, 12-20, 24, (Readings: p. 153-169, 346)

Descartes, Rene (1596-1650), 32-33, 34-36, 44, 64, 67, (Readings: p. 109-121, 249-273)
Digges, Thomas (d. 1595), 19

Engineers, 2, 4-7
Etaples, Jacques Letevre d'(ca. 1450-1536), 9
Eustachio (1520-74), 41

Fabricius of Aquapendente (1537-1619), 41
Fallopius (1523-62), 41
Forli, Jacopo da (fl. 1413), 54-55

Galen (A.D. 131-201), 40, 54
Galileo Galilei (1564-1642), 2, 24-32, 36-37, 51-52, 62, 64, 67, 70-71, 73-76, (Readings: p. 122-124, p. 125-136, p. 137-142, p. 186-204, p. 205-218, p. 245-248)
Gilbert, William (1546-1603), 27

Halley, Edmund (1656-1742), 38, 308-309
Harvey, William (1578-1657), 42-46, (Readings: p. 143-152)
Hermeticism, 2-3, (Readings: p. 312-321, 333-334)
Hero of Alexandria (ca. A.D. 62), 8
Hooke, Robert (1635-1703), 38
Hugo of Siena (fl. 1439), 55-56
Humanists, 7-10, 63

Kepler, Johannes (1571-1630), 2, 20, 22-24, 26-27, 30-32, 36-37, (Readings: p. 170-174, p. 175-185)

Leeuwenhoek, Antoni van (1632-1723), 45
Leibnitz, Gottfried Wilhelm (1646-1716), 32-34
Leonardo da Vinci (1452-1519), 5-6, 316

Machine metaphor, 6-7
Malpighi, Marcello (1628-94), 43
Mechanical philosophy, 39-40, 43-44, (Readings: p. 245-248, p. 249-273, p. 274-283, 335-336)
Moses, 2, 334-335

Navigation, 10, 308-309
Neo-Platonism, 2, 62-63, (Readings: p. 312-321, 347-348)
Newton, Sir Isaac (1642-1727), 2, 3, 26, 34, 36-40, 64, (Readings: p. 219-244, p. 284-286, p. 287-303, 322-332)
Nicholas of Cusa (1401-64), 1
Nifo, Agostino (fl. 1506), 56-59

Oresme, Nicholas (d. 1382), 1, 346

Paul of Venice (1429), 56
Peuerbach, George (1423-69), 14-15
Pietro d'Abano (fl. 1310), 52-54
Plato (427-347 B.C.), 2, 8
Ptolemy (fl. ca. A.D. 150), 9, 13-14, 17

Ray, John (1627-1705), 46-47
Reformation, 11-12

Scientific Revolution, 1-3, (Readings: p. 304-311, p. 339-348)
Servetius, Michael (ca. 1511-53), 41
Stellar parallax, 19

Tartaglia, Niccolo (1500-57), 32
Tournefort, Joseph Pitton de (1656-1708), 46

Vesalius, Andreas (1514-64), 40-41
Viete, Francois (1540-1603), 32

Zabarella, 59-63

NOTES

NOTES